International Series in Operations Research & Management Science

Volume 366

The book series **International Series in Operations Research and Management Science** encompasses the various areas of operations research and management science. Both theoretical and applied books are included. It describes current advances anywhere in the world that are at the cutting edge of the field. The series is aimed especially at researchers, advanced graduate students, and sophisticated practitioners.

The series features three types of books:

- Advanced expository books that extend and unify our understanding of particular areas.
- Research monographs that make substantial contributions to knowledge.
- Handbooks that define the new state of the art in particular areas. Each handbook will be edited by a leading authority in the area who will organize a team of experts on various aspects of the topic to write individual chapters. A handbook may emphasize expository surveys or completely new advances (either research or applications) or a combination of both.

The series emphasizes the following four areas:

Mathematical Programming: Including linear programming, integer programming, nonlinear programming, interior point methods, game theory, network optimization models, combinatorics, equilibrium programming, complementarity theory, multiobjective optimization, dynamic programming, stochastic programming, complexity theory, etc.

Applied Probability: Including queuing theory, simulation, renewal theory, Brownian motion and diffusion processes, decision analysis, Markov decision processes, reliability theory, forecasting, other stochastic processes motivated by applications, etc.

Production and Operations Management: Including inventory theory, production scheduling, capacity planning, facility location, supply chain management, distribution systems, materials requirements planning, just-in-time systems, flexible manufacturing systems, design of production lines, logistical planning, strategic issues, etc.

Applications of Operations Research and Management Science: Including telecommunications, health care, capital budgeting and finance, economics, marketing, public policy, military operations research, humanitarian relief and disaster mitigation, service operations, transportation systems, etc.

This book series is indexed in Scopus.

Fausto Pedro García Márquez • Benjamin Lev
Huchang Liao
Editors

Outsourcing Using Operations Research and Management Science Methods

From Theory to Practice

Springer

Editors
Fausto Pedro García Márquez
Ingenium Research Group
University of Castilla-La Mancha
Ciudad Real, Spain

Benjamin Lev
Drexel University
Philadelphia, USA

Huchang Liao
Sichuan University
Chengdu, China

ISSN 0884-8289 ISSN 2214-7934 (electronic)
International Series in Operations Research & Management Science
ISBN 978-3-031-91844-5 ISBN 978-3-031-91845-2 (eBook)
https://doi.org/10.1007/978-3-031-91845-2

This Springer imprint is published by the registered company Springer Nature Switzerland AG
The registered company address is: Gewerbestrasse 11, 6330 Cham, Switzerland

It has been a pleasure to participate in these two volumes of "Outsourcing in Management Science and Operations Research" with Springer, the authors and the editors, Prof. Benjamin and Prof. Huchang Liao, excellent colleagues but better friends. Editors are from Spain, the USA, and China, three continents. Also authors are from many countries, e.g., UK, USA, Mexico, Algeria, Slovakia, India, Ukraine,… with different religions, political ideas, cultures,… but something in common, the interest to contribute with their hard work done for the science to the acknowledgments of the humanity, which does not understand about borders. I feel very grateful and fortunate to be part of that process. My last words, but not least, I would like to dedicate this book to my mother, who will be always in my heart.

García Márquez

It is with an enormously grateful heart that I share the publication of these two volumes of "Outsourcing in Management Science and Operations Research." My academic journey on a quest to share information, improve the functions of humanity and gain wisdom in the process has been and continues to be an abiding source of joy in my life. I continue to enjoy watching the seeds of learning grow in unexpected directions around our beautiful planet with the inspirational generations of young people I have the privilege of teaching and learning from. Finally, as always, I want to recognize the greatest roles I ever played outside of academia and the classroom given to me by those I will forever hold most dear: husband, father, and grandfather. That first role began with my beloved wife Debbie 65 years ago whose memory remains a blessing in all our lives. Debbie gave me the precious gift of fatherhood through my loving son Ron (M.D) and devoted daughter Nurit (J.D., Lieutenant Colonel Retired, USAF). They in turn brought Melitza and Jim (Colonel Retired, USAF) into our lives leading to the paramount gift, our beloved grandchildren: Hannah (Carnegie Mellon University, B.S., Neuroscience), Jimmy (Virginia Polytechnic Institute, B.S. Clinical Neuroscience), Veronica, Sebastian, and Arya. I will close with a sincere thank you for the many years of continued professional and personal support and a wish that your journey for knowledge and wisdom be as rich and enduring.

BenjaminLev

It was a really brilliant and enjoyable journey to work with Professor Fausto and Professor Benjamin Lev for editing these two volumes of "Outsourcing in Management Science and Operations Research." The insightful thoughts shared in those chapters are just like a breath of fresh air for me. I would like to express my highest gratitude to the authors who supported these two volumes. The experience of working with Professor Fausto and Professor Benjamin Lev will be unforgettable for me forever.

HuchangLiao

Preface

This book aims to provide relevant theoretical frameworks and the latest empirical research findings in Outsourcing in Management Science and Operations Research. It has been written for professionals who want to improve their understanding of the strategic role of outsourcing at various levels of the information and knowledge organization, that is, outsourcing at the global economic level, at networks and organizations, at teams and work groups, of information systems and, finally, outsourcing at the level of individuals as players in the networked environments.

This book is intended for professionals in the field of energy, engineering, information science, mathematics, economics, etc., and researchers who wish to develop new skills in outsourcing, or who employ the outsourcing discipline as part of their work. The authors of this volume describe their original work in the area or provide material for cases and studies successfully applying the outsourcing discipline in real-life cases and theoretical approaches.

Ciudad Real, Spain — Fausto Pedro García Márquez
Philadelphia, PA, USA — Benjamin Lev
Chengdu, China — Huchang Liao

Introduction

Outsourcing is a valuable tool for industry, society, and governments, a research field that requires the use and application in Management Science (MS) and Operations Research (OR). In this book, the topics of MS and OR together with Outsourcing are introduced. The chapters start with a basic concept and discuss the benefits, advantages and disadvantages, present cases, applications, theory, and potential future. The book covers as wide an array of topics as space permits. Examples are from private and public industries. Future applications, trends, and the potential future of outsourcing are discussed.

Outsourcing is a widely used tool to get things done faster, reduce cost, share risk, increase efficiency, and flexible capacity. This book links the above to management science (MS) and operations research (OR) models. Specifically, this book provides an interface between the main disciplines of engineering/technology and the organizational, economic, administrative, and planning capabilities of managing outsourcing.

Facility Management (FM) outsourcing currently focuses on sustainability through the adoption of the newly recognized UN Sustainable Development Goals when making business decisions. Chapter 1 aims to validate the published Artificial Intelligence (AI)-based FM outsourcing relationship system using real business cases in the working environment in terms of sustainability. It briefly introduces the theory of the FM outsourcing relationship system by discussing how it can help FM seniors and strategists design their FM daily strategies wisely and make their businesses more effective and productive. It also introduces what the research is practically doing at the case-study stage for testing and verification. It is concluded that FM outsourcing categorization may help define the appropriate relationships between providers and clients. Further, the outcomes generated from the AI model can define and explain the existing outsourcing relationships between stakeholders and service providers.

Chapter 2 presents a comprehensive review of key dynamics in manufacturing outsourcing research, focusing on the relationship between an original equipment manufacturer (OEM) and a contract manufacturer (CM). The cooperation and coopetition relationships, along with modelling frameworks for various supply chain scenarios, are discussed. The chapter provides a seven-step analytical framework including echelons of the supply chain, players involved, outsourcing decisions, and decision sequences for outsourcing decision analysis. Demonstrations of deriving the optimal outsourcing strategies (in-house, turnkey, or consignment) are provided, identifying conditions for win-win or win-win-win outcomes. Furthermore, it includes three dynamic variations, including multi-vendor and multi-client outsourcing, private information, and product differentiation, to enrich outsourcing implications. Each variation is supported by relevant articles summarizing major focuses and modelling frameworks. Chapter 2 concludes with a general discussion of outsourcing relationships and highlights potential research areas that arise from new challenges in the changed business environments.

Outsourcing is a globally significant practice that takes different forms. Although there are practitioner guidelines for managing safety in outsourcing relationships, these are generic and fail to account for different forms of outsourcing and how the management of safety might be different in each. Adopting an embedded case design, Chapter 3 investigates the safety management practices in three different forms of outsourcing occurring in a single organization, a UK division of a global mechanical electrical engineering company. Data from 24 interviews with employees from both clients and contractors across the three subcases revealed 10 different safety management practices (selection and recruitment, induction, preparing risk assessment and method statements, permits to work, verbal and written communication, monitoring, auditing, reporting, and reviewing) that mapped onto the practitioner guidance. This overall similarity may be accounted for by three isomorphic pressures. However, different practices were emphasized in each of the three forms of outsourcing. Monitoring and auditing were prominent where entire functions were outsourced. Risk assessments, method statements, and permits to work were used where particular tasks were outsourced. Required skills were stipulated when agency workers were employed. These differences may reflect three different ways to coordinate and control work safely in these relationships.

Chapter 4 explores the critical decision-making process in selecting IT outsourcing service providers for public administrators, focusing on its impact on future public value creation. The research introduces a novel framework based on linear programming for stable matching, interval numbers, and a Matrix model procedure for addressing relational variables influencing service provider selection in public–private IT outsourcing. Drawing on empirical data from Mexico's public administration, the study identifies trust and knowledge interfaces as pivotal factors shaping public value in outsourcing projects. The methodology correlates public value with service provider selection criteria, offering valuable insights for decision-makers and practitioners. Computational experiments validate the stability of this approach, providing recommendations for optimizing selection processes and enhancing outcomes for citizens and stakeholders. The study's contributions extend beyond IT outsourcing, influencing discussions on methodologies for the service provider selection problem, outsourcing in public sector management, and value creation.

Outsourcing is considered a key factor for optimizing cost-efficiency and reinforcing competitiveness within the supply chain. Chapter 5 investigates the outsourcing from forward-loop and reverse supply chain. It addresses a single manufacturer in relationships with an upstream partner encompassing a raw material supplier and subcontractors with cutting-edge technology, while downstream partners consist of subcontractors' collection centers to deal with returns. The manufacturer involves subcontractor contracts for purchasing ready-to-use products besides leveraging comparative advantage. The latter focuses on returned products, with in-house remanufacturing and outsourcing. Outsourcing is justified by capacity and specific process requirements. A multi-objective mixed integer programming formulation is proposed in chapter 5 and implemented by the GAMS software for the elaboration of an integrated plan minimizing economic costs, carbon emissions, and system unavailability. On this basis, computational experiments reveal the benefits of integrated manufacturing/remanufacturing/outsourcing with CO2 emissions reduction in decreasing new product demand, which results in major resource savings.

The public provision of security is traditionally tied to the sovereignty and legitimacy of the modern state. In the meantime, private security actors are playing an increasingly substantial role in the domestic and international provision of public and private security. Against this background, Chapter 8 affirms the need to closely examine the globally expanding processes of privatizing security, and particularly some authoritarian states' decision to outsource the public provision of security. In this vein, the chapter examines how different states use, and abuse, the privatization of security and how this phenomenon impacts the expression and reconfiguration of state power as well as the relationship between the state and the citizenry. Moreover, in terms of studying the security market, especially amid an evolving security environment and under entrenched authoritarian states, Chapter 6 proposes the nodal-network framework of analysis as highly suitable for the study of outsourcing security in contemporary authoritarian states, and beyond. Acknowledging the value and strengths of the nodal and network models in studying contemporary security markets, the nodal-network framework of analysis essentially combines the two models into a holistic framework, which enables a more comprehensive study of individual cases as well as in-depth cross-case analysis.

In the complex manufacturing landscape, machine failures and unplanned stoppages frequently lead to production delays, energy wastage, and diminished product quality. Maintenance costs can represent a high portion of total production expenses, making efficient equipment maintenance crucial for operational success. The integration of cyber-manufacturing—marked by smart machines, the Internet of Things (IoT), and cloud computing—poses new challenges, as evidenced by a significant uptick in cyber-attacks. Chapter 7 develops models to evaluate the financial implications and benefits of cybersecurity within maintenance outsourcing agreements. It proposes strategies for aligning the interests of manufacturers, who are vulnerable to cyber threats, with contractors accounting for potential cyber-attack costs. The findings offer actionable insights for optimizing profitability under the dual threats of mechanical failures and cyber-attacks, providing comprehensive strategies for managing maintenance and cybersecurity investments. This research is vital for manufacturers seeking to safeguard their operations and maximize profits amidst increasing cyber threats.

The surge in e-commerce has revolutionized customer access to a global marketplace, offering a seamless experience from product selection to payment. Expectations for swift, competitively priced, and well-coordinated deliveries are high. However, the operational challenges posed by global supply chains, spanning extensive distances, are substantial. To meet these challenges, retailers often rely on dependable fourth-party logistics (4PL) providers for efficient and customer-centric goods delivery. Recognizing the significance of this, a comprehensive review of logistics providers becomes imperative, utilizing proper analytical techniques. Chapter 8 introduces a novel approach for assessing resilient 4PLs, using the intuitionistic fuzzy Dombi–Bonferroni (DOBI) method as its foundation. The methodology was validated and applied to evaluate resilient 4PL providers for an Indian online retailer based in Kochi, specializing in the delivery of live plants across the country. The results offered valuable insights, aiding the retailer in making informed decisions regarding their product delivery partnerships.

Outsourcing, its processes and efficiency, factors and barriers, risks and benefits, are most frequently analyzed for the conditions of private companies. However, outsourcing is very frequent also in the public sector, both on the level of public organizations and self-government. The objective of Chapter 9 is to analyze the outsourcing of ancillary services on the Slovak municipal level. According to the findings, the scale of outsourcing of ancillary services on the municipal level is relatively large (depending on the concrete service); however, the process of outsourcing and its results are rather problematic. The most critical aspects of the outsourcing process on the Slovak municipal level are the decision-making (decision in-house versus outsourcing), award process, and contract management. Chapter 9 provides critical lessons especially for developing countries and countries of post-transitional character, with a lack of accountability and lack of experience with outsourcing on the municipal level.

Bhagalpur, called the “Silk City” in India, is famous for its silk-weaving tradition and diverse products. However, the silk industry in Bhagalpur faces challenges because the yarn used in weaving has become expensive. The weavers, essential for making these designs, cannot afford to buy the costly yarn. It is not just the expensive yarn; there is also tough competition from cheaper synthetic fabrics like Chinese silk, Koria, Viscose, and synthetic staples. This change has made it harder for local weavers to earn good wages. Many Bhagalpur textile firms struggle to get enough money to grow and update their technology. Access to banks makes it even more challenging. Weavers also need help with issues like low pay, lack of recognition, and declining demand, discouraging young people from learning this craft. Overcoming these challenges is essential to keeping Bhagalpur’s silk tradition alive and passing on weaving skills to the next generation. These issues are covered in Chapter 10.

Ciudad Real, Spain — Fausto Pedro García Márquez
Philadelphia, PA, USA — Benjamin Lev
Chengdu, China — Huchang Liao

Contents

About the Editors

Fausto Pedro García Márquez works at UCLM as a Full Professor (Accredited as Full Professor from 2013), Spain, an Honorary Senior Research Fellow at Birmingham University, UK, a Lecturer at the Postgraduate European Institute, a Research Fellow at INTI International University & Colleges, Malaysia, and has been Senior Manager in Accenture (2013–2014). He obtained his European PhD with maximum distinction. He has been distinguished with the prices: Runner Prize (2023), Nominate Prize (2022), Gran Maestre (2022), Grand Prize (2021), Runner Prize (2020) and Advancement Prize (2018), Runner (2015), Advancement (2013) and Silver (2012) by the International Society of Management Science and Engineering Management (ICMSEM), First International Business Ideas Competition 2017 Award (2017), etc. He has published more than 283 journal papers (187 JCR: 92-Q1; 52-Q2; 39-Q3; 9-Q4), some recognized as: "Progress in Photovoltaics: Research and Applications" (Q1, IF. 8.49, one of the most downloaded in the first 12 months of publications, 2023), "Applied Energy" (Q1, IF 9.746, as "Best Paper 2020"), "Renewable Energy" (Q1, IF 8.001, as "Best Paper 2014"); "ICMSEM" (as "excellent"), "Int. J. of Automation and Computing" and "IMechE Part F: J. of Rail and Rapid Transit" (most downloaded), etc. He is the author and editor of over 55 books (Elsevier, Springer, Pearson, Mc-GrawHill, Intech, IGI, Marcombo, AlfaOmega,...), >115 international chapters, and 6 patents. He is the Editor of 5 Int. Journals, Committee Member more than 70 Int.

Conferences. He has been the Principal Investigator in 5 European Projects, 8 National Projects, and more than 150 projects for universities, companies, etc. He is being: Expert in the European Union in AI4People (EISMD), and ESF; Director of https://ingenium.uclm.es; Senior Member at IEEE, 2021–...; Honored Honorary Member of the Research Council of Indian Institute of Finance, 2021–...; Committee Chair of The International Society for Management Science and Engineering Management (ISMSEM), 2020–...; Research Fellow at INTI International University & Colleges, Malaysia, from 2023-...; Visiting Professor at Sheyang University (China) from 2024–2027; Advisory Board of the EU Project SunBio (Id: ID 101157493) 2024–2027. His main interests are: Artificial Intelligence, Maintenance, Management, Renewable Energy, Transport, Advanced Analytics, and Data Science. More information in https://blog.uclm.es/faustopedrogarcia

Benjamin Lev is the University Trustee Professor 2014–2021 at LeBow College of Business, Drexel University, Philadelphia, Pennsylvania, USA. He holds a PhD in Operations Research from Case Western Reserve University. Prior to joining Drexel University, Dr. Lev held academic and administrative positions at Temple University, University of Michigan-Dearborn, and Worcester Polytechnic Institute. He is the Editor-in-Chief of OMEGA—The International Journal of Management Science http://www.omegajournal.org/; Co-Editor-in-Chief of International Journal of Management Science and Engineering Management; and serves on several other journal editorial boards (INFORMS JAA (formerly Interfaces), IAOR, ORPJ, Financial Innovation, OPSEARCH, IDIM, IIE-Transactions, ERRJ, INFORMS JOR). He currently holds faculty appointments at seven Chinese universities (Beijing Jiaotong University, Chengdu University, Nanjing University of Aeronautics and Astronautics, Nanjing University of Information Science and Technology, Nanjing Audit University, Xidian University, Tianjin University). Professor Lev is the former TIMS VP-Meetings and INFORMS VP- Meetings. INFORMS Senior

Fellow since 2003. He has published eighteen books, numerous articles and organized many national and international conferences including ORSA/TIMS Philadelphia; INFORMS Israel; IFORS Scotland; ALIO-INFORMS Buenos Aires; ICMSEM Philadelphia. https://en.wikipedia.org/wiki/Benjamin_Lev

Huchang Liao is a Research Fellow at the Business School, Sichuan University, Chengdu, China. He received his PhD degree in Management Science and Engineering from the Shanghai Jiao Tong University, Shanghai, China, in 2015. He has published 4 monographs, and more than 300 peer-reviewed papers, many in high-quality international journals including *Decision Analysis*, *European Journal of Operational Research, Omega, IEEE Transactions on Fuzzy Systems, IEEE Transactions on Engineering Management, IEEE Transactions on Systems, Man, and Cybernetics: Systems*, *IEEE Transaction on Cybernetics,* etc. His main research interests include multiple criteria decision analysis, group decision analysis, fuzzy decision analysis, machine learning-based decision analysis and medical decision analysis. Prof. Liao has been elected to be the National Young Talent in China, the Fellow of IFSA, IET, and BCS. He is the Associate Editor or Editorial Board Member of many top-tier international journals, including *IEEE Transactions on Fuzzy Systems* and *Applied Soft Computing*.

Revolutionizing Facilities Management Outsourcing: AI Applications and Case Studies in Sustainable Outsourcing Relationships

Ka Leung Lok, Albert So, Alex Opoku, and Charles Chen

1 Introduction

In the Facility Management (FM) industry, Strategic Sustainable FM can assist in achieving the 17 United Nations Sustainable Development Goals (SDGs) across organizations. Outsourcing sustainable FM leads to better business decisions (Lok et al., 2023) and helps to reduce energy, water, and waste in building maintenance. However, the FM outsourcing sector faces challenges in applying these SDGs, making clear support essential for effective adoption. This chapter explores how facility management outsourcing contributes to the SDGs. Opoku (2024) examined the connection between the SDGs and the built environment, focusing on the 5Ps: people, planet, prosperity, peace, and partnerships. This framework guides future research and helps to measure FM's added value to core businesses and stakeholders. The chapter also discusses an AI-based facility management outsourcing system related to the SDGs, aiming to inspire FM professionals with new ideas about relationships between facility owners and service providers. Opoku and Lee (2022)

K. L. Lok (✉)
Faculty of Business and Creative Industries, University of South Wales, Cardiff, UK
e-mail: Ka.lok@southwales.ac.uk; K.L.Lok@edu.salford.ac.uk

A. So
Asian Institute of Built Environment, Hong Kong, China
e-mail: atpso@hku.hk

A. Opoku
Department of Architectural Engineering, College of Engineering, University of Sharjah, Sharjah, UAE
e-mail: aopoku@sharjah.ac.ae

C. Chen
Hawai'i Pacific University, Honolulu, HI, USA
e-mail: cxchen@hpu.edu

F. P. García Márquez et al. (eds.), *Outsourcing Using Operations Research and Management Science Methods*, International Series in Operations Research & Management Science 366, https://doi.org/10.1007/978-3-031-91845-2_1

emphasize using practices that support social, environmental, and economic benefits, showing how the FM sector can support the 17 SDGs at different organizational levels through data-driven technologies.

The ISO/TC 267 Technical Committee for Facilities Management was formed in 2012 (ISO, 2022). As of 2022, 51 countries are part of this committee. The recent ISO FM standards confirm that essential features of goods and services, like safety, quality, and reliability, are consistent. These standards also support the Sustainable Development Goals (ISO/TC 267). Facility Management (FM) is important for organizations that manage and maintain workplaces and assets (British Standards Institution, 2018). FM is now moving toward a strategic approach by including the United Nations Sustainable Development Goals, which encourage Sustainable Facility Management (SFM) in business choices. The Sustainable Development Goals (SDGs) create a baseline of established practices for sustainable FM. However, the FM sector may face challenges when trying to use these international sustainability goals. On the positive side, sustainable FM can show how FM adds value to core business operations, which emphasizes the significance of sustainability in the global FM industry. While technology and strategic methods can improve sustainability across many fields, teamwork and collaboration within the community are vital to tackle these challenges effectively. Sustainable facility management is important for the international facility management (FM) industry. Lok et al. (2018) highlighted that strong encouragement from organizations is vital for adopting sustainability practices successfully. By integrating sustainability, businesses can improve their efficiency and productivity. The development of sustainable facility management depends on FM professionals committing to it and effectively applying the new sustainable development goals (SDGs) set by the global FM community. However, to fully realize the benefits of sustainable facility management, it is essential to include the SDGs in daily FM services. Without this integration, significant improvements in FM services cannot be achieved.

Using environmentally friendly materials can improve indoor air quality, save water, and increase energy efficiency for comfort. Important strategies include sustainable renovation, flexible design, and circular practices (Lee & Kang, 2013). Good facility management can also boost productivity and service quality. However, the facility management community often overlooks sustainability. It makes us question whether we can effectively organize services without following relevant Sustainable Development Goals (SDGs). Integrating SDGs into facility management is essential for promoting sustainability. Today, everyone needs to stay informed about these trends, as all generations should understand and accept the UN goals. Many people are now seeking sustainable choices in their daily lives to enhance communication and productivity. This shift shows that adopting SDGs can help to create a more sustainable world and encourage best practices in workplaces.

This chapter looks at whether we need to encourage sustainable facility management (FM) and use Sustainable Development Goals (SDGs) in this area. The main focus is on how to improve FM services through these goals. FM is crucial for organizations because it involves managing, operating, and maintaining workplaces and their assets efficiently (British Standards Institution, 2018). To ensure a high quality of life, we must maintain strong performance in facility management. We will explore two key questions: Why are development goals in the built environment important? What barriers come up when trying to align FM services with these goals? This chapter investigates how sustainable facility management connects with the Sustainable Development Goals.

2 The United Nations Sustainable Development Goals (SDGs)

Opoku and Lee (2022) stressed that the facility management (FM) sector should take a key role in promoting sustainability in daily practices to improve customer service. Sustainable FM practices help reduce water, energy, and waste during building maintenance and operations. The International Organization for Standardization (ISO) has released over 22,000 standards and documents that provide important guidance based on global collaboration. These standards are vital for achieving the Sustainable Development Goals (SDGs) (ISO, 2022). Collins et al. (2019) attempted to connect sustainable buildings with sustainable FM. They highlighted the need to connect design, construction, and FM for better solutions based on life cycle assessments. Opoku and Lee (2022) noted a shift toward long-term thinking in business decisions, focusing on practices that consider social, environmental, and economic benefits. Sustainable facility management and the SDGs are increasingly important for building assets around the world. They influence and are influenced by sustainable development goals. Besides security, all aspects of FM relate to the environmental, social, and economic parts of sustainable development. Additionally, sustainable facility management aligns closely with the SDGs. This chapter examines how the FM sector can support various issues of the 17 Sustainable Development Goals at the organizational level by using data-driven management technologies.

2.1 Sustainable Facilities Management Incorporating SDGs

Sustainable Facility Management (SFM) focuses on managing and delivering essential and support services that promote economic, social, and environmental sustainability (Tucker, 2013). The facility management (FM) sector should lead the way in sustainability by making it part of daily practices, which can improve customer service. SFM anticipates reducing the negative environmental impact of business activities. This involves smart decision-making and adopting sustainable practices that consider customer experience, climate change, and competition. Opoku and Lee (2022) explain that SFM combines facility management with sustainable development. This is done by using technology and new business methods that balance social, economic, and environmental factors. Nielsen and Galamba (2010) looked into how sustainability affects core business functions and support roles, as well as their impact on local and global communities. SFM also focuses on using eco-friendly materials to improve indoor air quality, encourages water reuse, improves energy efficiency for thermal comfort, and supports sustainable renovation. It also promotes flexible designs that help create sustainable cities and communities and embrace circularity (Lee & Kang, 2013). Additionally, Strategic Sustainable FM can help to achieve the 17 Sustainable Development Goals (SDGs) at all levels of the FM sector. It assists in managing the built environment and facility management, especially during the challenges caused by the Covid-19 pandemic.

Facility managers make decisions that greatly affect the planet, both positively and negatively (Aceves-Avila & Berger-García, 2019). In facility management (FM), these managers play a key role in applying sustainability principles in buildings (Elmualim et al., 2012). To implement these principles successfully, they need to work together with important partners to create strategies that support health, safety, and well-being in organizations. At all levels—strategic, tactical, and operational—sustainable facility management (SFM) practices can address various challenges in FM. This needs practical implementation that includes administration, investment, space management, operations, and services. While many see SFM as focused solely on environmental issues (Lok et al., 2018), FM organizations are increasingly considering environmental, social, and economic factors together. Opoku and Lee (2022) note that SFM offers benefits like energy savings, water conservation, waste reduction, and lower carbon footprints. To understand how SFM impacts the planet, we must examine its link to the Sustainable Development Goals (SDGs).

Facility management (FM) can significantly help achieve development goals. However, according to Kwawu and Elmualim (2011), facility managers need to learn important skills to effectively include sustainability in their FM strategies and operations. They are key players in driving change within organizations and can influence employees at all levels (Elmualim et al., 2009). It is essential to understand that 80% of a building's climate change impact happens during its operational stage, showing how operations can harm the environment (Buser et al., 2018). The built environment contributes over 40% of material use, 33% of global energy use, and 40–50% of greenhouse gas emissions. Therefore, Sustainable Facility Management (SFM) is crucial for global sustainability, especially given the large number of existing buildings (Nielsen et al., 2009; Radebe & Ozumba, 2021). Nielsen et al. (2016) point out that SFM can solve important difficulties such as climate adaptation, energy efficiency, and sustainable development while creating innovative ways for both organizations and society. A study by the International Facility Management Expert Center (IFMEC, 2018) in the Netherlands found that effective SFM can help achieve the 17 Sustainable Development Goals (SDGs). The FM profession is well-positioned to integrate these SDGs at all levels of an organization and can promote individual behavior changes by creating a supportive environment for sustainable practices. Table 1 links sustainable facility management to the

Table 1 The role of FM in achieving the SDGs

The role of the FM	SDGs		SDG targets
Provide individual economic and social improvements for those in need	1	No poverty	1.2, 1.4
Catering influences the sourcing of food products, food security, nutritional value, and waste management	2	Zero hunger	2.1, 2.4
Co-creators of the workplace take responsibility for the working conditions of employees	3	Good health and well-being	3.7,3.8
Improving global education involves supplying proper school equipment and enabling new learning methods	4	Quality education	4.3,4.4
Facility management contributes to work-life balance by providing good and flexible working conditions	5	Gender equality	5.5,5.6
Responsible water management reduces water loss by controlling leakages and increasing efficiency	6	Clean water and sanitation	6.2,6.4
The primary task is to implement and maintain innovations through a continuous improvement process	7	Affordable and clean energy	7.2,7.3
Facility managers worldwide can significantly enhance the overall working conditions for employees	8	Decent work and economic growth	8.3
Key technological innovations are often related to smart buildings and workplaces	9	Industry, innovation, and infrastructure	9.5
Increasing number of multinationals are tendering maintenance and facility services on a European and global scale	10	Reduced inequalities	10.2,10.6
Contribute to sustainable growth by maintaining buildings, districts, and cities	11	Sustainable cities and communities	11.3,11.6
Source food resources using a circular procurement strategy	12	Responsible consumption and production	12.4,12.5
Sustainable business management is a high priority within the field of facility management	13	Climate action	13.3
Pollution from plastics is a major issue; FM helps through circular procurement policies & waste control	14	Life below water	14.2,14.4
Facility managers are often in direct contact with a significant portion of animal products and decrease their usage	15	Life on land	15.1,15.5
Peace and justice are not solely the responsibility of the government; strong institutions also play a key role	16	Peace, justice, and strong institutions	16.2,16.10
Facility management can play an important role in bringing together all supporting departments within organizations	17	Partnerships for the goals	17.7,17.9

Source: United Nations (2015) and IFMEC (2018)

Table 2 Interpretation of SDGs to ISO standards

SDGs		Interpretation of SDGs to ISO standards
1	No poverty	ISO International Standards offer a platform for best practices across all economic activities, ranging from agriculture to banking
2	Zero hunger	There are over 1600 ISO standards specifically designed for the food production sector to enhance confidence in food products
3	Good health and well-being	Access to healthcare is a fundamental human right. ISO has developed more than 1300 standards supporting safety and quality in healthcare
4	Quality education	ISO 21001 pertains to management systems for educational organizations, providing requirements along with guidance
5	Gender equality	Gender equality is a critical aspect of social responsibility, aiming for the empowerment of women and equality within society
6	Clean water and sanitation	Worldwide, over 80% of wastewater generated by society is discharged back into the ecosystem without treatment or reuse
7	Affordable and clean energy	ISO standards represent internationally agreed guidelines and requirements for solutions concerning energy efficiency and renewable energy
8	Decent work and economic growth	International Standards foster economic growth by establishing a common language and framework recognized globally
9	Innovation and infrastructure	Industrialization is achieved through agreed international specifications meeting requirements for quality, safety, and sustainability
10	Reduced inequalities	These standards ensure market efficiency, protect public health and safety, and contribute to environmental preservation
11	Sustainable cities and communities	The responsible use of resources, coupled with environmental preservation, aims to enhance the well-being of citizens
12	Consumption and production	Efforts are focused on reducing environmental impact and promoting the use of renewable energy sources
13	Climate action	ISO plays an essential role in addressing climate issues, helping monitor climate change and quantify greenhouse gas emissions
14	Life below water	The organization offers a unique opportunity to participate in the development of fisheries and aquaculture
15	Life on land	ISO standards aim to protect and promote biodiversity on land through better resource management
16	Peace, justice and institutions	Effective, accountable, and inclusive societies rely on strong governance at all levels
17	Partnerships for the goals	These standards are developed with the consensus of a wide range of stakeholders from around the globe, including representatives from the government

Source: United Nations (2015) and International Organization for Standardization (2018)

17 Sustainable Development Goals (SDGs). Table 2 shows the connection between the SDGs and ISO standards, while Table 3 lists the benefits of sustainable facility management.

The Facilities Management (FM) sector works with people, organizations, and authorities to keep spaces safe and secure. This aligns with Sustainable Development

Table 3 Benefits of sustainability facilities management

Perspectives	Benefits of Sustainable Facilities Management
Social	Add value to organizations and customers by effectively managing sustainability issues and practices Focus on long-term goals within organizations while maintaining continuity responsibilities Integrate the Sustainable Development Goals (SDGs) into a wide range of corporate practices Develop a leadership network aimed at promoting gender parity in executive management
Environmental	Evaluating profitability, productivity, energy management, waste management, employee well-being, and public perception of an organization Promoting work-life balance by providing good and flexible working conditions Ensuring the proper functioning of the market, protecting people's health and safety, and preserving the environment Aiming for a reduction in energy consumption, waste reduction, increased productivity, elimination of oil and air pollution, sustainable urbanization, reduction of deforestation, and decreasing carbon dioxide emissions
Economic	Technology is advancing beyond our wildest imaginations, while resources are becoming increasingly scarce. Customers are demanding higher operational efficiency Incorporating sustainable practices in building management not only helps preserve the environment but also reduces costs This approach lowers the operational expenses of organizations and decreases the carbon emissions of buildings. By focusing on lifecycle cost reduction, businesses can achieve financial gains and drive investments, ultimately improving profitability, remaining competitive, and expanding their market
Drivers for SFM	A growing awareness of the benefits and importance of integrating sustainability into Facilities Management (FM) practices is evident. Pressure from legislation, intense market competition, and rapidly changing business environments necessitate the pursuit of a competitive edge Interestingly, influences from stakeholders, employees, and lifecycle cost reduction were considered the least significant drivers for Sustainable Facilities Management (SFM) practices The main drivers identified for SFM include job creation for local communities, waste reduction, and the enhancement of relationships with stakeholders

Source: Abigo et al. (2012); Elmualim et al. (2012); Baaki Kurannen et al. (2016); IFMEC (2018) and International Organization.for Standardization (2018)

Goal 16 (Peace, Justice, and Strong Institutions) and Goal 17 (Partnership for the Goals). The FM sector can also support Sustainable Development Goal 12 (Responsible Consumption and Production) by encouraging sustainable and circular purchasing practices. This ensures that only eco-friendly products that are safe for health and the environment are used. For example, the FM sector should use wood products that have sustainable certifications. This helps to maintain biodiversity, which relates to Goal 15 (Life on Land, Biodiversity). By following these policies, the sector can reduce its carbon dioxide emissions and overall carbon footprint, which supports Goal 13 (Climate Action). These efforts are key to protecting our oceans and seas (Goal 14: Life Below Water), which are vital for the health of our planet.

Recently, scholars and researchers have started studying the UN Sustainable Development Goals (SDGs) in the built environment. Opoku and Lee (2022) found that facilities management (FM) can create jobs, which helps improve people's economic and social situations (SDG 8: Decent Work and Economic Growth) and addresses poverty (SDG 1: No Poverty). The FM industry is key to the food supply chain in various organizations, such as companies, schools, and hospitals. By working together to improve workplaces and employee conditions, the sector supports SDG 2 (Zero Hunger) and SDG 3 (Good Health and Well-Being). In addition, the FM sector helps maintain buildings sustainably in cities and communities (SDG 11: Sustainable Cities and Communities). This includes managing energy use in buildings (SDG 7: Affordable and Clean Energy) and better managing water resources (SDG 6: Clean Water and Sanitation) by reducing leaks. FM plays a significant role in improving the quality of education in international educational facilities (SDG 4: Quality Education). It also promotes diversity with a workforce from various nationalities (SDG 10: Reduced Inequalities) and provides equal pay and career opportunities for women, supporting gender equality (SDG 5). FM professionals have also embraced technologies like artificial intelligence (AI) and the Internet of Things (IoT) for smart buildings, helping achieve SDG 9 (Industry, Innovation, and Infrastructure) (IFMEC, 2018).

Facility managers should pay attention to the long-term environmental impact of their decisions instead of just short-term maintenance issues. Sustainable facilities management (SFM) aims to build net-zero energy buildings, improve energy solutions for existing buildings, and use data-driven management technologies. Using smart technologies in different facilities can make operations more efficient. To succeed in sustainability, it's important to train staff on best practices and policies while also informing end users. Sustainability should be part of daily operations. This includes reducing water usage with automated toilets, waterless urinals, and low-flow fixtures, sourcing local food, and adopting recycling and waste disposal strategies. Additionally, practices like hot-desking can support sustainability (Berardi, 2013).

3 Sustainable Facilities Management Outsourcing Relationships: AI Applications and Case Studies

This facilities management (FM) outsourcing system is helpful for FM services. Its success depends not only on FM researchers but also on how well FM practitioners and the community apply the system (Lok et al., 2021). Today, people of all ages need to learn and stay updated on modern IT techniques since digitalization affects us all. Lee et al. (2021) suggest that digitalization changes how we carry out daily tasks in both traditional and new industries, including FM. To improve communication and productivity, it is important for everyone to use IT applications in their daily lives. We increasingly use artificial intelligence (AI), machine learning (ML), and predictive maintenance systems to support decision-making for building maintenance (Villa et al., 2021). Clearly, IT applications can boost efficiency and productivity across all professions.

This chapter explains a system for managing sustainable relationships in facility management (FM) outsourcing using real case studies. Mannino et al. (2021) found that having inadequate data can slow down digital progress in FM. Collins et al. (2019) pointed out that there is a disconnection between sustainable buildings and FM. They stressed the need to connect design, construction, and FM more effectively. This connection requires better solutions based on life cycle assessments. Sustainable FM is related to building performance, tools and standards for sustainability, productivity, user satisfaction, and sustainability management (Nielsen et al., 2016). Good relationships between clients and service providers are crucial for successful FM outsourcing services (Lok & Baldry, 2015). The FM Contingency Outsourcing Relationship (CORE) model helps measure how well an FM service provider is currently performing and assesses future outsourcing plans. It looks at capabilities and capacities for specific contracts aligning with the identified relationships (Lok et al., 2020). By using and validating real data, this system can effectively support FM outsourcing services in the built environment.

A new model called the CORE model is now being used in the facilities management (FM) industry. The FORT model was originally created for the information technology sector. Lok et al. explained the CORE model, which is based on four types of outsourcing relationships identified in the FORT model. This study looked at simulated case studies within the CORE model's four categories: in-house management, technical expertise, commitment, and common goals. It primarily focused on the clients' perspective. The study builds on earlier research about the outsourcing relationships between FM service providers and clients. It also investigates the use of Artificial Neural Networks (ANNs) to support sustainable practices.

The CORE model describes four main outsourcing categories: *OC*1, *OC*2, *OC*3, and *OC*4 (Lok et al., 2020). However, in real life, things often don't fit perfectly into these categories. After examining actual case studies, the research introduced three new middle categories: *OC*1/2, *OC*2/3, and *OC*3/4. These new categories help to explain how the system works more clearly.

This study uses a survey to examine eight outsourcing strategies across seven different outsourcing relationships. It introduces rules for CORE related to four simulated outsourcing systems (Lok et al., 2021). The study looks at how to apply seven outsourcing categories effectively in facility management (FM) relationships using scientific Artificial Intelligence (AI). The results from the Artificial Neural Network (ANN) validation offer useful insights into the relationships between stakeholders and service providers. By following these rules, users and facility owners can better design their FM outsourcing strategies. This can lead to improved productivity, efficiency, and overall service in FM (Lok et al., 2022). In summary, categorizing FM outsourcing helps to clarify the right relationships within these systems.

4 Materials and Methods

To take advantage of Industry 4.0, businesses can use big data analytics, modeling, and simulation. This study confirms existing knowledge about how artificial intelligence can improve facilities management (FM) outsourcing. This approach helps FM companies gain a competitive edge and create real value. We used a survey to analyze eight outsourcing strategies across four types of outsourcing relationships. Our practical approach includes four specific categories of FM outsourcing. We designed the data collection process so each case study fits one of these categories.

The data collection was conducted from early August 2021 to the end of December 2021, covering 5 months. We originally planned to conduct four case studies, each focusing on a different type of outsourcing relationship. However, due to the COVID-19 pandemic, collecting primary data in Hong Kong became difficult because many industries faced lockdowns. This survey aimed to take a strategic approach within the construction and built environment sectors, where facilities management professionals understand the research topic better. There are two ways to find suitable case studies about companies or institutions through individual research connections. We have sent electronic invitations to local facility management (FM) and real estate professional networks, including several professional institutions. The respondents for this survey are FM facility owners and practitioners in the built environment. Each respondent's company or organization invited two or three colleagues to complete the survey in the same work setting. This method aims to focus on participants in the built environment, making the results stronger and more reliable. The practical case studies will include examples from Hong Kong and various international industries. These will cover property management, property development, building maintenance, leisure and culture, education, and exhibitions.

We used Artificial Neural Networks (ANN) to analyze raw data while we collected it. This was important for identifying the type of outsourcing relationship in a specific case study. As we examined the cases, we noticed that some outcomes did not fit neatly into the four main outsourcing categories: *OC*1, *OC*2, *OC*3, and *OC*4. These outcomes often fell near the borders between two categories. To solve this, we created three new hybrid categories: *OC*1/2, *OC*2/3, and *OC*3/4. For example, *OC*1/2 includes cases between *OC*1 and *OC*2. Now, we have a total of seven outsourcing categories. The final data about these categories is noted in the analysis section.

4.1 Data Collection Stage

Here are ten steps for companies or organizations that want to take part in this research as case studies:

1. The company should be recognized at a regional or international level.
2. The company can either own or use a facility.

3. The company must provide two to three people to complete the questionnaire on their own and without help to ensure accurate results.
4. We will prioritize senior or middle-level professionals from regional or international clients or companies.
5. Participants do not need to know their company's specific category.
6. We will brief participants before the questionnaire survey starts.
7. Participants can check their responses against an independent standard related to their company.
8. Different people from the same company should work together to ensure fair, objective, and reliable results.
9. The Artificial Neural Network (ANN) analysis gave positive scientific results.
10. The ANN analysis shows that no major parameter among the eight outsourcing strategies can be set to zero. If there is no rating provided in the questionnaire, we will assign a value of "1" to the outsourcing strategy and a weight of "0," meaning it will not affect the overall assessment.

These steps are important for ensuring the integrity and effectiveness of the research process.

4.2 Analysis of the Data

4.2.1 Outsourcing Categorization and Generation of Final OC Using ANN

This chapter looks at how to use an Artificial Neural Network (ANN) for Facilities Management (FM) outsourcing, building on what Lok et al. (2020) previously discussed about using quantitative data. We will measure eight outsourcing strategies along two axes. The X-axis shows how the outsourced FM portfolio affects the client's competitive position and long-term goals. The Y-axis assesses how much ownership and control of FM assets are transferred to service providers (Lok et al., 2021). This model can help predict the relationships between FM stakeholders in specific contracts, including building maintenance, security, cleaning, and catering. The ANN includes four input variables ($OC1$, $OC2$, $OC3$, and $OC4$) and one output variable (OC). We calculate $OC1$ to $OC4$ using raw data from various FM firms, and the final value of OC helps us categorize the outsourcing strategy.

We identified eight FM outsourcing strategies based on the FM CORE model (Lok & Baldry, 2015, 2016) and assigned each a value between 0% and 100%. The values include Substitution of Ownership ($SO1$, $SO2$) and Substitution of Control ($SC1$, $SC2$) on the Y-axis and Competitive Position ($CP1$, $CP2$) and Long-term Plan ($LP1$, $LP2$) on the X-axis. Next, we combined these eight values into four outsourcing category values, also ranging from 0% to 100%, using the mapping from Lok et al. (2021). We achieved this using four equations based on the Cobb-

Douglas Production Function (Cobb and Douglas, 1928). We classify the indices as high = 3, medium = 2, and low = 1.

$$\begin{aligned} OC1 &= \left(SO1^{3*}SO2^{2*}SC1^{*}SC2^{*}CP1^{3*}CP2^{2*}LP1^{*}LP2\right)^{\frac{1}{14}} \\ OC2 &= \left(SO1^{2*}SO2^{3*}SC1^{2*}SC2^{*}CP1^{2*}CP2^{3*}LP1^{2*}LP2\right)^{\frac{1}{16}} \\ OC3 &= \left(SO1^{*}SO2^{2*}SC1^{3*}SC2^{3*}CP1^{3*}CP2^{2*}LP1^{3*}LP2\right)^{\frac{1}{18}} \\ OC4 &= \left(SO1^{2*}SO2^{2*}SC1^{3*}SC2^{3*}CP1^{2*}CP2^{2*}LP1^{3*}LP2^{3}\right)^{\frac{1}{20}} \end{aligned}$$

Four values that represent outsourcing categories go into a well-trained artificial neural network (ANN), as explained by Lok et al. (2020). Each value ranges from 0% to 100%, which is then changed to a new range of [0.5, 5.5]. To do this, we divide each raw value by 20 and add 0.5. Each outsourcing category is rated on a scale from 1 to 5. For example, the range of [0%, 20%] is converted to [0.5, 1.5]. The output is limited to the range of [0.5, 4.5], based on the expert database used for training. This limit is because there are four outsourcing categories: *OC*1, *OC*2, *OC*3 and *OC*4. The final output category is determined using the following formula:

$$OC = \begin{cases} 1 & \text{if} \quad 0.5 \leq OC < 1.5 \\ 2 & \text{if} \quad 1.5 \leq OC < 2.5 \\ 3 & \text{if} \quad 2.5 \leq OC < 3.5 \\ 4 & \text{if} \quad 3.5 \leq OC < 4.5 \end{cases}$$

This section gives four examples of outsourcing and explains the framework clearly. Lok et al. (2021) identify four categories: *OC*1, *OC*2, *OC*3 and *OC*4. However, it isn't practical to assign *OC*1 to a company with a score of 1.49 and *OC*2 to another with a score of 1.51. To address this, we created three new categories: *OC*1/2, *OC*2/3 and *OC*3/4.

The real world is continuous, not just made up of separate parts. We recommend using a margin of 0.15, so the Transient Zone is ± 0.15. This study includes the main outsourcing categories *OC*1, *OC*2, *OC*3, *OC*4, as well as some cases that fall in between. For example, *OC*1/2 is between *OC*1 and *OC*2, *OC*2/3 is between *OC*2 and *OC*3, and *OC*3/4 is between *OC*3 and *OC*4. With this adjustment, the ranges for the seven outsourcing categories are as follows:

*OC*1:	[0.5000, 1.3499]
*OC*1/2:	[1.3500, 1.6500]
*OC*2:	[1.6501, 2.3499]
*OC*2/3:	[2.3500, 2.6500]
*OC*3:	[2.6501, 3.3499]
*OC*3/4:	[3.3500, 3.6500]
*OC*4:	[3.6501, 4.5000]

5 Summary

Lok et al. (2021) describe four kinds of outsourcing relationships between clients and service providers:

1. Outsourcing Category 1 (*OC*1): This type is called Support/In-house. It greatly affects hard facilities management (FM) by tackling challenges related to flexible facilities and offering a competitive edge.
2. Outsourcing Category 2 (*OC*2): This type is known as Alignment/Technical Expertise. It is important for soft FM to help build flexible relationships in service delivery and improve the value of the FM portfolio and business processes.
3. Outsourcing Category 3 (*OC*3): This type is called Reliance/Commitment. It has a strong impact on how managers control operations and make decisions about planning and development. It also involves replacing in-house FM staff, which adds to the competitive advantage.
4. Outsourcing Category 4 (*OC*4): This type is known as Alliance/Partner. It significantly boosts long-term competitiveness through strong partnerships and strategic relationships, leading to new revenue opportunities.

Each category highlights different aspects of the service relationship and its effects on facilities management (Tables 4 and 5).

5.1 Analysis of Outsourcing Category 1 (OC*1)*

*OC*1 comes from Case Study 5, which looks at the public sector in Exhibition and Education. This organization works regionally and has fewer than 50 employees. It aims to provide teaching and learning platforms that support a sustainable environment for the local community. The facilities management (FM) outsourcing service provider manages several subcontractors responsible for cleaning, building maintenance, and catering. The survey included two managers, and their raw output scores were 1.054 and 1.147.

Another *OC*1 is from Case Study 8, which examines the private sector in property management. This company employs between 100 and 200 people and offers property management services. The FM outsourcing provider also oversees subcontractors that provide services like security, cleaning, and renovation. The two survey respondents were associate directors and senior officers, with raw output scores of 1.058 and 1.107.

The analysis for Outsourcing Category 2 (*OC*2) is not available because the research team could not find a suitable company for this category. Although this is unfortunate, it is important to note that all cases were randomly selected, so it keeps the generality.

Table 4 Profile of details of the eight case studies of the seven outsourcing categories (data collection period: 20/8/21 to 5/12/21; 3.5 months)

Case study	Sector/size/number of employees/number of respondents/level of respondent/business nature	FM outsourcing services	Nature of FM services providers of the case Characteristics of outsourcing category	Final raw output	Confirmed (*OC*)
1	Private (Building maintenance)/regional/Below 50/2/Assistant Manager/ Provision on Maintenance services to residents	Maintenance works: services	**Repair and Maintenance of Building Assets** The Outsourcing Category 1/2 (*OC*1/2) describes a relationship between the Client (C) and the Service Provider (SP) that exists between in-house support and the SP's specialized expertise To justify this new category, it is essential to analyze the impacts of Ownership Substitution (SO1 and SO2) within Facilities Management (FM) Outsourcing strategies. The impacts of SO1 and SO2 can be categorized as high and medium. Similarly, for the strategic influence of FM Outsourcing strategies, the impacts of CP1 and CP2 also fall between high and medium When does a company fall into the Outsourcing Category 1/2 (*OC*1/2)? If a company is dynamically categorized as *OC*1 but is making progress towards *OC*2, it qualifies as being in the Outsourcing Category 1/2 (*OC*1/2), which includes in-house support and technical expertise. This dual categorization has a significant impact on SO1 (hard FM)—addressing the challenges of flexible facilities—and SO2 (soft FM)—which pertains to managing flexible relationships in service provision. Furthermore, it significantly influences CP1 (competitive advantage) and CP2 (value points for leveraging the FM portfolio and improving business processes) Service Providers (SPs) exhibit the following *OC*1 and *OC*2 characteristics: they can offer a high standard of mutually agreed-upon equipment to meet the Client's	1.573 1.449	1/2

			requirements and maintain strong daily relationships with Clients. This involves diligent work, professionalism, warm hospitality, close coordination, and a keen understanding of customer needs Additionally, SPs can deliver medium standards of tailored professional knowledge regarding building assets and uphold a general level of routine productivity in monthly operations. This encompasses security management, waste management, workplace cleanliness, and indoor environmental quality		
2	Private (Property development)/International/500 – 1000/2/Senior officer/ Provision on property development and management services	Office maintenance; IT hardware; cleaning and security	**Builder; E&M Works; Office Support; Hygiene and Security System** The Outsourcing Category 3 (*OC*3) refers to a relationship where the connection between the client (C) and the service provider (SP) is characterized by the SP's reliance and commitment The impacts of SC1 and SC2 regarding ownership substitution, along with CP1 and LP1 reflecting the strategic influence of facilities management (FM) outsourcing strategies, are considered quite significant Service providers can deliver sufficient or even superior standards of mutually agreed working timeframes for work orders and monthly operational confirmations, meeting the clients' requirements. They can also foster good daily relationships with clients through diligent work, professionalism, warm hospitality, close coordination, and understanding of customer needs Service providers can track their performance every month to improve customer satisfaction. This focus includes areas such as health, safety, maintenance, and operational management	3.261 3.487	3

(continued)

Table 4 (continued)

Case study	Sector/size/number of employees/number of respondents/level of respondent/business nature	FM outsourcing services	Nature of FM services providers of the case Characteristics of outsourcing category	Final raw output	Confirmed (*OC*)
3	Public (Leisure and culture of Government)/regional/ Below 50/3/Manager/ Provision on quality cultural services commensurating as a world-class city and events capital	Security; cleaning and antimicrobial	**Building Management Responsibilities: Patrol buildings and inspect visitors; Respond to emergencies; Vacuum, sweep, and mop floors; Empty trash cans; Spray antimicrobial coatings** The Outsourcing Category 4 (*OC*4) denotes a relationship where the Contractor (C) and Service Provider (SP) are part of an alliance or partnership The impacts of SC1 and SC2, relating to Ownership Substitution, along with LP1 and LP2 regarding Strategic Influence in Facilities Management (FM) Outsourcing strategies, are as significant as those in Outsourcing Category 3 (*OC*3) Service Providers can meet annual performance goals and improve customer satisfaction in areas like emergency planning, business continuity, and sustainability	3.889 3.875 3.907	4
4	Public (Construction and Maintenance)/regional/ 500–1000/2/ Property Officer/ Provision on construction and maintenance services to districts	Security; cleaning	**General Property Management Services** The Outsourcing Category 2/3 (*OC*2/3) represents a relationship where the service provider (SP) balances their alignment and technical expertise with their reliance and commitment to the client (C) To support the classification of this new group, it's essential to analyze the impacts of SO2, SC1, and SC2 within the Ownership Substitution of Facilities Management (FM) Outsourcing strategies, which range between high and medium levels. Additionally, the strategic influences of FM Outsourcing strategies, particularly CP1 and CP2, also display high and medium impacts, falling under	2.529 2.478	2/3

			Outsourcing Category 1/2 (*OC*1/2). The influence of LP1 is similarly categorized as in-between high and medium So, when does a company fall under Outsourcing Category 2/3 (*OC*2/3)? If a company is dynamically and marginally classified as *OC*2, with the potential progress to *OC*3, we would consider it within the *OC*2/3 category. This classification indicates a strong impact on SO2 (soft FM), emphasizing the challenges of maintaining flexible relationships in service provision, and on CP2, which links to the value points for leveraging the FM portfolio and enhancing business processes. There is an important impact on SC1 and SC2, which encompass managerial control and decision-making regarding operations, planning, development, and the replacement of in-house FM staff, as well as on CP1 (competitive advantage) and LP1 (competitiveness) Service providers (SPs) with *OC*2 and *OC*3 characteristics can offer tailored professional knowledge at intermediate to high standards for building assets. They can also maintain a mutually agreed-upon timeframe for work orders and address client concerns regarding confirmation of monthly operations. SPs are expected to uphold a high standard of customer satisfaction in areas such as health, safety, maintenance, and operation management Additionally, SPs should ensure a sufficient, if not superior, standard for working timeframes and performance metrics. They are expected to build strong, daily relationships with clients through diligent work, professionalism, warm hospitality, close coordination, and a deep consideration of customer needs		

(continued)

Table 4 (continued)

Case study	Sector/size/number of employees/number of respondents/level of respondent/business nature	FM outsourcing services	Nature of FM services providers of the case Characteristics of outsourcing category	Final raw output	Confirmed (*OC*)
5	Public (Education and exhibition)/ regional/ Below 50/2/ Manager/Provision on teaching and learning platform about the sustainable environment to the local community	Cleaning; building maintenance and catering	**The FM Management contractor oversees a number of subcontractors** In the Outsourcing Category 1 (*OC*1), the relationship between the contractor (C) and the service provider (SP) is classified as part of a supportive in-house group The impacts of both SO1 (Ownership Substitution) and CP1 (Strategic Influence of FM Outsourcing strategies) are considered quite significant Service providers (SPs) are capable of delivering at least a satisfactory or even superior standard of mutually agreed equipment to meet the daily operational requirements of contractors (Cs). They also maintain strong relationships with the contractors through their diligent work, professional demeanor, warm hospitality, close coordination, and deep consideration of customer needs	1.054 1.147	1
6	Public (Property management)/ national/500–1000/ 2/ Works supervisors/ Provision of housing supply services	Security, cleaning, customer and maintenance services/ general building maintenance works	**Cleaning Service; Maintenance/Building Management** The Outsourcing Category 3/4 (*OC*3/4) defines the relationship between the Client (C) and Service Provider (SP) as one that lies between reliance/commitment and alliance/partnership To justify the establishment of this new category, it is essential to analyze the SC1 and SC2 components of Ownership Substitution within Facility Management (FM) Outsourcing strategies. The impacts of SC1 and SC2 are as significant as those of Outsourcing Category 3 (*OC*3) and Outsourcing Category 4 (*OC*4). Regarding the Strategic Influence of FM Outsourcing strategies, the impacts of CP1	3.695 3.410 3.370 3.434	3/4
7	Private (Building surveying consultancy)/ International/50–100/2/Assistant building surveyor/Building surveying consultancy				

			fall between high and medium, similar to Outsourcing Categories 1/2 (*OC*1/2) or 2/3 (*OC*2/3). Conversely, the impacts of LP1 are comparable in significance to those in OC3 and OC4, while the impacts of LP2 are also substantial When does a company fall into the Outsourcing Category 3/4 (*OC*3/4)? If a company is dynamically and marginally categorized at *OC*3 but is progressing towards *OC*4, we would classify it within *OC*3/4 (Commitment/Partnership). This classification indicates a high impact on managerial control and decision-making over operations, planning, development, and implementation, especially concerning in-house FM staff. It also reflects a competitive advantage (CP1) and overall competitiveness (LP1), along with a focus on long-term competitiveness, fostering close partnerships, strategic inter-organizational relationships, and new revenue streams Service Providers (SPs) exhibit the following characteristics of *OC*3: they can consistently maintain monthly performance and customer satisfaction concerning health, safety, maintenance, and operations management For the OC4 category, SPs demonstrate the ability to sustain yearly performance and customer satisfaction in areas such as emergency planning, business continuity, and sustainability		
8	Private (Property management)/regional/100–200/2/Associate Director/Provision of property management services	Security, cleaning, renovation	Comprehensive hard and soft PFM services ditto	1.058 1.107	1

(continued)

Table 4 (continued)

Case study	Sector/size/number of employees/number of respondents/level of respondent/business nature	FM outsourcing services	Nature of FM services providers of the case Characteristics of outsourcing category	Final raw output	Confirmed (*OC*)
X	X	X	The Outsourcing Category 2 (*OC*2) indicates that the relationship between the Client (C) and the Service Provider (SP) falls within a group that aligns with the SP's technical expertise The impacts of SO2 concerning Ownership Substitution and CP2 regarding the Strategic Influence of Facility Management (FM) outsourcing strategies are considered quite significant Service Providers can offer sufficient or even superior levels of customized professional knowledge for managing building assets. It is crucial for the Client and Service Provider to mutually agree on the daily operations to ensure they meet the client's requirements. The Service Provider can maintain a high level of general routine productivity for the Client on a monthly basis. Examples of this include security management, waste management, workplace cleanliness, and maintaining indoor environmental quality.	X X	2

Table 5 Raw data of the eight case studies of the seven outsourcing categories

Case study	Industry	Officer	SO1	SO2	SC1	SC2	CP1	CP2	LP1	LP2	Input *OC1*	Input *OC2*	Input *OC3*	Input *OC4*	Output (raw)	Confirmed *OC*
1	Private (building maintenance)	1 (X)	78.18	44.83	101.72	8.61	61.94	132.74	78.60	20.00	**3.430**	**3.630**	3.020	2.820	1.573	*OC1/2*
		2 (Y)	87.27	62.07	89.44	4.73	60.00	137.76	68.84	20.00	**3.450**	**3.650**	2.770	2.630	1.449	*OC1/2*
2	Private (property development)	1 (X)	63.64	100.00	78.94	81.23	66.45	98.72	64.47	10.00	3.810	4.020	**3.950**	3.340	3.261	*OC3*
		2 (Y)	63.64	100.00	91.32	81.23	73.55	117.23	100.41	10.00	4.110	4.460	**4.450**	3.690	3.487	*OC3*
3	Public (leisure and cultural services)	1 (X)	58.18	20.69	100.00	100.00	63.87	92.33	73.06	75.79	3.560	3.560	4.000	**4.010**	3.889	*OC4*
		2 (Y)	45.45	27.59	100.00	100.00	70.97	89.90	73.06	75.79	3.580	3.660	4.120	**4.050**	3.875	*OC4*
		3 (Z)	60.00	20.69	100.00	100.00	66.45	88.66	73.06	75.79	3.590	3.560	4.010	**4.020**	3.907	*OC4*
4	Public (construction & maintenance)	1 (X)	81.82	48.28	86.85	34.86	72.90	94.76	88.40	13.20	3.650	**3.730**	**3.590**	3.160	2.529	*OC2/3*
		2 (Y)	87.27	51.72	76.42	42.49	73.55	85.97	80.55	13.20	3.680	**3.690**	**3.580**	3.160	2.478	*OC2/3*
5	Public (education & Exhibition)	1 (X)	83.64	96.55	27.63	7.07	75.48	72.33	52.22	10.00	**3.130**	3.040	2.360	2.140	1.054	*OC1*
		2 (Y)	81.82	82.76	35.02	6.15	72.26	73.80	60.46	10.00	**3.090**	3.060	2.390	2.170	1.147	*OC1*
6	Public (property management)	1 (X)	70.91	62.07	100.00	81.23	76.77	82.33	118.91	23.52	4.090	4.270	**4.500**	**4.020**	3.695	*OC3/4*
		2 (Y)	63.64	75.86	123.95	82.78	87.10	80.63	112.28	19.04	4.190	4.430	**4.710**	**4.070**	3.410	*OC3/4*
7	Private (building surveying consultancy)	1 (X)	36.36	24.14	100.00	100.00	56.13	109.67	59.28	26.39	3.080	3.250	**3.650**	**3.330**	3.370	*OC3/4*
		2 (Y)	34.55	20.69	100.00	100.00	77.42	112.42	59.28	31.04	3.210	3.310	**3.800**	**3.440**	3.434	*OC3/4*
8	Private (property management)	1 (X)	12.73	55.17	5.00	4.78	24.52	123.49	48.32	25.51	**1.760**	1.940	1.520	1.510	1.058	*OC1*
		2 (Y)	7.27	37.93	1.00	3.68	20.65	146.97	84.84	10.00	**1.390**	1.530	1.210	1.150	1.107	*OC1*

5.2 Analysis of Outsourcing Category 3 (OC3)

*OC*3 is based on Case Study 2, which looks at an international private sector company that provides property development services. The company has between 500 and 1000 employees. They hire a facilities management (FM) service provider to handle building maintenance, electrical work, office support, hygiene services, and security systems. The FM services include general office decoration, fixture maintenance, IT hardware management, cleaning services, and security. Two senior officers took part in the survey, giving raw scores of 3.261 and 3.487.

5.3 Analysis of Outsourcing Category 4 (OC4)

OC 4 refers to Case Study 3, which examines a public sector organization that focuses on culture and leisure. This organization has fewer than 50 employees and operates in a specific region. Its goal is to provide high-quality cultural services to support its reputation as an international city and event destination. The facilities management (FM) outsourcing service provider handles various building management tasks. These tasks include patrols, visitor inspections, emergency responses, vacuuming, sweeping, mopping floors, emptying trash cans, and applying antimicrobial coatings. The FM services cover cleaning, security, and antimicrobial treatments. Three managers took part in a survey and provided scores of 3.889, 3.875, and 3.907.

New outsourcing categories need to be established as the current four categories do not cover all real-world situations. To address this, it is suggested to introduce three new categories—1/2, 2/3, and 3/4—to better analyze and support the existing categories: *OC*1, *OC*2, *OC*3 and *OC*4. The details for these new groups are as follows:

5.4 Analysis of Outsourcing Category 1/2 (OC1/2)

Case Study 1 looks at a private building maintenance company that operates in a specific region and has fewer than 50 employees. This company provides maintenance services to residents. The facilities management (FM) outsourcing provider handles the repair and maintenance of building assets and delivers various outsourcing services, including maintenance work. Two managers took part in the survey and reported raw output scores of 1.573 and 1.449.

5.5 Analysis of Outsourcing Category 2/3 (OC2/3)

*OC*2/3 comes from Case Study 4, which looks at a public sector organization in the maintenance and construction industry. This organization operates regionally and employs between 500 and 1000 people. It mainly provides maintenance and construction services to different districts. An FM outsourcing service provider handles general property management services, such as security and cleaning. Two property officers participated in the survey, giving raw output scores of 2.529 and 2.478.

5.6 *Analysis of Outsourcing Category 3/4 (OC3/4)*

*OC*3/4 includes Case Study 6 and Case Study 7. Case Study 6 features a public property management organization operating nationally, with 500 to 1000 employees. This organization focuses on housing supply services. An FM outsourcing provider manages building maintenance and offers services like security, cleaning, and customer support. Two supervisors from this study reported raw scores of 3.695 and 3.410.

Case Study 7 looks at a private building surveying consultancy that operates internationally. This organization has between 50 and 100 employees and specializes in building survey consultancy services. An FM outsourcing provider oversees building management, including maintenance and cleaning. Two building survey respondents gave raw scores of 3.434 and 3.370.

6 Discussion

IFMEC (2018) notes that the facilities management (FM) industry has made great strides by using technologies like artificial intelligence (AI) and the Internet of Things (IoT) for smart-building projects. These efforts support the UN's Sustainable Development Goals (SDGs), particularly SDG 9, which focuses on industry, innovation, and infrastructure. The digitalization of FM, especially in outsourcing, is a recent trend that fits with the Fourth Industrial Revolution.

This chapter examines FM services related to real estate and soft-user services. Opoku and Lee (2022) emphasize the importance of partnerships in reaching one of the 17 goals. They argue that the FM sector must take a leading role in promoting engagement and integrating sustainability into daily practices to improve customer service. Sustainable FM merges facilities management principles with sustainable development by adopting new technologies and practices that balance social, economic, and environmental impacts.

Our well-trained Artificial Neural Network (ANN) was applied to eight real-world cases, confirming the effectiveness of our approach. The actual results matched the outsourcing categories identified by the ANN. FM service providers can improve their outsourcing services continuously based on these categories. The CORE model assists in assessing and managing FM outsourcing relationships with an eye on sustainable performance in environmental, social, and economic areas. This model supports both short-term and long-term FM plans, enhancing outsourcing results.

This chapter offers valuable insights into the firms tested, allowing facility owners to use the CORE model to measure and evaluate outsourced services systematically. This ensures a substantial database for further analysis and helps increase service productivity while reducing costs linked to FM contracts.

One challenge of this study is the limited number of companies willing to participate, resulting in only eight case studies. Additionally, using artificial neural networks (ANNs) has its drawbacks. As the number of cases increases, the learning capabilities of ANNs may slightly alter the underlying framework. While this adaptability has advantages, facility owners may need to invest time and effort to verify outsourced goods and services, which could delay commercial implementation.

To enhance the study's credibility, it would help to include more real-life case samples from FM experts and conduct structured interviews with them. However, we did not cover the financial aspects of FM outsourcing contracts, as these details are usually confidential. Future research could benefit from including quantitative on-site measurements along with AI analyses for a clearer evaluation of FM outsourcing categories.

6.1 FM Sector Incorporation with SDGs

The Sustainable Development Goals (SDGs) are important standards that facility managers can utilize to improve their operations. Nevertheless, the facility management (FM) sector struggles to fully understand and implement these goals. Sustainability and security/emergency management are increasingly linked in organizations. When managed well, they can significantly enhance facility management operations (Roper & Richard, 2014). This section looks at sustainable development in facility management and its connection to sustainable facility management and the SDGs. Recent studies have explored topics like green technologies and innovative building practices (Olawumi & Chan, 2018). These studies also discuss trends in sustainability, such as sustainability indicators, sustainable urban development, environmental assessments, and public policy. It's important to combine theoretical and practical knowledge to guide this document and assess building operations. This assessment should consider social, environmental, and economic impacts, including the use of sustainability standards and tools (Nielsen et al., 2016).

The SDGs can assist in showing the added value of FM to core business operations and the FM industry as a whole. This is especially true regarding ISO standards and the roles of clients, service providers, and researchers. However, the pace of developing sustainable facility management has been still slow. The connection between sustainable FM and the SDGs is still developing. Several FM ISO standards exist, but these pose challenges for international FM stakeholders. Aligning ISO standards with the SDGs aims to improve FM services. However, how to implement these standards and goals is still unclear. Potential risks exist for FM stakeholders, making it crucial to understand these issues thoroughly.

6.1.1 Role of Clients

Regardless of whether they are private, public, or non-governmental organizations, it is essential to consider the requirements of their facilities. To align with the recently published FM ISO standards, organizations must grasp these standards fully and implement them effectively. However, integrating FM standards into their operations can be challenging. Moreover, the Sustainable Development Goals (SDGs) hold significant value for organizations. The relationship between ISO standards and SDGs can be mutually beneficial, allowing organizations to align their strategies with both sets of criteria. Unfortunately, some clients are hesitant to adopt these standards and goals, as they view them as a potential waste of short-term resources, which can hinder their overall business improvement. Establishing a connection between these standards and goals can be complex.

Conservative clients may not see how important it is to include new Facility Management (FM) Sustainable Development Goals (SDGs) for improving their assets and organizations. This lack of awareness can cause them to fall behind in global progress. Many established companies think they can operate well without the SDGs, but ISO FM practitioners stress the need to pursue these goals.

The ISO 41001 Annex, called "Guidance on the Use of This Document," provides clear steps for using the standard. It explains the process and lists specific functions for assessment and assignment. Each organization may have different needs, but a general framework applies to all (Reynolds, 2022). Nevertheless, many stakeholders show little interest in how these SDGs can benefit their businesses, which can harm FM productivity worldwide.

Various industries, especially international companies, are in a good position to adopt new FM sustainable development goals. They often hesitate to spend money and resources on these standards, thinking they are not urgent or beneficial. Many organizations already use established ISO management system standards, such as ISO 9001, 14001, and 55001. If FM focuses more on reducing costs than on creating strategic value, this remains a problem (Lok & Baldry, 2015). Often, the added value of the goals is not obvious, making it hard to justify adding another management system.

6.1.2 Role of Service Providers

To implement standards and goals effectively, service providers need to organize their resources carefully. They may find it challenging to operate efficiently, even within their own organizations. However, their main job is to meet both goals and standards to satisfy their clients' needs. Achieving this can be tough, as they must work both inside and outside their organizations to meet client requirements and policies. Some companies may not see the Sustainable Development Goals (SDGs) as important in building assets. However, the SDGs can create a better environmental system for the industry worldwide. If these companies use new digital techniques for data management with the right governance, they may find financial support to address social and economic challenges (Linkov et al., 2018). All investments should be sustainable, including extra financing, technology, and resources. These issues can hinder environmental progress and lead to questions about whether organizations can achieve positive results and increased productivity after implementing the SDGs.

First, organizations must prepare to adopt both internal and external goals and standards that match their clients' requirements. Second, they need to recognize that different clients may have different concerns related to these goals and standards. Therefore, it is important to create comprehensive plans and strategies to meet clients' complex requirements sustainably. Psychological barriers can lead people to overlook development goals. Some individuals may be reluctant to invest time and effort in supporting the SDGs within their businesses. This reluctance can prevent them from understanding what users need and expect from these goals. Users may feel that their experiences are not valued, leading to a lack of trust in the SDGs and their potential to improve business success. They may also worry about changes in new technologies. However, it is essential to establish standardized and strategic support for successfully adopting sustainable facilities management.

6.1.3 Role of Researchers

Researchers aim to understand standards and goals related to investigations. They help clients and service providers see why these standards and goals matter. However, researchers face challenges when trying to present these standards and goals fairly, especially concerning their scientific value. It can be hard to find useful data and analyze their importance. To improve this, researchers need to conduct more studies and use updated data. They also need real-world examples to back up their findings. Unfortunately, researchers and practitioners often do not collaborate effectively. Researchers can run objective studies, while practitioners can share relevant case studies.

Researchers also understand that people may face challenges with Sustainable Development Goals (SDGs). Important questions include: How can facilities management (FM) support SDGs worldwide? How do FM professionals see the importance of SDGs for business? How can they connect their understanding of new sustainable development goals to their services? Despite these questions, researchers often lack the case studies and support that they need to improve their research.

6.2 Recommendations on Sustainable Facility Management Outsourcing in SDGs

The Sustainable Development Goals (SDGs) are important for the facility management (FM) community. When we manage risks well, we can achieve these goals and improve the quality of FM services in buildings. However, the SDGs have not been implemented as quickly as expected. One reason for this delay is the connection between FM and other sectors like IT and HR, especially when focusing on sustainable facility management. Collaboration among all stakeholders is key to successfully implementing the SDGs in this area. FM service providers and clients should integrate the SDGs into their FM strategies and policies. By working together, they can find effective ways to meet these goals, knowing that communication and trust are essential.

Regular reviews of Sustainable Development Goals (SDGs) commitments are important. This helps keep efforts relevant and effective. Researchers should also explore how to improve the relationship between facility management (FM) and SDGs. However, reaching these goals still presents significant challenges.

Recently, facility management has increasingly prioritized sustainability by incorporating the newly recognized UN Sustainable Development Goals into business decisions. This chapter validates an AI-based outsourcing relationship system for facility management (FM) by examining various real business cases, including building maintenance, property development, leisure and cultural services, construction, education, exhibitions, and building surveying consultancy, all within the context of sustainability.

Big data is important for improving AI-driven facilities management (FM) outsourcing systems. Analyzing more case studies helps us give better advice to FM service providers. By testing more case studies, we can make the model more accurate. The AI model's results help to analyze the current outsourcing relationships between clients and service providers. Clients with clear and integrated FM outsourcing relationships can expect better services from their providers.

Additionally, the variety of case studies is significant. In the future, AI FM outsourcing could be applied to specialized types of buildings, such as data centers. In conclusion, categorizing FM outsourcing can help define appropriate relationships among all parties involved. This increased accuracy and precision will ultimately benefit end users—who may not always be direct clients—service providers and governing bodies.

7 Conclusion

This chapter looks at the Sustainable Development Goals (SDGs) in facility management (FM). While there is already some focus on sustainable facility management (SFM), FM professionals need to do more to implement these goals successfully. By using the SDGs, FM experts and academics can improve SFM practices. The SDGs can also help connect sustainable management practices with FM systems and emphasize the need to reduce waste in a sustainable way. Several important performance indicators (KPIs) related to FM and SFM have been identified through literature reviews. These include aspects like functionality, user experience, physical features, and financial factors. Research mainly focuses on efficiency, productivity, resource allocation, customer service, asset management, and cost control. The chapter is divided into two sections. The first section talks about how to apply sustainable facility management with the FM SDGs, while the second section shares case studies about AI-driven FM outsourcing systems.

In conclusion, understanding SFM and the FM SDGs can lead to better cost and resource efficiency. It can also improve user satisfaction through higher quality and reliable FM services. We encourage further research in important areas. It is essential to combine SFM and the FM SDGs into a united model that reflects the importance of services from three main FM stakeholders. Also, SFM should not just assess performance based on functionality; it should also look at how these services impact daily operations in buildings. Given how crucial these services are, implementing development goals for facility management should use availability-based strategies already in practice in the worldwide FM industry. This will help confirm that services continue without unrealistic efficiency expectations.

This study has limitations because it relies on the literature of recent FM publications and may reflect narrow perspectives from the researchers. Despite these limitations, the findings still hold value. New international SDGs in FM could lead to larger research projects that produce more general results. In summary, this chapter examines how SFM brings both opportunities and challenges in applying the new Sustainable Development Goals in the FM industry, representing a significant step toward sustainability in SFM outsourcing.

References

Abigo, A., Madgwick, D., Gidado, K., & Okonji, S. (2012). Embedding sustainable facilities management in the management of public buildings in Nigeria. In *EPPM 2012* (pp. 369–380). University of Brighton.

Aceves-Avila, C. D., & Berger-García, M. A. (2019). Sustainable facility management in higher education institutions. In W. Leal Filho (Ed.), *Encyclopedia of sustainability in higher education*. Springer Cham Germany.

Baaki Kurannen, T., Rizal Baharum, M., & Shah Ali, A. (2016). *A review of sustainable facilities management knowledge and practice*. University of Malaysia.

Berardi, U. (2013). Sustainability assessment of urban communities through rating systems. *Environment Development Sustainability, 15*, 1573–1591.

British Standards Institution. (2018). *Facility management – Management systems – Requirements with guidance for use* (ISO 41001:2018) UK.

Buser, M., Støre-Valen, M., Olsen, E. B., Straub, M., & Lauridsen, K. A. (2018). Improving the implementation of sustainable facility management: The role of end-users in realising energy efficient solutions. In *Proceedings of the 17th EuroFM Research Symposium EFMC, EuroFM, Sofia, Bulgaria*. Available online: https://www.semanticscholar.org/chapter/Improving-the-implementation-of-sustainable-the-of-Buser-St%C3%B8re-Valen/3dfcfb546283bc205703c89c1b96088ed66e263b. Accessed 1 Feb 2022.

Cobb, C. W., & Douglas, P. H. (1928). A Theory of Production. *The American Economics Review, 18*, 139–165.

Collins, D., Haugen, T., Lindkvist, C., & Aamodt, C. (2019). Bridging the gap between sustainable FM and sustainable buildings – An exploratory study of six public buildings in Norway. *Facilities, 37*, 639–652.

Elmualim, A. A., Czwakiel, A., Valle, C. R., Ludlow, G., & Shah, S. (2009). The practice of sustainable facility management: Design sentiments and the knowledge chasm. *Architectural Engineering Design Management, 5*, 91–102.

Elmualim, A., Valle, R., & Kwawu, W. (2012). Discerning policy and drivers for sustainable facility management practice. *Journal of Sustainability Built Environment, 1*, 16–25.

IFMEC. (2018). *Facility management approach to realizing the Sustainable Development Goals.* International Facility Management Expert Centre (IFMEC).

International Organization for Standardization. (2018). *Contributing to the UN Sustainable Development Goals with ISO standards, Switzerland*, ISO Central Secretariat.

International Organization for Standardization. (2022). *How ISO standards help meet the SDGS.* Available at: https://www.iso.org/sdgs.html. Accessed 23 June 2022.

Kwawu, W., & Elmualim, A. (2011). Sustainability in facility management: A review of drivers and policy issues. In C. Egbu & L. ECW (Eds.), *Proceedings of the 27th Annual ARCOM Conference, Bristol UK, 5–7 September* (pp. 1185–1194). Association of Researchers in Construction Management.

Lee, J. Y., & Kang, M. (2013). Innovation characteristics and intention to adopt sustainable facility management practices. *Ergonomics, 56*, 480–491.

Lee, J. Y., Irisboev, I. O., & Ryu, Y.-S. (2021). Literature review on digitalization in FM and FM performance measurement: Contribution of industry 4.0 in the global era. *Sustainability, 13*(23), 13432. https://doi.org/10.3390/su132313432

Linkov, I., Trump, B. D., Poinsatte-Jones, K., & Florin, M. V. (2018). Governance strategies for a sustainable digital world. *Sustainability, 10*(2), 440. https://doi.org/10.3390/su10020440

Lok, K. L., & Baldry, D. (2015). Facility management outsourcing relationships in the higher education institutes. *Facilities, 33*(13/14), 819–848.

Lok, K. L., & Baldry, D. (2016). Demand and supply of FM outsourcing services. *Journal of Facility Management, 14*(3), 221–248.

Lok, K. L., Opoku, A., & Baldry, D. (2018). Design of sustainable outsourcing services for facility management: Critical success factors. *Sustainability, 10*(7), 2292–2307.

Lok, K. L., So, A., Opoku, A., & Song, H. (2020). Globalized service providers' perspective for FM outsourcing relationships: Artificial neural networks. *Management Decision, 59*(1), 134–151. https://doi.org/10.1108/MD-01-2019-0102

Lok, K. L., So, A., Opoku, A., & Charles, C. (2021). A sustainable facility management outsourcing relationships system: Artificial neural networks. *Sustainability, 13*, 4740. https://doi.org/10.3390/su13094740

Lok, K. L., So, A., Opoku, A., & Chen, C. (2022). A sustainable artificial intelligence facility management outsourcing relationships system: Case studies. *Frontier Psychology, 13*, 920625. https://doi.org/10.3389/fpsyg.2022.920625

Lok, K. L., Opoku, A., Smith, A. J., van der Pool, I. & Cheung, K. L. (2023). Sustainable facility management in UN development goals. In *IOP Conference Series: Earth and Environmental Science, Vol. 1176, CIB W070 Conference on Facility Management and Maintenance, 08/05/2023 – 11/05/2023, Trondheim, Norway*. https://doi.org/10.1088/1755-1315/1176/1/012022.

Mannino, A., Dejaco, M. C., & Re Cecconi, F. (2021). Building information modelling and internet of things integration for facility management – Literature review and future needs. *Applied Sciences, 11*(7), 3062. https://doi.org/10.3390/app11073062

Nielsen, S. B., & Galamba, K. R. (2010). Facility management – When sustainable development is core business. In *9th EuroFM Research Symposium EFMC Madrid Spain.*

Nielsen, S. B., Jensen, J. O., & Jensen, P. A. (2009). Delivering sustainable facility management in Danish housing estates. In *Proceedings of the CIMNE 2009 International Conference on Sustainability Measurement and Modelling Barcelona Spain 5–6 November.*

Nielsen, S. B., Sarasoja, A. L., & Galamba, K. R. (2016). Sustainability in facilities management: An overview of current research. *Facilities, 34*, 535–563.

Olawumi, T. O., & Chan, D. W. M. (2018). A scientometric review of global research on sustainability and sustainable development. *Journal of Cleaner Production, 183*, 231–250.

Opoku, A. (2024). *The Elgar companion to the built environment and the sustainable development goals*. Edward Elgar Publishing.

Opoku, A., & Lee, J. Y. (2022). The future of FM: Managing facilities for sustainable development. *Sustainability, 14*(3), 1705. https://doi.org/10.3390/su14031705

Radebe, S., & Ozumba, A. O. U. (2021). Challenges of implementing sustainable facility management in higher institutions of learning. In *IOP Conference Series: Earth and Environmental Science*. IOP Publishing Bristol UK.

Reynolds, D. (2022). Facility management – ISO 41000 series in brief with emphasis on ISO 41001. *Global Facility Management Alliance.*

Roper, K. O., & Richard, P. (2014). *The facility management handbook*. AMACOM.

Tucker, M. (2013). Sustainable facility management. In A. Cotgrave & M. Riley (Eds.), *Total sustainability in the built environment*. Palgrave Macmillan.

United Nations. (2015). *Transforming our world: The 2030 Agenda for Sustainable Development. Department of Economic and Social Affairs*, United Nations. https://sdgs.un.org/2030agenda

Villa, V., Naticchia, B., Bruno, G., Aliev, K., Piantanida, P., & Antonelli, D. (2021). IoT open-source architecture for the maintenance of building facilities. *Applied Science, 11*(12), 5374. https://doi.org/10.3390/app11125374

Outsourcing Fundamentals: The Supply Chain Analysis of Manufacturing Outsourcing Relationship

Yuwen Chen, Jiayuan Zhang, and Gulver Karamemis

1 Introduction

1.1 From Transactional to Strategic Outsourcing

In today's dynamic and globally interconnected business landscape, the strategic decision to outsource manufacturing and service operations has emerged as a cornerstone for numerous industries. Businesses are increasingly recognizing the imperative of concentrating on core competencies to maintain competitive edges. Many businesses entrust specific aspects of production or service delivery to external partners while focusing on specialized expertise, cost efficiencies, and agility enhancement. From the assembly lines of manufacturing to customer support and IT services, outsourcing has become a strategy empowering organizations to streamline processes, focus on core competencies, and navigate the ever-evolving demands of a competitive market. Its pervasive influence spans industries in electronics, apparel, pharmaceuticals, automobiles, beverage and food (Chen et al., 2021).

The landscape of outsourcing has undergone a transformative journey since the 1980s, marked by notable shifts and advancements. Initially, outsourcing was predominantly driven by cost considerations, with companies in the PC and

Y. Chen (✉)
University of Rhode Island, Kingston, RI, USA
e-mail: yuwen@uri.edu

J. Zhang
University of Wisconsin at Whitewater, Whitewater, WI, USA
e-mail: zhangji@uww.edu

G. Karamemis
Georgia Southern University, Statesboro, GA, USA
e-mail: gkaramemis@georgiasouthern.edu

F. P. García Márquez et al. (eds.), *Outsourcing Using Operations Research and Management Science Methods*, International Series in Operations Research & Management Science 366, https://doi.org/10.1007/978-3-031-91845-2_2

electronic industries (Wang et al., 2014) seeking to reduce operational expenses. Business Process Outsourcing (BPO), where companies delegate non-core functions such as customer support and human resources (HR) to specialized service providers, became popular in the 1990s. The pressure of a globally competitive business environment, technological advancements, and the maturation of outsourcing service providers have further propelled this evolution. Notably, the shift from transactional, ad-hoc outsourcing to a strategic, partnership-oriented model has become a hallmark of the contemporary outsourcing landscape (Domberger, 1998).

In a review article by Lacity et al. (2011), research in BPO decisions primarily focused on make-or-buy decisions, degree of outsourcing, offshore practices, and supplier selections. Kremic et al. (2006) categorize the motivations of outsourcing into three types: cost-driven, strategic-driven, and politics-driven. The 2000s saw a surge in Information Technology Outsourcing (ITO), exemplified by the globalization of software development and IT support services. IT outsourcing services include application development, system integration, infrastructure and software support and maintenance, data center management, systems design/planning, and telecommunication/network (Loh & Venkatraman, 1992). The market size of global ITO in 2015 was estimated at $274.2 billion, and it surged to a substantial $440 billion in 2022 (Research and Markets, 2023).

Over time, businesses that seek outsourcing started recognizing other benefits and pursuing outsourcing not just from a cost-cutting perspective. This transition was evidenced by the seminal work of Quinn and Hilmer (1994) in the exploration of strategic outsourcing as a means of gaining competitive advantages. Quinn and Hilmer (1994) emphasize the importance of aligning outsourcing decisions with broader organizational strategic goals and highlight the partnerships between the client and their outsourcing providers. The early form of outsourcing was exemplified in business collaborations where enterprises engaged external entities for specialized tasks. For example, business logistics involves substantial investments in infrastructure, technology, and workforce, contributing to fixed costs that can strain company resources. Logistics is often the function that businesses choose to outsource first since it allows businesses to leverage economies of scale, access advanced technologies, and benefit from the expertise of specialized logistics professionals. According to a survey conducted by Armstrong & Associates, Inc. (2013), 86% of U.S. domestic Fortune 500 companies use 3PLs, demonstrating that strategic outsourcing has become common in current business settings.

1.2 Outsourcing Relationship

The strategic outsourcing paradigm recognizes the interdependence between the client and the outsourcing partners and emphasizes shared goals and collaborative decision-making. This alignment ensures that outsourcing practices fulfill organizational objectives and promote a symbiotic relationship that goes beyond transactional interactions among supply chain partners. Strategic outsourcing enhances the overall effectiveness of supply chain management and reflects the adaptability of organizations in response to changing global business environments.

The outsourcing relationship is between the client and the outsourcing providers, and sometimes upstream suppliers are also involved. When outsourcing providers—such as UPS as 3PL provider, Amazon, Microsoft and Google as IaaS, PaaS, and SaaS[1] providers for many businesses—do not compete directly with the client, outsourcing decisions in such situations are less complex. In logistics, strategic outsourcing decisions revolve around selecting the right transportation modes and optimizing areas in warehousing, operational capabilities, geographical coverage, and cost structure (Zailani et al., 2017). In cloud server outsourcing, critical strategic decisions include service level agreement, penalty for service interruptions, data security and compliance with regulations, scalability and flexibility, pricing structure and cost transparency, data management and ownership, and customer support (Gozman & Willcocks, 2019). When business manufacturing is outsourced, we often refer to original equipment manufacturers (OEMs) as the clients and contract manufacturers (CMs) as the outsourcing providers. OEMs are normally firms of established brands with higher cost structures. CMs are firms specializing in manufacturing with cost advantages that are further enhanced by producing in low-cost countries. When CMs (e.g., Acer, Asus, and Samsung) enhance their capabilities, they eventually enter into key markets with their own brand products and compete with the OEM (Kemahlıoğlu-Ziya, 2015).

Outsourcing in manufacturing becomes intricate as the CM must coordinate with various suppliers providing components or parts for the OEM. This complexity arises from the multi-tiered structure of modern supply chains involved in production and product development, and manufacturing outsourcing will include coordination with the suppliers as well. There are two major approaches to manufacturing outsourcing. In the *consignment* approach, the OEM and its supplier engage in direct negotiations regarding the sourcing price of components, and the CM is responsible for manufacturing and/or assembling products for the OEM. In the *turnkey* approach, also known as *delegation*, the outsourcing cost paid by the OEM to the CM encompasses both the components supplied by the OEM's suppliers and the manufacturing costs incurred by the CM (Karamemis et al., 2023). Conventional outsourcing wisdom often believes that the OEM prefers consignment due to better cost control, and the CM prefers turnkey due to the fact that it may enjoy increased profit margins by directly interacting with the suppliers. Karamemis et al. (2023) analyze different power dynamics between an OEM and a CM and find counterintuitive outcomes that may occur under certain conditions.

With manufacturing capability, CMs that pursue a profit margin higher than manufacturing outsourcing often start selling their own products in their home countries and do not directly compete with the OEM in key markets. The OEM

---

[1] IaaS (Infrastructure as a Service), PaaS (Platform as a Service) and SaaS (Software as a Service) are common IT services provided by companies like Amazon, Google, Microsoft, IBM, Oracle, Salesforce, Adobe, ... etc.

then might be concerned about the potential threat posed by the CM to its brand. PC brands Acer and Asus and electronic product brands Samsung and Haier all started as CMs and eventually competed with their corresponding OEMs in key markets. It is reasonable for the OEM to worry about the CM's cost advantages and the proximity gained through learning experiences, as well as the risk of losing manufacturing know-how, even if there are no concerns about intellectual property infringement. IBM's PC business sold to Lenovo (Arruñada & Vázquez, 2006) serves as a notable example where a CM evolved into a direct competitor and replaced the OEM. When making outsourcing decisions for cost-cutting purposes, OEMs should be mindful of the potential threat of CMs' competition in the long term.

In this chapter, we investigate manufacturing outsourcing and how firms have an intricate relationship with their outsourcing providers. In such a situation, the outsourcing relationship and the choice of outsourcing approach (turnkey or consignment) will also impact upstream suppliers. For service (like logistics, billing, and HR) and IT outsourcing where service providers do not compete with their clients or do not overtake core business know-how, please refer to Lacity et al. (2012) and Iqbal and Dad (2013).

1.3 Benefits and Risks of Outsourcing Practices

The strategic outsourcing approach aligns decisions with core business objectives and emphasizes long-term value creation beyond mere cost reduction. Such long-term values include reducing capital investment, sharing development costs and risks, and shortening product development and production ramp-up time (Kemahlıoğlu-Ziya, 2015; Guo et al., 2010; Liao et al., 2009; Arruñada & Vázquez, 2006).

Logistics and IT outsourcing are good examples of reducing the burden of capital investment on non-core business functions. Both logistics and IT functions need human and physical asset capabilities and investments, which prove to be ineffective if they are not part of the business's core competency (Zailani et al., 2017). Firms outsourcing these functions can preserve capital for key business operations, lower fixed cost expenditure, and maintain a flexible cost structure. Though cost saving is a common goal for outsourcing, different outsourcing practices may have different motivations that later determine the performance. For example, Lacity et al. (2012) find that ITO and BPO are pursued in different ways. They revealed that 56% of ITO clients were firms with poor financial performance, while only 20% of BPO clients were indicated with poor financial performance. Such differences might be the result of large-scale ITO decisions that involve the sale and transfer of expensive assets and can improve financial performances more quickly; thus, ITO is chosen when businesses are under deep financial stress. In another study, Brewer et al. (2013) find that firms with "high commitment to growth and cost strategies tend to achieve cost-related performance at higher levels than firms with a lower commitment to the same," and a "balanced" outsourcing plan that emphasizes multiple strategies achieves higher cost-saving performance than a "non-balanced" one.

Outsourcing needs closer coordination with upstream suppliers, especially when part of product development and design needs suppliers' inputs. In the fashion industry, many brands have outsourced the design to Original Design Manufacturers (ODMs), since the fashion industry is very competitive (Shen et al., 2016), and the ODMs can be more sensitive to market trends and styles. As agility and innovation are paramount to businesses in the twenty-first century, working closely with key suppliers can make use of the best-in-world resources and capabilities. For example, Boeing's defense operations collaborated with hundreds of suppliers to develop component modules, and they introduced two prototypes of its Joint Strike Fighter (Quinn, 2000) with fewer internal workers. Wasti and Liker (1997) point out that firms that sell complex products depend heavily on suppliers to gain competitive advantages through collaboration in product development. Though there exist risks when sharing product development secrets with suppliers, they find that the supplier's in-house technology capability is important to the client, and the risk of outsourcing is offset by less OEM investment in R&D and a shortened product development cycle.

Earl (1996) investigates 11 risks of IT outsourcing: the possibility of weak management, inexperienced staff, business uncertainty, outdated technology skills, endemic uncertainty, hidden costs, lack of organizational learning, loss of innovative capacity, dangers of an eternal triangle, technology indivisibility, and fuzzy focus. Earl believes firms should ask why they should not insource IT service first before outsourcing, and businesses should ponder, "Why does outsourcing make sense and why does it work?" Earl recommends businesses to consider, "If the risks of outsourcing are real, do the benefits of outsourcing outweigh the risks?" When asking such questions, firms may selectively outsource important functions. One way to mitigate risk is through experience as there is a learning curve in outsourcing (Barthélemy, 2001). Barthélemy believes that outsourcing can only be done better by experiencing it through a learning curve and provides recommendations for various stages of the outsourcing learning curve.

Garaventa and Tellefsen (2001) warn of three hidden costs when businesses choose to outsource. First, outsourcing induces different administrative costs, which include the need for detailed situational analysis, the preparation of requests for proposals (RFP), holding pre-bid conferences, pre-qualification of bidders, bid evaluation and contract award processes, and contract monitoring. Second, outsourcing may damage employees' loyalty and trust to the organization as a human cost. Finally, employees of the outsourcing clients may feel betrayed (ethical cost) from outsourcing due to job security concerns. For example, after selling its PC business to Lenovo in 2005, IBM sold its x86 server business in China to Lenovo in 2014 (Bradsher, 2014). Though employees can choose to stay under terms and conditions comparable to their current jobs, Chinese IBM workers chose to strike against the deal.

In the next section, we discuss the supply chain of business manufacturing outsourcing and focus on the relationship (cooperative vs. coopetitive) between the OEMs and the CMs. In the end, we provide several key factors in the scope of the supply chain when businesses engage in manufacturing outsourcing.

2 The Supply Chain of Manufacturing Outsourcing

In manufacturing outsourcing, the turnkey (delegation) or consignment approach requires different levels of engagement in outsourcing management. We can classify supply chains by differentiating the relationship between the OEMs and the CMs from an outsourcing point of view. The firms are cooperative in achieving their individual goals without direct competition, or they can form a coopetition relationship in which the CM manufactures for the OEM and competes with the OEM. Competition can also exist among several OEMs, who aim to achieve competitive advantage through contracting with a common CM, or among several CMs competing for outsourcing opportunities by a common OEM. In this section, for each case, we will include a discussion on whether there exists any competition between the firms within the same echelon of the supply chain, i.e., competition between OEMs or between CMs. Furthermore, in studying outsourcing decisions, the scope of the outsourcing supply chain can be analyzed by the number of echelons, the number of players, and the type of sourcing strategy. These topics will be further discussed in the subsections below.

2.1 Cooperation in Outsourcing Supply Chains

In one of the simplest outsourcing supply chains, there exists one OEM and one non-competitive CM (NCM) that cooperate in production. The CM owns manufacturing strength and does not offer its own products, and thus, there is no direct conflicting interest between the OEM and the NCM. For example, Gray et al. (2009) study the outsourcing decision between the two players in a two-period game. In this two-echelon, two-player supply chain, choices that the OEM evaluates are full outsourcing, partial outsourcing, or foregoing the outsourcing option and producing in-house. Since outsourcing is a strategic decision for both players, both the OEM and the CM are assumed to be capable of reducing production cost via learning-by-doing, and they can change their decisions in their two-period model. They find that partial outsourcing can be an optimal strategy. Dynamic outsourcing strategies where the OEM changes outsourcing strategy from one period to the next can be optimal. They also find that the CM and the OEM can benefit from each other's learning-by-doing.

While considering cooperation in an outsourcing supply chain, factors outside of the outsourcing contract may influence the players' decisions. For example, the CM can invest in technology to gain advantages and win outsourcing contracts, which in turn also determines the quality of outsourced products for the OEM. Kaya (2011) explores the OEM's relationship with a non-competing CM when the CM's investment in product quality may influence the market demand. In the model, coordinating and non-coordinating contracts are compared when the OEM has a production cost disadvantage as well as a disadvantage in improving product quality. The CM has greater leverage since its investment in technology and quality can be "averaged" through its multiple OEM clients. They find that if the OEM relies on CM's effort in quality improvement, only a simultaneous revenue and cost-sharing contract can coordinate the outsourcing supply chain.

In practice, CM may produce for several OEMs,[2] who compete with one another for CM's capacity. Multi-client outsourcing (MCO), or one outsourcing vendor (CM) vs. multiple clients (OEMs), is common in the IT, apparel, and logistics industries (Ni et al., 2009). For example, in the semiconductor industry, firms like Apple, Nvidia and Qualcomm compete with each other while they rely on wafer fabrication production from companies like TSMC (Taiwan Semiconductor Manufacturing Company); and in the mobile phone market, Foxconn produces smartphones for Apple, Nokia, and Motorola (Karamemis et al., 2023; Troianovski & Clark, 2012). Many outsourcing papers extend the OEM-CM cooperation to include more than one OEM with different settings in component resale options, production costs, quantity vs. price competitions, and risk preferences (Boulaksil & Fransoo, 2009; Lv, 2019; Wu & Zhang, 2014; Chen et al., 2012; Arya et al., 2008; Feng & Lu, 2013; Ülkü et al., 2007).

On the other hand, there are several reasons (such as supply risk, product lines from different providers, leveraging suppliers) that may prompt an OEM to outsource to more than just one CM. Such a single client (OEM) vs. multiple vendors (CMs) is called multi-vendor outsourcing (MVO). For example, in Apple's ecosystem, Foxconn and Pegatron serve as significant CMs for products like iPhone, Apple Watch, and Augmented Reality (AR) devices, with China's Luxshare joining as the third supplier in 2023 (Li & Cheng, 2023). Such multi-outsourcing relationships were explored by Yan et al. (2010), Xue et al. (2016), and Chen and Liu (2021). These papers differ in their models on factors of inventory systems, order compliance (forced or voluntary), the existence of demand uncertainty, and the existence of player coordination. In Sect. 4.1, we discuss multi-client or multi-vendor outsourcing relationships in more detail.

We can further consider the involvement of upstream partners in the supply chain and analyze three-echelon supply chains consisting of an OEM, a CM and a supplier (Guo et al., 2010). With added suppliers, OEMs can choose different sourcing approaches (turnkey or consignment) when managing their outsourcing supply chain. In turnkey, the CM negotiates component costs with suppliers directly and charges the OEM an outsourcing cost that covers component costs paid to the suppliers. In this situation, the OEM simplifies supplier management but also faces the disadvantage of losing contact with its upstream suppliers. Some OEMs (e.g.,

[2]Turnkey is the assumed outsourcing approach when the supplier is not included in the consideration. The CM will be in charge of component sourcing for the OEM in this case.

Apple) prefer consignment outsourcing to have better quality and cost controls for the products, but the OEMs will have more challenging supplier management. Turnkey consignment decisions, in reality, can be more complex. For example, Wang et al. (2014) discuss the turnkey-consignment decision in different order contract structures. The order contract structures may change the outsourcing strategy preferences for both the OEM and the CM.

While considering the suppliers in the supply chain, similar to the two-echelon supply chains, we can analyze the optimal outsourcing strategy of the OEMs when they compete with each other in a three-echelon supply chain. Bolandifar et al. (2016) study the optimal component procurement strategies of two competing OEMs selling substitutable products. In their model, they have two OEMs who can choose turnkey or consignment as their outsourcing strategy from an NCM and a supplier. When the component cost of the supplier is exogenously given, both OEMs either control (consignment) or delegate (turnkey) their component procurement. When the component cost is determined by the supplier, the supplier's pricing decision influences the outcome, where the larger OEM always prefers turnkey while the smaller OEM may prefer turnkey or consignment. Furthermore, Xu et al. (2018) study a multinational firm's procurement strategy under the impacts of competition of a local OEM outsourcing to a common CM with considerations of a supplier and import/export taxes in China that may influence the outsourcing game. They consider a profit maximization game with four players, which include a multinational firm, a local OEM, a CM, and a supplier. They find that the multinational firm's procurement strategy is influenced by the thresholds of the domestic market size and the import/export taxes that players pay.

A three-tier outsourcing supply chain can further extend to include multiple suppliers that compete to be chosen. Yang et al. (2017) consider a three-tier supply chain with an OEM, a CM and multiple suppliers with various quality levels. They analyze whether the OEM should produce in-house or delegate its outsourcing to the CM while minimizing the unit cost of outsourcing due to quality issues. Kayis et al. (2013) study a three-tier supply chain where the OEM can delegate the procurement of a component from a tier-2 supplier to its tier-1 supplier (turnkey) or can control the procurement of the component itself (consignment). The tier-2 supplier produces the components, and the tier-1 supplier transforms the components into a final product. They provide conditions that the OEM prefers a consignment strategy over turnkey.

2.2 Coopetition in Outsourcing Supply Chains

As the CMs become larger and their bargaining power increases, this could pose potential threats to the OEMs. The CMs may directly compete with the OEMs by offering their own brand products in the same market while manufacturing for the OEMs. It is often assumed that the OEMs enjoy some brand image advantages (Niu et al., 2019b) or that consumers see the CM's product as inferior to the OEM's product. However, depending on the substitutability of the CM's product, the intensity of the competition between the OEM and the CM could be weak or strong. For example, Samsung competed with Apple in the smartphone market when it produced OLED displays and flash memory chips to Apple.

When a CM offers its own branded products to the market, the OEM may consider outsourcing to an NCM. Should the OEMs avoid competitive CMs (CCMs) and only collaborate with NCMs? There are several studies that investigate OEM's CCM and NCM selection decisions under different settings. For example, Yan et al. (2019) model the NCM to passively accept OEM's quantity decisions without any supply issues; Niu et al. (2015) allow a second-mover advantage that the late CM may undercut the price of the first CM when the CMs may have a strong or weak marketing power; Li et al. (2020) explore the endogenous and exogenous quality decision between an OEM and a CCM while an NCM is present. In the apparel industry, Li et al. (2023) study the sourcing decision of an Original Brand Manufacturer (OBM) and consider whether OBM can produce in-house or outsource its production to a CCM or an unreliable NCM. The unreliability of the NCM stems from its delivered quantity that is less than the order size. They consider the technology spillover if the OBM outsources its production to a CCM. In the apparel industry, the designs are easily copied, and the barrier of technology spillover is easily broken. They find that when the investment cost for in-house production is low, the OBM prefers producing in-house regardless of the manufacturing level. Specifically, when the manufacturing level is high or medium, and the consumers' product preference level is high, the OBM prefers outsourcing to the NCM; otherwise, the OBM prefers outsourcing to the CCM.

The power dynamics between the OEM and the CM can be further studied in different game settings. Wang et al. (2013) consider a two-echelon supply chain where the OEM collaborates and competes with the CM at the same time. The two players can engage in a simultaneous game, or the OEM (or the CM) can act as the Stackelberg leader. The OEM's leader position depends on the outsourcing cost or the proportion of production outsourced to the CM. They find that the CM may set outsourcing cost sufficiently low to allow both parties to coexist in the market, and the OEM outsources its entire production to the CM.

In most cases, the CM normally is a follower of the branded OEM's move. However, some OEMs enter the market with their brand without any manufacturing know-how and have to rely on CMs for production. Also, the CMs may be capable of co-designing the product with the OEMs or even being in charge of the whole design since the CM leads in technology or patents relevant to the market (Yan et al., 2019). A Taiwanese computer CM, Asustek, led the market to launch low-cost laptop models in 2007, and its OEM client, Dell, entered the same market 1 year later (Vilches, 2007; Dannen, 2008). To incorporate scenarios where the CM or the OEM may be the leader, there are some studies that compare the outcomes between CM-leading and OEM-leading dynamics. For example, Karamemis et al. (2023) compare outsourcing strategy (turnkey vs. consignment) and outsourcing cost determination when either the CM or the OEM can decide the outsourcing cost or the outsourcing strategy. Their findings demonstrate that the outsourcing outcomes depend on who (CM or OEM) makes sourcing decisions and who determines the outsourcing cost, and counterintuitive outcomes may occur in certain conditions. Readers can refer to Karamemis et al. (2023) for different combinations of OEM-CM power dynamics.

2.3 The Scope of Outsourcing Supply Chain

Finally, we suggest that prior to delving into diverse outsourcing models, readers should pose the following inquiries. The seven-step inquiries below serve to narrow the focus of the outsourced supply chain, enabling a more precise analysis of the intricate dynamics involved.

1. What is the extent of the supply chain echelons considered in the outsourcing context? Should the examination solely encompass the CM and the OEM in a two-tier scenario and concentrate on outsourcing decisions? Or should it extend to a three-tier configuration that involves suppliers?
2. Within each echelon of the supply chain, how many active decision-making players exist? Do these players proactively make decisions, or do they predominantly react to the decisions of others?
3. What type of sourcing approach will be adopted by these entities (e.g., turnkey or consignment)? Are there variations in this approach?
4. What decisions are made by which specific players? These decisions may encompass quantity determinations by the OEM and/or CM, outsourcing costs (typically determined by the CM), component costs (typically managed by the supplier), sourcing approaches (often determined by the OEM), and occasionally encompass quality and product positioning when product differentiation factors into the model.
5. Is there a competitive dynamic between the OEM(s) and CM(s)?
6. What is the chronological sequence of decision-making in the timeline? Is it a scenario where a leader dictates decisions and followers respond, or does it involve simultaneous decision-making in a competitive setting?

How do varying power dynamics, such as those between strong and weak players or among key stakeholders, influence the outsourcing relationships? In the next section, we provide ten in-house or outsourcing production models that involve an OEM and a CM if a two-tier echelon (as base models) is considered or added with a supplier if a three-tier echelon (as extended models) is considered. The outsourcing can be in either a cooperative or coopetitive relationship or in a turnkey or consignment outsourcing contract if a three-tier outsourcing supply chain is considered. We provide key assumptions that are used for all models to derive analytical decisions for the purpose of model comparison. The optimal decisions for each model are provided, and we demonstrate an example that an OEM is considering either producing in-house or outsourcing (turnkey or consignment) in a three-tier echelon setting.

3 Outsourcing Models

In this section, we provide several outsourcing models that mathematically formulate different parties' profit/cost functions in outsourcing supply chains. We first focus on the supply chain of outsourcing that consists of one OEM and one CM, in which their outsourcing decisions are made either without (the base model) or with a supplier (the extended model) that supplies a key component for the products. The OEM and the CM can be in cooperation (the CM only manufactures for the OEM) or coopetition (the CM manufactures for the OEM and also competes with the OEM by producing its own branded products), and they are in quantity competition in the same market. These models are summarized from various outsourcing studies cited in this chapter. To maintain consistency and for the purpose of model comparison, we use terms that might be named differently from some studies. For example, the cost of manufacturing outsourcing for the OEM pays to the CM is called wholesale price (Niu et al., 2015) or unit cost (Li et al., 2020), which is normally assumed to be determined by the CM and thus named. In this chapter, we call it "outsourcing cost." Similarly, the cost of components, which is normally set by the supplier, can be called component price (Chen et al., 2012) or input cost (Xu et al., 2018). In this chapter, we call it "component cost."

When an outsourcing relationship is formed, we assume the CM decides on outsourcing cost (w) while the OEM decides on turnkey (T) or consignment (G) strategy since such a setting is most commonly discussed in outsourcing research. Under turnkey, the outsourcing cost covers CM's component cost that the CM pays to the supplier (thus, the OEM pays to the supplier indirectly through the CM); under consignment, the outsourcing cost only covers the manufacturing cost of the CM since the OEM pays component cost directly to the supplier. In the next section, we will further discuss outsourcing strategies in different settings. Note that the OEM can always manufacture in-house without the CM, which we label as the benchmark case. We assume that the OEM has a production cost disadvantage, such that its unit production cost is higher than the CM, and thus, outsourcing is considered. In addition, we assume that all other per-unit production costs are zero without losing generality for all players to simplify analytical outcomes. Please refer to Table 1 for variable notations used in this chapter.

Figure 1 illustrates ten different cases that are commonly discussed in various outsourcing relationships. We call the two-tier supply chain (OEM and CM) as the base case when the supplier is not actively involved (Fig. 1a–d). When a supplier is included as the extra tier in the outsourcing supply chain, the OEM may choose turnkey (Fig. 1f, i) or consignment outsourcing strategy (Fig. 1g, j). Figure 1a, c, e, h are cases that OEM chooses to produce in-house without outsourcing to the CM. If the CM offers its branded products while outsourcing for the OEM, then the two players are in coopetition (Fig. 1d, i, j.); otherwise, they are in cooperation (Fig. 1b, f, g.). The variables in Fig. 1 are the decisions of players, in which the superscript denotes turnkey (T) or consignment (G), and the subscript denotes the player i ($i = O$, C, or S representing the OEM, the CM and the Supplier, respectively).

Table 1 Variable notations used in the chapter

Parameters	
a	Market potential
b	Product substitution effect between OEM's and CM's products
p_i	Player i's product price derived from quantity competition
z	OEM's production cost disadvantage (extra in-house production cost) compared to the CM
f_i	Fixed cost for player i ($i \in \{O, C, S\}$)
v	Component cost in cases A, B, C and D when no supplier is present
Decision variables	
q_i^j	Player i's production quantity ($i \in \{O\}$ for Fig. 1a, b, e–g, and $i \in \{O, C\}$ for Fig. 1c, d, h–j) under turnkey ($j = T$), consignment ($j = G$) or in-house ($j = I$)
w^j	Outsourcing cost under turnkey ($j = T$) or consignment ($j = G$)
v_C^j	Component cost the supplier charges the CM under turnkey ($j = T$) or consignment ($j = G$)
v_O^G	Component cost the supplier charges the OEM under consignment
v_i^I	Component cost the supplier charges player i under in-house production ($i \in \{O, C\}$)

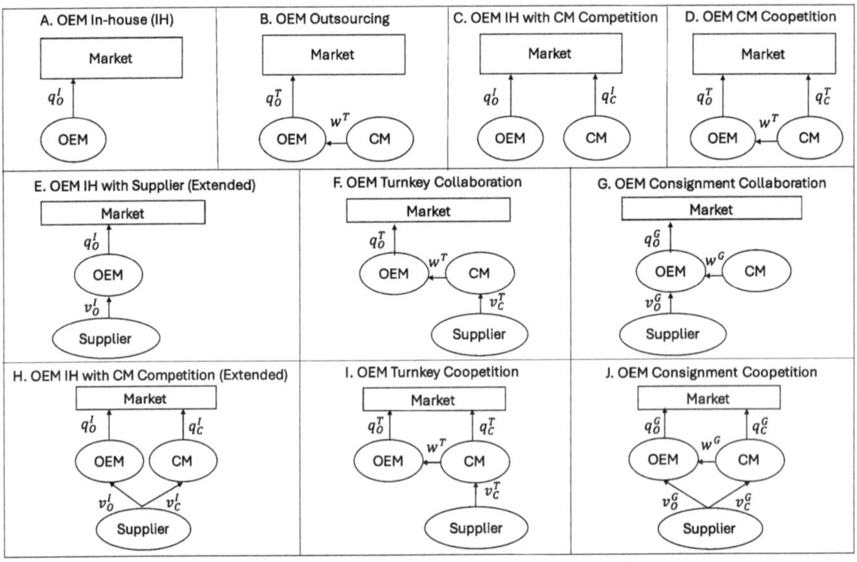

Fig. 1 Outsourcing structure and decisions between supply chain partners

Under turnkey, the CM acts as the delegate of the OEM and sources the components directly from the supplier; thus, the supplier only decides v_C^T. Under consignment, the OEM sources the components directly from the supplier; thus, the supplier charges v_C^G and v_O^G to the CM and the OEM, respectively. We assume all parameters are known to all players, who are rational by maximizing their profits. Note that

Table 2 Timeline and player i's ($i \in \{O, C, S\}$) decisions for different cases

Case	Stage 1	Stage 2	Stage 3
A	N/A	N/A	O: q_O^I
B	N/A	C: w^T	O: q_O^I
C	N/A	N/A	O: q_O^I, C: q_C^I
D	N/A	C: w^T	O: q_O^T, C: q_C^T
E	S: v_O^I	N/A	O: q_O^I
F	S: v_C^T	C: w^T	O: q_O^T
G	S: v_O^G	C: w^G	O: q_O^G
H	S: v_C^I, v_O^I	N/A	O: q_O^I, C: q_C^I
I	S: v_C^T	C: w^T	O: q_O^T, C: q_C^T
J	S: v_C^G, v_O^G	C: w^G	O: q_O^G, C: q_C^G

when no supplier is present in the base case, the CM will charge an outsourcing cost that covers all its costs, which is equivalent to turnkey strategy if outsourcing is formed.

We assume the product price is linear to the total quantities offered to the market (where a is the market potential) since this is the most commonly used demand model for outsourcing modeling research. The market price of the OEM's product is $p_O = a - q_O^T$ (Bernstein & Federgruen, 2004; Farahat & Perakis, 2011) when the CM cooperates only. In competitive cases, $p_O = a - q_O^j - bq_C^j$ and $p_C = a - bq_O^j - q_C^j$ are the prices for OEM's and CM's products, respectively, when the CM competes with the OEM in outsourcing strategy j ($j \in \{T, G\}$). Parameter b ($0 < b < 1$) indicates that OEM's and CM's products are not totally identical and the substitution effect from competitor's product is less than one (Wang et al., 2013; Chen et al., 2021). Each player i has a fixed cost f_i ($i \in \{O, C, S\}$ in all models and OEM has $f_O = 0$ when it chooses to outsource. We assume all fixed costs are in reasonable ranges so that there will not be trivial cases where players end up with negative profits. The timeline of the game and the decisions of players for each case are summarized in Table 2. To make comparisons among different cases on the same basis, we assume the component cost is v in the base case (1A and 1C) for the OEM and the CM. This v is for model comparison purposes and is assumed as a given market value similar to the component cost when a supplier is an active player.

We assume that each player at each stage knows relevant parameters and decisions made from earlier stages. All players in each case use backward induction at different stages to derive their optimal decisions to maximize profits accordingly. Using this approach, we obtain optimal decisions and derive the players' profits in each case. In the base model (cases A, B, C and D), the OEM and the CM compare their corresponding profits from outsourcing and from in-house (I) production. If both players (the OEM and the CM) have higher profits in outsourcing, then an outsourcing relationship will be formed. If any player is worse off in outsourcing, then no outsourcing will be formed, and the OEM will manufacture in-house. In the extended model, the OEM and the CM will compare their corresponding profits from turnkey (T), consignment (G) and in-house (I) production (a three-way comparison).

The OEM will choose an outsourcing strategy (T or G) that has the highest profit for itself when the CM is also better off in outsourcing. Since outsourcing can only be formed when the OEM and the CM are both better off in outsourcing, we can call such an outcome a win-win scenario. Note that though the supplier is an active player setting the component cost to maximize its profit in extended models, it cannot directly influence the outsourcing approach. If the supplier is present and also better off in outsourcing, then such a scenario will be a win-win-win scenario for all three players.

In the following subsections, we provide the profit functions in ten outsourcing cases for all players in the game. Due to page limits, we provide detailed derivations for cases H, I and J and demonstrate how an optimal outsourcing strategy can be determined since they are the most complicated cases in a three-tier outsourcing supply chain. In other cases, readers can apply proper procedures to derive the outcome accordingly. We provide the details of optimal solutions for all ten cases that readers can refer to.

3.1 *Operational Outsourcing Decisions*

3.1.1 OEM In-house Production (Benchmark Cases)

In case A (Fig. 1a), the OEM will do the production in-house and is the only player in the set-up. The component cost is assumed to be v. As we mentioned, the OEM has a production cost disadvantage compared to the CM. Parameter z ($z > 0$) represents the OEM's extra per-unit production cost in in-house production. Also there is a fixed cost when the OEM chooses to produce in-house (all fixed costs discussed in other cases will be omitted thereafter). Here we assume that the CM's profit is 0 because it is not competing with the OEM in the specific product market. The profit function of the OEM is presented below:

$$\pi_O = q_O^I\left(a - q_O^I - z - v\right) - f_O$$

In case E (Fig. 1e), we include a supplier in the game. When the supplier is involved, the supplier charges the OEM component cost v_O^I. The profit of the supplier comes from selling the components to the OEM.

$$\pi_O = q_O^I\left(a - q_O^I - z - v_O^I\right) - f_O$$

$$\pi_S = q_O^I v_O^I - f_S$$

In case C (Fig. 1c), we include the CM who is competing with the OEM. Both players sell products to the market and compete. Since the supplier is not present, the component cost is v for both players. The profit functions for the OEM and the CM are provided below:

$$\pi_O = q_O^I\left(a - q_O^I - bq_C^I - z - v\right) - f_O$$
$$\pi_C = q_C^I\left(a - bq_O^I - q_C^I - v\right) - f_C$$

If the supplier is present and the OEM produces in-house with a coopetitive CM who offers its products in the market (Fig. 1h), the supplier charges the OEM and the CM component prices v_O^I and v_C^I, respectively. The profit functions for all players are:

$$\pi_O = q_O^I\left(a - q_O^I - bq_C^I - z - v_O^I\right) - f_O$$
$$\pi_C = q_C^I\left(a - bq_O^I - q_C^I - v_C^I\right) - f_C$$
$$\pi_S = q_O^I v_O^I + q_C^I v_C^I - f_S$$

3.1.2 Turnkey Cooperation (Base Case)

In the turnkey cooperation case (Fig. 1b), the OEM outsources the production and delegates component sourcing to the CM. The CM charges the OEM a per-unit outsourcing cost w^T that covers the component cost in stage 2. The OEM then decides the quantity outsourced to the CM for production in stage 3. The OEM's profit comes from selling products to the market, and the CM's profit comes from outsourcing for the OEM after deducting the component cost. Given the decisions both players made, the profit functions of the OEM and the CM are provided below:

$$\pi_O = q_O^T\left(a - q_O^T - w^T\right)$$
$$\pi_C = q_O^T\left(w^T - v\right) - f_C$$

3.1.3 Turnkey Cooperation (Extended Case)

In the extended case of turnkey cooperation (Fig. 1f), the CM sources the components from the supplier and makes the products for the OEM. The supplier charges the CM per-unit component cost v_C^T in stage 1. Given the component cost v_C^T, the CM decides the outsourcing cost w^T in stage 2. The OEM decides the quantity outsourced to the CM in stage 3. The profit of the OEM comes from selling products to the market. The CM's profit comes from outsourcing for the OEM. The supplier's profit comes from selling components to the CM. The profit functions of the OEM, the CM, and the supplier are provided below:

$$\pi_O = q_O^T\left(a - q_O^T - w^T\right)$$

$$\pi_C = q_O^T\left(w^T - v_C^T\right) - f_C$$

$$\pi_S = q_O^T v_C^T - f_S$$

3.1.4 Consignment Cooperation (Base Case)

In the consignment cooperation (Fig. 1g), the OEM sources from the supplier directly on the components and delivers the components to the CM. The CM provides manufacturing outsourcing for the OEM and charges the OEM with outsourcing cost (w^G) only. In the timeline of the game, the supplier first decides the component cost v_O^G in stage 1. The CM decides the per-unit outsourcing cost w^G in stage 2. In stage 3, the OEM decides the production quantity. The revenue of the OEM comes from selling products to the market. In such a case, the OEM pays the CM per-unit outsourcing cost and pays the supplier per-unit component cost. The CM's profit comes from manufacturing outsourcing for the OEM, while the supplier's profit comes from selling the components to the OEM. The profit functions of the OEM, the CM, and the supplier are provided below:

$$\pi_O = q_O^G\left(a - q_O^G - w^G - v_O^G\right)$$

$$\pi_C = q_O^G w^G - f_C$$

$$\pi_S = q_O^G v_O^G - f_S$$

3.1.5 Turnkey Coopetition (Base Case)

In the Turnkey coopetition base case (Fig. 1d), the CM outsources and competes with the OEM in the same market. In the timeline of the game, the CM first decides the outsourcing cost w^T for OEM's products. Given the outsourcing cost, the OEM and the CM decide the quantities q_O^T and q_C^T, respectively, in stage 3. The profit of the OEM comes from selling products to the market. The CM's revenue has two parts: the revenue from selling its own products to the market and the revenue from outsourcing for the OEM. The profit functions of the OEM and the CM are provided below:

$$\pi_O = q_O^T\left(a - q_O^T - bq_C^T - w^T\right)$$

$$\pi_C = q_C^T\left(a - bq_O^T - q_C^T - v\right) + q_O^T\left(w^T - v\right) - f_C$$

3.1.6 Turnkey Coopetition (Extended Case)

In this case (Fig. 1i), the CM sources the components from the supplier for its own products and the OEM's products. The supplier gains its profit by selling the components to the CM, which includes OEM's and CM's quantities. In the timeline of the game, the supplier first charges the CM with component cost v_C^T in stage 1. The CM then charges the OEM per-unit outsourcing cost w^T in stage 2. In stage 3, the OEM and the CM decide the quantities q_O^T and q_C^T, respectively. The profit of the OEM comes from selling products to the market. The CM's profit includes the revenue from selling its own products, the revenue from outsourcing for the OEM, and the component cost and the fixed cost. The profit of the supplier comes from selling components to the CM. The profit functions of all players are provided below:

$$\pi_O = q_O^T\left(a - q_O^T - bq_C^T - w^T\right)$$

$$\pi_C = q_C^T\left(a - bq_O^T - q_C^T\right) + q_O^T w^T - \left(q_O^T + q_C^T\right)v_C^T - f_C$$

$$\pi_S = \left(q_O^T + q_C^T\right)v_C^T - f_S$$

3.1.7 Consignment Coopetition (Extended Case)

In this case (Fig. 1j), the CM and the OEM source from the supplier on the components separately, and the OEM outsources the manufacturing to the CM. The OEM buys from the supplier at component cost v_O^G, and the CM buys from the supplier at component cost v_C^G. In the timeline of the game, the supplier decides component costs v_O^G and v_C^G in stage 1. The CM decides unit outsourcing cost w^G for the manufacturing outsourcing only in stage 2. After the outsourcing cost is decided, both the OEM and the CM decide their quantities in stage 3. The profit of the OEM comes from selling products to the market. The CM's profit includes the revenue from selling its own products, the revenue from outsourcing for the OEM, and the component cost from its own products and the fixed cost. The profit of the supplier comes from selling components to the CM and the OEM. The profit functions of all players are provided below:

$$\pi_O = q_O^G\left(a - q_O^G - bq_C^G - w^G - v_O^G\right)$$

$$\pi_C = q_C^G\left(a - bq_O^G - q_C^G\right) + q_O^G w^G - q_C^G v_C^G - f_C$$

$$\pi_S = q_O^G v_O^G + q_C^G v_C^G - f_S$$

3.2 Strategic Outsourcing Decision

Given the profit functions in the ten cases, we apply the backward induction method to solve the optimal solutions for each case. Here, we use cases H, I and J (since they are the most complicated cases) as examples to illustrate how the backward induction method works in finding optimal solutions for all players. First, we solve the optimal quantities of the OEM and the CM. We then substitute the optimal quantities in CM's profit function, and the CM optimizes its profit by deciding the optimal outsourcing cost. Further, we substitute the optimal quantities and outsourcing cost in the supplier's profit function, and the supplier decides the optimal component cost that optimizes its profit. The optimal component cost is then used to update mathematical expressions of optimal quantities and outsourcing costs in later stages. When the optimal quantity and cost solutions from all players are in the most updated forms, we derive the optimal profits for all players. Readers can use the timeline and decisions made in different stages in Table 2 for other cases. Table 3 below provides the mathematical expressions of the optimal decisions of the players in ten cases.

Given the derived solutions provided in Table 3, we can compare different cases to derive the optimal outsourcing strategy for the OEM. We assume that CM's cooperation or coopetition is determined already (not a CM's decision in the game), and the discussion for optimal outcomes is based on the active OEM that determines outsourcing strategy. Readers can refer to Karamemis et al. (2023), which allows situations when the CM has a stronger power and determines turnkey or consignment strategy. The comparison between cases A and B explores the outsourcing decision of the OEM to the CM when the CM is not competing with the OEM and the supplier is not involved. In this case, the OEM only considers whether it is more profitable to outsource. The comparison between cases C and D explores the outsourcing decision of the OEM to the CM when the CM is competing with the OEM and the supplier is not involved. In this case, the OEM considers whether it is more profitable to outsource to the CM even when the CM competes in the same market.

The comparison among cases E, F, G explores the outsourcing decision of the OEM to the CM without CM's competition and the supplier is involved. The OEM can decide whether to produce in-house, allocate the production and procurement functions to the CM (turnkey sourcing), or allocate only the production function to the CM (consignment sourcing). The comparison among cases H, I, and J explores the outsourcing decision of the OEM to the CM with CM's competition, and a supplier is present. Below, we illustrate the comparison among cases H, I, and J since the OEM may choose to produce in-house (Case H), turnkey outsourcing to the CM (Case I), or consignment outsourcing to the CM (Case J).

To find out OEM's optimal strategy among cases H, I and J, OEM needs to compare its derived profits from these three cases given the optimal decisions made in Table 3. Let us label OEM's profits in Cases H, I, and J as π_O^H, π_O^I and π_O^J, respectively. When $(\pi_O^J > \pi_O^H) \cap (\pi_O^J > \pi_O^I)$, OEM will choose a consignment

Table 3 Optimal solutions for the players in different cases

Case	Optimal solutions		
	OEM	CM	Supplier
A. OEM In-house (IH)	$q_O^{I*} = \frac{a-v-z}{4}$ $\pi_O^{I*} = \frac{1}{4}(a-v-z)^2 - f_O$	NA	NA
B. OEM Outsourcing (Base)	$q_O^{T*} = \frac{a-v}{4}$ $\pi_O^* = \frac{1}{16}(a-v)^2$	$w^{T*} = \frac{a+v}{2}$ $\pi_C^* = \frac{1}{8}(a-v)^2 - f_C$	NA
C. OEM IH with CM Competition (Base)	$q_O^{T*} = \frac{a(2-b)+bvc-2(v+z)}{4-b^2}$ $\pi_O^* = \frac{(a(2-b)+bvc-2(v+z))^2}{(4-b^2)^2} - f_O$	$q_C^{T*} = \frac{a(2-b)-2vc+b(v+z)}{4-b^2}$ $\pi_C^* = \frac{(a(2-b)-2vc+b(v+z))^2}{(4-b^2)^2} - f_C$	NA
D. OEM CM Coopetition (Base)	$q_O^{T*} = \frac{2(1-b)(a-v)}{8-3b^2}$ $\pi_O^* = \frac{4(1-b)^2(a-v)^2}{(8-3b^2)^2}$	$w^{T*} = \frac{a(8-(4-b)b^2)+(8-b^2(2+b))v}{16-6b^2}$ $q_C^{T*} = \frac{(2-b)(4+b)(a-v)}{16-6b^2}$ $\pi_C^* = \frac{(6-b)(2-b)(a-v)^2}{4(8-3b^2)} - f_C$	NA
E. OEM IH with Supplier (Extended)	$q_O^{I*} = \frac{a-z}{4}$ $\pi_O^{I*} = \frac{1}{16}(a-z)^2 - f_O$	NA	$v_O^* = \frac{a-z}{2}$ $\pi_S^* = \frac{(a-z)^2}{8} - f_S$
F. OEM Turnkey Cooperation (Extended)	$q_O^{T*} = \frac{a}{8}$ $\pi_O^* = \frac{a^2}{64}$	$w^{T*} = \frac{3a}{4}$ $\pi_C^* = \frac{a^2}{32} - f_C$	$v_C^* = \frac{a}{2}$ $\pi_S^* = \frac{a^2}{16} - f_S$
G. OEM Consignment Cooperation (Extended)	$q_O^{T*} = \frac{a}{8}, \pi_O^* = \frac{a^2}{64}$	$w^{T*} = \frac{a}{4}$ $\pi_C^* = \frac{a^2}{32} - f_C$	$v_O^* = \frac{a}{2}$ $\pi_S^* = \frac{a^2}{16} - f_S$
H. OEM IH with CM Competition (Extended)	$q_O^{T*} = \frac{a(2-b)-2z}{2(4-b^2)}$ $\pi_O^* = \frac{(a(2-b)-2z)^2}{4(4-b^2)^2} - f_O$	$q_C^{T*} = \frac{2a-ab+bz}{8-2b^2}$ $\pi_C^* = \frac{(a(2-b)+bz)^2}{4(4-b^2)^2} - f_C$	$v_C^* = \frac{a}{2}$ $v_O^* = \frac{a-z}{2}$ $\pi_S^* = \frac{a^2(2-b)-a(2-b)z+z^2}{2(4-b^2)} - f_S$

(continued)

Table 3 (continued)

Case	Optimal solutions		
	OEM	CM	Supplier
I. OEM Turnkey Coopetition (Extended)	$q_O^{T*} = \frac{a(1-b)}{8-3b^2}$ $\pi_O^* = \frac{a^2(1-b)^2}{\left(8-3b^2\right)^2}$	$w^{T*} = \frac{a\left(24-(10-b)b^2\right)}{4\left(8-3b^2\right)}$ $q_C^{T*} = \frac{a(2-b)(4+b)}{4\left(8-3b^2\right)}$ $\pi_C^* = \frac{a^2(6-b)(2-b)}{16\left(8-3b^2\right)} - f_C$	$v_C^* = \frac{a}{2}$ $\pi_S^* = \frac{a^2(12-b(6+b))}{8\left(8-3b^2\right)} - f_S$
J. OEM Consignment Coopetition (Extended)	$q_O^{T*} = \frac{a(32-(2-b)b(18+b(18+b)))}{256-200b^2+39b^4}$ $\pi_O^* = \frac{a^2(32-(2-b)b(18+b(18+b)))^2}{\left(256-200b^2+39b^4\right)^2}$	$w^{T*} = \frac{a(256-b(32+b(2+b)(104-b(76-b(14+b)))))}{4\left(256-200b^2+39b^4\right)}$ $q_C^{T*} = \frac{a\left(256-b^2(152-b(4+b(16+b)))\right)}{4\left(256-200b^2+39b^4\right)}$ $\pi_C^* = \frac{k}{16\left(32-13b^2\right)^2\left(8-3b^2\right)} - f_C$	$v_C^* = \frac{a(2+b)(16-(12-b)b)}{64-26b^2}$ $v_O^* = \frac{2a(8+b(1-4b))}{32-13b^2}$ $\pi_S^* = \frac{a^2\left(1024-944b^2+216b^4-b^6\right)(12-b(6+b))}{8\left(32-13b^2\right)^2\left(8-3b^2\right)} - f_S$

Note: $k = (a^2(12288 - b(5120 + b(10176 - b(5184 + b(1744 - b(1376 - b(168 + b(32 + b))))))))$

strategy; when $\left(\pi_O^I > \pi_O^H\right) \cap \left(\pi_O^I > \pi_O^J\right)$, OEM will choose a turnkey strategy; and when $\left(\pi_O^H > \pi_O^I\right) \cap \left(\pi_O^H > \pi_O^J\right)$, OEM will produce in-house. However, for outsourcing to be chosen, CM's total profit from outsourcing needs to be better than without outsourcing for the OEM. Let π_C^H, π_C^I and π_C^J represent CM's profits in Cases H, I, and J, respectively, given the optimal decisions made in Table 3. The CM will provide turnkey outsourcing for the OEM when $(\pi_C^I > \pi_C^H)$, and consignment outsourcing for the OEM when $(\pi_C^J > \pi_C^H)$. The CM will not provide turnkey (or consignment) outsourcing when $\pi_C^H > \pi_C^I$ (or $\pi_C^H > \pi_C^J$) even if the OEM prefers turnkey (or consignment) outsourcing. By comparing OEM's and CM's profits in cases H, I, and J, we can obtain the conditions that win-win outsourcing in either turnkey or consignment will be formed. Since the OEM in-house production is the benchmark case, we use OEM's in-house production cost disadvantage, z, to identify such conditions. When $z > \min\{z_1, z_2\}$,[3] the OEM prefers outsourcing instead of in-house. Here z_1 is the threshold of the in-house production cost disadvantage for the OEM to select turnkey $(\pi_O^I > \pi_O^H)$ or in-house $(\pi_O^I < \pi_O^H)$, and z_2 is the threshold of the production cost disadvantage for the OEM to select consignment $(\pi_O^J > \pi_O^H)$ or in-house $(\pi_O^J < \pi_O^H)$. When z is small ($z < \min\{z_1, z_2\}$), the OEM will be more profitable to produce in-house. Only when the z is larger than $\min\{z_1, z_2\}$, the OEM will be more profitable to select turnkey or consignment. For the CM, the CM will be more profitable to produce for the OEM when $z < \min\{z_3, z_4\}$, where z_3 is the threshold of z for the CM to provide turnkey outsourcing $(\pi_C^I > \pi_C^H)$, and z_4 is the threshold of z for the CM to provide consignment outsourcing $(\pi_C^J > \pi_C^H)$. The CM is not willing to outsource for the OEM when OEM's in-house production cost is high ($z > z_3$ or $z > z_4$) since the CM will have a higher profit for not outsourcing for the OEM. To conclude, the win-win turnkey (consignment) outsourcing condition for the OEM and the CM to select outsourcing is $z_1 < z < z_3$ ($z_2 < z < z_4$.). Note that the supplier only determines its component cost(s) to the CM and the OEM in cases H, I and J, and it cannot influence OEM's outsourcing strategy. As a result, the supplier may be better- or worse-off when the OEM and the CM form a turnkey or consignment outsourcing contract based on their best interests. If the supplier is better off under turnkey or consignment outsourcing, then a win-win-win outcome occurs in such outsourcing arrangement.

For other cases, readers can use similar approaches to derive the conditions that outsourcing (turnkey or consignment) may be chosen by the OEM and the CM between cases A and B, between cases C and D, and among cases E, F and G.

---

[3] $z_1 = a - \frac{ab}{2} - \frac{\left(4-b^2\right)^2}{\left(32-20b^2+3b^4\right)} \sqrt{a^2(1-b)^2 + \left(8-3b^2\right)^2 f_O}$,

$z_2 = a - \frac{ab}{2} - \left(4-b^2\right) \sqrt{\frac{a^2\left(32-b(2-b)(18+b(18+b))\right)^2}{\left(256-200b^2+39b^4\right)^2} + f_O}$,

$z_3 = -\frac{a(2-b)}{b} + \frac{a\left(4-b^2\right)}{2b} \sqrt{\frac{(6-b)(2-b)}{\left(8-3b^2\right)}}$, and

$z_4 = -\frac{a(2-b)}{b} + \frac{\left(4-b^2\right)^2}{2b\left(128-84b^2+13b^4\right)} \sqrt{\frac{\left(a^2(12288-b(5120+b(10176-b(5184+b(1744-b(1376-b(168+b(32+b))))))))+16\left(32-13b^2\right)^2\left(8-3b^2\right)f_C\right)}{\left(8-3b^2\right)}}$.

4 Outsourcing Environmental Factors and Model Variations

The analyses and discussions above are limited to examining an outsourcing relationship involving an OEM, a CM, and potentially a supplier. However, outsourcing decisions and strategy selection are influenced by numerous factors in the broader business environments. In this section, we present several variations of outsourcing relationships that managers should consider when making decisions about outsourcing. First, the cost advantages of a CM are derived from economies of scale, suggesting that a CM can offer outsourcing services to multiple OEMs concurrently. Similarly, relying on a single CM exposes the OEM to substantial supply risks. To mitigate this risk, an OEM may choose multiple CMs for different product lines or for different markets. Examining the dynamics of such one-to-multiple players in both directions (OEM-to-CM and CM-to-OEM) in an outsourcing relationship will be important. Second, the analyses presented above presuppose information symmetry among various outsourcing entities. However, in reality, possessing private information (such as part procurement costs and rebates from suppliers) is common in outsourcing and crucial for attaining leverage in contractual negotiations (Chen et al., 2012). We will discuss how private information may influence outsourcing relationships. Third, avoiding direct competition between the OEM and the CM can improve both players financially. Under coopetition, the OEM and the CM may seek differentiating their products horizontally through channel management or vertically through quality positioning while maintaining their outsourcing partnership in productions (Caldieraro, 2016). Below, we discuss each variation in the outsourcing relationship separately and propose approaches to resolve the challenges players may face. At the end of each subsection, we propose a simple model framework to capture the OEM-CM outsourcing dynamics to readers as a reference. Such frameworks lay the foundations for detailed analysis that can be derived further. Readers can also revise the model frameworks with other variations for their unique business problem.

4.1 *Multi-Client or Multi-Vendor Outsourcing Relationship*

When production outsourcing prevailed in many industries in the 90's, CMs' unique manufacturing know-hows attracted many OEMs and helped them grow at an astonishing rate. According to Sturgeon (2002), the leading five electronic CMs in the U.S. experienced an average annual growth rate of 43% between 1995 and 2002. As a result, multi-client outsourcing (MCO) is common in the IT, apparel, and logistics industries (Ni et al., 2009). In the PC industry, we provide a visualization of the many-to-many OEM-CM outsourcing relationship in Fig. 2.

Competing OEMs outsourcing from a common CM are prevalent in the outsourcing supply chain. Chen et al. (2012) study a large OEM's outsourcing

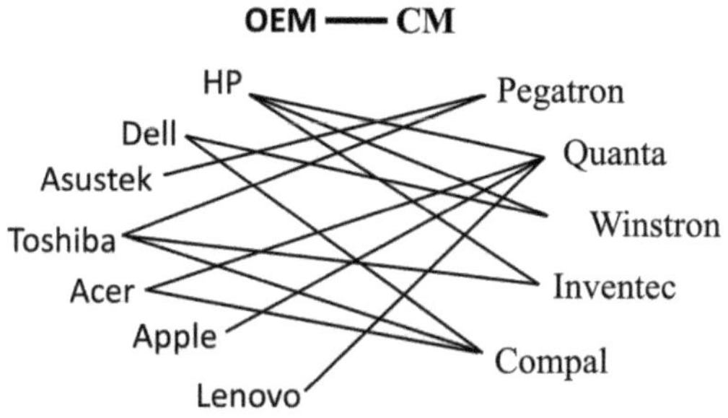

Fig. 2 Visualization of many-to-many OEM-CM outsourcing relationship in the PC industry. (Source of the many-to-many OEM-CM outsourcing relationship in the PC industry, https://www.theguardian.com/technology/blog/2008/jun/27/didquantaorcompalmakeyour, accessed on12/30/2023)

decision (turnkey vs. consignment) with a CM who also serves a small OEM. The large OEM and the CM may have different purchasing power to the supplier on the components, which may influence the sourcing outcomes. They show that under the consignment case, the larger OEM's optimal strategy is to resell (buy then sell) components at the highest possible component cost to the CM. CM's outsourcing preferences depend on its purchasing power on the component cost, and it can be better off to accept turnkey outsourcing for the larger OEM while accepting consignment outsourcing for the smaller OEM. The large OEM's preferences depend on component cost, the volatility of the CM's component cost, and substitutability between two OEMs' products. Ni et al. (2009) explore the situation that the CM has both scale and scope economies if it provides manufacturing for multiple OEMs. By manufacturing for two OEMs, the CM achieves a lower unit production cost than that when the CM only has a single client. Each OEM may choose turnkey (buy) or in-house production (make), which causes uncertainty to CM's profit. Their findings conclude that if an outsourcing vendor has a high economy of scope and the OEMs have high in-house production costs, then MCO can be the equilibrium outsourcing outcome.

Arya et al. (2008) study the outsourcing decisions of two competing OEMs and a monopolistic CM who manufactures for both OEMs. They state that "conventional wisdom suggests that a firm will not buy an input for a price above its in-house cost of production." However, they find that one OEM may be willing to pay a premium (higher than its in-house production cost) in CM's outsourcing production in order to increase the opportunity cost of the rival OEM. Feng and Lu (2013) study the impact of outsourcing contracts on quantity/price competition of two OEMs in a two-tier supply chain where the OEMs can choose to outsource to a common CM or an exclusive CM. They consider two types of outsourcing contracts: (i) wholesale contracts, and (ii) a two-part tariff contract where the OEM pays a unit price and a fixed fee to the supplier. For determining the outsourcing cost of the contracts, they find that OEM's profit is always higher when outsourcing to an exclusive CM compared with outsourcing to a common CM. Interestingly, in two-tariff contracts, when the OEMs' bargaining power is sufficiently strong (weak), OEMs' profits are higher under quantity (price) competition by outsourcing to a common CM than to an exclusive one.

When multiple entities are involved in an outsourcing supply chain, a firm may not be willing to share information to gain negotiation leverage and have more control. Boulaksil and Fransoo (2009) study order release strategy when a CM with a capacitated production line serves two OEMs. When the CM is not willing to share its capacity information, how the OEMs release their orders critically influences the outcomes such as capacity reservation and cancellations. Ülkü et al. (2007) study MCO from a risk-taking perspective. The study compares the supply chain profits in two scenarios: (i) the OEM takes on the risk of under- or over-investment into productive resources, and (ii) the CM takes on the risk. They also consider the case where both the OEM and the CM take on the risk together. They find that, from the supply chain point of view, there is no unique situation where it is always better to assume risks. If the CM does not have a good understanding of end demand, it is preferable for the OEM to bear the risks.

For the OEM, the yield uncertainty from its CM poses a severe threat to its business. Factors of yield uncertainty include quality issues, capacity limits, labor shortage, and natural calamity and supply disruptions triggered by Covid-19 pandemic in the past several years (Chen & Liu, 2021). To reduce operational disruption, some OEMs adopt multi-vendor outsourcing (MVO) strategy and choose multiple CMs for different product lines or for different markets (Li & Cheng, 2023; Fig. 2 above). These papers differ in their models on factors of inventory systems, order compliance (forced or voluntary), existence of demand uncertainty, and existence of player coordination. Chen and Liu (2021) claim that, in multi-outsourcing cases, individual agents making local optimizations without considering their impacts on others can result in a decline in the overall supply chain profit. They present a model of a multi-outsourcing relationship where an OEM encounters uncertain market demands, and each of its multiple CMs faces yield uncertainty. In their Stackelberg game, the OEM sets the ordering quantities first, and the CMs respond with production quantities, which can be larger than the ordering quantities due to yield uncertainty.

In the topic of MVO, there are studies that focus on OEM's selection when it can choose outsourcing from a CCM or an NCM. Yan et al. (2019) explore the coopetition relationship between the OEM and a CCM while other NCMs are present. They assume the OEM outsources only a portion of its production quantity to the CCM and the leftover quantity is outsourced to the NCMs. Niu et al. (2015) study the outsourcing decisions between an OEM and a CCM and an NCM. They investigate a two-stage endogenous pricing game. In the first stage, the competitive players decide on the timing of the pricing of the competitive products and in the second stage they decide on the prices of the products. They find that, regardless of the CCM's marketing power, the CCM should continue manufacturing products for the OEM. Hence, coopetition is preferred over competition by the CM.

Among the OEMs that adopt MVO, we can extend the discussion to when the OEMs are also competing with each other in the same market with substitutable products. Wu and Zhang (2014) study the reshoring/outsourcing decisions of two competing OEMs who can outsource their production to one of the two CMs in a two-stage game. In their model, they consider a sole-sourcing strategy; either efficient sourcing (from an overseas firm) or responsive sourcing (from a domestic firm). They extend their model to include more than two OEMs and study the impact of one firm's reshoring strategy on the rest of the firms' profits. They find that, "in certain competitive settings, firms may outsource to a long lead-time CM to reduce competition rather than to take advantage of low sourcing cost." One of the counterintuitive results they find is that when labor and logistics costs in emerging economies increase, all competing OEMs' profits may improve. If an OEM chooses to reshore due to increased costs, this can result in a new equilibrium sourcing structure that can alleviate market competition. Table 4 below compares the model settings and the focuses from studies that address multi-client or multi-vendor OEM-CM relationships.

Here, we propose a general model for a single period MVO model with one OEM and $\boldsymbol{n}$ separate CMs ($\boldsymbol{i} \in \{\mathbf{1}, \mathbf{2}, \ldots, \boldsymbol{n}\}$) in collaborative outsourcing without a supplier in a similar turnkey outsourcing framework proposed in the previous section. We assume the OEM determines production quantity $\boldsymbol{q}_{Oi}^{T}$ to CM $\boldsymbol{i}$, and the market price is set by all quantities that enter the same market. We also assume CM $\boldsymbol{i}$ sets its outsourcing cost $\boldsymbol{w}_i^T$ with a unique fixed cost $\boldsymbol{f}_{Ci}$ and variable component cost $\boldsymbol{v}_{Ci}^{T}$. Thus the OEM's profit function can be formulated as $\mathbf{max}_{\boldsymbol{q}_{Oi}^{T}} \boldsymbol{\pi}_O = \boldsymbol{Q}(\boldsymbol{a} - \boldsymbol{Q}) - \sum_{i=1}^{n} \boldsymbol{q}_{Oi}^{T} \boldsymbol{w}_i^T$, where $\boldsymbol{Q} = \sum_{i=1}^{n} \boldsymbol{q}_{Oi}^{T}$, and $\boldsymbol{Q}(\boldsymbol{a} - \boldsymbol{Q})$ and $\sum_{i=1}^{n} \boldsymbol{q}_{Oi}^{T} \boldsymbol{w}_i^T$ are the total revenue and total production costs, respectively. The CM $\boldsymbol{i}$'s profit function can be expressed as $\mathbf{max}_{\boldsymbol{w}_i^T} \boldsymbol{\pi}_{Ci} = \boldsymbol{q}_{Oi}^{T} \left(\boldsymbol{w}_i^T - \boldsymbol{v}_{Ci}^{T} \right) - \boldsymbol{f}_{Ci}, \boldsymbol{i} \in \{\mathbf{1}, \mathbf{2}, \ldots, \boldsymbol{n}\}$. Using the backward induction methods, such a multiple sourcing model can be solved in an OEM-lead, CMs-lead Stackelberg game or simultaneous decision game.

4.2 Private Information in Outsourcing Supply Chain

While outsourcing offers numerous advantages to OEMs, it also exposes the OEMs' business knowledge and supplier relationships to the CMs, which can potentially pose risks to the OEMs in the long run (Guo et al., 2010; Lv, 2019). Key contract details such as component costs and rebates between the OEMs and their suppliers are sensitive information that the OEMs prefer to keep confidential while entrusting the manufacturing process to the CMs. The consignment approach emerges as a strategy for the OEM to retain control over its relationships with suppliers. Guo et al. (2010) investigate a three-tier outsourcing supply chain (an OEM, a CM, and a supplier) where the production costs might be private information to other players. They compare three sourcing approaches: consignment (C), turnkey (T) and integrated turnkey (I, an alliance is formed by the CM and the supplier) and explore the conditions that OEM may choose one over others. They find that when the

Table 4 Model comparison for outsourcing models focusing on multi-client or multi-vendor outsourcing relationship

Paper	Objective function	Players involved	Decisions	Model focus
Chen et al. (2012)	Profit maximization	1CM, 2 OEMs (1 large, 1 small)	OEMs: quantities, CM: outsourcing cost	The large OEM and the CM have different purchasing powers to the supplier, and the OEMs may choose turnkey or consignment (buy-sell).
Arya et al. (2008)	Profit maximization	1CM, OEM 1 (incumbent) and OEM 2 (new entrant)	OEM1: quantity of turnkey (buy) or in-house (make) OEM2: turnkey quantity CM: two outsourcing costs to two OEMs	The impact of the incumbent OEM's in-house cost on the new OEM's outsourcing costs
Feng and Lu (2013)	Profit maximization	2 OEMs, 1 common CM or two exclusive CMs	OEMs: prices or quantities, CM(s): outsourcing cost (s)	Each OEM bargains with its exclusive CM vs. both OEMs bargain with a common CM.
Ni et al. (2009)	Profit maximization	1CM, 2 OEMs	OEMs: turnkey (buy) quantity or in-house quantity (make) CM: outsourcing cost	The CM has economies of scope and scale and different risk preference (averse or neutral) while the OEM may make or may not outsource.
Boulaksil and Fransoo (2009)	Cost minimization	1 CM, 2 OEMs	OEMs: aggregate quantity, per variant quantities, and cancellation depending on the order release strategy.	The impact of order release strategies (quantity reservation and cancellation) when the CM has capacity limits
Chen and Liu (2021)	Cost minimization	1 OEM, multiple CMs	OEM: ordering quantities to all CMs, CMs: production quantity	Quantity decisions when the OEM faces uncertain demand, and the CMs have yield uncertainty.
Wu and Zhang (2014)	Profit maximization	2 CMs (one responsive in time, one efficient in cost), 2 OEMs	OEMs: quantities to each CM, CMs: outsourcing cost	Two OEMs in quantity competition game with demand uncertainty, the efficient CM has cost advantage and time disadvantage compared to the responsive CM.

production costs are private information, the CM and the supplier tend to distort such information to obtain higher profits from outsourcing and selling components, respectively. However, if the production costs are public information, the OEM is always better off under integrated turnkey strategy.

In a different setting, Lv (2019) studies an outsourcing scenario in which two OEMs compete in the same market, and both outsource to a common CM that has private information in its own procurement cost in turnkey strategy. Each OEM may choose turnkey or consignment sourcing strategy. The model then characterizes the equilibrium on two OEMs' decisions and finds that OEM's assessment on the CM's procurement cost distribution and the market size play critical roles in the equilibrium outcome.

Price negotiation is a critical business secret, and an outsourcing relationship may reveal some price agreements to other parties that later harms one of the players. According to Deshpande et al. (2011), OEM brands like IBM and HP use "price-masking mechanism" and hide component price information with the suppliers from its CM, and around 40% of OEMs use similar techniques based on iSuppli's OEM survey in 2004. Deshpande et al. (2011) propose techniques from secure multiparty computation (SMC) and game theory for an OEM with multiple CMs to determine its outsourcing agreement to one of the CMs. In such a mechanism, the OEM can mask component prices from the selected CM while making sure the CM will bid on its true cost without adding extra margins. They also find that participating CMs will not be able to derive any private cost information from other players in the bidding game, in which private information is maintained. Note that such outsourcing contract practices only occur when the OEM is large enough that it has advantages in component costs. For small OEMs that do not have leverage over its component suppliers, such strategies will not work.

Yang et al. (2017) investigate OEM's component procurement strategy (in-house procurement vs. delegation to the CM) when both the OEM and the CM have different negotiation powers over suppliers that have different quality levels. The OEM can choose one of the suppliers for its in-house procurement or delegate the sourcing to the CM. In their model, the OEM's power over suppliers is public information, but the CM's power over suppliers might be private. The OEM has to make procurement decisions under risks and uncertainties. They find that a proficiently crafted procurement outsourcing agreement can incentivize the CM to opt for superior quality materials, and thus propose a quality assurance and inspection strategy for fraud prevention. However, their findings are based on CM's and OEM's cost functions that only include the "procurement cost" rather than the whole outsourcing cost, thus their conclusion may not hold when the objective functions are more comprehensive to include other outsourcing costs.

Table 5 below compares the model settings for outsourcing relationships with private information. Among them, three out of four outsourcing papers related to private information above investigate MCO or MVO relationships since private information is used to leverage one's negotiation power against other players. Note that each model has a unique objective function, players involved, decisions and model focus; thus, their conclusions should not be compared directly. Such

Table 5 Model comparison for outsourcing models focusing on private information

Paper	Objective function	Players involved	Decisions	Model focus
Guo et al. (2010)	Profit maximization	1 CM, 1 OEM, and 1 supplier (not an active decision maker)	Wholesale cost, component cost by the OEM, or component cost by the CM.	Comparison of the effectiveness of different outsourcing structures.
Lv (2019)	Profit maximization	2 OEMs, 1 common CM	Each OEM decides quantity and consignment vs. turnkey decision	The CM has private information on the procurement cost
Deshpande et al. (2011)	Profit maximization	1 OEM, multiple CMs	Component costs bidding by CMs, and the OEM chooses who wins and how much to pay the winning CMs	CMs bid confidentially with private component cost information, the OEM picks the winner(s) and how much the CMs are paid
Yang et al. (2017)	Cost minimization for component cost	1 OEM, multiple CMs	Outsourcing or in-house production by the OEM, quality nonconformance rate by CMs	OEM's powers over suppliers are public information, but the CM's powers over suppliers might be private.

comparison highlights critical factors that managers should consider when they conduct an analytical framework.

Here, we propose a general model based on Lv's setup (Lv, 2019) with one CM and two competing OEMs ($i \in \{1, 2\}$) in a turnkey outsourcing framework (we skip consignment here to simplify the model) proposed in the previous section. We assume that OEM i determines production quantity q_{Oi}^T. to the common CM, and the CM charges OEM i with w_i as the outsourcing cost. In turnkey, outsourcing cost w_i will cover the component cost. We assume the CM keeps its information on component cost v_C^T private, which both OEMs only know the binomial distribution of v_C^T with two possible outcomes: v_L and v_H, where v_L and v_H are the low and high cost estimates for the component, respectively, and $v_H > v_L > 0$. Both OEMs share the same knowledge of such component cost in a binomial distribution, where the probabilities are $P(v_C^T = v_L) = \beta$, $P(v_C^T = v_H) = 1 - \beta$ and $0 < \beta < 1$. The market price for OEM i is $p_{ik} = a - q_{Oik}^T - bq_{Ojl}^T$, where b is the product substitution effect between two OEMs' products, $0 < b < 1$, $i,j \in \{1, 2\}$, $i \neq j$ and $k,l \in \{L, H\}$. Here q_{OiL}^T and q_{OiH}^T represent different production quantities that OEM i sets when it thinks CM's component cost is v_L and v_H, respectively. And two OEMs may have different assessments on CM's component cost, which means OEM i may offer q_{OiH}^T but OEM j may offer q_{OjL}^T, or vice versa. Let $\pi_{OiL}^T = q_{OiL}^T \left(a - q_{OiL}^T - bq_{Ojl}^T - w_i\right)$ and

$\pi^T_{OiH} = q^T_{OiH}\left(a - q^T_{OiH} - bq^T_{Ojl} - w_i\right)$, which are the profit functions of OEM i ($i \in \{1, 2\}$) when it thinks CM's component cost is v_L and v_H, respectively. Then, the expected profit function for OEM i will be $E\left(\pi^T_{Oi}\right) = \beta\pi^T_{OiL} + (1-\beta)\,\pi^T_{OiH}$. The CM's profit function[4] can be expressed as $\max_{w_i, w_j} \pi^T_C = \beta^2\pi^T_{C,LL} + \beta\,(1-\beta) \times \left(\pi^T_{C,HL} + \pi^T_{C,LH}\right) + (1-\beta)^2\pi^T_{C,HH}$, where $\pi^T_{C,kl}(k, l \in \{L, H\})$ represents CM's profit function when OEM i and OEM j set production quantities q^T_{Oik} and q^T_{Ojl}, respectively. Using the backward induction methods, such MCO sourcing models with private information can be solved in an OEM-lead, CMs-lead Stackelberg game, or simultaneous decision game.

4.3 *Product Differentiation in Competing Outsourcing Relationship*

When an OEM competes with a CM or with another OEM in the same market, it will be beneficial if it can avoid direct competition; thus, firms may want to utilize horizontal (e.g., product positioning) or vertical differentiation to achieve this. Caldieraro (2016) investigates a complex dual channel case where an incumbent OEM faces a CM's possible entry and explores how both players choose high or low product quality (vertical) and position them when the consumers may or may not have homogeneous preference (taste). Facing the threat of CM's possible entry, the OEM can choose to produce in-house, outsource to the CM, or outsource to an independent supplier. They find that if both the OEM and the CM compete for consumers and there exists horizontal differentiation, then it is optimal for the new entrant CM to join the market with its own brand while concurrently establishing an outsourcing arrangement with the existing incumbent OEM. When two firms can endogenously select their product lines and provide productions for each other, they will eventually differentiate their product models (one chooses high quality; the other chooses low quality) and outsource for each other because such arrangement softens direct competition. Under certain conditions, vertical conflicts can be totally eliminated, and they claim their outcome is more efficient than the traditional way that maximizes differentiations. They also find that if both firms demonstrate horizontal differentiation and consumers share uniform vertical preferences (all consumers are either low or high type), the entrant will always enter in the market. If consumers do not see differences between firms' brands (no horizontal differentiation), the entrant will stay out of the market and will outsource for the incumbent OEM when the CM has cost advantage.

---

[4]The expressions of the four parts of π^T_C are: $\pi^T_{C,LL} = q^T_{OiL}\left(w_i - v^T_C\right) + q^T_{OjL}\left(w_j - v^T_C\right) - f_C$, $\pi^T_{C,HL} = q^T_{OiH}\left(w_i - v^T_C\right) + q^T_{OjL}\left(w_j - v^T_C\right) - f_C$, $\pi^T_{C,LH} = q^T_{OiL}\left(w_i - v^T_C\right) + q^T_{OjH}\left(w_j - v^T_C\right) - f_C$, and $\pi^T_{C,HH} = q^T_{OiH}\left(w_i - v^T_C\right) + q^T_{OjH}\left(w_j - v^T_C\right) - f_C$.

Xiao et al. (2014) study the strategic outsourcing decisions of two competing OEMs under vertical and horizontal product differentiation. In their setting, they have two OEMs competing with each other and two CMs produce for the OEMs respectively. They study the symmetric case (where both OEMs decide to produce in-house or to outsource) or the asymmetric case (where one OEM decides to produce in-house, the other decides to outsource). The OEMs decide different quality investment levels. They find that symmetric outsourcing is a subgame perfect Nash equilibrium (SPNE) if the production costs of both OEMs are sufficiently high, and asymmetric sourcing is an SPNE if the production cost of one OEM is relatively high compared to the other OEM's. They particularly find that the quality investment level by the OEMs will influence the equilibrium results of the OEMs selecting asymmetric or symmetric outsourcing strategies. The higher the quality investment efficiency, the smaller chance of symmetric outsourcing; the greater the horizontal differentiation, the larger the chance of symmetric outsourcing.

The product quality can influence CM's decision to become an entrant that competes with the OEM. Mandal and Jain (2021) study partial outsourcing decision between an OEM and a CCM, where the qualities of the products from the OEM and the CCM are different. The CCM decides whether to compete with the OEM or not. They find that whether the CCM decides to compete with the OEM depends on the product quality differentiation. Within a moderate range of product quality differentiation, CCM's competition can be beneficial to both players. This finding is consistent under both symmetric and asymmetric information scenarios. Li et al. (2020) study the sourcing strategy of an OEM in the presence of a CCM. The OEM can sell products with a high-quality brand and has three strategy options: producing in-house, outsourcing to a CCM that sells its own low-quality brand, or outsourcing to an NCM. They find that when the product qualities are exogenous, the OEM's sourcing strategy depends on the OEM brand's efficiency in producing and selling the product, and both the OEM and the CCM prefer outsourcing arrangements. When the product qualities are endogenous, the OEM prefers to in-house or outsource to an NCM.

With escalating competition, the "time-to-market" factor becomes important to businesses. An Original Design Manufacturer (ODM), functioning as a CM with design and manufacturing capabilities, can streamline the product development cycle for OEMs. Nevertheless, when multiple OEMs opt to outsource to the same ODM, this practice has the potential to diminish product differentiation, and subsequently increases market competition among OEMs. Some ODMs divide their outsourcing divisions separately to serve different OEM clients and each division has its own R&D teams, sales force, and factories. Feng and Lu (2010) build a competitive game model that has two OEMs competing in the same market and outsourcing to a common ODM. They employ the Hotelling model to represent horizontal product differentiation, where consumers exhibit distinct preferences for products and experience transportation costs (or disutilities) when consuming a product located farther from their ideal points. They also allow asymmetry between two OEMs' bargaining powers and see how it will impact OEMs' outsourcing decisions. They find that an OEM with strong negotiation power tends to insource design to retain its pricing advantage, but a weak OEM normally has a lower profit margin and intends to outsource product design to the ODM. If the ODM pools its division resources, it can have a cost advantage (the economy of scale), but by doing so two OEMs' products become less differentiated. Also, the equilibrium of OEMs' product positions can be asymmetric (one product located at one end of the Hotelling line but the other located interiorly) even when two OEMs are symmetric. As the market share difference between the two OEMs increases, it alleviates price competition and the ODM can have a higher profit.

Yang et al. (2022) study outsourcing strategies of the OEMs between predefined strategy or custom strategy from a common CM. In the custom strategy, the CM is responsible for all the activities, including product production, product design, and the R&D of the key components, in which case the CM is similar to an ODM. In the predefined strategy, only the component procurement and product assembly are entrusted to the CM. They study decisions of two OEMs, who are assumed to have different market powers, and then one is the leader and other is the adopter (follower). They explore the conditions of quality cost and R&D expenses where the leading OEM will select predefined or custom strategy, and the adopter OEM responds with a high- or low-quality product selection. They identify the ranges of conditions in the quality cost level and R&D expenses that the leading OEM benefits from the predefined or custom mode, given the adopter OEM selecting a high-quality (or low-quality) product. They also discuss the range of conditions in quality cost where the adopter OEM will select high-quality or low-quality products. The CM's maximum profit scenario shares the conditions that favor the adopter OEM, and the CM can benefit from the leader OEM selecting the custom mode.

Another paper that considers horizontal product differentiation by focusing on the quality of the product is Niu et al. (2019a). They study the OEM's sourcing strategies on whether to rely on a domestic CM for metal material purchasing and manufacturing services (domestic sourcing), or to purchase scrap metal abroad (cross sourcing). In this paper, the OEM and the CM compete with each other in the market, while the OEM has a higher market potential. Different from the earlier presented papers, the government's preferences on sourcing strategies are considered in this model. They find win-win sourcing strategies for the OEM and the CM: when the quality of the scrap metal is high and CM's procurement cost is also high, both the OEM and the CM prefer cross-border sourcing. However, when the quality of the scrap and CM's procurement cost are both low, both the OEM and the CM prefer domestic sourcing.

Below Table 6 compares the model settings for outsourcing relationship with product differentiation. Note that each model has a unique objective function, players involved, decisions and model focus, thus, their conclusions should not be compared directly. Such comparison highlights critical factors that managers should consider when they conduct an analytical framework.

Here we propose a model setup for quality differentiation between two OEMs based on Xiao et al. (2014) in a turnkey outsourcing framework (we skip consignment here to simplify the model) proposed in the previous section. We assume the OEM i determines production quantity q_{Oi}^{T}. The market price for OEM i is

Table 6 Model comparison for outsourcing models focusing on product differentiation

Paper	Objective function	Players involved	Decisions	Model focus
Caldieraro (2016)	Profit maximization	1 OEM (incumbent) and 1 CM (new entrant)	OEM: outsourcing or not, and pricing decision. CM: entry or not, outsourcing or not, and price decision.	The model focuses on whether both firms will differentiate their products vertically and horizontally when consumers may have low- and high-end quality preference (vertically), and/or may have brand preference (horizontally).
Feng and Lu (2010)	Profit maximization	1 ODM (CM with design capability) and 2 OEMs.	OEMs: production quantities. CM: outsourcing costs.	The ODM has economy of scope of due to its ODM's capability sharing, which may reduce product differentiation
Xiao et al. (2014)	Profit maximization	2 OEMs and 2 CMs	OEMs: outsourcing or not, quality investment level, and pricing decisions. CMs: outsourcing costs.	The model focuses on whether OEMs select symmetric or asymmetric sourcing under vertical and horizontal product differentiation.
Yang et al. (2022)	Profit maximization	1 CM and 2 OEMs	OEMs: sourcing strategies, quality level, production quantities. CM: outsourcing costs.	The CM produces for competing OEMs who determine quality levels and select different sourcing strategies.
Mandal and Jain (2021)	Profit maximization	1 CM (new entrant) and 1 OEM (incumbent)	OEM: production quantities, fraction of products produced in-house. CM: component quality level, and contract structure.	The OEM can decide the fraction of products outsourced to the competing CM, who decides the component quality.
Li et al. (2020)	Profit maximization	An OEM, a competing CM, and a noncompeting CM	OEM: sourcing strategies, pricing decisions, and product quality. Competing CM: wholesale price, pricing decision, product quality. Noncompeting CM: Wholesale price	The sourcing strategy of an OEM to produce in-house, to outsource to a competing CM, or to outsource to a noncompeting CM when the quality of brand is considered.

$p_i = a - q_{Oi}^T - b\, q_{Oj}^T + x_i - x_j$, where x_i and x_j are the quality impacts on the market potential of OEMs i and j $(i,j \in \{1,2\}, i \neq j)$, respectively. The quality improvement cost of OEM i is in a quadratic form as $\frac{s_i^2}{k_i}$, where s_i is the quality cost coefficient, and $k_i(k_i > 0)$ is the diminishing return coefficient on such quality investment. The CM determines the outsourcing cost w_i for OEM i. The profit function of OEM i is $\max_{q_{Oi}^T} \pi_{Oi} = q_{Oi}^T \left(a - q_{Oi}^T - bq_{Oj}^T + x_i - x_j - w_i\right) - \frac{s_i^2}{k_i}$ and the profit function of the CM is $\max_{w_1,w_2} \pi_C = \sum_{i=1}^2 q_{Oi}^T w_i - f_C$. Using the backward induction method, this product differentiation problem between two OEMs can be solved in a one-leading-one-following game or a simultaneous decision game between two OEMs.

5 Conclusion and Future Directions

Outsourcing has become a critical business practice that improves financial performance. Over the last 3 years, the upheavals from the pandemic and geopolitical conflicts have compelled numerous organizations to confront vulnerabilities within their intricate and extensive global supply networks. From several surveys with business executives, Alicke et al. (2022) found that businesses use three ways to improve supply chain resilience to cope with current challenges. First, firms ask end-to-end supply chain visibility from suppliers. Second, proactive firms redesign their supply chain footprint with a robust scenario planning. Third, successful scenario planning relies on comprehensive, accurate master data for better analysis, and 74% of firms plan to invest in digital technologies for demand and supply planning. Thus, although supply disruptions were severe in many industries, businesses did not shy away from manufacturing and service outsourcing (Karamemis et al., 2023). Revenue in the BPO market is projected to reach US$134.3 bn in 2024[5].

Given the increased reliance on outsourcing, we provide a discussion on the dynamics of outsourcing fundamentals. This chapter mainly focuses on the outsourcing of manufacturing and production. We address the echelons of outsourcing supply chain and players involved in the outsourcing setup. We start with a typical and simple setup of two players (an OEM and a CM) in a two-tier echelon, then extend our exploration to include a supplier in a three-tier echelon outsourcing setup. In the three-tier supply chain with an active supplier, the OEM can choose to delegate part/component sourcing to the CM (turnkey) or negotiate directly with the supplier (consignment) to have better control for its supplier.

When the CM with manufacturing capability is a potential competitor to the OEM, the cooperation or coopetition relationship formed between the OEM and the CM is considered next. Integrating "cooperation or coopetition" relationships with the levels of echelons, we establish ten different models (case A to case J) for various

[5]https://www.statista.com/outlook/tmo/it-services/business-process-outsourcing/united-states

scopes and dynamics in manufacturing outsourcing supply chain and provide optimal decisions players should make for each model. We demonstrate the procedures to derive optimal outsourcing strategies (turnkey, consignment, or in-house) that OEM may choose (cases H, I, and J) and the decisions players should make for a three-tier coopetitive outsourcing supply chain. We then provide the conditions that favor each outsourcing strategy and demonstrate when a win-win or win-win-win outsourcing result may occur. Readers can apply the seven-step analytical framework above to construct suitable outsourcing dynamics and derive the optimal outsourcing strategy and decisions for other comparative outsourcing scenarios.

After the analysis for a "one-OEM-one-CM" two-tier or three-tier outsourcing supply chain, we extend our discussions to include three more complex outsourcing dynamics: multi-client or multi-vendor outsourcing (MCO or MVO) relationship, private information of outsourcing players, and product differentiation (horizontally or vertically) in competitive outsourcing relationship. These more complex dynamics are common in the outsourcing supply chains and deserve attention for involved firms before signing outsourcing and supply contracts. We provide readers a modeling framework and exemplary objective functions for all players involved in each complex outsourcing dynamics. Readers can revise model setups according to their specific outsourcing problems and apply similar approaches in Sect. 3 to obtain further insights.

There are still many outsourcing challenges that are not covered in this chapter. Below, we provide readers references to construct their analytical model in case such challenges are of their interests. We list each outsourcing challenge first and provide the research that may be helpful to readers: different purchasing powers among the players, please see Chen et al. (2012); different types of outsourcing contracts, please see Arya et al. (2008); information sharing among players, please see Boulaksil and Fransoo (2009); risk preferences (risk averse vs. risk neutral) of the players, please see Ülkü et al. (2007); price negotiation, please see Deshpande et al. (2011). We recommend a "balanced" approach when readers want to include more complexity in analytical models. After deriving preliminary outcomes from a complex analytical model, if a variable's impact can be "decoupled" from other factors and such impacts do not render surprising outcomes that deviate from previous studies with that variable as a major factor, we recommend removing that variable from a complex outsourcing model since there exist no interactions between that variable and other variables in the model setup. In this way, we can ensure the final analytical model that contains factors of our utmost interests is still manageable (thus is "balanced") to obtain meaningful business insights.

The contemporary business landscape is confronted with multifaceted challenges stemming from the unprecedented disruptions caused by the Covid-19 pandemic, trade wars and tariffs, and geopolitical conflicts in regions such as Ukraine, Israel and Gaza Strip, and the Red Sea. These global events have significantly impacted the manufacturing sector and introduced a myriad of hurdles for business operations. The pandemic has disrupted supply chains, leading to material shortages and logistical constraints, while geopolitical conflicts have introduced uncertainties in strategic outsourcing decisions when the supply chain stretches too far. In a survey conducted by Alicke et al. (2022), businesses revealed a shift towards adopting dual or multiple sourcing strategies for crucial materials and manufacturing suppliers. Forty-four percent of businesses expressed a desire to diversify their supplier network and enhance sourcing within their respective regions. Ninety-seven percent of respondents say they will increase the inventory levels of both components and finished products. The findings indicate a trend of transitioning from global to regional supply networks, with nearshore or onshore supply chain of reduced just-in-time practices. Production facilities are to be built closer to home markets, reducing dependency on distant suppliers and fostering greater control over production processes. Since 2025, the trade wars among major global economies have escalated and added great uncertainty to business sourcing decisions due to pending tariff negotiations. The outcomes of such negotiations will lead to new global economic orders and international trade alliances, thus definitely will redraw future business sourcing and outsourcing landscapes.

Another new trend is ecosystem-based outsourcing that focuses on building collaborative ecosystems of partners and service providers. Himmelreich et al. (2021) point out that orchestrating a large supplier ecosystem is taxing, expensive and complicated to businesses, and selective and deep partnerships are far more productive. Such ecosystems have been in logistics and IT outsourcing environments. Providers of compatible business applications, cloud services and hardware and software systems in the IT industries often form informal alliances. With proper outsourcing arrangement, OEMs can obtain quality manufacturing and services from suppliers. If the OEM has strong powers to the suppliers (e.g., Apple), it can have the major CM coordinate these suppliers while exerting direct control. For an OEM that has less powers or are not capable, the CM can be the leader creating such an outsourcing ecosystem. For example, wafer fabrication companies have pioneered Semiconductor Backend Turnkey Service (SBTS), a comprehensive solution that consolidates services from either the CM's internal facility or external partners. SBTS proves to be a cost-effective and time-saving option for OEMs by minimizing coordination efforts, which are commonly referred to as "supplier maintenance cost" (Chen et al., 2023).

In addition, technological advances in artificial intelligence (AI) and the allure of automation, data-driven insights, and enhanced productivity propels businesses to strategically integrate AI solutions. It triggered a wave of investments from tech giants (Alphabet, Microsoft, Amazon and Meta, etc.) into Large Language Models (LLM) and AI engines (Leswing, 2023). The majority of businesses aspiring to adopt AI lack the in-house capacity to develop their AI engines. As per the IBM Global AI Adoption Index report (Tsekov, 2023), a quarter of companies are embracing artificial intelligence (AI) through outsourcing in response to shortages in skillful workers with AI capabilities. Consequently, the ongoing trend in IT outsourcing is anticipated to expand to encompass AI and automation outsourcing in the coming years. Service providers in the IT sector are gradually integrating AI-driven solutions into their offerings, enhancing their service portfolio, and providing clients with advanced intelligence and data-driven insights.

References

Alicke, K., Barriball, E., Foster, T., Mauhourat, J., and Trautwein, V. (2022). Taking the pulse of shifting supply chains, McKinsey.com, 08/26/2022. https://www.mckinsey.com/capabilities/operations/our-insights/taking-the-pulse-of-shifting-supply-chains#/. Accessed 24 Jan 2024.

Armstrong & Associates, Inc. (2013). 3PL customers report identifies service trends, 3PL market segment sizes and growth rates. 3plogistics.com, 07/22/2013. https://www.3plogistics.com/3pl-customers-report-identifies-service-trends-3pl-market-segment-sizes-and-growth-rates-2/. Accessed 31 Dec 2023.

Arruñada, B., & Vázquez, X. H. (2006). When your contract manufacturer becomes your competitor. *Harvard Business Review, 84*(9), 135–140.

Arya, A., Mittendorf, B., & Sappington, D. E. M. (2008). The make-or-buy decision in the presence of a rival: Strategic outsourcing to a common supplier. *Management Science, 54*(10), 1747–1758.

Barthélemy, J. (2001). The hidden costs of it outsourcing. *Sloan Management Review, 42*(3), 60–69.

Bernstein, F., & Federgruen, A. (2004). Comparative statics, strategic complements and substitutes in oligopolies. *Journal of Mathematical Economics, 40*(6), 713–746.

Bolandifar, E., Kouvelis, P., & Zhang, F. (2016). Delegation vs. control in supply chain procurement under competition. *Production and Operations Management, 25*(9), 1528–1541.

Boulaksil, Y., & Fransoo, J. C. (2009). Order release strategies to control outsourced operations in a supply chain. *International Journal of Production Economics, 119*(1), 149–160.

Bradsher, K. (2014). Chinese IBM workers strike amid Lenovo sale unrest. Financial review. https://www.afr.com/technology/chinese-ibm-workers-strike-amid-lenovo-sale-unrest-20140307-ixmsn. Accessed 04 Jan 2024.

Brewer, B., Ashenbaum, B., & Ogden, J. A. (2013). Connecting strategy-linked outsourcing approaches and expected performance. *International Journal of Physical Distribution & Logistics Management, 43*(3), 176–204.

Caldieraro, F. (2016). The role of brand image and product characteristics on firms' entry and OEM decisions. *Management Science, 62*(11), 3085–3391.

Chen, Z., & Liu, F. (2021). Multi-outsourcing supply chain coordination under yield and demand uncertainties. *Expert Systems with Applications, 181*, 115177.

Chen, Y. J., Shum, S., & Xiao, W. (2012). Should an OEM retain component procurement when the CM produces competing products? *Production and Operations Management, 21*(5), 907–922.

Chen, Y., Karamemis, G., & Zhang, J. (2021). A win-win strategy analysis for an original equipment manufacturer and a contract manufacturer in a competitive market. *European Journal of Operational Research, 293*(1), 177–189.

Chen, J. C., Chen, T. L., Huang, W. C., Peng, P., & Lin, T. (2023). Supply chain planning for IC design house back-end production network with turnkey service. *IEEE Transactions on Semiconductor Manufacturing, 36*(3), 458–475.

Dannen, C. (2008). Dell announces low-cost sub-notebook. Fastcompany.com, 05/29/2008. https://www.fastcompany.com/872217/dell-announces-low-cost-sub-notebook. Accessed 12 Jan 2024.

Deshpande, V., Schwarz, L. B., Atallah, M. J., Blanton, M., & Frikken, K. B. (2011). Outsourcing manufacturing: Secure price-masking mechanisms for purchasing component parts. *Production and Operations Management, 20*(2), 165–180.

Domberger, S. (1998). *The contracting organization: A strategic guide to outsourcing*. Oxford University Press.

Earl, M. J. (1996). The risks of outsourcing IT. *Sloan Management Review, 37*(3), 26–32.

Farahat, A., & Perakis, G. (2011). A comparison of Bertrand and Cournot profits in oligopolies with differentiated products. *Operations Research, 59*(2), 507–513.

Feng, Q., & Lu, L. X. (2010). Design outsourcing in a differentiated product market: The role of bargaining and scope economies. Available at SSRN 2986185.

Feng, Q., & Lu, L. X. (2013). The role of contract negotiation and industry structure in production outsourcing. *Production and Operations Management, 22*(5), 1299–1319.

Garaventa, E., & Tellefsen, T. (2001). Outsourcing: The hidden costs. *Review of Business, 22*, 28–31.

Gozman, D., & Willcocks, L. (2019). The emerging cloud dilemma: Balancing innovation with cross-border privacy and outsourcing regulations. *Journal of Business Research, 97*, 235–256.

Gray, J. V., Tomlin, B., & Roth, A. V. (2009). Outsourcing to a powerful contract manufacturer: The effect of learning-by-doing. *Production and Operations Management, 18*(5), 487–505.

Guo, P., Song, J. S., & Wang, Y. (2010). Outsourcing structures and information flow in a three-tier supply chain. *International Journal of Production Economics, 128*(1), 175–187.

Himmelreich, H., Hrishikesh, H., Scherp, E., & Oshri, I. (2021). Reimagining outsourcing after Covid-19, Computeweekly.com, 03/15/2021. https://www.computerweekly.com/opinion/Reimagining-outsourcing-after-Covid-19. Accessed 20 Dec 2023.

Iqbal, Z., & Dad, A. M. (2013). Outsourcing: A review of trends, winners & losers and future directions. *International Journal of Business and Social Science, 4*(8), 91–107.

Karamemis, G., Zhang, J., & Chen, Y. (2023). Consignment and turnkey sourcing and outsourcing analysis for a three-player supply chain in various power dynamics. *European Journals of Operational Research, 311*(1), 125–138.

Kaya, O. (2011). Outsourcing vs. in-house production: A comparison of supply chain contracts with effort dependent demand. *Omega, 39*(2), 168–178.

Kayis, E., Erhun, F., & Plambeck, E. L. (2013). Delegation vs. control of component procurement under asymmetric cost information and simple contracts. *Manufacturing & Service Operations Management, 15*(1), 45–56.

Kemahlıoğlu-Ziya, E. (2015). Contracting for capacity under renegotiation: Partner preferences and the value of anticipating renegotiation. *Production and Operations Management, 24*(2), 237–252.

Kremic, T., Icmeli Tukel, O., & Rom, W. O. (2006). Outsourcing decision support: A survey of benefits, risks, and decision factors. *Supply Chain Management: An International Journal, 11*(6), 467–482.

Lacity, M. C., Solomon, S., Yan, A., & Willcocks, L. P. (2011). Business process outsourcing studies: A critical review and research directions. *Journal of Information Technology, 26*, 221–258.

Lacity, M. C., Willcocks, L. P., & Solomon, S. (2012). Robust practices from two decades of ITO and BPO research. In M. C. Lacity & L. P. Willcocks (Eds.), *Advanced outsourcing practice: Rethinking ITO, BPO and cloud services* (pp. 1–24). Palgrave Macmillan.

Leswing, K. (2023). Tech giants are pouring money into A.I. as they cut costs elsewhere, Cnbc.com, 04/28/2023. https://www.cnbc.com/2023/04/28/tech-earnings-calls-show-mega-cap-companies-going-big-on-ai-.html. Accessed 24 Jan 2024.

Li, L., & Cheng, T. -F. (2023). Apple taps China's Luxshare to develop augmented reality device. Nikkei.com, 02/23/2023. https://asia.nikkei.com/Spotlight/Supply-Chain/Apple-taps-China-s-Luxshare-to-develop-augmented-reality-device. Accessed 31 Dec 2023.

Li, W., Chen, J., & Chen, B. (2020). Sourcing strategy of original equipment manufacturer with quality competition. *Decision Sciences, 51*(5), 1110–1130.

Li, G., Wu, H., & Dai, J. (2023). Production sourcing strategy for an apparel original brand manufacturer in the presence of technology spillover. *IEEE Transactions on Engineering Management, 7*(4), 1283–1294.

Liao, Y., Liao, K., & Hutchinson, R. (2009). A conceptual framework for prototyping outsourcing in new product development: A knowledge-based view. *Journal of Manufacturing Technology Management, 21*(1), 122–138.

Loh, L., & Venkatraman, N. (1992). Determinants of information technology outsourcing: A cross-sectional analysis. *Journal of Management Information Systems, 9*, 7–24.

Lv, F. (2019). Should competing original equipment manufacturers outsource procurement activities under asymmetric cost information? *International Journal of Production Research, 57*(14), 4561–4578.

Mandal, P., & Jain, T. (2021). Partial outsourcing from a rival: Quality decision under product differentiation and information asymmetry. *European Journal of Operational Research, 292*(3), 886–908.

Ni, D., Li, K. W., & Tang, X. (2009). Production costs, scope economies, and multi-client outsourcing under quantity competition. *International Journal of Production Economics, 121*(1), 130–140.

Niu, B., Wang, Y., & Guo, P. (2015). Equilibrium pricing sequence in a co-opetitive supply chain with the ODM as a downstream rival of its OEM. *Omega, 57*, 249–270.

Niu, B., Liu, Y., Luo, H., & Feng, B. (2019a). Domestic sourcing vs. cross-border sourcing: Impact of the quality of the scrap metal and government's tariff policies. *Journal of Cleaner Production, 208*, 1281–1293.

Niu, B., Mu, Z., Chen, L., & Lee, C. K. (2019b). Coordinate the economic and environmental sustainability via procurement outsourcing in a co-opetitive supply chain. *Resources, Conservation and Recycling, 146*, 17–27.

Quinn, J. B. (2000). Outsourcing innovation: The new engine of growth. *Sloan Management Review, 41*(4), 13–28.

Quinn, J. B., & Hilmer, F. G. (1994). Strategic outsourcing. *Sloan Management Review, 35*(4), 43–55.

Research and Markets. (2023). Global IT outsourcing market. Researchandmarkets.com, January 2024. https://www.researchandmarkets.com/report/it-outsourcing. Accessed 25 Jan 2024.

Shen, B., Li, Q., Dong, C., & Quan, V. (2016). Design outsourcing in the fashion supply chain: OEM versus ODM. *Journal of the Operational Research Society, 67*(2), 259–268.

Sturgeon, T. (2002). Modular production networks: A new American model of industrial organization. *Industrial Corporate Change, 11*(3), 451–496.

Troianovski, A., & Clark, D. (2012). Inside Nokia's struggle against Apple's iPhone. Wsj.com, 05/12/2012. https://www.wsj.com/articles/SB10001424052702303640104577436443119293310. Accessed 27 Dec 2023.

Tsekov, P. (2023). How AI is influencing the IT outsourcing business. Forbes.com, 09/07/2023. https://www.forbes.com/sites/forbestechcouncil/2023/09/07/how-ai-is-influencing-the-it-outsourcing-business/. Accessed 24 Jan 2024.

Ülkü, S., Toktay, L. B., & Yücesan, E. (2007). Risk ownership in contract manufacturing. *Manufacturing & Service Operations Management, 9*(3), 225–241.

Vilches, J. (2007). Asus Eee PC now available to US buyers. Techspot.com, 10/31/2007. https://www.techspot.com/news/27698-asus-eee-pc-now-available-to-us-buyers.html. Accessed 12 Jan 2024.

Wang, Y., Niu, B., & Guo, P. (2013). On the advantage of quantity leadership when outsourcing production to a competitive contract manufacturer. *Production and Operations Management, 22*(1), 104–119.

Wang, Y., Niu, B., & Guo, P. (2014). The comparison of two vertical outsourcing structures under push and pull contracts. *Production and Operations Management, 23*(4), 610–625.

Wasti, S. N., & Liker, J. K. (1997). Risky business or competitive power? Supplier involvement in Japanese product design. *Journal of Product Innovation Management, 14*(5), 337–355.

Wu, X., & Zhang, F. (2014). Home or overseas? An analysis of sourcing strategies under competition. *Management Science, 60*(5), 1223–1240.

Xiao, T., Xia, Y., & Zhang, G. P. (2014). Strategic outsourcing decisions for manufacturers competing on product quality. *IIE Transactions, 46*(4), 313–329.

Xu, J., Hsu, V. N., & Niu, B. (2018). The impacts of markets and tax on a multinational firm's procurement strategy in China. *Production and Operations Management, 27*(2), 251–264.

Xue, W., Choi, T.-M., & Ma, L. (2016). Diversification strategy with random yield suppliers for a mean-variance risk-sensitive manufacturer. *Transportation Research Part E: Logistics and Transportation Review, 90*, 90–107.

Yan, X., Zhang, M., & Liu, K. (2010). A note on coordination in decentralized assembly systems with uncertain component yields. *European Journal of Operational Research, 205*(2), 469–478.

Yan, Y., Zhao, R., & Lan, Y. (2019). Moving sequence preference in coopetition outsourcing supply chain: Consensus or conflict. *International Journal of Production Economics, 208*, 221–240.

Yang, D., Liu, S., Zhang, Z., Huang, F., & Wang, J. (2022). Strategic interaction of original equipment manufacturers between outsourcing and purchasing in a quality-differentiated market. *PloS one, 17*(1), e0262678.

Yang, F. X., Zhang, R. Q., & Zhu, K. (2017). Should purchasing activities be outsourced along with production? *European Journal of Operational Research, 257*(2), 468–482.

Zailani, S., Shaharudin, M. R., Razmi, K., & Iranmanesh, M. (2017). Influential factors and performance of logistics outsourcing practices: An evidence of Malaysian companies. *Review of Managerial Science, 11*, 53–93.

Do the Different Forms of Outsourcing Affect the Management of Safety? A Comparative Case Study in a Single Organization

Colin Pilbeam

1 Introduction

Outsourcing is a common occurrence in both private and public sector organizations around the world and may take different forms, which include firms engaging with other firms and individuals (Connelly & Gallagher, 2004; Davis-Blake & Broschak, 2009). Outsourcing does, however, have consequences, not least through the introduction of a variety of risks into the activities of both parties. These can adversely affect organizational safety performance. While outsourcing and chains of contractor relationships have been implicated in many catastrophic incidents across industrial sectors, for example, the Deep Water Horizon blowout in 2010, the AZF Chemical Factory explosion, Toulouse in 2001, and the derailment at Hatfield in 2000, "the connection between this contemporary organizational phenomenon and safety is less well studied" (Hayes & Tillement, 2022, p. v). This chapter addresses this deficiency.

Guidance on the safety management of contractor relationships does exist (e.g., HSE, 2011; ISSA, 2018), but this is largely generic. It does not accommodate the variety of outsourcing relationship types that occur in practice (Ashford et al., 2007; Connelly & Gallagher, 2004), which may each require a differentiated approach to safety management. This study therefore investigated how safety was managed in the three different, but frequently occurring, forms of outsourcing identified by Davis-Blake and Broschak (2009) in their review and found in different businesses within a single division of a global mechanical electrical engineering company operating in the UK (identified here as EngCo). The design of this study matches the single case study with embedded subcases adopted by Dubois and Gadde (2002)

C. Pilbeam (✉)
Safety and Accident Investigation Centre, Cranfield University, Cranfield, UK
e-mail: colin.pilbeam@cranfield.ac.uk

F. P. García Márquez et al. (eds.), *Outsourcing Using Operations Research and Management Science Methods*, International Series in Operations Research & Management Science 366, https://doi.org/10.1007/978-3-031-91845-2_3

in their investigation of outsourcing in a truck manufacturer. The case company, its situation, and its organization and control of outsourced activities constitute a common frame around the three subcases. By limiting organizational variation, the effects of different outsourcing arrangements on safety management practices could be more easily identified, permitting a more effective answer to the question, "What are the safety management practices occurring in different outsourcing arrangements?"

The chapter is organized as follows. A brief literature review defines outsourcing, noting the wide variety of forms possible. It synthesizes and compares guidance on the safety management of contractors available to practitioners and identifies some of the empirical investigations that support this guidance. The section on methods outlines the research design, introduces the case organization and the three embedded cases, and then describes the data collection and analysis. Findings from the three sub-cases, each representing a different form of outsourcing arrangement, are presented separately and then compared. The discussion suggests theoretical explanations for both the apparent similarities and differences in safety management practices between these three commonly occurring but different forms of outsourcing.

2 Literature Review

Outsourcing is one of the most significant and enduring strategic organizational activities of the modern era (Belcourt, 2006; Hätönen & Eriksson, 2009), which Davis-Blake and Broschak (2009; p. 322) define as "the act of obtaining goods or services from individuals or organizations outside of a firm's boundaries when these goods or services could be created internally by a firm's own employees and managers." Many different activities may be outsourced, including, for example, routine cleaning, specialist advice, bespoke product manufacturing, HR and IT functions, transportation, maintenance, and minor construction.

Arrangements for the outsourcing of goods or services take three forms (Davis-Blake & Broschak, 2009). The first arrangement is to locate the whole process or function beyond the boundary of the lead firm, for example, the outsourcing of facilities management, which includes cleaning, general site maintenance and minor works (Atkin & Bildsten, 2017). By externalizing these peripheral services, the lead firm can focus on core competencies or leverage limited resources and reduce risk. A second arrangement involves locating parts of the process outside of the firm. These may be the more mundane or routine tasks, or conversely, tasks that require specialist expertise, for example, the servicing and repair of critical machinery or instruments. Contingent working is a third type of arrangement (Connelly & Gallagher, 2004). This involves the procurement of human resources through employment agencies or search firms. Outsourcing in these three arrangements occurs either between two firms or organizations, where processes are outsourced, or directly between a firm and an individual, where staffing (and so the acquisition of skills) is outsourced (Davis-Blake & Broschak, 2009).

Outsourcing processes inevitably requires a re-allocation of tasks within the client firm or between the client firm and the contractor (Davis-Blake & Broschak, 2009). Employees in the client firm may retain more complex tasks and more mundane tasks may be outsourced. The reverse is also possible. Specialist tasks may be outsourced, and client firm employees maintain the basic tasks. Outsourcing may also require client firm employees to coordinate the activities and monitor the performance of contractors, thus adding to their workload. These additional responsibilities may demand new skills. Such changes can lead to tensions between client firm employees and contractors (Clarke, 2003), arising from differences between organizations in their physical, social or cognitive processes (Pilbeam, 2024). These negative interpersonal relationships have deleterious consequences for work-group dynamics. Moreover, outsourcing affects not only the composition of work groups but also the coordination of work processes, and such changes can introduce risks adversely affecting the management of safety. For example, a recent study of outsourced maintenance of operations in a glass manufacturing plant (Grusenmeyer, 2022) illustrated risks associated with disorganization of task distribution and coordination between staff in the different organizations and weaknesses in communication.

Contingent working is common in the construction industry. Data from surveys or secondary sources in this sector regularly show that contingent workers encounter greater risks (e.g., Mehta & Theodore, 2006) and suffer more injuries than permanent employees (Hintkikka, 2011). A point reinforced by a comparative study across construction, childcare, logistics and hospitality by Mayhew et al. (1997, p. 171) who noted that while the pattern of injury and illness varied by sector, these rates were higher for individual contractors than employees, because "all these workers are dispersed, relatively powerless and insecure." Despite this evidence there is little direct information on how safety might be managed amongst these contingent workers. General guidance on safety management in construction (e.g., Hallowell & Gambatese, 2009) does not explicitly deal with safety management in outsourcing relationships, although it does suggest that subcontractor selection and management are important activities.

Practical guidance for managing safety in outsourcing relationships, for example by the UK's Health and Safety Executive (HSE, 2011), is often provided in the form of a checklist. Inevitably, these are generic, although some provide greater detail than others. Four sets of practitioner guidance are compared in Table 1. While they adopt a similar staged approach, there are notable differences. Those provided by the National Safety Council (2015) are brief. In contrast, a more recent set provided by the International Social Security Association (ISSA) (2018) contains more details, emphasizing particularly the planning, selection, contracting and preparation stages before work commences. Variation in the detail provided for these early stages can potentially lead to safety issues as the work progresses. Control of work on-site is variously specified, implying judgment in the extent of engagement needed between the client and the contractor. In all cases, there is much less detail provided about the

Table 1 A comparison of practical guidance on the safety management of contractors

HSE (2011; pp. 22–23)	Indicator (2015; p. 10)	National Safety Council (2015)	ISSA (2018)	A priori coding template
Step 1: Planning Identify hazards Assess risks Eliminate and reduce the risks Specify H&S conditions Discuss with contractor	1. When choosing the contractor, make reasonable checks that they are competent to carry out the work safely 2. To enable them to plan the work, notify the contractor in advance of any constraints, site safety rules and other information of relevance	1. Pre-qualification 2. Pre-job task and risk assessment	1. *Project preparation* (project definition, planning, tender, procurement) 2. *Choice of contractor* (pre-qualification process, selection criteria, final selection) 3. *Contractual arrangements* (project definition, guideline for contractors, coordinating persons, subcontractors, risk assessment, operational plan)	1. *Selection & recruitment*
Step 2: Choosing a contractor What competence is needed? Get evidence Go thru' information about the job and site Ask for Methods Statement	3. For significant jobs, request a risk assessment and method statement. Read this on receipt and identify any hazards which are likely to affect your staff, visitors etc.		4. *Collective preparation* (guideline of contractors, coordinating persons, risk assessment, information and communication management, appointment of contractor's workforce)	
Step 3: Contractors working on site All contractors sign in and out Name a site contact Reinforce H&S information and site rules Check the job and allow work to begin	4. Arrange any special measures with the contractor which will help the job run smoothly and protect them or others from harm 5. When the contractor's workers arrive on site, brief them on the site safety rules, hazards and emergency procedures. Check what they are planning to do. Identify areas they'll work in. Get them to sign in and tell them they must sign out.	3. Contractor training and orientation	5. *Management of contract* (protective measures, safety information, operational plan, identification of workforce) 6. *Control and sign-off/completion* (implementation of protective measures, supervision measures, incident management, contract infractions, testing and acceptance)	2. *Induction* 3. *Risk assessment and methods statements (RAMS)* 4. *Permits to work* 5. *Verbal communication* 6. *Written communication*

	6. If they are conducting higher hazard activities, e.g., hot work using a blow torch, issue a permit to work			
Step 4: Keeping a check Assess the degree of contact needed How is the job going? Are any special arrangements needed?	7. Monitor periodically to check that the contractor's staff are working safely and to identify unexpected issues that need to be resolved	4. Monitoring of job		7. *Monitor/safety walkabout* 8. *Inspect/audit* 9. *Report*
Step 5: Reviewing the work Review the job and the contractor Record the lessons	8. After the work is complete, make sure that it's of adequate quality and you receive any certification required, e.g., commissioning certificate	5. Post-job evaluation	7. *Review*	10. *Review*

closure of the job and its review, which would allow opportunities for performance improvement to be captured.

Empirical studies of safety management in outsourcing arrangements in different industries in different locations support the steps outlined generally in the practitioner guidance but suggest there is more subtlety and nuance than some of the guidelines reveal. To illustrate, some authors (Hasle, 2007; Rebitzer, 1995) recommend that prior safety performance should be an important criterion in the selection process for appointing contractors. Kochan et al. (1994) concur but note that it is rarely done and suggest that on-site visits to potential contractors during the tendering stage could also be adopted. In the guidelines much attention is given to developing safety plans, hazard analysis and risk assessments. Lingard et al. (2020) note that appropriate checks of competence and review of statements of proposed methods of working are crucial. These then drive the documentation of statements of methods of work and the development of permits to work. These specific safety task-related practices are also evident in the empirical studies (e.g., Glazner et al., 1998; Manu et al., 2013), but other management practices such as training and supervision, which are not safety specific, are also found. For example, induction training is necessary but more especially for new and inexperienced workers (Lowrey et al., 1998). Continuous supervision and positive role modelling of safety behaviours, particularly by members of the senior management team (Glazner et al., 1999; Schubert & Dijkstra, 2009), are considered important. Involving the senior management team and their signalling of the importance of safe working improves safety performance (Lingard et al., 2010; Vassie & Fuller, 2003). Insights like these are not evident in the available generic guidance. Other valuable practices for managing safety in outsourced relationships were evidenced in several other empirical studies, but these were not always indicated explicitly in several of the guidelines. Examples include monitoring the flow of information, including safety-related information (Rousseau & Libuser, 1997), and the ongoing monitoring of contractor safety performance to support the continuous feedback needed for performance improvement (Gochfeld & Mohr, 2007; Nenonen & Vasara, 2013), and to ensure compliance with the contract (O'Brien, 1999). In addition, studies have shown that monitoring minor injuries reduces major ones (Lowrey et al., 1998), and the reporting and investigation of near misses and accidents and subsequently sharing this information encourage learning (Kongsvik et al., 2012).

Combining the practitioner guidance with the empirical studies of safety management practices in outsourced relationships highlights three deficiencies. Firstly, as noted above, the available practical guidance is generic and fails to account for the richness and diversity of practices inherent in any particular case. Different outsourcing arrangements, including the three forms noted above, might warrant some safety management practices and not others. Secondly, while some studies have compared safety management practices in outsourcing activities within or across sectors using surveys (e.g., Glazner et al., 1998; Nenonen et al., 2015; Rebitzer, 1995), there has been no detailed systematic comparison of safety management practices in different types of outsourcing arrangement. Thirdly, while some studies have investigated safety management practices in an outsourcing relationship in a single organization, these are relatively few and often from safety-critical industries, notably the oil and gas industry. Examples include Collinson's (1999) study of workers on a North Sea oil rig, Vassie and Fuller's (2003) study of offshore oil exploration, Milch and Laumann's (2018) study of offshore drilling in the Norwegian petroleum industry, and McDermott and Hayes (2018) study of risk shifting in excavation of a gas pipeline in Australia. Studies in other sectors include Drupsteen et al.'s (2015) exploration of safety issues in a logistics company and Garner's (2006) partial re-examination of the Columbia disaster.

This study addresses these three deficiencies by identifying the safety management practices occurring in a single organization that deployed the three different outsourcing arrangements to support different aspects of its business. Using a case study approach, with three subcases embedded in a single case (Dubois & Gadde, 2002), we explore a "contemporary phenomenon in a real-life setting" (Gibbert & Ruigrok, 2010: p. 712) and uncover the diversity of safety management practices occurring across the life of different types of outsourcing arrangement in a single organization.

3 Methods

3.1 Research Design

Ridder (2017) identified and compared four different approaches to conducting case study research, deploying different designs to serve different purposes. The approach adopted here is a descriptive comparison of the practices of safety management identified from qualitative data obtained from interviews with those working in three different types of outsourcing arrangements in a single organization. Interviews with several employees and contractors in a particular type of outsourcing arrangement helped to confirm the reliability of the data, giving assurance of the regularity of the safety management practices in that specific type of contracting arrangement. This allowed the construction of a configuration of safety management practices for each outsourcing type, which could then be compared, providing an empirical foundation for creating a new theory (Tsang, 2014). This comparison does not seek statistical generalizability to a larger population of all outsourcing relationships but heuristic generalization (Tsoukas, 2009) in the absence of existing theory on what processes and practices are adopted for safety management in different types of outsourcing relationships.

3.2 Outsourcing Arrangements in EngCo

EngCo is a global mechanical, electrical engineering company headquartered in Europe that has been in operation for more than 150 years. In consultation with the

Head of Governance in one of EngCo's UK divisions, three different outsourcing arrangements were identified that aligned with the three recognised outsourcing arrangements noted above:

1. *Externalizing a whole process or function.* EngCo had approximately 120 operational sites in the UK ranging in size from small depots to large manufacturing hubs. A facilities management company (FMCo) had recently won the contract to manage these EngCo facilities (including maintenance and sub-contracted work). A small Real Estate Division within EngCo oversaw this 3-year contract.
2. *Outsourcing parts of a process.* This was found in the relationship between an established engineering plant at an EngCo site in the Northeast of England, and its long-standing contractual relationships with several smaller companies providing specialist engineering and maintenance services (SpecialistCos)
3. *Procurement of contract workers through an employment agency.* EngCo employed trained personnel recruited from an agency (AgencyCo) to enable it to fulfil contractual obligations with two energy providers to install SMART energy meters on customer premises (homes and businesses) as part of the UK Government's plans to "offer" SMART meters to all by the end of 2020.

3.3 Data Collection

In the first three months of 2018, the Head of Governance facilitated access to both employees and contractors in these different outsourced arrangements arranging 24 semi-structured interviews with key informants having a variety of roles (Table 2). In EngCo, these included EHS managers or advisors, as well as business

Table 2 Details of the number and roles of interviewees in three different outsourcing arrangements with EngCo

Contractor	Contractor activity	Number of interviews/role of interviewees	
		EngCo staff	Contractors/agency workers
FMCo. (Case 1)	FMCo provides facilities management services across EngCo's portfolio of UK sites	4 (Location Managers)	3 (Technical Services Manager; FMCo Regional Manager; Asbestos and L8 coordinator)
SpecialistCos (Case 2)	SpecialistCos provide technical services to support the engineering activities at one of EngCo's established sites	5 (Head of Operations; Head of Supply Chain; H&S Adviser—site; H&S Adviser—field; Procurement Assistant)	5 (representatives from 4 different organizations)
AgencyCo (Case 3)	AgencyCo employs individual contractors to fit SMART meters on behalf of EngCo	4 (Head of Managed Services; Head of Operations; Head of EHS; Field Manager)	3 (2 Dual fuel meter engineers; Technical coach)

and location managers. In the contracted companies, participants had a range of roles, including specialist contractor, site engineer and function manager, or temporary workers from the agency. This wide variety of experience amongst the interviewees makes it more likely that the breadth of important issues on the topic will be surfaced and that consensus will be achieved quickly (Guest et al., 2006). Interviews with key informants lasted from between 17 to 38 minutes. They were recorded with permission and transcribed verbatim by a third party under contract, giving a total of almost 11 hours of recorded data. Interviews were conducted face-to-face in the cases of outsourcing with specialist contractors and with agency workers. They were conducted by telephone in the cases of outsourcing with FMCo because of the mobility of this cadre of employees. Topic areas discussed in the interview included an overview of the general safety performance of the site and outsourced activity (to provide context for the outsourcing arrangement), the safety practices for managing the outsourced activity (including a discussion of where these do or do not work well), the history and nature of the relationship between client and contractor, and any notable challenges including how these have impacted safety, ways that contractors contribute to improving safety performance of the client organization, and ways that changes are made to improve the practices of maintaining safety in the client organization.

3.4 Data Analysis

Our data analysis followed procedures recommended for template analysis (Brooks et al., 2015), a form of thematic analysis. Thematic analysis is a widely adopted "method for identifying, analysing and reporting patterns (themes) within data" (Braun & Clarke, 2006; p. 79). Initial readings of all the transcripts tentatively indicated the adoption of practices used regularly to manage safety in these different outsourcing relationships. The author was attuned to this possibility through a prior reading of empirical studies and the four practitioner guidelines on the management of safety in contactor relationships. Each transcript from within a case was coded semantically using the language of the interviewees to generate first-order codes. These free codes were then collated for each case using a template of safety practices used in the management of safety in outsourcing relationships developed a priori from an integration of different practitioner guidance (Table 1). This was an iterative process where the veracity of codes and the accuracy of placement to the coding structure were repeatedly checked with reference to the context being described in the interview and re-reading of the category descriptions in the guidance from which each template was derived. Quotes from interviewees have been used as illustrations in the findings.

In line with recommendations for conducting rigorous case-based research (Tsang, 2014), several different tactics were used to ensure validity and reliability. Specifically, the literature was used to develop (i) the framework for selecting the three cases, (ii) the research protocol and (iii) the a priori coding template.

Commonalities in the quotes within cases and patterns in the data between cases ensured internal validity. Case study reports were verified by a project steering group of five practitioners, including the Head of Governance of the EngCo division in which this study occurred.

4 Findings

4.1 Case 1: Outsourcing Facility Management Across UK to FMCo

At each site, FMCo employed sub-contractors to support the management of EngCo facilities. FMCo also managed the contractors EngCo brought onto all their sites, having a managing agent role. Both sets of contractors were selected from those available on an EngCo-preferred supplier list maintained and updated by the procurement function within EngCo. Health and safety (H&S) management and performance were part of the evaluation criteria used in the tendering process for the outsourced task.

Arriving onsite contractors undertook not only FMCo inductions but also EngCo inductions under the instruction of the site supervisor. The production of Risk Assessments and Methods Statements (RAMS) was an essential part of FMCo control of contractors but was often pre-specified by EngCo because they own the risk.

> So, our site supervisors would review the risk assessments, methods statements, and competencies to ensure suitability to the work and then, as I say, write and issue, and fully induct. So, we do fully induct all sub-contractors onto site as well. (Regional Manager, FMCo)

The RAMS were reviewed by FMCo's site supervisors, and this allowed them to check the competency of the contractors coming onsite. Access permits and permits to work were another vital mechanism for controlling contractor activities and these were issued by FMCo but closely audited by EngCo.

> But we work very closely with FMCo on the permits to make sure that at least the risk has been identified and covered with their RAMS, etc. It's not just a paper exercise that these things are done correctly. (Location Manager 4)

A different location manager commented that "recently we did have an issue with a contractor where I found out that they weren't working with the correct permits, which I then escalated, and they got chucked off site" (Location Manager 1).

Meetings were a routine and frequent vehicle for communication. EngCo required FMCo to hold regular meetings with contractors onsite to disseminate H&S messages and for reporting and updating. Often this took the form of daily short toolbox talks. The sharing of H&S information via social media complemented formal communication at meetings between EngCo and FMCo.

EngCo location managers held monthly meetings with FMCo's regional management team, in which they went through "things like statutory mandatory compliance and any issues" (Location Manager 3). They also undertook two spot checks and site walk-rounds per month. It provided "a fresh pair of eyes" (Location Manager 2) to spot any safety issues that may have been overlooked. These checks were against a pre-specified checklist of criteria.

> We've got a form that we used that are for us to check ... we check high level stuff. ... So, it's prescriptive, but obviously if you find something you just start to dig a little bit deeper. It's just a typical audit document. (Location Manager 3)

This helped to ensure FMCo was compliant with the terms of its contract.

> [The compliancy documentation] is a, you could call it a huge tick list if you will, but every piece of compliance under every heading that you can think of, and each of the sites are listed and it's been either passed, failed, done, not done, and what the actions are. ... It's a huge document, absolutely massive documentation, but it's very clever, it's a one-stop shop. (Location Manager 2)

These standard monitoring reports formed the basis of monthly audits of FMCo performance by EngCo to ensure compliance with the KPIs specified in the contract and provided a "very strict governance process" (Location Manager 4).

There was limited evidence of learning. There was no mention of near-miss/incident reporting. One interviewee mentioned that close-out meetings were documented and that lessons learned were "done," suggesting these activities were performed in a perfunctory manner with little anticipation of sustained change.

4.2 Case 2. Outsourcing Specialist Activities at a Single Site

A number of smaller companies provided specialist engineering and maintenance services to the work at one of EngCo's established engineering plants. Over time, these smaller companies had been acquired by larger national companies, but the business units dealing with this particular EngCo site had endured. Some of these relationships had lasted for more than 50 years, and many of the respondents had working relationships spanning decades. The long-term continuity of these relationships developed trust at a local level.

> You have a good communication with them, because you get to know them that many time on different jobs you've been on. You get to know all the engineers and you have a good rapport with them. It's a good setup with them. (SpecialistCo 1)

This rapport ensured a succession of contracts with EngCo and ongoing employment in the specialist companies. Despite their familiarity with the operations onsite and familiarity with the EngCo staff, all contractors were inducted at the beginning of each new engagement.

"Every contractor coming on site must have a risk assessment and method statement. That's the procedure whatever they're doing" (EngCo H&S Adviser—

Site). These were submitted to EngCo in advance, scrutinised carefully, and amendments were requested and made prior to induction.

> We then produced our RAMS and COSHH and electronics takes it to site. They'll review it and say, 'yay' or 'nay' or 'can you tweak that', 'we don't quite understand there', 'we don't understand that there', 'tweak that there'. The RAMS get issued. We come to site and do our stuff in a safe manner. (SpecialistCo 1)

These RAMS were often supplemented by a point-of-work assessment to cater to the dynamic nature of the factory environment.

> **Contractor**: *You've got to get your permit. You go and review the area. They look at it properly nowadays where, in the past, prior to the incident certainly, then you would be issued your permit with your risk assessment and off you'd go, and there was no real live review of that prior to the work commencing.*
>
> **Interviewer**: *But this has now changed?*
>
> **Contractor**: *Yes, and even our technicians now have a live document which is a point of work risk assessment, so even though the risk assessment's been done perhaps by somebody like myself, or one of the project engineers or the service manager for the site, then when our engineer turns up, he's also got an A4 size [sheet] and he goes through his risk assessment.* (SpecialistCo 2).

EngCo staff hosting the contractor-issued permits to work. These lasted for a maximum of 12 h, after which a continuation permit was required. These were displayed at the work site so that activities could be easily monitored against expectations during safety walkabouts.

> The safety department sometimes have a safety walkaround on certain days and if they come across your area, they'll come in there and make sure your permit's in order, that your risk assessment's up to date and that you've got copies of those documents. (SpecialistCo 3)

Verbal communication was a natural part of the relationship and was seen as an essential albeit informal part of ensuring safe working on site.

Although EngCo procedures specified that there should be weekly inspections or checks of all contractors to ensure safe working, for some specialist companies, this was delayed:

> They've always come to me monthly. I'll have an [EngCo] department manager walk around, boots on the ground I think they call it. They'll come in and have a nosey, have a look. (SpecialistCo 4)

While others reported that they had never experienced an inspection:

> I'll be honest here, and the times I've worked onsite, and I'm speaking personally, I've not had an [EngCo] person come up and just have a check to say, have you got this and that in place. Have you got your RAMS or just a spot-check to see that you're working safely. (SpecialistCo 3)

Audits were uncommon and conducted by the client company rather than EngCo.

> We also have our own internal auditing process where some of the managers and project engineers will visit a site and just audit our own people on site. (SpecialistCo 2).

Incidents were reported when they occurred. Individual contractor firms conducted internal reviews on the completion of the projects to promote their own learning, but these were rarely done with EngCo staff to feed into a cycle of continuous improvement for EngCo more widely.

> It depends generally on the size of it. Sometimes we'll have close-out meetings where we will attend site. That tends to be if the site has had an issue and then that tends to be more, I think end client driven, rather than EngCo driven. (SpecialistCo 1)

4.3 *Case 3. Outsourcing Recruitment of Temporary Workers to AgencyCo*

Overall, EngCo spent c. £180 m on temporary labour each year because of the seasonality of many of its activities. Much of this is procured through agencies. Procurement managers work with employment agencies to agree on contracts specifying requirements. These included qualifications and skills, as well as health and safety requirements to ensure the temporary labour had the correct PPE and tools before arriving on site. While EngCo provided some equipment, for example, hard hats and hi-viz vests, there is a limit to what they provide. "We can't keep giving away £1000" (EHS adviser to procurement), as jackets and flame-retardant overalls, for example, are not redistributed to new starters but discarded. Agencies were also required to provide feedback to EngCo on incident rates of their employees and to conduct drug and alcohol tests. One of the biggest challenges with using agency workers is their habit of seeking another position during their current contract and leaving before the end of the contracted period. Replacing individuals can be problematic and introduces risk into the work. When contracts end, this provides the opportunity to retain those temporary workers who have performed well, "we get introduced to them through the agency, we see how they work, they see how we work and if it's a happy marriage then after probably two years then they'll join us" (Field manager).

Negotiations with AgencyCo to provide workers to support the SMART meter rollout in 2017 ensured that contractors had terms and conditions that were similar to permanent EngCo employees. The decision by EngCo not to employ directly was to avoid the need to make large numbers of employees redundant at the completion of the SMART meter rollout. By remaining on AgencyCo's books, EngCo argued that these contractors had a better chance of redeployment after the known end date of the project. These terms and conditions gave the temporary workers more security and greater assurance. EngCo, by taking responsibility for all aspects of the individuals' employment, other than payroll, sought to build enduring relationships and reduce churn in the workforce.

Individual recruits had to be fully trained prior to their deployment in the field and this basic training was done prior to working for EngCo. Upon commencing work for EngCo, the individual contractors had an intense one-week induction in the field to prepare them for working alone subsequently. This induction involved working alongside a mentor. Together with the tools, items of PPE and other equipment,

EngCo provided AgencyCo staff with an electronic device containing all the necessary risk assessments, methods statements, and other policies and procedures essential for completing the task of installing SMART meters safely. They also introduced safety coaches to provide ongoing day-to-day support to the operatives in the field.

Communications with recruits seeking advice from EngCo team managers and coaches were frequent, often daily. Social media provided an effective tool for raising and responding to questions and keeping track of progress on the job. Face-to-face team meetings were planned but occurred erratically, given the geographic dispersion of the team and the rapid influx of new recruits. Bulletins and newsletters were sent to the contractors' home addresses, although there was no formal check that they had been read. Regular quarterly toolbox talks on a variety of safety topics driven by safety reports were recorded by a safety advisor for consistency of delivery and disseminated on the electronic devices.

Work was monitored regularly and almost continuously by EngCo's managers and supervisors through ongoing online conversations. This complemented more formal inspections, where the SMART team coach would "drop into site on a regular basis and carry out work-in-progress audits. And from a coaching and mentoring perspective they can guide that guy" (Head of Operations). Work was also audited by an independent company employed by EngCo. These inspections and audits formed the basis for ongoing individual performance reviews, and enabled managers to check both the understanding and competency of the individual contractors. These auditing activities were planned in advance and were detailed on the work schedule for individual managers.

Any incidents and accidents were investigated by supervisors and were reported. These reports were reviewed by the manager together with the individual concerned to support both individual and organizational learning.

4.4 Cross Case Comparison

Practices for managing safety in each of the three outsourcing arrangements are indicated in Table 3 against the coding categories derived a priori from the practitioner guidance. The number of different interviewees mentioning the occurrence of a practice is indicated by the percentages in Table 3, with higher percentages indicating a greater number of people mentioning a practice and suggesting a wider appreciation of the importance of this practice in the outsourcing arrangement.

In this organization, safety management practices were described by the Head of Managed Services as a "Vanilla service offering that could be adapted" to suit different client arrangements. They were generally similar in each case. Collectively interviewees in each case mentioned most of the 10 categories of practices for managing safety, with a few exceptions noted in Table 3. However, some codes were mentioned more often than others in each outsourcing arrangement, and closer inspection of these patterns of codes and the underlying narratives of the interviews in a particular outsourcing arrangement suggested a consistent differential emphasis

Table 3 Comparison of safety management practices in three different outsourcing arrangements (emphasis indicated by % frequency of interviewees in a case mentioning practice)

Practices	Case 1 (outsourcing the whole function)	Case 2 (outsourcing specialist activities)	Case 3 (recruitment of temporary workers)
Selection & recruitment	57	40	**100**
Induction	43	50	**86**
Risk assessment methods statements	**86**	**80**	71
Permits to work	57	**60**	0
Verbal communication	43	**60**	43
Written communication	0	10	71
Monitor/safety walkabout	57	40	57
Inspect/audit	**86**	20	**86**
Report	29	40	43
Review	0	20	0

in each arrangement (noted in bold in Table 3). Where the whole function (in this case facility management) was outsourced (Case 1) interviewees emphasized the use of RAMS and auditing through regular reports of performance against a set of pre-determined KPIs and service-level agreements. Interviewees in case 2, which focused on the outsourcing of specialist activities, emphasized the preparation and use of RAMS and permits to work to manage safety. In the third case, involving the recruitment of temporary workers, the emphasis was on the selection and recruitment of workers with appropriate skills, their effective induction into the job role, and subsequent inspection of their work.

5 Discussion

Practices for managing the safety of outsourced activities are documented generically, to a greater or lesser extent, in several practitioner guidelines (Table 1). Moreover, each of the individual practices has been the subject of academic investigation. However, Davis-Blake and Broschak (2009) identified three distinct types of outsourcing and to date there has been no comparative analysis of safety management practices across these three types. The study reported in this chapter addresses this deficiency by examining the practices for safety management in each of these three types of outsourcing arrangement in the context of a single organization, allowing the identification of differences and similarities between them. It identified 10 practices for managing safety which align with those found in the practitioner guidance.

5.1 Differences in Safety Management Between Outsourcing Arrangements

Most safety management practices indicated in the guidelines and academic research were evidenced in each of the three types of outsourcing, although some practices were more prominent in some arrangements than others (see Table 3). In case 1, where the whole function was outsourced, EngCo placed considerable emphasis on the practices of monitoring and auditing the safety performance of FMCo against previously agreed safety KPIs. Breaching these incurred a financial penalty. Unfortunately, as noted by the EngCo Location Managers, the complexity of EngCo operations and the number and variability of the sites created significant challenges for FMCo when they took over the contract which resulted in frequent breaches of the contract. To resolve these frequent breaches a "KPI-holiday, which is a breach without a fine" (Location Manager 2) was called, allowing EngCo and FMCo together to identify and remedy the problems. Case 2 illustrated the outsourcing of specific tasks to specialist contractors. Here EngCo emphasized the control of the work onsite through safety inductions, the preparation of RAMS and the issuing of permits to work. Where outsourcing involved the recruitment of temporary workers through an employment agency, EngCo emphasized the recruitment of workers with required skills and their appropriate induction together with an on-going programme of performance monitoring. According to the Head of EHS, "they work to our processes, they work to our procedures, they work to our training standards, and they're managed by our people." These data suggest that the focus of safety management practices is different in each of these three different forms of outsourcing.

According to Mintzberg (1983) the coordination and control of work may be achieved in at least three different ways, namely standardization of skills, standardization of work processes and standardization of outcomes. Each of these different ways of coordinating and controlling work would also seem to apply to the management of safety in these three different forms of outsourcing, with a different approach in each case. EngCo standardized outputs through the specification of safety-related KPIs in the contract, where the whole function (in this case, facility management) was outsourced. The safe working of specialist contractors was closely controlled through the use of RAMS and permits to work, which specified what could be done, by whom and how (i.e., the control of work processes). Standardization of skills in the training prior to the recruitment of temporary workers ensured subsequent safe working, which was further controlled by auditing of outputs. Investigating whether these different ways of coordinating and controlling work are applied to the management of safety in outsourcing relationships in other organizations and sectors merits further study, which may permit the development of practitioner guidance specific to different forms of outsourcing.

5.2 *Similarities in Safety Management Between Outsourcing Arrangements*

Although a different emphasis on safety management practices could be seen across these three different forms of outsourcing, there was nevertheless a strong commonality between them. While this similarity may be a consequence of the constraining influence of the company setting, Pilbeam et al. (2016) observed a conformity of safety practices across organizations operating in low-hazard service sectors. Such similarity of practices was inevitable, they argued, because safety is a highly institutionalized domain of organizational activity (Meyer & Rowan, 1977) and therefore susceptible to the institutionalizing forces, both political and cultural, operating in the wider environment (Ashworth et al., 2009). These may have been active in this study.

Three isomorphic pressures act on institutional domains (DiMaggio & Powell, 1983). Coercive pressures emanate from legal or regulatory requirements. For example, the Health and Safety at Work, etc., Act (HSAW, 1974) requires all firms operating in the UK to provide a safe place for people to work. External pressures may also be exerted by contractual obligations (Ashworth et al., 2009). These were evident in case 1, where FMCo was held to account strongly by the obligations stipulated in the contract with EngCo.

Normative isomorphism encourages organizations to voluntarily adopt safety management practices considered legitimate by others relevant to the organization (or, in this study, a division within EngCo). Any deviation from these normative practices calls into question the competence of the organization and its compliance. The recently published HSE report on the "Blue-Tape" agenda (HSE, 2019) demonstrates the existence of these pressures and their impact. Organizations succumb to normative pressures and are persuaded to adopt unnecessary practices "just in case." In this case the perceived influence of other businesses in the division or of other divisions in EngCo may have encouraged a standardized way of working, and so the occurrence of a common set of safety management practices.

Organizations may copy or emulate the safety practices of others, especially in uncertain situations in order to improve safety performance, an issue considered in more detail in Pilbeam and Karanikas (2023). Such mimetic isomorphism is likely when contracts change. It is easier to replicate the practices embedded in the previous contract and currently operating than to reevaluate the circumstances and make changes to more effectively match the competencies of the new partner with the evolving requirements of the task. This simple replication will be encouraged through the transfer of staff from one firm to another. Naturally, this stifles innovation and the pursuit of performance improvement. EngCo staff commented on the failure of successive changes in outsourced partners to deliver tangible improvements in the safety performance of facilities management.

5.3 Practices for Safety Task and Relationship Management

Practical guidance (e.g., HSE, 2011; ISSA, 2018) on the management of safety in outsourcing relationships follows a temporal process, beginning with planning and ending with reviewing the work. An alternative arrangement to this temporal sequence of safety management practices is to differentiate safety management practices into two separate albeit interconnected categories, namely safety task-related practices and specific relationship management practices. Safety task-related practices focus on the delivery of safety in the context of an outsourcing relationship. These include the assessment of risk, the writing of methods statements, the issuing of permits to work and safety walkabouts. General relationship management practices include selection, recruitment, communication, monitoring, inspecting, auditing, reporting, and reviewing. Here these relationship management practices are executed in the context of safety. This distinction resembles the differentiation between the leadership of tasks and the leadership of relationships noted in earlier studies of leadership (Parry & Bryman, 2006), and similarly is helpful in clarifying and identifying areas of potential improvement in the management of safety in outsourcing relationships. Improving safety task-related practices needs to draw on safety expertise whereas relationship management practices can be improved through training drawing on insights from organizational behaviour, psychology, or leadership, for example. Typically, training in one set of practices rarely acknowledges and incorporates training in the other set of practices. This suggests that the curricula of safety management training need to be revised and expanded.

5.4 Limitations of Empirical Study

The limitations of this study are those common to case study-based research that adopts "cross-sectional designs based on interviews" (Ridder, 2017; p. 284). First, we only investigated some outsourcing arrangements in a single UK division of a global mechanical electrical engineering company. The extent to which other organizations share these characteristics limits the heuristic generalizability (Tsoukas, 2009), but obvious exceptions include organizations in the public sector where contracting and procurement arrangements differ and small and medium-sized enterprises which lack the resources to monitor and audit the practices of other organizations. Nevertheless, the data suggest that the safety management practices in use were supported by general practitioner guidance, so it is likely that other companies may operate in the same way. Second, data collection was based solely on semi-structured interviews, in common with other case studies in the field of safety (e.g., Collinson, 1999), although triangulation with other data sources is encouraged (Eisenhardt & Graebner, 2007). Here triangulation was aimed for by interviewing people in different roles and from both organizations to gain different perspectives on the safety management practices in any particular outsourcing arrangement.

6 Conclusion

Outsourcing increases safety risks in organizations and accidents and injuries are frequently reported in outsourcing relationships. Current practitioner guidance on the management of safety in outsourced relationships is generic and does not differentiate between the three commonly occurring forms of outsourcing. This embedded case study in a single organization identified a common set of 10 safety management practices operating across all three forms of outsourcing. These were selection and recruitment, induction, preparing risk assessment and method statements, permits to work, verbal and written communication, monitoring, auditing, reporting, and reviewing. However, it also revealed a difference in emphasis of these practices between each of the three forms, which may reflect three different ways to coordinate and control work safely. Where a whole process or function was outsourced, monitoring and auditing were emphasized to control work outputs. Work processes were coordinated and controlled by the use of RAMS and permits to work, when parts of a process were outsourced. Outsourced activities that involved the procurement of workers through an agency were controlled by stipulating required skills. Furthermore, these 10 safety management practices can be broadly categorised into safety task-related practices, specifically assessment of risk, writing method statements, issuing of permits to work and safety walkabouts, and relationship management practices, including, for example, selecting, communicating, reporting and reviewing. This differentiation may enable the development of more effective safety management training for managing outsourcing relationships and help to reduce accidents and fatalities associated with this universal and enduring business strategy.

References

Ashford, S. J., George, E., & Blatt, R. (2007). Old assumptions, new work. *The Academy of Management Annals, 1*(1), 65–117.

Ashworth, R., Boyne, G., & Delbridge, R. (2009). Escape from the iron cage? Organizational change and isomorphic pressures in the public sector. *Journal of Public Administration and Theory, 19*, 165–187.

Atkin, B., & Bildsten, L. (2017). A future for facility management. *Construction Innovation, 17*(2), 116–124.

Belcourt, M. (2006). Outsourcing – The benefits and the risks. *Human Resource Management Review, 16*, 269–279.

Braun, V., & Clarke, V. (2006). Using thematic analysis in psychology. *Qualitative Research in Psychology, 3*, 77–101.

Brooks, J., McCluskey, S., Turley, E., & King, N. (2015). The utility of template analysis in qualitative psychology research. *Qualitative Research in Psychology, 12*(2), 202–222.

Clarke, S. (2003). The contemporary workforce: Implications for organisational safety culture. *Personnel Review, 32*(1), 40–57.

Collinson, D. L. (1999). "Surviving the rigs": Safety and surveillance on North Sea oil installations. *Organisation Studies, 20*(4), 579–600.

Connelly, C. E., & Gallagher, D. G. (2004). Emerging trends in contingent work research. *Journal of Management, 30*(6), 959–983.

Davis-Blake, A., & Broschak, J. P. (2009). Outsourcing and the changing nature of work. *Annual Review of Sociology, 35*, 321–340.

DiMaggio, P. J., & Powell, W. W. (1983). The iron cage revisited: Institutional isomorphism and collective rationality in organizational fields. *American Sociological Review, 48*, 147–160.

Drupsteen, L., Rasmussen, H. B., Ustailieva, E., & van Kampen, J. (2015). Key aspects in managing safety when working with multiple contractors: A case study. *Work, 51*(4), 715–720.

Dubois, A., & Gadde, L.-E. (2002). Systematic combining: An abductive approach to case research. *Journal of Business Research, 55*, 553–560.

Eisenhardt, K. M., & Graebner, M. E. (2007). Theory building from cases: Opportunities and challenges. *Academy of Management Journal, 50*(1), 25–32.

Garner, J. T. (2006). Masters of the universe? Resource dependency and interorganisational power relationships at NASA. *Journal of Applied Communications Research, 34*, 368–385.

Gibbert, M., & Ruigrok, W. (2010). The "what" and "how" of case study rigor. *Organizational Research Methods, 13*(4), 710–737.

Glazner, J. E., Borgerding, J., Lowrey, J. T., Bondy, J., Mueller, K. L., & Kreiss, K. (1998). Construction injury rates may exceed national estimates: Evidence from the construction of Denver International Airport. *American Journal of Industrial Medicine, 34*, 105–112.

Glazner, J. E., Borgerding, J., Bondy, J., Lowrey, J. T., Lezotte, D. C., & Kreiss, K. (1999). Contractor safety practices and injury rates in construction of the Denver International airport. *American Journal of Industrial Medicine, 35*, 175–185.

Gochfeld, M., & Mohr, S. (2007). Protecting contract workers: Case study of the US department of energy's nuclear and chemical waste management. *American Journal of Public Health, 97*(9), 1607–1613.

Grusenmeyer, C. (2022). Maintenance outsourcing and safety. A case study of disorganization phenomena in a reticular organization. *Safety Science, 153*, 105801.

Guest, G., Bunce, A., & Johnson, L. (2006). How many interviews are enough? An experiment with data saturation and variability. *Field Methods, 18*(1), 59–82.

Hallowell, M. R., & Gambatese, J. A. (2009). Construction safety risk management. *Journal of Construction Engineering and Management, 135*(12), 1316–1323.

Hasle, P. (2007). Outsourcing and employer responsibility: A case study of occupational health and safety in the Danish public transport sector. *Industrial Relations, 62*(1), 96–117.

Hätönen, J., & Eriksson, T. (2009). 30+ years of research and practice of outsourcing – exploring the past and anticipating the future. *Journal of International Management, 15*, 142–155.

Hayes, J., & Tillement, S. (2022). Outsourcing and safety – an introduction. In J. Hayes & S. Tillement (Eds.), *Contracting and safety: Exploring outsourcing practices in High-Hazard Industries* (pp. 1–7). Springer.

Health and Safety at Work etc Act. (1974). http://www.legislation.gov.uk/ukpga/1974/37/pdfs/ukpga_19740037_en.pdf

Hintkikka, N. (2011). Accidents at work during temporary agency work in Finland – Comparisons between certain major industries and other industries. *Safety Science, 49*, 473–483.

HSE. (2011). *Managing contractors. A guide for employers* (2nd ed.). Health and Safety Executive.

HSE. (2019). *Understanding the impact of business-to-business health and safety 'rules'*. Health and Safety Executive.

Indicator. (2015). *Managing contractors – How to get it right*. Indicator.

International Social Security Association. (2018). *Guidance on the safe management of contracts: A contract life-cycle approach*. BG Energie Textil Elektro Medienerzeugnisse, Gustav-Heinemann-Ufer, Germany.

Kochan, T. A., Smith, M., Wells, J. C., & Rebitzer, J. B. (1994). Human resource strategies and contingent workers: The case of safety in the petrochemical industry. *Human Resource Management, 33*(1), 55–77.

Kongsvik, T., Fenstad, J., & Wendelborg, C. (2012). Between a rock and a hard place: Accident and near-miss reporting on offshore service vessels. *Safety Science, 50*, 1839–1846.
Lingard, H. C., Cooke, T., & Blismas, N. (2010). Safety climate in conditions of construction subcontracting: A multi-level analysis. *Construction Management and Economics, 28*(8), 813–825.
Lingard, H., Wakefield, R., & Walker, D. (2020). The client's role in promoting work health and safety in construction projects: Balancing contracts and relationships to effect change. *Construction Management and Economics, 38*(11), 993–1008.
Lowrey, J. T., Borgerding, J. A., Zhen, B., Glazner, J. E., Bondy, J., & Kreiss, K. (1998). Risk factors for injury among construction workers at Denver international airport. *American Journal of Industrial Medicine, 34*, 113–120.
Manu, P., Ankrah, N., Proverb, D., & Suresh, S. (2013). Mitigating the health and safety influence of sub-contracting in construction: The approach of main contractors. *International Journal of Project Management, 31*, 1017–1026.
Mayhew, C., Quinlan, M., & Ferris, R. (1997). The effects of subcontracting/outsourcing on occupational health and safety: Survey evidence from four Australian industries. *Safety Science, 25*(1–3), 163–178.
McDermott, V., & Hayes, J. (2018). Risk shifting and disorganization in multi-tier contracting chains: The implications for public safety. *Safety Science, 106*, 263–272.
Mehta, C., & Theodore, N. (2006). Workplace safety in Atlanta's construction industry: Institutional failure in temporary staffing arrangements. *The Journal of Labor and Society, 9*, 59–77.
Meyer, J. W., & Rowan, B. (1977). Institutionalized organizations: Formal structures as myth and ceremony. *American Journal of Sociology, 83*, 340–363.
Milch, V., & Laumann, K. (2018). Sustaining safety across organizational boundaries: A qualitative study exploring how interorganizational complexity is managed on a petroleum-producing installation. *Cognition, Technology & Work, 20*, 179–204.
Mintzberg, H. (1983). *Structure in fives: Designing effective organizations*. Prentice-Hall.
National Safety Council. (2015). *Best practices in contractor management*. Campbell Institute Technical Report.
Nenonen, S., & Vasara, J. (2013). Safety management in multiemployer worksites in the manufacturing industry: Opinions on cooperation and problems encountered. *International Journal of Occupational Safety and Ergonomics, 19*(2), 167–183.
Nenonen, S., Kivistö-Rahnasto, J., & Vasara, J. (2015). Safety considerations during different stages of a project life cycle in the manufacturing industry. *Human Factors and Ergonomics in Manufacturing, 25*(1), 12–27.
O'Brien, M. E. (1999). Contractor safety. *Professional Safety, 44*(2), 32–35.
Parry, K. W., & Bryman, A. (2006). Leadership in organizations. In I. S. R. Clegg, C. Hardy, T. Lawrence, & W. R. Nord (Eds.), *The SAGE handbook of organization studies* (2nd ed., pp. 447–468). SAGE.
Pilbeam, C. (2024). Boundaries: Their influence on managing safety in outsourcing. In J.-C. Le Coze & B. Journé (Eds.), *Safe performance in a world of global networks. Springer Briefs in Safety Management* (pp. 75–86). Springer.
Pilbeam, C., & Karanikas, N. (2023). Effective transfer of safety interventions within and between organizations: Leveraging translation theory to achieve improved outcomes. *Safety Science, 168*, 106318.
Pilbeam, C., Doherty, N., Davidson, R., & Denyer, D. (2016). Effect of isomorphic forces on safety practices in service organisations: Are there dangers to homogeneity? *Policy and Practice in Health and Safety, 14*(1), 50–64.
Rebitzer, J. B. (1995). Job safety and contractor workers in the petrochemical industry. *Industrial Relations, 34*(1), 40–57.
Ridder, H.-G. (2017). The theory contribution of case study research designs. *Business Research, 10*, 281–305.

Rousseau, D. M., & Libuser, C. (1997). Contingent workers in high-risk environments. *California Management Review, 39*(2), 103–121.
Schubert, U., & Dijkstra, J. J. (2009). Working safety with foreign contractors and personnel. *Safety Science, 47*, 786–793.
Tsang, E. W. K. (2014). Generalizing from research findings: The merits of case studies. *International Journal of Management Reviews, 16*, 369–383.
Tsoukas, H. (2009). Generality and small-N studies. In I. D. A. Buchanan & A. Bryman (Eds.), *SAGE handbook of organizational research methods* (pp. 285–301). SAGE.
Vassie, L. H., & Fuller, C. W. (2003). Assessing the inputs and outputs of partnership arrangements for health and safety management. *Employee Relations, 25*(5), 492–503.

Optimizing Service Provider Selection in Public-Private IT Outsourcing for Public Value

Nancy M. Arratia-Martínez, Isis Gutiérrez-Martínez, François Duhamel, and Luis Felipe Luna-Reyes

1 Introduction

The selection of an appropriate IT outsourcing service provider represents a critical strategic decision for public administrators, conditioning future public value creation through outsourcing collaborations. This chapter delves into the variety of relational factors that may positively impact various facets of public value creation in public-private IT outsourcing relationships to optimize service provider selection processes. The research question in this chapter is: How can the combination of relational variables influencing service provider selection in a public-private IT outsourcing relationship be optimized to create public value in this context?

In this chapter, we propose to study the service provider selection problem under a novel framework based on the equivalent linear programming model of the stable matching problem. This framework aims at delineating strict order preference lists of service providers according to the congruence between their characteristics and the characteristics expected from service providers in general to obtain specific

N. M. Arratia-Martínez · I. Gutiérrez-Martínez (✉)
School of Business and Economics, Business Administration Department, Universidad de las Américas Puebla, Puebla, Mexico
e-mail: nancy.arratia@udlap.mx; isis.gutierrez@udlap.mx

F. Duhamel
School of Business and Economics, International Business Department, Universidad de las Américas Puebla, Puebla, Mexico
e-mail: francois.duhamel@udlap.mx

L. F. Luna-Reyes
Rockefeller College of Public Affairs and Policy, University at Albany, Albany, NY, USA

Universidad de las Américas Puebla, Puebla, Mexico
e-mail: lluna-reyes@albany.edu

F. P. García Márquez et al. (eds.), *Outsourcing Using Operations Research and Management Science Methods*, International Series in Operations Research & Management Science 366, https://doi.org/10.1007/978-3-031-91845-2_4

dimensions of public value in outsourcing projects. Interval numbers are defined to express the importance given to the outcomes and service providers' characteristics to capture the margin of imprecision in the estimation of the corresponding values by the agents involved. The strength of the correlation between the characteristics expected from service providers and public value has been obtained from an empirical study of public-private IT Outsourcing projects in Mexico's public administration. In this way, service provider selection processes can be optimized to reach a certain type of public value between efficacy, citizen-centric values, and political benefits.

Drawing on a literature review and empirical data, this study reveals the relational variables influencing public value in public-private IT outsourcing arrangements, i.e., trust (benevolence, competence, and honesty) and knowledge interfaces (pragmatic and semantic). Relational variables, such as trust, are crucial for public value creation for several reasons: first, trust increases transparency, collaboration, open communication, and feedback between service providers and the public administration (see, for example, Picazo-Vela et al., 2022 for that matter). These dimensions are supposed to enhance the efficiency and effectiveness of public services by identifying areas for improvement in the development of IT systems that save costs and fulfill citizen needs. Second, trust would strengthen long-term relationships, allowing the combination of resources and expertise to tackle complex challenges related to public value through public-private collaborations.

It also exhibits which factors are desirable in orientating service provider selection to reach a certain type of public value in public-private IT outsourcing projects. Our computational experiments, based on empirical data, suggest that the stable matching approach performs well in establishing preference ranks of service providers to be assigned to new projects, given public value objectives attributed by public administrators to those projects.

This research represents significant contributions: it addresses relational variables influencing service provider selection in public-private IT outsourcing, while most related literature focuses on technical criteria based on expertise, quality, cost, and risk (Rajaeian et al., 2017). In terms of methodological approach, this study is the first, up to our knowledge, which considers public value as a driver for preferences to achieve stability in a project-service provider matching, using empirical evidence from Mexico's public administration IT outsourcing projects to reinforce the results. The proposed approach has a distinctive advantage over other existing methods dealing with the service provider selection problem, as it allows to deal simultaneously with the imprecision in inputs and with the construction of a strict order list of preferences for projects based on relational values characteristics and public value-related outcomes.

The findings of this research provide valuable insights for public sector decision-makers, IT outsourcing practitioners, and policymakers alike. By shedding light on the relationship between IT outsourcing service provider selection criteria and public value, this article offers a framework for optimizing service provider selection processes and enhancing better outcomes for citizens and various stakeholders. The implications of this study extend beyond IT outsourcing and contribute to the broader discourse on public sector management, innovation, and value creation in public settings.

This chapter is organized as follows. First, it presents a literature review regarding service provider selection problems in public-private outsourcing context, key variables that influence public value in public-private IT outsourcing, and modeling methods for service provider selection. Next, it describes the research methodology related to the approach for service provider selection and assignment chosen. Then, this chapter offers the results of the decision model approach for IT outsourcing service provider selection, based on the congruence between service providers' relational characteristics and public value objectives for new projects under the stable matching problem structure. Finally, in the discussion and conclusion section, the authors highlight the importance of public value dimensions and their determinants to optimize IT outsourcing service provider selection, reveal managerial implications, and offer recommendations for future research.

2 Literature Review

Public-private outsourcing involves intensive collaboration between two entities bound by a service contract, with the public administrative entity acting as the client and the private entity as the service provider. The relationship between these entities must be actively managed to enhance public value (Swar et al., 2012). The primary challenge in making these collaborations effective lies in navigating the inherent complexity of aligning initial conditions, structures, processes, outcomes, and accountabilities to reflect public value on both sides (Bryson et al., 2015). This complexity makes performance assessment particularly difficult, given the diverse service level agreements (SLAs) and dispute resolution mechanisms that must align with the broad objectives and goals of public administration (Bai et al., 2022). Private sector service providers, in particular, need to understand public value concerns to avoid negatively impacting decisions and coordination. Therefore, selecting a service provider based on multiple criteria that account for the complexity of the public sector is crucial for the success of public-private IT outsourcing projects.

Service provider selection is a process of multicriteria decision-making (MCDM), which consists of selecting or ranking candidate service providers based on various criteria, numerical values, interval numbers, and linguistic variables (Feng, 2012). The goal is to select a portfolio with a reasonable number of service providers to match clients' aspirations and available service provisions. Service provider selection is crucial for project management in general (Bai et al., 2022; Choi & Contractor, 2019) and outsourcing in particular (Chang et al., 2012). Studies addressing service providers' selection problems mostly focus on technical variables related to expertise, quality, cost, and risk and, more seldom, on relational issues between clients and service providers (Rajaeian et al., 2017). The main relational variables usually envisaged in existing literature regarding interorganizational collaborations are related to trust, knowledge, and communication (Ansell & Gash, 2008; Burnes & Anastasiadis, 2003; Fusiripong et al., 2017; Lee & Kim, 2007; Swar et al., 2012). Recent perspectives on IT Outsourcing stress the importance of client-vendor relationships in achieving outsourcing success (Lee, 2001; Duhamel et al., 2021). In fact, much of the contemporary ITO literature has emphasized the crucial role of the relational aspects of outsourcing (Duhamel et al., 2023; Fan & Luna-Reyes, 2016).

There still exists a lack of empirical studies to support service provider selection processes in the context of public administration (Orlu et al., 2021), where objectives in terms of public value prevail (Gantman, 2011). Moreover, there do not exist, in the extant literature, studies that apply selection methods matching service providers and IT projects using data measuring relational capabilities of service providers and public administrators' preferences regarding their objectives in IT outsourcing projects.

Research on service provider selection in purchasing is quite extended, with methodologies ranging from conceptual to empirical and using a variety of methods with different levels of complexity. Examples of methods used include case-based reasoning, Simple Multi-Attribute Rating Technique (SMART) and Analytic Hierarchy Process (AHP). AHP, for example, arranges decision attributes and alternatives in a hierarchical structure and ranks alternatives using a series of pairwise comparisons. The calculation of priority scales usually relies on experts' judgments. Analytic Network Process (ANP) generalizes AHP for interdependent decision attributes (Liou et al., 2011). The preference Ranking Organization Method for Enrichment of Evaluations (PROMETHEE) provides a ranking of choices/alternatives based on preference degrees. Simple Additive Weighting (SAW) or Weighted Sum Model (WSM) determines a weighted score for each alternative by adding contributions of each attribute multiplied by their weights. Goal programming refers to an application of linear programming to solve problems with multiple potentially conflicting objects. We can also find neural networks or a combination of the latter with other methods (i.e., AHP and DEA) (Ho et al., 2010; Hosseininasab & Ahmadi, 2015).

However, research on service provider selection applied to outsourcing operations has been relatively more limited (Bai et al., 2022; Feng, 2012). Feng (2012), more particularly, presents a decision method for multi-sourcing service provider selection in service outsourcing, combining a technique for order preference by similarity to ideal solution (TOPSIS) with a bi-objective 0–1 linear programming model and calculates Pareto-optimal solutions for services provider portfolios. In TOPSIS (Technique for Order of Preference by Similarity to Ideal Solution), alternatives are chosen according to the shortest geometric distance from the positive ideal solution and the longest geometric distance from the negative ideal solution. It has the advantage of allowing trade-offs between criteria. Qin et al. (2017) mobilize the linear programming technique for the multi-dimensional analysis of preferences (LINMAP) method to solve multi-attribute service provider selection issues in an interval type-2 fuzzy environment. LINMAP uses the comparison of pairwise alternatives given by the decision maker as input and generates the best compromise alternative (or solution) that has the shortest distance to the positive ideal solution.

AHP-goal programming remains the most popular approach to address those issues (Ho et al., 2010). Fuzzy set theory, on its part, aims at mathematically representing uncertainty, dealing with the imprecision stemming from subjective evaluation indices through formalized tools (Rajaeian et al., 2017).

Existing modeling methods focus on clients' objectives and neglect the perspective of service providers, insofar as service providers possess their own criteria when selecting projects (Pan et al., 2023; Feng, 2012). To address this gap, sound decision methods based on matching processes are needed (Feng, 2012). One approach to accomplish optimal service provider selection (in the perspective of maximizing public value in public administration in our case) lies in the incorporation of the principles of stable matching theory and in the integration of a robust form to express both sides' preferences (Pan et al., 2023), also taking into account the imprecision in the estimation of those preferences (Feng, 2012). Matching theory has emerged as a tool for analyzing the design of matching markets (Che et al., 2019; Gale & Shapley, 1962). Pan et al. (2023) studied the problem of selection between project bidding and construction subcontractors, using the Ordinal Priority Approach (OPA) method to determine the order of preference between the two sides. Gharote et al. (2015) proposed a methodology to predict preferences for both trainees and software project requirements using utility theory. They compared the unstable solutions provided by a greedy algorithm and showed the importance of using stable matching, reaching significantly higher satisfaction average values (on trainees and project requirements) compared to the percent increase in the additional cost. Several generalizations and variations of the stable matching problem have been studied due to the potential applications to labor markets (Sethuraman et al., 2006). In the engineering field, contractor selection for the subcontractors is a crucial task where the choosing of a qualified partner may produce satisfactory results for both sides (Pan et al., 2023). One of the well-known cases where stable matching mechanisms are applied is in the National Resident Matching Program (NRMP) (Lee, 2016).

Regarding effectiveness in decision-making, information systems must handle imprecision and thereby emulate human-like approximate reasoning (Eshragh, 1980; Zemankova & Kandel, 1985). In mathematical programming problems, data are commonly represented as real numbers based on the experience or knowledge of specialists. However, it is often necessary to address inaccuracies and uncertainty in the input information (Lai et al., 2002; Nakahara et al., 1992). Interval numbers and interval programming have become key approaches to managing such environments, as they allow decision-makers to express imprecision or uncertainty simply and effectively. These methods also offer a more natural way to represent vagueness or inaccuracies in data (Garajová et al., 2019).

Therefore, in this research we propose a new approach that involves the equivalent linear program of stable matching problem (one-to-one case) to assign service providers to projects driven by public value. This approach involves determining the preferences for projects using a Matrix Model procedure with the use of interval values to capture the imprecision of estimations when selecting the most suitable service providers for projects.

3 Methodological Approach

Our approach is based on a stable matching process to analyze the service provider selection problem. To do so, basic definitions and notations for stable matching are described in the following section. In this section, we also introduce the proposed approach.

3.1 *Basic Definitions and Notation for Stable Matchings*

Consider the set of projects denoted by $P = \{p_1, p_2, \ldots, p_n\}$ and the set of IT outsourcing service providers $R = \{r_1, r_2, \ldots, r_m\}$. Hereinafter we will refer to an element from any of the two sets as an *agent*, which, in the set of projects P, could indicate the leader, the project director or the project by itself, while an agent from the set of service providers R could indicate the IT service provider company, the service provider's team or the project leader.

Given the sets of projects (P), the preference from each agent is denoted by $>_p$. For example, if $r_1 >_p r_2$, it means the agent p privileges the service provider r_1 to r_2. Complementarily, $r_1 \geq_p r_2$ indicates that p prefers r_1 or it has equal preference for r_1 and r_2.

In equivalent form, if $p_1 >_r p_2$, the service provider r prefers the project p_1 to project p_2. Complementarily, $p_1 \geq_r p_2$ indicates that service provider r prefers p_1 to p_2 or that the provider r has an equal preference for p_1 than to p_2. The previous description leads to the structure provided in Fig. 1, where each agent of a set presents its preference order list of the elements of the opposite set.

The new approach introduced in this chapter—represented in Fig. 1—establishes preferences on the project side using desirable outcomes for public value as drivers, while assuming the references of IT outsourcing service providers to be known.

Once preferences are established, we continue with the stable matching problem model. To do so, we present the concept of acceptable pairs; then we present the one-to-one stable matching problem and finally the integer linear programming problem.

1	A	C	B	E	D
2	B	A	E	D	C
3	E	D	A	B	C
4	D	C	A	E	B
5	C	A	D	B	E

A	2	1	4	5	3
B	1	2	3	4	5
C	3	4	1	2	5
D	2	1	3	4	5
E	4	5	3	1	2

Fig. 1 Structure of the preference order lists from both sets, projects (1, 2, 3, 4 and 5), and IT service providers (A, B, C, D and E)

3.1.1 Acceptable Pairs

An agent from one set is considered *acceptable* to an agent from the opposite set if the latter appears on the preference list of the former (Manlove et al., 2002).

Let's denote μ as a match, constituted by acceptable pairs, that is, $\mu \subseteq T$, where T is the set of all acceptable pairs (r, p). A pair is acceptable if both agents consider the other as acceptable.

3.1.2 One-to-One Stable Matching Problem

In the one-to-one problem, the main objective is to find a pairing that assigns each agent from one set exactly to one agent from the opposite set in such a way that there exist no r and p elements, preferring each other more than the pair assigned to them in the matching. Additionally, a matching μ is *individually rational* when there are no agents preferring not to be matched instead of being paired with any other agent. When those conditions are satisfied, then the matching is stable (Roth et al., 1993).

3.1.3 Integer Linear Programming Problem

Under the equivalent integer program of the two-side stable matching and the one-to-one scheme, x_{rp} denotes the decision if the pair (r, p) is in μ. In such a case, $x_{rp} = 1$.

This is,

$$x_{rp} = \begin{cases} 1 \ (r,p) \in \mu, \\ 0 \text{ otherwise.} \end{cases}$$

The agent matched with the service provider r is denoted by $\mu(r)$ and similarly $\mu(p)$ denotes the match of p.

The valid set of matchings is defined by the group of constraints that ensure that:

- No more than one IT service provider is assigned to each project (Eq. 1).
- Each IT service provider has no more than one project assigned to it (Eq. 2).
- The stability condition for each acceptable pair (r, p) must be satisfied (Eq. 3).
- The constraints to keep the decision variables are under a binary, 0–1, form. (Eq. 4).

$$\sum\nolimits_{i:(i,p) \in T} x_{ip} \leq 1, \forall p \in P \tag{1}$$

$$\sum\nolimits_{j:(r,j)\in T} x_{rj} \leq 1, \forall r \in R \tag{2}$$

$$x_{rp} + \sum\nolimits_{i >_p r} x_{ip} + \sum\nolimits_{j >_r p} x_{rj} \geq 1, \forall (r,p) \in T \tag{3}$$

$$x_{rp} \in \{0, 1\}, \forall (r,p) \in T \tag{4}$$

The objective function to be maximized is given in Eq. (5) and represents the total sum of the assignments.

$$\text{Maximize} \sum_{(r,p)\in T} x_{rp} \tag{5}$$

3.2 Proposed Approach

In this chapter, public value is considered to drive preferences for stability in a project-service provider matching problem. The empirical data comes from a research project study dealing with the outsourcing of information technology in public administration in Mexico. As part of that research project, a survey was sent to public managers (decision-makers) responsible for the outsourcing of information technology contracts at the state level. Data coming from 62 participants representing 26 out of 32 states in Mexico was obtained. Most outsourcing technology information project contracts of the public sector with service providers were related to software development and data center operations. Measurement of relational variables in the survey included trust (benevolence, competence, honesty), quality of semantic and pragmatic interfaces and public value (efficacy, citizen-centric values, and political benefits).

Trust-related dimensions (competence, benevolence, and honesty) were measured using existing scales from Lee and Kim (2007). To measure the quality of semantic and pragmatic interfaces, own scales were elaborated based on extant literature (Carlile, 2002, 2004), as none exist so far. Public value measurement was done with items coming from Picazo-Vela et al. (2022), integrating public value dimension's related to efficacy (cost reduction, access to competencies and the quality of the information system produced), citizen-centric values (government transparency, faster response, and ease of use) and political benefits (promotional purpose, hierarchical promotion, and state level impact). (See Appendix 1 for the description of the items). Table 1 shows correlation results from the empirical study.

The proposed approach in this chapter uses the correlations in Table 1 to produce the preference matrices needed as input to the one-to-one stable matching problem. The implementation of this approach is guided by the following three assumptions:

Table 1 Correlations between relational factors and public value attributes

	Public value								
	Efficacy			Citizen-centric values			Political benefits		
Characteristics	Cost reduc.	Access to compet.	Quality of IS	Gover. Transp	Fast resp.	Ease of use	Prom. purpose	Hierar. prom.	State impact
Benevolence	0.407	0.472	0.494	0.688	0.544	0.593	0.110 (ns)	0.240 (ns)	0.415
Competence	0.636	0.761	0.613	0.751	0.853	0.645	0.040 (ns)	0.098 (ns)	0.442
Honesty	0.638	0.718	0.634	0.777	0.741	0.780	0.049 (ns)	0.231 (ns)	0.532
Pragmatic interface	0.595	0.442	0.531	0.375	0.420	0.417	0.150 (ns)	0.026 (ns)	0.227 (ns)
Semantic interface	0.340	0.378	0.511	0.320	0.332	0.362	−0.114 (ns)	0.122 (ns)	0.275

Assumption 1 One side of the market (IT outsourcing) possesses an adequate level of information that allows it to define preferences over agents on the opposite side as a strict order preference list.

This chapter does not discuss the aspirations sought by external IT service providers when submitting preferences for projects or contracts. We suppose such aspirations can be driven by competitive capability development, as well as economic and political considerations (Könning et al., 2019).

Assumption 2 The opposite side of the market (projects, leaders, public or private administrators) can express the degree to which it expects to achieve one or more outcomes related to public value.

Assumption 3 It is assumed that all IT outsourcing service providers provide similar services.

The following development explains the proposed procedure for matching projects with IT outsourcing service providers. This involves empirical information coming from Table 1, service provider evaluations, and the significance of each outcome related to public value, expressed as interval values. It is important to note that in terms of scalability, more dimensions, outcomes and characteristics can be used to incorporate other drivers of the provider selection process. More projects can also be incorporated to address actual needs in the context under study.

3.2.1 Proposed Procedure for Service Provider Selection and Assignment

The proposed procedure described here below is delineated in four stages: Data preparation, evaluation using Matrix Models for a multi-project environment (Gregory, 1986; Youssef et al., 1996), preference establishment, and the application of the one-to-one stable matching programming model.

(1) Data Preparation

Step 1. Choose the outcomes associated with a public value that are sought for the projects. In this chapter's context, the selection of outcomes is conducted by considering those associated with different dimensions of public value that are sought or fall within the scope of the projects at hand.

If the primary considerations for selecting and assigning service providers revolve around efficacy, citizen-centric values, and political benefits, we will focus on the following outcomes: cost reduction, access to competencies, quality of the IS produced, transparency, faster response, ease of use, promotional purposes, hierarchical promotion, and state impact. In the following, we denote the set of outcomes as $O = \{w_1, w_2, \ldots, w_{|O|}\}$.

Step 2. Select characteristics of IT outsourcing service providers that are correlated with the outcomes sought. This selection will address specific conditions sought by decision-makers, serving as a bridge that connects the expected outcomes with the service provider's qualities that drive or contribute to their achievement.

In this research, the correlations provided in Table 1 are used to describe the alignment between the characteristics of service providers and the desired outcomes associated with dimensions of public value.

It is important to note that sometimes public administrators may want to consider the whole set of criteria to measure or only consider a subset for practical reasons (such as limited information or decision-makers preferences). In both situations, our proposed approach allows them to obtain a valid solution for the matching problem.

The set of service provider characteristics used as part of the proposed approach are those given in Table 1; this set is denoted by $K = \{k_1, k_2, \ldots k_{|K|}\}$.

Step 3. Assign weights to outcomes and characteristics of service providers, by project. Using a scale of 0–1 as a basis, project directors or administrators determine the degree of emphasis that projects place on each public-value-related outcome. These weights are expressed as interval numbers and denoted by $e_{pw} = \left[e_{pw}^-, e_{pw}^+\right] = \left\{x | e_{pw}^- \le x \le e_{pw}^+, x \in R\right\}$ where $p \in P$ serves as the index of the project, and w is the index of the outcome. Interval numbers help to capture imprecision or vagueness in estimations (Garajová et al., 2019), providing a way to express not just one but a range of possible values.

Sometimes, actions in a project or plan can indirectly affect more than one objective that wasn't set as a primary objective or to be achieved. For this reason, we do not discount the fact that a project will impact more than one outcome, even in a reduced value.

To assign weights to service providers' characteristics, we defined a scale of 0–10 also provided as an interval number. Considering that each service provider will be assessed based on these characteristics, it is necessary to establish a weight that is consistent in terms of importance and specific to the project.

The relative importance or weight that a characteristic k has with respect to the outcome w and project p is denoted by $q_{pwk} = \left[q_{pwk}^-, q_{pwk}^+\right]$.

(2) Evaluation using Matrix Models for Multi-project Environment.

Step 4. Use of the structure of the Matrix Models procedure. This step involves organizing data into the correct format prior to the calculation of scores.

The Matrix Models (Gregory, 1986; Youssef et al., 1996) provide a straightforward and structured method for expressing scores using factors, subfactors, and candidate evaluations. In this context, we define factors as outcomes and subfactors as characteristics. We extend the Matrix Model structure to assess service providers in a multi-project environment using interval numbers.

In this step, service providers need to be assessed on each of the considered characteristics. For this, we propose expressing the extent to which a service provider satisfies a characteristic as an interval value in the range of 0–1. Let $g_{rk} = \left[g_{rk}^-, g_{rk}^+\right]$ be the degree in which an IT outsourcing service provider r satisfies a characteristic $k \in K$.

Step 5. Compute Service Provider-Outcomes Scores. These values will reflect the grade to which a service provider satisfies a specific characteristic in a project, with the resulting value being an interval number as a fraction of the maximum possible to reach.

For each project, the score of the service provider with an outcome (f_{prw}) here is expressed as the weighted sum divided by the sum of weights. This is,

$$f_{prw} = \frac{\sum_{k \in K} q_{pwk} \cdot g_{rk}}{\sum_{k \in K} q_{pwk}}, \quad \forall w \in O, r \in R, p \in P \tag{6}$$

Expressing the values in Eq. (6) as intervals and applying the arithmetic for interval numbers, Eq. (6) can be formulated to the one in Eq. (7). Refer to Kulisch (2009) for a complete description of the interval's arithmetic.

$$f_{prw} = \left[\frac{\sum\limits_{k \in K} q_{pwk}^{-} \cdot g_{rk}^{-}}{\sum_{k \in K} q_{pwk}^{+}}, \frac{\sum\limits_{k \in K} q_{pwk}^{+} \cdot g_{rk}^{+}}{\sum_{k \in K} q_{pwk}^{-}} \right] \quad \forall w \in O, r \in R, p \in P \tag{7}$$

The latter result is given by the conditions: $\sum\limits_{k \in K} q_{pwk}^{-} \cdot g_{rk}^{-} \geq 0$ and $\sum\limits_{k \in K} q_{pwk}^{+} \cdot g_{rk}^{+} \geq 0$, and $\sum_{k \in K} q_{pwk}^{-} > 0$, $\sum_{k \in K} q_{pwk}^{+} > 0$.

This process represents a way to evaluate cross-projects and involves a differentiation from the original model proposed by Gregory (1986), where the score at factor level was obtained as the sum of evaluations of service providers divided by the sum of weights.

Step 6. Compute Project-Service Provider Scores. Once the Service Provider-Outcomes Scores were obtained, we utilized the importance weights for outcomes (provided by each project) to calculate the weighted sum. This sum is then divided by the total weight sum to derive a score in relation to a service provider for each project. This is,

$$\alpha_{pr} = \frac{\sum_{w \in O} e_{pw} f_{prw}}{\sum_{w \in O} e_{pw}}, \forall p \in P, r \in R. \tag{8}$$

Eq. (8) can be transformed using the same arithmetic for interval values and the resultant is expressed in Eq. (9).

$$\alpha_{pr} = \left[\frac{\sum_{w \in O} e_{pw}^{-} \cdot f_{prw}^{-}}{\sum_{w \in O} e_{pw}^{+}}, \frac{\sum_{w \in O} e_{pw}^{+} \cdot f_{prw}^{+}}{\sum_{w \in O} e_{pw}^{-}} \right], \forall p \in P, r \in R. \tag{9}$$

The latter result is given by the conditions: $\sum_{w \in O} e_{pw}^{-} \cdot f_{prw}^{-} \geq 0$ and $\sum_{w \in O} e_{pw}^{+} \cdot f_{prw}^{+} \geq 0$, and $\sum_{w \in O} e_{pw}^{-} > 0$, $\sum_{w \in O} e_{pw}^{+} > 0$.

1	A	C	F	B	E	D
2	B	A	E	D	F	C
3	E	D	F	B	C	A
4	D	C	A	F	B	E
5	C	A	D	B	E	F

1	A	C	B	E	D
2	B	A	E	D	C
3	E	D	B	C	A
4	D	C	A	B	E
5	C	A	D	B	E

Fig. 2 Example of a preference order list for projects, the original lists (at left) and lists for projects after the elimination of the agent F (at right)

(3) Preference Establishment

Step 7. Defuzzify and compare the Project-Service Provider Scores. This entails transforming interval values to facilitate comparison, applying an optimistic or pessimistic attitude in the case of ties. To this end, the resultant values α_{pr} are processed using the definition of the mid-point and half-width of interval numbers to get a strict order of preference over service providers.

Then, the policy to define superiority is, for all $p \in P$ we say that r is valued as superior to r', when $\alpha_{pr} \neq \alpha_{pr'}$ and if mid-point $(\alpha_{pr'}) <$ mid-point (α_{pr}). When mid-point (α_{pr})=mid-point $(\alpha_{pr'})$, then, we will say that r is valued as superior to r' if half-width$(\alpha_{pr'}) <$ half $-$ width(α_{pr}). The latter can be applied to break ties in an optimistic outlook, while in a pessimistic outlook, we will select as superior to others the agent with the smaller half-width. These rules will define the preference order. If both the midpoint and half-width were equal (tie), then we will solve it arbitrarily.

Step 8. Generate strict order preference lists. Explicitly establish the strict preference order lists for each project over each service provider, considering the previously defined comparison policies.

(4) Application of the One-to-One Stable Matching Model.

Step 9. Service provider selection and list trimming. When the set of service providers is larger than the projects' set, we will trim it to include only the service providers that hold the best positions in terms of an overall position measure across projects. Let us explain this with a basic example.

Figure 2 shows the preference lists for five projects (left); this is an instance with unequal cardinality. Next, to shorten the lists, we will eliminate the agents that occupy the worst positions in the overall ranking. The overall position of a service provider is obtained as the sum of the rank numbers it obtained for each one of the five projects. For example, service provider B obtained a score of 18 (4 + 1 + 4 + 5 + 4 = 18). The service providers with the highest value will be eliminated (i.e., in the worst positions). In this example, the selected service providers are A, B, C, D and E. Consequently, F will be discarded.

Step 10. Solve the one-to-one stable matching programming model. For this step, we will employ the integer linear program of the one-to-one stable matching to determine the assignment of service providers to projects. The model aims to maximize Eq. (5) under the constraints (1)–(4).

The final assignment will ensure the stability condition; in a practical context, the preferences from both sides of the market have been considered, with preference on the side of projects driven by public value.

4 Results from the Proposed Framework

In this section, we present the results of the proposed approach in this chapter through a numerical example.[1] This example considers a set of 4 projects in the public sector that involve the selection of IT outsourcing service providers as part of the activities to be carried out.

For this numerical example, based on the correlation results between relational factors and public value attributes obtained in the empirical study (see Table 1 in the methodology section), we considered from the efficacy and external public value dimensions two expected outcomes: quality of IS produced and government transparency. The association between outcomes and service provider characteristics was determined as follows: pragmatic and semantic interfaces were characteristics of service providers assessed for the quality of IS produced, while benevolence, competence, and honesty were considered for government transparency. For its part, the number of considered IT outsourcing service providers was six.

Table 2 presents the values of weight or importance of each expected outcome for projects.

In Table 3 we present the weight of characteristics with respect to outcomes by project. Subsequently, the satisfaction degree or evaluation of service providers over characteristics related to public value outcomes (g_{rk}) are presented in Table 4.

The numerical scale to evaluate information in all Tables is continuous; for Table 2 we applied an evaluation between 0 and 10. In Tables 2 and 4, the scale of evaluation is between 0 and 1. Particularly for values in Table 4, the continuous

Table 2 Degree of relative importance of outcomes by project

	Degree of impact over public value outcomes (e_{pw})		
Project no.	Quality of IS produced (ω_1)	Government transparency (ω_2)	SUM
1	[0.5,0.6]	[0.9,1]	[1.4,1.6]
2	[0.4,0.55]	[0.8,0.95]	[1.2,1.5]
3	[0.9,1]	[0.76,0.8]	[1.66,1.8]
4	[0.7,0.75]	[0.8,0.9]	[1.5,1.65]

[1] The template file to replicate the numerical example in this chapter can be available upon request from the corresponding author.

Table 3 Relation between service provider characteristics and expected outcomes by project

	Outcomes and service providers' characteristics					
	Quality of IS produced (ω_1)		Government transparency (ω_2)			
Project no.	Pragmatic interface (k_1)	Semantic interface (k_2)	Benevolence (k_3)	Competence (k_4)	Honesty (k_5)	SUM
1	[4.1,4.5]	[6.4,6.5]	[6.4,6.5]	[2.9,3.5]	[6,6.5]	[25.8,27.5]
2	[6.5,7.5]	[2,3]	[4,4.5]	[8,9]	[5,5.5]	[28.1,29.5]
3	[3,3.5]	[8,8.5]	[7,7.5]	[6,6.5]	[9,9.5]	[33,35.5]
4	[9,9.5]	[4,5]	[2,2.5]	[3,4]	[8,8.5]	[26,29.5]

Table 4 Valuation of service provider characteristics (g_{rk})

	Service provider characteristics					
Service provider r_i	Pragmatic interface (k_1)	Semantic interface (k_2)	Benevolence (k_3)	Competence (k_4)	Honesty (k_5)	SUM
1	[0.6,0.75]	[0.8,0.9]	[0.25,0.5]	[0.4,0.5]	[0.2,0.25]	[2.25,2.9]
2	[0.9,1]	[0.6,0.75]	[0.7,0.75]	[0.5,0.6]	[0.43,0.55]	[3.13,3.65]
3	[0.5,0.65]	[0.5,0.55]	[0.5,0.55]	[0.7,0.85]	[0.9,0.95]	[3.1,3.55]
4	[0.7,0.76]	[0.8,0.84]	[0.4,0.5]	[0.5,0.55]	[0.7,0.89]	[3.1,3.54]
5	[0.9,0.93]	[0.94,0.97]	[0.54,0.65]	[0.8,0.85]	[0.9,0.93]	[4.08,4.33]
6	[0.5,0.6]	[0.7,0.7]	[0.6,0.67]	[0.9,0.92]	[0.6,0.7]	[3.3,3.59]

0–1 scale provides an independent scale related to the projects since the values in Table 4 can be established as a fraction of the values given for the project in Table 3.

The information from Tables 2, 3, and 4 is then processed to evaluate service providers over projects. To this end, we organized the data for each project as shown in Tables 5, 6, 7, and 8. The first column of Tables 5, 6, 7, and 8 includes the names of outcomes and characteristics; then in column 2 we present the weight of the characteristic k_i related to outcomes and projects; in columns 3–8 the evaluation of each service provider is given.

Table 5 shows the evaluation of providers for project 1. For this first project, column 2 shows that more weight is given to the semantic interface, benevolence, and honesty, and it has a higher weight to the outcome of government transparency.

Table 6 shows that, for project 2, the most important outcome is government transparency with a weight of [0.8, 0.95], and the higher weight is given to the service provider characteristic of competence, in contrast with project 1.

Table 7 presents a high weight to both outcomes for project 3 (quality of IS produced and government transparency) as well as a high weight to the characteristics: semantic interface and honesty.

Finally, Table 8 presents a similar weight to both outcomes for project 4, with pragmatic interface and honesty with the highest weights.

In Tables 5, 6, 7, and 8, the inputs of service providers remain equal since those values are given for characteristics that are assessed but without differentiating in

Table 5 Matrix models: calculation of the total score of service providers according to characteristics' weights and service provider evaluation for project 1

		Service providers					
Project 1	Weights	r_1	r_2	r_3	r_4	r_5	r_6
Outcome 1: Quality of IS produced (w_1)							
Pragmatic interface (k_1)	[4.1,4.5]	[0.6,0.75]	[0.9,1]	[0.5,0.65]	[0.7,0.76]	[0.9,0.93]	[0.5,0.6]
Semantic interface (k_2)	[6.4,6.5]	[0.8,0.9]	[0.6,0.75]	[0.5,0.55]	[0.8,0.84]	[0.94,0.97]	[0.7,0.7]
	Score:	[0.69,0.88]	[0.68,0.89]	[0.48,0.62]	[0.73,0.85]	[0.88,1]	[0.59,0.69]
Outcome 2: Government transparency (w_2)							
Benevolence (k_3)	[6.4,6.5]	[0.25,0.5]	[0.7,0.75]	[0.5,0.55]	[0.4,0.5]	[0.54,0.65]	[0.6,0.67]
Competence (k_4)	[2.9,3.5]	[0.4,0.5]	[0.5,0.6]	[0.7,0.85]	[0.5,0.55]	[0.8,0.85]	[0.9,0.92]
Honesty (k_5)	[6,6.5]	[0.2,0.25]	[0.43,0.55]	[0.9,0.95]	[0.7,0.89]	[0.9,0.93]	[0.6,0.7]
	Score:	[0.46,0.71]	[0.52,0.69]	[0.64,0.83]	[0.50,0.72]	[0.68,0.87]	[0.61,0.79]
Overall evaluation							
Outcome 1	[0.5,0.6]	[0.69,0.88]	[0.68,0.89]	[0.48,0.62]	[0.73,0.85]	[0.88,1]	[16.58,19.38]
Outcome 2	[0.9, 1]	[0.46,0.71]	[0.52,0.69]	[0.64,0.83]	[0.50,0.72]	[0.68,0.87]	[0.61,0.79]
Service provider-project score (α_{pr})		[0.47,0.88]	[0.51,0.87]	[0.51,0.86]	[0.51,0.88]	[0.66,1.05]	[0.53,0.86]

Table 6 Matrix models to calculate the total score of service providers according to characteristics weights and service provider evaluation for project 2

		Service providers					
Project 2	Weights	r_1	r_2	r_3	r_4	r_5	r_6
Outcome 1: Quality of IS produced (w_1)							
Pragmatic interface (k_1)	[6.5,7.5]	[0.6,0.75]	[0.9,1]	[0.5,0.65]	[0.7,0.76]	[0.9,0.93]	[0.5,0.6]
Semantic interface (k_2)	[2,3]	[0.8,0.9]	[0.6,0.75]	[0.5,0.55]	[0.8,0.84]	[0.94,0.97]	[0.7,0.7]
	Score:	[0.52,0.98]	[0.67,1.15]	[0.40,0.77]	[0.59,0.97]	[0.74,1.16]	[0.44,0.78]
Outcome 2: Government transparency (w_2)							
Benevolence (k_3)	[4,4.5]	[0.25,0.5]	[0.7,0.75]	[0.5,0.55]	[0.4,0.5]	[0.54,0.65]	[0.6,0.67]
Competence (k_4)	[8,9]	[0.4,0.5]	[0.5,0.6]	[0.7,0.85]	[0.5,0.55]	[0.8,0.85]	[0.9,0.92]
Honesty (k_5)	[5,5.55]	[0.2,0.25]	[0.43,0.55]	[0.9,0.95]	[0.7,0.89]	[0.9,0.93]	[0.6,0.7]
	Score:	[0.43,0.69]	[0.47,0.69]	[0.64,0.90]	[0.48,0.71]	[0.69,0.92]	[0.66,0.82]
Overall evaluation							
Outcome 1	[0.4,0.55]	[0.52,0.98]	[0.67,1.15]	[0.40,0.77]	[0.59,0.97]	[0.74,1.16]	[0.44,0.78]
Outcome 2	[0.8, 0.95]	[0.43,0.69]	[0.47,0.69]	[0.64,0.90]	[0.48,0.71]	[0.69,0.92]	[0.66,0.82]
Service provider-project score (α_{pr})		[0.37,1]	[0.43,1.07]	[0.45,1.07]	[0.41,1.01]	[0.57,1.26]	[0.47,1.06]

Table 7 Matrix models calculating the total score of service providers according to characteristics weights and service provider evaluation for project 3

		Service providers					
Project 3	Weights	r_1	r_2	r_3	r_4	r_5	r_6
Outcome 1: Quality of IS produced (w_1)							
Pragmatic interface (k_1)	[3,3.5]	[0.6,0.75]	[0.9,1]	[0.5,0.65]	[0.7,0.76]	[0.9,0.93]	[0.5,0.6]
Semantic interface (k_2)	[8,8.5]	[0.8,0.9]	[0.6,0.75]	[0.5,0.55]	[0.8,0.84]	[0.94,0.97]	[0.7,0.7]
	Score:	[0.68,93]	[0.63,0.90]	[0.46,0.63]	[0.71,0.89]	[0.85,1.05]	[0.59,0.73]
Outcome 2: Government transparency (w_2)							
Benevolence (k_3)	[7,7.5]	[0.25,0.5]	[0.7,0.75]	[0.5,0.55]	[0.4,0.5]	[0.54,0.65]	[0.6,0.67]
Competence (k_4)	[6,6.5]	[0.4,0.5]	[0.5,0.6]	[0.7,0.85]	[0.5,0.55]	[0.8,0.85]	[0.9,0.92]
Honesty (k_5)	[9,9.95]	[0.2,0.25]	[0.43,0.55]	[0.9,0.95]	[0.7,0.89]	[0.9,0.93]	[0.6,0.7]
	Score:	[0.48,0.71]	[0.5,0.67]	[0.67,0.85]	[0.51,0.72]	[0.71,0.87]	[0.64,0.8]
Overall evaluation							
Outcome 1	[0.9,0.1]	[0.68,93]	[0.63,0.90]	[0.46,0.63]	[0.71,0.89]	[0.85,1.05]	[0.59,0.73]
Outcome 2	[0.76,0.8]	[0.48,0.71]	[0.5,0.67]	[0.67,0.85]	[0.51,0.72]	[0.71,0.87]	[0.64,0.8]
Service provider-project score (α_{pr})		[0.54,0.90]	[0.53,0.87]	[0.51,0.79]	[0.57,0.88]	[0.72,1.05]	[0.57,0.83]

Table 8 Matrix models calculating the total score of service providers according to characteristics weights and service provider evaluation for project 3

		Service providers					
Project 4	Weights	r_1	r_2	r_3	r_4	r_5	r_6
Outcome 1: Quality of IS produced (w_1)							
Pragmatic interface (k_1)	[9,9.95]	[0.6,0.75]	[0.9,1]	[0.5,0.65]	[0.7,0.76]	[0.9,0.93]	[0.5,0.6]
Semantic interface (k_2)	[4,5]	[0.8,0.9]	[0.6,0.75]	[0.5,0.55]	[0.8,0.84]	[0.94,0.97]	[0.7,0.7]
	Score:	[0.59,89]	[0.72,0.1.02]	[0.45,0.69]	[0.66,0.88]	[0.82,1.05]	[0.50,0.71]
Outcome 2: Government transparency (w_2)							
Benevolence (k_3)	[2,2.5]	[0.25,0.5]	[0.7,0.75]	[0.5,0.55]	[0.4,0.5]	[0.54,0.65]	[0.6,0.67]
Competence (k_4)	[3,4]	[0.4,0.5]	[0.5,0.6]	[0.7,0.85]	[0.5,0.55]	[0.8,0.85]	[0.9,0.92]
Honesty (k_5)	[8,8.5]	[0.2,0.25]	[0.43,0.55]	[0.9,0.95]	[0.7,0.89]	[0.9,0.93]	[0.6,0.7]
	Score:	[0.54,0.84]	[0.42,0.69]	[0.69,0.99]	[0.53,0.85]	[0.71,0.99]	[0.58,0.87]
Overall evaluation							
Outcome 1	[0.7,0.75]	[0.59,89]	[0.72,0.1.02]	[0.45,0.69]	[0.66,0.88]	[0.82,1.05]	[0.50,0.71]
Outcome 2	[0.8,0.9]	[0.54,0.84]	[0.42,0.69]	[0.69,0.99]	[0.53,0.85]	[0.71,0.99]	[0.58,0.87]
Service provider-project score (α_{pr})		[0.51,0.95]	[0.51,0.92]	[0.53,0.94]	[0.54,0.95]	[0.69,1.12]	[0.49,0.88]

projects. The differentiation is given on the calculus of the scores for the specific weights by project.

The scores of each outcome are obtained through Eq. (7), which is given by the sum product of the service provider valuation and the characteristic weight, then divided by the sum of the weights of characteristics. This is, for project 1, outcome 1 (Quality of IS produced), and service provider 1, the calculus is given as follows,

$$\begin{aligned} f_{r_1 w_1} &= \frac{[4.1, 4.5] \times [0.6, 0.75] + [6.4, 6.5] \times [0.8, 0.9]}{[4.1, 4.5] + [6.4, 6.5]} \\ &= \frac{[4.1 \times 0.6 + 6.4 \times 0.8, 4.5 \times 0.75 + 6.5 \times 0.9]}{[4.1 + 6.4, 4.5 + 6.5]} \\ &= \frac{[7.58, 0.9225]}{[10.5, 11]} \\ &= \left[\frac{7.58}{11}, \frac{0.9225}{11}\right] \\ &= [0.69, 0.88] \end{aligned}$$

The score for outcome 2 is obtained in the same way, using the evaluations of service provider 2. The overall evaluation is obtained using the Eq. (10). This implies the sum product of weights of outcomes with the evaluation of a service provider divided by the sum of weights.

For example, the value [0.47,0.88] is the score of the service provider 1 in project 1, and it was obtained as follows,

$$\begin{aligned} \alpha_{p_1 r_1} &= \frac{([0.5,0.6] \times [0.69,0.88] + [0.9, 1] \times [0.46,0.71])}{[0.5,0.6] + [0.9, 1]} \\ &= \left[\frac{0.5 \times 0.69 + 0.9 \times 0.46}{0.6 + 1}, \frac{0.6 \times 0.88 + 1 \times 0.71}{0.5 + 0.9}\right] = [0.47, 0.88] \end{aligned}$$

As can be seen in Tables 5, 6, 7, and 8, we obtained service provider-project scores as intervals, which, in many cases, are intersected. For this reason, we apply a "defuzzification" method based on the center of each interval. Once the score service provider-projects have been obtained, we continue with step 7 (*Defuzzify and compare the Project-Service Provider Scores*), obtaining the midpoint and the half-width when necessary.

The interval mid-points for the evaluation of service providers in project 1 are presented in Table 9. When mid-points are equal, half-width will be used to establish an order of preference of one service provider over another, as indicated above. For example, when results are equal, to break the tie, we select the service provider superior to others, considering the interval with the highest half-width.

This process will result in the preference list shown in Fig. 3 (left). The fifth service provider is preferred for all projects, based on outcomes and characteristic evaluation, followed by the fourth and sixth service providers.

Table 9 Mid-point for the values of service provider-project

	Service providers					
	r_1	r_2	r_3	r_4	r_5	r_6
Project 1	[0.47,0.88]	[0.51,0.87]	[0.51,0.86]	[0.51,0.88]	[0.66,1.05]	[0.53,0.86]
Midpoint	0.679	0.690	0.684	0.694	0.854	0.694
Half-width	0.205	0.185	0.174	0.185	0.196	0.166
Position	6	4	5	2	1	3

Projects							
	1	5	6	4	2	~~3~~	~~1~~
	2	5	6	2	~~3~~	4	~~1~~
	3	5	4	~~1~~	2	6	~~3~~
	4	5	4	~~3~~	~~1~~	2	6

Projects					
	1	5	6	4	2
	2	5	6	2	4
	3	5	4	2	6
	4	5	4	2	6

Fig. 3 The order preference lists for projects (left) and the shortened preference lists (right)

Service providers					
	2	1	3	4	2
	4	2	1	4	3
	5	3	4	1	2
	6	3	2	1	4

Fig. 4 Order preference lists of service providers

To conclude the process, the stable matching programming model is applied to find the assignation of projects with service providers. For this, we shortened the list of preferences to have only four service providers as candidates to be assigned.

For this case, the eliminated service providers were service provider number 1 with a sum of positions equal 19 and service provider 3 with a sum of positions equal 17. To solve this instance, we considered the list of the preference order of service providers over projects presented in Fig. 4.

The instance was solved through the stable matching problem equivalent programming model implemented with ILOG CPLEX Optimization Studio version 20.1 on a conventional computer. The obtained solution results in the assignment of the pairs: (service provider 2, project 4), (service provider 4, project 1), (service provider 5, project 3) and (service provider 6, project 6). This appears in the preference lists in Fig. 5.

The obtained solution ensures that there is no pair of service provider-project that prefer each other more than the one that was assigned to them. It is important to note that a different method to defuzzify and compare the interval numbers will possibly result in a different solution.

Furthermore, the service provider selected for project 4 (number 2) was initially ranked in a less favorable position compared to the two excluded service providers, 1 and 3 (refer to Fig. 3). This can be attributed to the procedure for narrowing down

Service providers					
	2	1	3	4	2
	4	2	1	4	3
	5	3	4	1	2
	6	3	2	1	4

Projects					
	1	5	6	4	2
	2	5	6	2	4
	3	5	4	2	6
	4	5	4	2	6

Fig. 5 Order preference lists of service providers (left) and projects (right) and the stable matching (circled)

the selection, which relies on comprehensive assessments of public value rather than individual evaluations alone.

5 Discussion

Service provider selection to enhance public value in IT Outsourcing projects is one of the most important issues in the public management literature (Bryson et al., 2015; Swar et al., 2012). From this perspective, this research provides important insights for the optimization of service provider selection in public-private IT Outsourcing. The method presented in this chapter helps to identify in a novel way the selection criteria to adequately allocate IT outsourcing service providers to specific projects in the perspective of public value.

This chapter provides several key insights. First, we introduce relational factors such as benevolence, competence, honesty, and semantic and pragmatic interfaces, while most of the literature considers more traditional technical factors such as quality, cost and risk (Rajaeian et al., 2017). In addition, relational factors used in our study were validated by an empirical study in Mexico. Trust, in the form of benevolence, honesty and technical capabilities, enhances the efficiency and effectiveness of public services, saving costs and fulfilling citizens' needs in terms of transparency, fast response, and ease of use. Thus, the resources and expertise of both partners can be combined to tackle the complex challenges that public administrators have to face in the development and delivery of public services, especially digital services.

Second, we propose and illustrate with a numerical example the service provider selection problem considering four projects in the public sector and six IT outsourcing service providers. The results show that the stable matching programming model ensures an optimal pairing of service providers with assigned projects, respecting public managers' preferences. The methodology chosen offers a template that can accommodate various criteria of selection that fit clients' goals and service provider's concerns (Feng, 2012; Pan et al., 2023).

Third, this paper presents an original approach incorporating the use of interval numbers to calculate scores to assess public service providers over a set of service providers. The project-service provider assignment is performed by applying the programming model of the stable matching problem to find the optimal matching between projects and service providers in terms of public value. The choice of using interval numbers to represent the inputs of the problem enables administrators and evaluators to convey their judgments by expressing a range of numbers rather than being confined to a precise, crisp definition. These intervals are expressed by defining the minimum and maximum possible values for the intended estimation.

Fourth, to our knowledge, there is no other research that addresses the relational factors of public value associated with the selection of IT service providers in a multi-project environment. The multi-project environment adds complexity to the problem under study due to the amount of information required, which involves measuring the degree to which capabilities are required in a service provider, as well as estimating the impacts of the project on a given objective or dimension of public value. Added to this is the implicit need to apply methods that handle imprecise information. In decision problems related to project management, methodologies in a multi-project environment that consider making decisions independently per project lead to sub-optimal solutions. By this, the proposed method is robust in its ability to effectively integrate these elements into the decision-making process of the service provider selection problem.

Finally, the stable matching problem's structure is applied to establish a selection method that considers the preferences of both parties and allows for a long-term sustainable relationship. In this chapter, we focused on the one-to-one stable matching structure. However, if other configurations are needed to accurately represent the real context (such as many-to-one or many-to-many), our proposed approach can be smoothly adapted.

6 Conclusion

This chapter emphasized the critical role of service provider selection in maximizing public value within public sector IT outsourcing projects. It offers valuable insights to optimize this selection process. A comprehensive and adaptable method for selecting service providers was presented, fostering trust, technical capabilities, and ultimately, the maximization of public value.

The proposed framework departs from traditional factors like cost and quality by incorporating relational factors like trust and communication. This aligns with contemporary ITO literature (Duhamel et al., 2023; Fan & Luna-Reyes, 2016), highlighting the importance of strong partnerships built on trust and effective communication for achieving public value. Moreover, as an additional contribution, the chapter presented a practical method for assigning service providers to projects using a stable matching model. This model ensured optimal pairings based on public managers' preferences and project requirements. This methodology offers a flexible framework that can be adapted to accommodate various selection criteria, making it valuable for diverse public sector applications. Finally, the approach used interval numbers to account for the inherent uncertainties in public service provider evaluation. This allows decision-makers to express judgments as ranges rather than single-point values, leading to more robust and realistic assessments.

In the following paragraphs, we indicate managerial recommendations derived from our results. We then propose some research limitations and suggest future research directions.

6.1 Managerial Recommendations

In terms of managerial recommendations, we argue that stable matching solutions may provide longer-lasting, solid relations between service providers and clients as they consider the preferences of both sides, while usual methods tend to privilege only one side of the collaboration. The solution proposed here could help to optimize selection processes and enhance positive outcomes for citizens and stakeholders. The practical application of the method to be used as a decision support system would require the development of user-friendly applications. Public managers should also consider the importance of maintaining, through formal processes, a strong database of service provider evaluations to keep an organizational memory of past assessments.

6.2 Research Limitations

Regarding research limitations, we specifically adopted the structure provided by the one-to-one stable matching problem to offer an accurate depiction of the Mexican context, where a public administration oversees a set of projects managed by various service providers, none of which dominate the entire market. The proposed approach is limited by the fact that, in the end, every service provider keeps a project. This implies a sense of fairness, which may not always be verified in real practice. This method is optimal in the sense of fairness and equal opportunities, but some service providers may not necessarily deserve to be given the opportunity to keep a project. If there is a necessity to assign a service provider to multiple projects, exploring the problem of many-to-one stable matching in such scenarios becomes relevant.

6.3 Future Research Directions

Concerning future research directions, the numerical example developed in this chapter illustrates how the proposed approach can be applied to select IT outsourcing service providers. Given the specific context in which this approach is applicable, adjustments could be made to enhance flexibility and address alternative contexts.

The inclusion of additional variables may also be relevant: for example, communications systems, commitment, and past experiences working with service providers could be considered, as they condition trust among clients and service providers. Moreover, adding more projects or criteria could reveal itself to be a complex endeavor in using this method (in terms of scalability), but this could be eventually handled by AI-based solutions. Additionally, alternative ordering methods could be implemented for interval comparison, based on service providers' assessments of key characteristics.

Finally, fuzzy numbers can also be considered to express imprecision in estimating preference weights (Rajaeian et al., 2017). It would be important to take into account more levels of possibility than we do, such as triangular fuzzy numbers, to express the minimum possible value, the maximum possible value, and the "most possible value," which is the value in between. The final comparison and selection will depend on the ranking method adopted to use for fuzzy numbers among the different possible approaches (Rajaeian et al., 2017).

Appendix 1: Measurement Items

Category	Item
Benevolence	
BENE 1	The service provider considers the welfare of my organization, as well as its own, when making important decisions in this project.
BENE 2	The service provider considers the interests of my organization and his/her organization when problems arise.
BENE 3	The service provider makes beneficial decisions to us under any circumstances.
Competence	
COMP 1	My service provider is very capable of performing his/her job in this project.
COMP 2	My service provider is known to be successful at the things s/he does.
COMP 3	My service provider has specific technological capabilities that can increase our performance.
Honesty	
HON_1	The service provider keeps the promises made regarding the project.
HON_2	The service provider is honest and sincere with us.
HON_3	The service provider can be relied upon to do the right thing to ensure the success of the project.
Pragmatic interface	
PRAGMA 1	My service provider and I have a different understanding of our project goals.
PRAGMA 2	Often, during the collaboration with the service provider, I initially think I understand my service provider, but afterwards this turns out not to be correct.
PRAGMA 3	I have a different perception of solutions to problems than my service provider.
PRAGMA 4	It is hard to come to a joint solution with my service provider.
Semantic interface	
SEM 1	We and our service provider share manuals, models, and methodologies with each other.

(continued)

Category	Item
SEM 2	We and our service provider share know-how from work experience with each other.
SEM 3	We and our service provider share each other's know-where and know-whom if decisions need to be taken.
Efficacy	
PV_E_CR 1	During the course of the collaboration, we have been able to reduce the cost of operations in our organization in this project.
PV_E_AC 1	During the course of the collaboration, we have been able to get access top-class, state of the art IT capabilities in this project.
PV_E_QIS 1	The systems or services developed through our collaboration are easy to use.
PV_E_QIS 2	Information systems developed through collaboration are useful.
PV_E_QIS 3	The information systems developed through collaboration respond to our needs.
PV_E_QIS 4	Information systems developed through collaboration are secure
Citizen-centric values	
PV_CC_GT 1	During the course of the collaboration, we have been able to create a more transparent government thanks to this project.
PV_CC_FR 1	During the course of the collaboration, we have been able to increase systems' timeliness for the citizen thanks to this project.
PV_CC_EU 1	During the course of the collaboration, we have been able to increase systems' user friendliness for the citizen thanks to this project.
Political benefits	
PV_PB_PP 1	The project has been used by the government for promotional purposes.
PV_PB_HP 1	The project was beneficial for the hierarchical progression of the project leaders.
PV_PB_SI 1	The project has had a high impact at the state level.

References

Ansell, C., & Gash, A. (2008). Collaborative governance in theory and practice. *Journal of Public Administration Research and Theory, 18*(4), 543–571. https://doi.org/10.1093/jopart/mum032

Bai, L., Zheng, K., Wang, Z., & Liu, J. (2022). Service provider portfolio selection for project management using a BP neural network. *Annals of Operations Research, 308*, 41–62. https://doi.org/10.1007/s10479-020-03878-0

Bryson, J. M., Crosby, B. C., & Stone, M. M. (2015). Designing and implementing cross-sector collaborations: Needed and challenging. *Public Administration Review, 75*(5), 647–663. https://doi.org/10.1111/puar.12432

Burnes, B., & Anastasiadis, A. (2003). Outsourcing: A public-private sector comparison [electronic version]. *Supply Chain Management: An International Journal, 8*(4), 355–366. https://doi.org/10.1108/13598540310490116

Carlile, P. (2002). A pragmatic view of knowledge and boundaries: Boundary objects in new product development. *Organization Science, 13*(4), 442–455. https://doi.org/10.1287/orsc.13.4.442.2953

Carlile, P. R. (2004). Transferring, translating, and transforming: An integrative framework for managing knowledge across boundaries. *Organization Science, 15*(5), 555–568. https://doi.org/10.1287/orsc.1040.0094

Chang, S. I., Yen, D. C., Ng, C. S. P., & Chang, W. T. (2012). An analysis of IT/IS outsourcing provider selection for small-and medium-sized enterprises in Taiwan. *Information & Management, 49*(5), 199–209. https://doi.org/10.1016/j.im.2012.03.001

Che, Y. K., Kim, J., & Kojima, F. (2019). Stable matching in large economies. *Econometrica, 87*(1), 65–110. https://doi.org/10.3982/ECTA13547

Choi, J., & Contractor, F. J. (2019). Improving the progress of research & development (R&D) projects by selecting an optimal alliance structure and partner type. *British Journal of Management, 30*(4), 791–809. https://doi.org/10.1111/1467-8551.12267

Duhamel, F., Gutiérrez-Martínez, I., Picazo-Vela, S., & Luna-Reyes, L. F. (2021). Strategic alignment, process improvements and public value in public-private IT outsourcing in Mexico. *International Journal of Public Sector Management, 34*(5), 489–507. https://doi.org/10.1108/IJPSM-07-2020-0183

Duhamel, F., Gutiérrez-Martínez, I., & Luna-Reyes, L. F. (2023, July 11–14). A relational view of knowledge sharing in public-private IT outsourcing relationships. *Proceedings of the 24th annual international conference on digital government research: Together in the unstable world: Digital government and solidarity*. (pp. 468–477). Gdańsk, Poland.

Eshragh, F. (1980). Subjective multi-criteria decision making. *International Journal of Man-Machine Studies, 13*(1), 117–141. https://doi.org/10.1016/S0020-7373(80)80039-3

Fan, L. & Luna-Reyes, L. F. (2016, June 8–10). Theoretical foundations to information technology outsourcing research in the public sector. In *Proceedings of the 17th annual international conference on digital government research dg.O 2016* (pp. 136–145). Shanghai, China.

Feng, B. (2012). Multisourcing service providers selection in service outsourcing. *Journal of the Operational Research Society, 63*, 582–596. https://doi.org/10.1057/jors.2011.61

Fusiripong, P., Baharom, F., & Yusof, Y. (2017). Determining multi-criteria supplier selection towards sustainable development of IT project outsourcing. *International Journal of Supply Chain Management (IJSCM), 6*(3), 258–270. https://doi.org/10.59160/ijscm.v6i3.1772

Gale, D., & Shapley, L. S. (1962). College admissions and the stability of marriage. *The American Mathematical Monthly, 69*(1), 9–15. https://doi.org/10.1080/00029890.1962.11989827

Gantman, S. (2011). IT outsourcing in the public sector: A literature analysis. *Journal of Global Information Technology Management, 14*(2), 48–83. https://doi.org/10.1080/1097198X.2011.10856537

Garajová, E., Hladík, M., & Rada, M. (2019). Interval linear programming under transformations: Optimal solutions and optimal value range. *Central European Journal of Operations Research, 27*, 601–614. https://doi.org/10.1007/s10100-018-0580-5

Gharote, M., Patil, R., Lodha, S., & Raman, R. (2015). Assignment of trainees to software project requirements: A stable matching based approach. *Computers & Industrial Engineering, 87*, 228–237. https://doi.org/10.1016/j.cie.2015.05.017

Gregory, R. E. (1986). Source selection: A matrix approach. *Journal of Purchasing and Materials Management, 22*(2), 24–29. https://doi.org/10.1111/j.1745-493X.1986.tb00159

Ho, W., Xu, X., & Dey, P. K. (2010). Multi-criteria decision making approaches for supplier evaluation and selection: A literature review. *European Journal of Operational Research, 202*(1), 16–24. https://doi.org/10.1016/j.ejor.2009.05.009

Hosseininasab, A., & Ahmadi, A. (2015). Selecting a supplier portfolio with value, development, and risk consideration. *European Journal of Operational Research, 245*(1), 146–156. https://doi.org/10.1016/j.ejor.2015.02.041

Könning, M., Westner, M., & Strahringer, S. (2019). A systematic review of recent developments in IT outsourcing research. *Information Systems Management, 36*(1), 78–96. https://doi.org/10.1080/10580530.2018.1553650

Kulisch, U. W. (2009). Complete interval arithmetic and its implementation on the computer. In *Numerical validation in current hardware architectures: International Dagstuhl Seminar,*

Dagstuhl Castle, Germany, January 6–11, 2008. Revised Papers (pp. 7–26). Berlin/Heidelberg: Springer Berlin Heidelberg.

Lai, K. K., Wang, S. Y., Xu, J. P., Zhu, S. S., & Fang, Y. (2002). A class of linear interval programming problems and its application to portfolio selection. *IEEE Transactions on Fuzzy Systems, 10*(6), 698–704. https://doi.org/10.1109/TFUZZ.2002.805902

Lee, J. N. (2001). The impact of knowledge sharing, organizational capability and partnership quality on IS outsourcing success. *Information and Management, 38*(5), 323–335. https://doi.org/10.1016/S0378-7206(00)00074-4

Lee, S. (2016). Incentive compatibility of large centralized matching markets. *The Review of Economic Studies, 84*(1), 444–463. https://doi.org/10.1093/restud/rdw041

Lee, J., & Kim, J. (2007). Grounded theory analysis of e-government initiatives: Exploring perceptions of government authorities. *Government Information Quarterly, 24*(1), 135–147. https://doi.org/10.1016/j.giq.2006.05.001

Liou, J. J., Wang, H. S., Hsu, C. C., & Yin, S. L. (2011). A hybrid model for selection of an outsourcing provider. *Applied Mathematical Modelling, 35*(10), 5121–5133. https://doi.org/10.1016/j.apm.2011.04.020

Manlove, D. F., Irving, R. W., Iwama, K., Miyazaki, S., & Morita, Y. (2002). Hard variants of stable marriage. *Theoretical Computer Science, 276*(1–2), 261–279. https://doi.org/10.1016/S0304-3975(01)00206-7

Nakahara, Y., Sasaki, M., & Gen, M. (1992). On the linear programming problems with interval coefficients. *Computers & Industrial Engineering, 23*(1–4), 301–304. https://doi.org/10.1016/0360-8352(92)90121-Y

Orlu, G. U., Pa, N. C., Amtan, R. B., & Amdan, H. B. (2021). Outsourcing provider selection model in public sector. *Turkish Journal of Computer and Mathematics Education (TURCOMAT), 12*(3), 1832–1841. Retrieved from https://turcomat.org/index.php/turkbilmat/article/view/1012

Pan, P., Jin, A., Mahmoudi, A., Li, X., & Wang, Y. (2023). A matching model for construction subcontractor selection in engineering bid decisions using ordinal priority approach. *Journal of Asian Architecture and Building Engineering*, 1–14. https://doi.org/10.1080/13467581.2023.2270009

Picazo-Vela, S., Luna, D. E., Gil-Garcia, J. R., & Luna-Reyes, L. F. (2022). Creating public value through inter-organizational collaboration and information technologies. *International Journal of Electronic Government Research (IJEGR), 18*(1), 1–18. https://doi.org/10.4018/IJEGR.288069

Qin, J., Liu, X., & Pedrycz, W. (2017). An extended TODIM multi-criteria group decision making method for green supplier selection in interval type-2 fuzzy environment. *European Journal of Operational Research, 258*(2), 626–638. https://doi.org/10.1016/j.ejor.2016.09.059

Rajaeian, M. M., Cater-Steel, A., & Lane, M. (2017). A systematic literature review and critical assessment of model-driven decision support for IT outsourcing. *Decision Support Systems, 102*, 42–56. https://doi.org/10.1016/j.dss.2017.07.002

Roth, A. E., Rothblum, U. G., & Van de Vate, J. H. (1993). Stable matchings, optimal assignments, and linear programming. *Mathematics of Operations Research, 18*(4), 803–828. https://doi.org/10.1287/moor.18.4.803

Sethuraman, J., Teo, C. P., & Qian, L. (2006). Many-to-one stable matching: Geometry and fairness. *Mathematics of Operations Research, 31*(3), 581–596. https://doi.org/10.1287/moor.1060.0207

Swar, B., Moon, J., Oh, J., & Rhee, C. (2012). Determinants of relationship quality for IS/IT outsourcing success in public sector. *Information Systems Frontiers, 14*(2), 457–475. https://doi.org/10.1007/s10796-010-9292-7

Youssef, M. A., Zairi, M., & Mohanty, B. (1996). Supplier selection in an advanced manufacturing technology environment: An optimization model. *Benchmarking for Quality Management & Technology, 3*(4), 60–72. https://doi.org/10.1108/EUM0000000004286

Zemankova, M., & Kandel, A. (1985). Implementing imprecision in information systems. *Information Sciences, 37*(1–3), 107–141. https://doi.org/10.1016/0020-0255(85)90008-8

Outsourcing Decisions in Both Forward-Loop and Reverse Supply Chains: An Integrated Approach

Mohammed Haoues, Toufik Bentrcia, Mohammed Merghem, and Mohammed Dahane

1 Introduction

In the last few years, an increasing complexity trend in supply chain management has taken place because of the growing focus on both sustainable strategies and operational performance. The forward supply chain denotes the set of operations needed to manufacture new items from raw materials and deliver them to clients, while the reverse supply chain involves gathering used items and reprocessing them to enhance their properties. Known also as remanufacturing, it can be defined as returning a used product in failure, end-of-life, obsolete, or waste states to a level of performance identical to or better than the original state. Seeking fully combined technical and environmental dedicated tools into a competitive and reliable framework showcases the vital nature of integrated planning. This can be accomplished via including managing in-house manufacturing costs, outsourcing, demand variations, inventory levels, availability, and ecological constraints (Haoues et al., 2023). Outsourcing is a key component in supply chain management as it improves cost-efficiency and allows companies to concentrate on their main competencies, which yields an overall competitiveness enhancement in the global market (Lee & Choi, 2011). Moreover, it offers access to specific skills, resources, and scalability whilst moderating risks in connection to supply chain disruptions (Haoues et al., 2019). Industrial plants are currently recommended to cover product recovery management in their production processes, guided by environmental legislation, eco-friendly

M. Haoues (✉) · T. Bentrcia · M. Merghem
Industrial Engineering Department, LAP—Batna 2 University, Batna, Algeria
e-mail: m.haoues@univ-batna2.dz; t.bentrcia@univ-batna2.dz; m.merghem@univ-batna2.dz

M. Dahane
Université de Lorraine, LGIPM, Metz, France
e-mail: mohammed.dahane@univ-lorraine.fr

F. P. García Márquez et al. (eds.), *Outsourcing Using Operations Research and Management Science Methods*, International Series in Operations Research & Management Science 366, https://doi.org/10.1007/978-3-031-91845-2_5

insights, and the potential economic benefits of product recovery. Remanufacturing is recognized to be of paramount utility since it not only saves time, resources and energy but also reduces both CO2 emission and solid waste. Such practice can be considered a crucial component within the outsourcing strategy of the company. Hence, more gains are realized in terms of the preservation of nonrenewable resources and the reduction of daily greenhouse gas emissions. To this end, it is worth implementing comprehensive approaches that integrate outsourcing in manufacturing, remanufacturing, reliability and environmental considerations. By doing so, companies can efficiently balance manufacturing and remanufacturing tasks, optimize material utilization, and dispatch sustainable practices along the whole supply chain. In this context, our work focuses on elaborating an integrated framework supporting multi-objective, multi-product, multi-period maintenance scheduling and CO2 emission requirements. Thus, our basic objective is to get a balanced plan in terms of economic costs, system unavailability, and Carbon dioxide emission levels. To the best of our knowledge, this problem has not been previously tackled in the available literature.

The rest of the chapter is structured as follows: Sect. 2 introduces a literature review elucidating the research gap and the positioning of our research. In Sect. 3, the identified problem is described besides the implementation of its associated mathematical model. Section 4 conducts numerical experiments on a case study and inspects the obtained results by adopting a sensitivity analysis approach. Finally, the last section recapitulates the main findings, underscores practical implications, and proposes directions for future study.

2 Literature Review

Manufacturing/remanufacturing operations are widely used in practice with many case studies emphasized in the literature, including renewable energy, the electronics industry and the automotive industry (Dahane et al., 2017; Belhocine et al., 2021; Harris et al., 2023). These operations emerging in Hybrid Manufacturing and Remanufacturing Systems (HMRS) have been recognized for their sustainable and effective nature. The flexibility of HMRS implementations makes it possible to combine many facets, such as strategic planning, maintenance and sustainability, contributing to a more systematic production. Our aim in this section is to disclose the interconnection of manufacturing/remanufacturing operations to other aspects of interest, namely, reliability and maintenance, outsourcing strategies and CO2 emission constraints so that the research gap to be tackled can be clearly ascertained.

2.1 Manufacturing/Remanufacturing Operations Under Reliability and Maintenance

The available contributions are basically motivated by the increasing recognition of the preventive maintenance (PM) role in boosting HMRS and maintenance planning.

A thorough understanding of such impact brings additional benefits in terms of performance optimization and cost reduction. In light of this, Polotski et al. (2019a) extended a coordination problem encompassing manufacturing/remanufacturing within a closed-loop supply chain network. The introduced extension is built upon the incorporation of disposal cost and rate as decision variables. Polotski et al. (2019b) considered an optimization problem of integrated production for an HMRS, where a single product is delivered with setup transitions between manufacturing and remanufacturing modes. Besides, the returned products demonstrate large variability in both type and quality as recovery procedures alter machine operation during remanufacturing. Furthermore, it is assumed that the age dynamics of the machines are basically impacted by their remanufacturing intensity. Therefore, in order to restore the system availability a maintenance strategy involving minimal repair (MR) in the case of failure and perfect PM should be adopted.

A production plan and replacement problem in a system integrating manufacturing and remanufacturing processes with random breakdowns and repairs is analyzed by Ouaret et al. (2019). The complexity generated by a diverse range of returned products is also supported in this study. Due to imperfect repairs, the authors supposed the continuous degradation of the remanufacturing machine over time implies its replacement. Assid et al. (2020) addressed a system with two facilities prone to arbitrary failures and repairs. The first facility is specifically reserved for manufacturing and transforming raw materials into finished products. The second facility operates in both manufacturing and remanufacturing modes in addition to handling shared resources and setups. In the same scope, Assid et al. (2023) manipulated a failure-prone system containing two production facilities. Within this framework, several constraints are introduced, namely, limitations on in-house production capacity, disposal activities, and switching between different modes.

2.2 *Manufacturing/Remanufacturing Operations with Outsourcing Strategies*

The actual supply chains are subject to severe vulnerabilities and disturbances, causing reliability menaces to deliveries. In order to remedy these shortcomings and set up efficient supply chain networks, it is mandatory to exploit various management strategies, including outsourcing, as a potential candidate to reach this goal (Haoues et al., 2021). From this perspective, a remanufacturing system receiving returned products from customers was investigated by Kim et al. (2006). The developed model focused on maximizing total remanufacturing savings by optimizing the allocation of products to remanufacturing facilities and subcontractors. Following a similar reasoning, Wang et al. (2011) dealt with the dynamic lot-sizing problem associated with single-item systems, including remanufacturing and outsourcing modules. It is assumed in the model that the demand and the return over a finite horizon are deterministic.

Amin and Zhang (2013) suggested a three-stage approach for the assessment and selection of optimal providers, remanufacturing subcontractors, and renovation locations. The selection procedure criteria are based on both qualitative and quantitative features. Furthermore, Ghassemi et al. (2018) inspected a closed-loop supply chain involving a manufacturer and several processing centers, where the resulting finished products are integrated next to those acquired from an external supplier into inventory. Nevertheless, the capacity limitations of the manufacturer can yield this method holding costs or the necessity of remanufacturing subcontractors.

An increasing interest was dedicated to the intersection of integrated production maintenance policies subject to outsourcing constraints. In this context, numerous works have substantially contributed to providing insights on such a complex subject. For instance, Dahane et al. (2011) implemented a combined maintenance policy integrating just-in-time manufacturing and maintenance decisions in an outsourcing setting. The manufacturing system under study comprises two pieces of equipment prone to breakdowns and manufacturing a single product. Haoues et al. (2019) explored integrated production and maintenance in a two-echelon supply chain. So, several outsourcers and subcontractors are involved in the network and manipulate a single product machine. The elaborated model allows for determining optimal configuration in terms of production rates, maintenance periods and suitable outsourcing strategies.

As can be deduced from the aforementioned studies, an exclusive focus is centered on the manufacturing process without taking into account the remanufacturing aspect. Hence, these works missed a critical dimension needed for elaborating industrial processes in accordance with resource conservation and environmental sustainability. Only a few papers attempted to bridge this gap by addressing both manufacturing and remanufacturing viewpoints within a unique approach. As an example, Merghem et al. (2023) treated a combined production/maintenance planning problem in a hybrid manufacturing and remanufacturing system with an outsourcing option. The authors shed light on the efficient coordination of these vital components and offer valuable insights into optimizing process performance.

2.3 Manufacturing/Remanufacturing Operations with CO2 Emission Constraints

Nowadays, environmental sustainability is attracting tremendous importance, as reflected by the wide acknowledgment of mitigating carbon emissions from industrial plants. In the literature, the main policies cover many fields such as emissions threshold, carbon pricing and carbon/emissions trading. Absi et al. (2013) investigated four CO2 emissions constraint types. The carbon emissions for each supplying mode are expressed by a linear function of the supplied amount. Such constraints offer a structured vision to manage and limit carbon emissions under distinct operating scenarios. The work of Zouadi et al. (2018) was focused on carbon emission reduction in an HMRS, where limitations on carbon emissions stemming from manufacturing, remanufacturing and transportation tasks were introduced. In the same context, Mishra et al. (2020) analyzed a closed-loop network model including a single manufacturer, a single retailer, and a one-third party. This model implements a carbon cap-and-trade mechanism for emissions control from storing, shipping and procurement processes. Ndhaief et al. (2020) elaborated a joint environmental production maintenance framework for manufacturing and remanufacturing systems using subcontractor solutions. A CO2 tax is paid if the system surpasses predefined thresholds, while the manufacturing or the remanufacturing processes have the option to engage a subcontractor. Alegoz's study (2021) studied production and sustainability-related decisions by assessing economic and environmental performance metrics. This is accomplished by comparing the entire system and individual supply chain elements under four scenarios. Works of Lahmar et al. (2022a, b) were oriented to the integration of economic considerations and environmental sustainability. This contributes to facilitating the implementation of reliable decision-making strategies in the context of manufacturing and remanufacturing operations. Haoues et al. (2023) addressed the problem of combined manufacturing and remanufacturing with maintenance planning while minimizing CO2 emissions.

2.4 Research Gap and Our Contributions

Our research differs from that of Haoues et al. (2023) by incorporating outsourcing strategies into the management of both forward-loop and reverse supply chain. In contrast to Merghem et al. (2023), our approach considers the multi-product dimension and emphasizes environmental factors, i.e., CO2 emissions reduction. Notably, our contribution remedies the knowledge gap in available literature where outsourcing is addressed exclusively in the remanufacturing process with a single subcontractor. Moreover, outsourcing in our study is exploited across the entire direct and reverse chain, which is a departure from Merghem's work not handling specialty outsourcing and environmental considerations. Regarding Lahmar et al. (2022a, b), our research integrates reliability, maintenance aspects, and outsourcing strategies which are excluded in the referenced work.

In comparison to Ndhaief et al. (2020), our research extends the maintenance policy by considering a plan of scheduling imperfect maintenance to mitigate the risk of failures occurring. Furthermore, we introduce an "emissions threshold" type CO2 emissions reduction policy together with multiple subcontractors in both direct and reverse logistics chains.

While the work published by Ghassemi et al. (2018) ignores maintenance and CO2 emission reduction aspects, our work provides some amendments by including the reliability and maintenance considerations. Zouadi et al. (2018) tackled a multi-objective planning problem for an HMRS producing a single product. Our approach

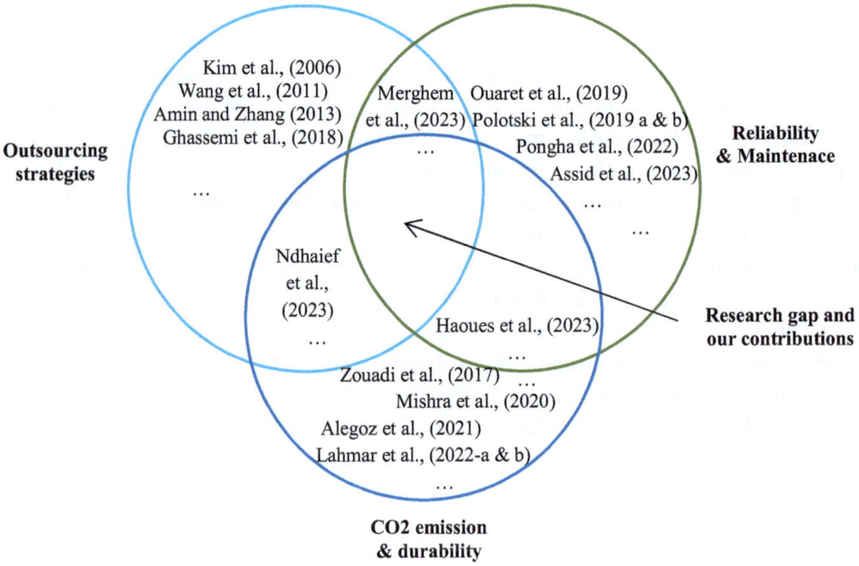

Fig. 1 Research gap identification

is similar to Zouadi's work in terms of CO_2 emissions minimization and subcontracting incorporation into both forward and reverse supply chains with multiple subcontractors.

Figure 1 depicts the intersections between different areas of literature and clearly underlines the research gap, presenting a new challenge for integrated management approaches in the context of HMRS. Compared to the available literature, our study devises a mathematical scheme addressing multi-objective, multi-product, and multi-period scenarios jointly with maintenance scheduling and CO_2 emission aspects. In this setting, the key goal is to identify an optimal combined strategy for coping with economic costs, system unavailability, and Carbon dioxide emissions. As far as we know, no previous works have treated such combined requirements and goals.

According to (Haoues et al., 2012, 2019, 2021; Zouadi et al., 2018; Merghem et al., 2023), outsourcing in both downstream loop and reverse supply chain is involved in our work not only as a strategic element but also as:

2.4.1 A Means of Capacity Expansion

Outsourcing manufacturing or remanufacturing tasks to external partners can be a means of expanding capacity during peak periods, which helps satisfy varied demands without approving significant investments.

2.4.2 An Outcome of Expertise and Specialization

Our model takes into account the outsourcing of defined tasks to specialized suppliers or remanufacturers with advanced capabilities and leverages their expertise.

2.4.3 Cost Optimization Strategies and Measures

Overall cost optimization within the HMRS can be achieved by outsourcing some manufacturing or remanufacturing tasks, particularly if external partners are able to realize scale economies or offer competitive pricing.

2.4.4 A Means of Flexibility and Adaptability

Due to demand fluctuations and varying requirements for manufacturing and remanufacturing in HMRS, outsourcing brings many benefits in terms of flexibility and quick adaptability to perturbations.

2.4.5 A Means to Take into Account Environmental Considerations

There is no doubt that by outsourcing certain pollutant manufacturing or remanufacturing tasks to specialized companies, including eco-friendly procedures, advantages are gained for HMRS basically when targeting waste reduction and carbon emissions.

2.4.6 A Means of Collaboration and Partnerships

Cooperation with external partners, such as suppliers or remanufacturers, promotes innovation and development exchange, yielding more income to the HMRS.

Two vital components need to be addressed before outsourcing is planned. Firstly, a meticulous evaluation of external partnerships is recommended to ensure the quality and fulfillment of environmental protection rules, as well as compatibility with the overall goals of the HMRS. Secondly, strategic decision-making for tasks partitioned into outsourcing and in-house sets is required to preserve a fixed level of control and quality measures.

In Table 1, we summarize the main contributions related to outsourcing strategies in addition to the associated characteristics and classification criteria, i.e., hypotheses, which provide a clear specification of the research gap to be tackled throughout our present research. The following abbreviation is used.

Table 1 A summary of classification hypotheses related to the main literature

Hypothesis	Objective function				System			Time scale		Product		Return						Demand		Perspective's study			Maintenance				CO2 emission policies				Outsourcing features											
Author	min	max	mono-objective	Multi-objective	Manufacturing	Remanufacturing	Hybrid	Discrete	Continues	Single	Multiple	Rework	Disposed	Deterministic	Stochastic	As new product	Not as new product	Deterministic	Stochastic	Manufacturer's point of view	Upstream sub perspective	Downstream sub perspective	Minimal repair	Imperfect PM	Perfect PM	Emissions threshold	Carbon pricing	Carbon emissions trading	Carbon offsets policy	Manufacturing	Remanufacturing	Single subcontractor	Multiple subcontractors	Forward-loop SC	Reverse SC	Capacity expansion	Specific process outsourcing	Cost optimization	Environmental Considerations	collaboration and Partnerships	Model type	Resolution approach
Kim et al., (2006)					■	■		■			■		■	■		■		■													■	■									MILP	Gams
Wang et al., (2011)					■	■		■		■				■		■		■												■		■									MILP	DP
Amin and Zhang (2013)				■	■	■		■			■		■	■		■		■																							MILP	Gams
Polotski et al., (2019-a)	■						■		■	■		■		■		■		■		■			■																		MILP	A
Zouadi et al., (2017)	■		■				■	■		■		■		■		■		■		■																					MILP	A, GA
Ghassemi et al., (2018)		■		■	■	■		■			■	■	■	■		■		■		■						■				■	■		■	■	■						MILP	AUGMECON
Ouaret et al., (2019)	■		■				■		■		■	■	■	■			■	■		■			■	■							■		■		■						S-MM	A, S
Polotski et al., (2019-b)	■						■		■			■		■			■	■		■			■																		MILP	A
Mishra et al., (2020)	■		■		■	■			■	■		■		■				■		■					■																MINLP	A
Ndhaief et al., (2020)	■		■		■	■		■		■		■			■				■				■					■													SO	A
Assid et al., (2020)	■		■				■		■	■		■	■	■		■		■		■					■		■				■	■						■	■		SP, S	S
Assid et al., (2023)	■		■				■		■	■		■	■	■		■		■		■			■																		SP, S	S
Lahmar et al., (2022-a&b)	■			■			■	■		■		■	■	■			■	■		■						■															MILP	NSGA
Merghem et al., (2023)	■		■				■	■		■		■	■	■		■		■		■			■	■							■	■			■	■		■		■	MILP	Gams
Haoues et al., (2023)	■			■			■	■			■	■	■	■		■		■		■			■	■		■															MILP	Gams
This chapter	■			■			■	■			■	■	■	■		■		■		■			■	■		■				■	■		■	■	■	■	■	■	■	■	MILP	Gams

A analytic, *AUGMECON* augmented ε-constraint method, *DP* dynamic programming, *GA* genetic algorithm, *Gams* general algebraic modeling system, *SO* stochastic optimization, *MILP* mixed-integer linear programming, *MINLP* mixed-integer non linear programming, *NSGA* non-dominated sorting genetic algorithm, *S* simulation, *S-MM* semi Markovien model, *SP* stochastic programming

3 Problem Statement

Based on the conducted literature review, we consider the following problem to constitute a major challenge for modern companies. In this plan, we investigate outsourcing in a product supply chain constituted of a manufacturer with an HMRS represented by a single machine. The latter is assumed to be prone to random failures, which requires immediate MR to restore the system to its operational state before the failure. The system produces multiple product types $p \in \{1, \ldots, P\}$ over a finite horizon H comprising $t \in \{1, \ldots, T\}$ periods with equal length τ. At the end of a period t, a demand $d_{p,\ t}$ is satisfied by both novel and remanufactured products without scarcities or backlogs. Nevertheless, imperfect PM is planned to reduce the occurrence of the breakdown and decrease the system's age and re-establish it to a configuration between "As Bad As Old" and "As Good As New" states. The manufacturer maintains relationships with upstream and downstream partners. So, we have the upstream partner with a supplier of raw materials and multiple subcontractors $s \in \{1, \ldots, S\}$ having cutting-edge technology for manufacturing/remanufacturing specific products. While for downstream partners, we have multiple subcontractors' collection centers $l \in \{1, \ldots, L\}$ responsible for collecting returned products from customers. Furthermore, each maintenance action will need a certain quantity of HMRS capacity defined by G. In addition, we suppose that any manufacturing, remanufacturing or transportation activity yields CO2 emissions.

Outsourcing is approached in the chain from two viewpoints. The first relies on the downstream loop supply chain, where the manufacturer contracts with several subcontractors to purchase products already manufactured and ready for employment. This option is built upon the principle of comparative advantage between the internal production of new products and the internal remanufacturing of returned products. The second viewpoint is the reverse supply chain, where customers return products to the collection centers. A percentage of returned products are remanufactured in-house. However, the remaining percentage of returned products requires specific operations from upstream subcontractors. The adoption of outsourcing in this situation is justified respectively by two major reasons: capacity outsourcing and specific process outsourcing. Besides, outsourcing is studied within an integrated maintenance/environment-based approach.

With regards to integrated maintenance planning, numerous objectives are acknowledged involving the minimization of the overall anticipated maintenance cost and the maximization of the system availability. The simultaneous optimization of the total expected maintenance cost and availability in the same plan might be unfeasible as suggested by Zhao et al. (2014). This makes the elaboration by the manufacturer of an integrated plan minimizing total economic cost and CO2 emissions while decreasing the system's unavailability an intractable goal. Therefore, a multi-objective mathematical formulation based on Mixed Integer Programming (MIP) is proposed to combine in-house manufacturing/remanufacturing, maintenance, environment, and outsourcing decisions in traditional forward and reverse supply chains. We elucidate in Fig. 2 the structure of the investigated supply chain.

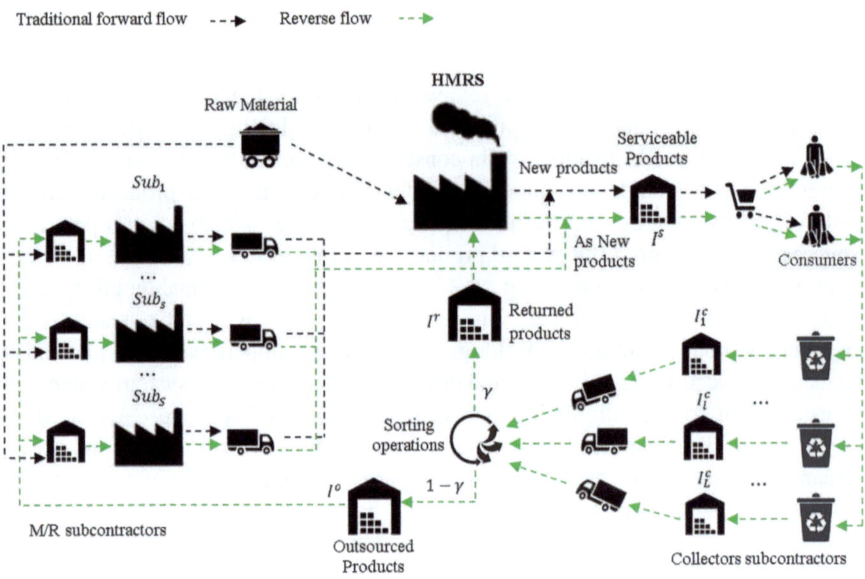

Fig. 2 Structure of the investigated supply chain

3.1 Notations

The following notations are exploited for the accurate formulation of our mathematical model.

Set elements	
t	Element from the set of periods
p	Element from the set of product types
l	Element from the set of collectors subcontractors
s	Element from the set of manufacturers/remanufacturers subcontractors
Parameters	
H	Length of planning horizon
P	Product number
T	Period number
C	Number of collectors subcontractors
S	Number of manufacturers/remanufacturers subcontractors
$d_{p,\,t}$	Demand of product p during period t
$o^{c}_{p,t,l}$	Cost of ordering returned product p during period t from subcontractor collection center l
$o^{om}_{p,t,s}$	Ordering cost of outsourced manufactured product p during period t from manufacturing subcontractor s
$o^{or}_{p,t,s}$	Ordering cost of outsourced remanufactured product p during period t from remanufacturing subcontractor s
$s^{m}_{p,t}$	Manufacturing setup cost of product p during period t

(continued)

$s^r_{p,t}$	Remanufacturing setup cost of product p during period t
$c^m_{p,t}$	Cost of manufacturing product p during period t
$c^r_{p,t}$	Cost of remanufacturing product p during period t
$T^{om}_{p,t,s}$	Transportation cost per unit from manufacturing subcontractor s for outsourced manufacturing product p during period t
$T^{or}_{p,t,s}$	Transportation cost per unit from remanufacturing subcontractor s for outsourced remanufacturing product p during period t
$T^c_{p,t,l}$	Transportation cost for return per collector subcontractor l of collected product p during period t
$h^s_{p,t}$	Cost of holding serviceable product p during period t
$h^r_{p,t}$	Cost of holding returned product p during period t
$h^o_{p,t}$	Cost of holding outsourced product p during period t
$R^c_{p,t,l}$	Quantity of returned products p at the subcontractor collection center l at the end of the period t
$e^c_{p,l}$	Unit emission per transported product p from subcontractor collection center l
$e^{om}_{p,s}$	Unit emission per transported product p from manufacturing subcontractor s
$e^{or}_{p,s}$	Unit emission per transported product p from remanufacturing subcontractor s
e^m_p	Amount of emissions generated by manufacturing one product p
e^r_p	Amount of emissions generated by remanufacturing one product p
$E_{\max}$	Maximum environmental impact allowed by the HMRS
T_{cm}	Time of MR tasks
T_{pm}	Time of PM tasks
ρ^m_p	Manufacturing time of one product p
ρ^r_p	Remanufacturing time of one product p
G	Nominal capacity of HMRS
γ	Fixed returned products percentage for in-house remanufacturing by the manufacturer
η	Factor of age reduction due to an imperfect PM action
τ	Period length
M	A big number
Decision variables	
$y^m_{p,t}$	Binary variable for manufacturing product p during period t
$y^r_{p,t}$	Binary variable for remanufacturing product p during period t
$q^m_{p,t}$	Quantity of products p manufactured during period t
$q^r_{p,t}$	Quantity of products p remanufactured during period t
$q^c_{p,t,l}$	Quantity of collected products p from collector subcontractor l at period t
$q^{om}_{p,t,s}$	Outsourced manufacturing quantity of products p from manufacturing subcontractor s at period t
$q^{or}_{p,t,s}$	Outsourced remanufacturing quantity of products p from remanufacturing subcontractor s at period t
$I^s_{p,t}$	Stock level of serviceable products p at end of period t
$I^r_{p,t}$	Stock level of returned products p at the end of period t
$I^o_{p,t}$	Stock level of outsourced products p at the end of period t
$I^c_{p,t}$	Stock level of collected products p at the end of period t

(continued)

$I^{cc}_{p,t,l}$	Stock level of collected products p at the end of period t from the collector subcontractor l
Z_t	Binary variable for scheduling PM at the start of period t
$r(t)$	Hazard rate function of HMRS at time t
a_t	Effective age of hybrid manufacturing remanufacturing system at the end of period t
ω_t	Factor of capacity reduction in period t
a^z_t	Linearized variable, with $a^z_t = Z_t a_{t-1}$

3.2 Mathematical Model

The implemented integrated maintenance in hybrid manufacturing and remanufacturing system with outsourcing strategies and CO2 emissions can be expressed as the multi-objective constrained optimization problem given below:

$$\min \mathrm{ECC} = \sum_{p=1}^{P}\sum_{t=1}^{T}\left(s^m_{p,t}y^m_{p,t} + c^m_{p,t}q^m_{p,t} + h^s_{p,t}I^s_{p,t} + s^r_{p,t}y^r_{p,t} + c^r_{p,t}q^r_{p,t} + h^r_{p,t}I^r_{p,t} + h^o_{p,t}I^o_{p,t}\right)$$
$$+\sum_{p=1}^{P}\sum_{t=1}^{T}\sum_{s=1}^{S}\left(o^{om}_{p,t,s}q^{om}_{p,t,s} + T^{om}_{p,t,s}q^{om}_{p,t,s} + o^{or}_{p,t,s}q^{or}_{p,t,s} + T^{or}_{p,t,s}q^{or}_{p,t,s}\right)$$
$$+\sum_{p=1}^{P}\sum_{t=1}^{T}\sum_{l=1}^{L}\left(o^{c}_{p,t,l}q^{c}_{p,t,l} + T^{c}_{p,t,l}q^{c}_{p,t,l}\right) \tag{1}$$

$$\min \mathrm{UNAVs} = 1 - \frac{T\tau - \sum_{t=1}^{T}\left(T_{pm}Z_t + T_{cm}\int_{a_t}^{a_t+\tau} r(t)dt\right)}{T\tau} \tag{2}$$

$$\min \mathrm{EVE} = \sum_{p=1}^{P}\sum_{t=1}^{T}\left(q^m_{p,t}e^m_p + q^r_{p,t}e^r_p\right) + \sum_{p=1}^{P}\sum_{t=1}^{T}\sum_{s=1}^{S}\left(q^{om}_{p,t,s}e^{om}_{p,s} + 2q^{or}_{p,t,s}e^{or}_{p,s}\right)$$
$$+\sum_{p=1}^{P}\sum_{t=1}^{T}\sum_{l=1}^{L}\left(q^c_{p,t,l}e^c_{p,l}\right) \tag{3}$$

St:

$$a_t = a_{t-1} - \eta a^z_t + \tau, \forall t \tag{4}$$

$$a^z_t \le a_{t-1}, \forall t \tag{5}$$

$$a^z_t \le MZ_t, \forall t \tag{6}$$

$$a_t^z \geq a_{t-1} + M(1 - Z_t), \forall t \tag{7}$$

$$I_{p,t}^s = I_{p,t-1}^s + q_{p,t}^m + q_{p,t}^r + \sum_{s=1}^{S} \left(q_{p,t,s}^{om} + q_{p,t,s}^{or} \right) - d_{p,t}, \qquad \forall p, t \tag{8}$$

$$I_{p,t}^o = I_{p,t-1}^o + (1-\gamma) \sum_{l=1}^{L} q_{p,t,l}^c - \sum_{s=1}^{S} \left(q_{p,t,s}^{om} + q_{p,t,s}^{or} \right), \qquad \forall p, t \tag{9}$$

$$I_{p,t}^r = I_{p,t-1}^r + \gamma \sum_{l=1}^{L} q_{p,t,l}^c - q_{p,t}^r, \qquad \forall p, t, l \tag{10}$$

$$I_{p,t-1,l}^{cc} + R_{p,t,l} - q_{p,t,l}^c = I_{p,t,l}^{cc}, \qquad \forall p, t, l \tag{11}$$

$$\omega_t = \frac{T_{pm} Z_t + T_{cm} \int_{a_t}^{a_t+\tau} r(t) dt}{\tau}, \qquad \forall t \tag{12}$$

$$\sum_{p=1}^{P} \left(q_{p,t}^m \rho_p^m + q_{p,t}^r \rho_p^r \right) \leq \tau\, G(1 - \omega_t), \qquad \forall t \tag{13}$$

$$q_{p,t}^m \leq \left(\sum_{\substack{k=1 \\ k \geq t}}^{K} d_{p,k} \right) y_{p,t}^s, \qquad \forall p, t \tag{14}$$

$$q_{p,t}^r \leq \left(\sum_{\substack{k=1 \\ k \geq t}}^{K} d_{p,k} \right) y_{p,t}^r, \qquad \forall p, t \tag{15}$$

$$\sum_{p=1}^{P} \sum_{t=1}^{T} \left(q_{p,t}^m e_p^m + q_{p,t}^r e_p^r \right) + \sum_{p=1}^{P} \sum_{t=1}^{T} \sum_{s=1}^{S} \left(q_{p,t,s}^{om} e_{p,s}^{om} + 2 q_{p,t,s}^{or} e_{p,s}^{or} \right) + \sum_{p=1}^{P} \sum_{t=1}^{T} \times \sum_{l=1}^{L} \left(q_{p,t,l}^c e_{p,l}^c \right) \leq \sum_{p \in P} \sum_{t \in T} d_{p,k} E_{\max} \tag{16}$$

$$I_{p,0}^s = I_{p,0}^r = I_{p,0}^o = I_{p,0,l}^{cc} = 0, \qquad \forall p, t, l, s \tag{17}$$

$$y_{p,t}^s, y_{p,t}^r, Z_t \in \{0, 1\}, \qquad \forall p, t, l, s \tag{18}$$

$$a_t, a_t^z, \omega_t, r(t), \text{ECC}, \text{UNAVs}, \text{EVE} \in \mathrm{R}^+, \qquad \forall p, t \tag{19}$$

$$q^{m}_{p,t}, q^{r}_{p,t}, q^{c}_{p,t,l}, q^{or}_{p,t,s}, q^{om}_{p,t,s}, I^{s}_{p,t}, I^{r}_{p,t}, I^{o}_{p,t}, I^{cc}_{p,t,l} \in \mathbb{Z}^{+}, \qquad \forall p, t, l, s \tag{20}$$

Through the planning, function (1) is designed to concurrently minimize the global cost associated with manufacturing, remanufacturing, and holding, minimize the unavailability of the HMRS (2), and minimize the overall emissions (3). Constraint (4) articulates the equation of virtual age of the hybrid manufacturing and remanufacturing system at the end of each time period. The bi-linear term $a_{t-1}Z_t$ is linearized through the inequalities (5), (6), and (7). Constraints (8), (9), (10) and (11) provide the inventory equilibrium equalities for serviceable, outsourced, returned and collected products, respectively. The factor of capacity reduction is defined by Eq. (12), while constraint (13) serves as the capacity restriction inequality, ensuring that the time required for manufacturing, remanufacturing, and all related activities satisfies the capacity of HMRS. Constraints (13) and (14) establish the relationships between the manufacturing and remanufacturing variables ($q^{m}_{p,t}$ and $q^{r}_{p,t}$ respectively) and the binary setup variables ($y^{m}_{p,t}$ and $y^{r}_{p,t}$). The restriction in the carbon emission over the planning horizon is ensured by the inequality (16). It includes emissions linked to manufacturing, remanufacturing and transportation among the different echelons of the network. Eqs. (17) represent the initial quantities in different stocks. Constraints (18) define the binary values associated with manufacturing and remanufacturing, and preventive maintenance activities. Finally, Constraints (19) and (20) provide the definition domains for the remaining variables.

4 Resolution Methodology

To tackle the elaborated multi-objective optimization problem, the resolution methodology is conducted in two stages. First, the Pareto front solutions are determined while a compromise solution is then picked by assessing some decision preferences.

4.1 *Objective Functions Reduction*

With the aim of reducing the computational burdens, the weighted sum approach has been widely investigated in multi-objective optimization literature to merge the set of objective functions (OF) in a single figure of merit. However, a normalization procedure is initially recommended due to the difference in OFs scales (Soroudi, 2017). In this context, Eqs. (21) and (22) are used for minimization and maximization problems, respectively.

$$\frac{F_i - F_i^{\min}}{F_i^{\max} - F_i^{\min}} \quad \text{For minimizing objective} \tag{21}$$

$$\frac{F_i^{\max} - F_i}{F_i^{\max} - F_i^{\min}} \quad \text{For maximizing objective} \tag{22}$$

Hence, a weighting factor is assigned to each OF according to its importance yielding the weighted OF given by this formula:

$$\min Z = \sum_{i=1}^{k} w_i F_i thickmathspace \text{and} \sum_{i=1}^{k} w_i = 1 \tag{23}$$

By doing so, the original multi-objective model reduces to an easy-to-solve mono-objective problem where only a single solution is associated with each configuration of weights. It should be mentioned that Pareto set solutions can be deduced by weight variation. Nevertheless, shortcomings may arise in the case of the problem's non-convexity, for which some Pareto solutions cannot be recognized (Marler & Arora, 2010). In addition, numerous roughly identical solutions are often generated so that only a single representative value needs to be preserved.

4.2 Selection of a Compromise Solution

Once the Pareto optimal front solutions are identified, a compromise solution is deduced by investigating some decision preferences. Based on (Soroudi, 2017), we exploit the fuzzy-satisfying technique. In this framework, a legend in the top right cornermembership function expressed by $\mu^{Z_k(S_n)}$ is elaborated to every solution from the Pareto front. This grade within the interval [0, 1] measures the distance between S_n and the set minimizing the OFZ_k. To each OF, a linear membership function is adopted:

$$\mu^{Z_k(S_n)} = \begin{cases} \dfrac{Z_k^{\max} - Z_k^{(S_n)}}{Z_k^{\max} - Z_k^{\min}}, & Z_k^{\min} \le Z_k(S_n) \le Z_k^{\max} \\ 0, & \text{otherwise} \end{cases} \tag{24}$$

Therefore, the final solution is obtained by maximizing the minimum satisfaction or minimizing the maximum dissatisfaction amongst all goals as follows:

$$\max{}_{n=1}^{N}\left(\min{}_{k=1}^{K} \mu^{Z_k(S_n)}\right) \tag{25}$$

5 Numerical Experiments

This section is devoted to the description of various numerical aspects regarding the considered system. In this scope, two elementary components are addressed namely the analysis of a basic case besides the sensitivity analysis performed to delve into the effect of some key factors.

5.1 *Basic Case Analysis*

Let us consider a supply chain constituted of a manufacturer equipped with a single machine-based HMRS and having a minimal capacity $G = 50$. Two types of products are slated for either manufacturing or remanufacturing over a finite horizon comprising eight periods; each is distinguished by demands and returns as outlined in Tables 2 and 3. The percentage of returned products for in-house remanufacturing by the manufacturer is set to 60%. The manufacturer is in relationships with a raw material supplier, four upstream M/R subcontractors, and three downstream subcontractors' collection centers. Additionally, it is assumed that the timings for any PM or MR actions are provided by $T_{cm} = 0.02$ and $T_{cm} = 0.1$, respectively. The factor of age decreases because of an imperfect PM action is fixed at $\eta = 0.5$. Moreover, it is presumed that the HMRS is susceptible to random failures, following a 2-parameters Weibull law with shape and scale parameters $\alpha = 2$ and $\beta = 3$. The maximum environmental impact allowed by the HMRS is set to 4.

The CO2 emission per product, the unitary costs of transportation and ordering for return per collector are summarized in Table 4.

Table 2 Periodic demand for each product

Period		1	2	3	4	5	6	7	8
Product	1	22	22	22	22	23	22	20	20
	2	25	25	22	25	23	22	20	20

Table 3 Periodic product returns

Period			1	2	3	4	5	6	7	8
Product	1	$l = 1$	12	12	12	12	12	12	12	12
		$l = 2$	11	11	11	11	11	11	11	11
		$l = 3$	10	10	10	10	10	10	10	10
	2	$l = 1$	7	7	7	7	7	7	7	7
		$l = 2$	11	11	11	11	11	11	11	11
		$l = 3$	10	10	10	10	10	10	10	10

Table 4 Unit emission, ordering and transportation costs of return per collector for each product

Collectors			1	2	3		1	2	3		1	2	3
Product	1	$e^c_{p,l}$	1.2	1.2	1.2	$o^c_{p,l}$	20	15	12	$T^c_{p,l}$	20	15	12
	2		1.5	1.5	1.5		10	15	12		20	15	12

Table 5 Unit costs of transportation and ordering for outsourced M/R products

M/R			1	2	3	4		1	2	3	4
Product	1	$T^{om}_{p,s}$	15	10	12	11	$T^{or}_{p,s}$	7	11	8	6
		$o^{om}_{p,s}$	270	280	285	275	$o^{or}_{p,s}$	120	130	135	125
	2	$T^{om}_{p,s}$	15	10	12	11	$T^{or}_{p,s}$	7	11	8	6
		$o^{om}_{p,s}$	270	280	285	275	$o^{or}_{p,s}$	120	130	135	125

Table 6 Unit emissions for outsourced M/R products transportation

M/R			1	2	3	4		1	2	3	4
Product	1	$e^{om}_{p,s}$	2.2	2.2	2.2	2.2	$e^{or}_{p,s}$	1.2	1.2	1.2	1.2
	2		2.5	2.5	2.5	2.5		1.5	1.5	1.5	1.5

Table 7 A summary of parameters employed for numerical experiments

Parameter		s^m_p	s^r_p	c^m_p	c^r_p	h^s_p	h^r_p	h^o_p	ρ^m_p	ρ^r_p	e^m_p	e^r_p
Product	1	1100	500	80	45	40	20	20	0.8	0.4	2.5	1
	2	1000	550	90	40	40	20	20	1	0.5	2	1.5

The CO2 emission per product and the unitary costs of transportation and ordering for each M/R subcontractor are summarized in Tables 5 and 6.

The remaining input data are detailed in Table 7.

The solution to the model is obtained using CPLEX solver within GAMS software, executed on a PC equipped with an i5 CPU and 16 GB of RAM.

The Pareto front solutions, obtained through the weighted sum technique, are detailed in Table 8 and schematized in Fig. 3.

Subsequently, the procedure entailed determining the most appropriate solution from the non-dominated ones, and this was achieved via the utilization of the Fuzzy Satisfying Method. In our specific scenario, solution S18 emerges as the optimal choice.

The analysis outcomes, which depict the optimally combined in-house M/R, maintenance and outsourced M/R plan with a focus on CO2 emissions reduction in different stages, are outlined in Table 9. This program seamlessly integrates the manufacturing of novel items with the remanufacturing of returned items to fulfill demand. Notably, outsourcing incorporation is critical for the emissions delivered throughout the entire manufacturing, remanufacturing and transportation processes.

To depict such influence, Fig. 4 is created to underline the correlation among the overall emissions and those specifically produced by in-house manufacturing/remanufacturing and transportation processes. We note that the evolution of these indicators, except the transportation process, is mainly linked to the in-house plan and the quantities of unit emissions generated by the manufacturing/remanufacturing and very closely linked to the outsourcing plan. However, transportation emissions are only linked to the outsourcing plan.

Table 8 Optimal Pareto solutions

Solution	ECC	UNAVs	EVE
S1	43,853	0.0856	1044.7
S2	43,853	0.0675	1045.7
S3	43,853	0.0675	1044.7
S4	125,978	0.0675	843
S5	43,853	0.0707	1044.7
S6	98,484	0.0675	731
S7	43,853	0.0842	1044.7
S8	43,890	0.0675	1012.7
S9	44,000	0.0675	972.7
S10	44,014	0.0675	968.7
S11	43,853	0.0756	1044.7
S12	43,886	0.0675	1015.7
S13	44,201	0.0675	924.2
S14	43,890	0.0756	1012.7
S15	43,890	0.0828	1012.7
S16	44,003	0.0675	971.7
S17	44,014	0.0711	968.7
S18	44,743	0.0701	861.5
S19	98,484	0.0678	731

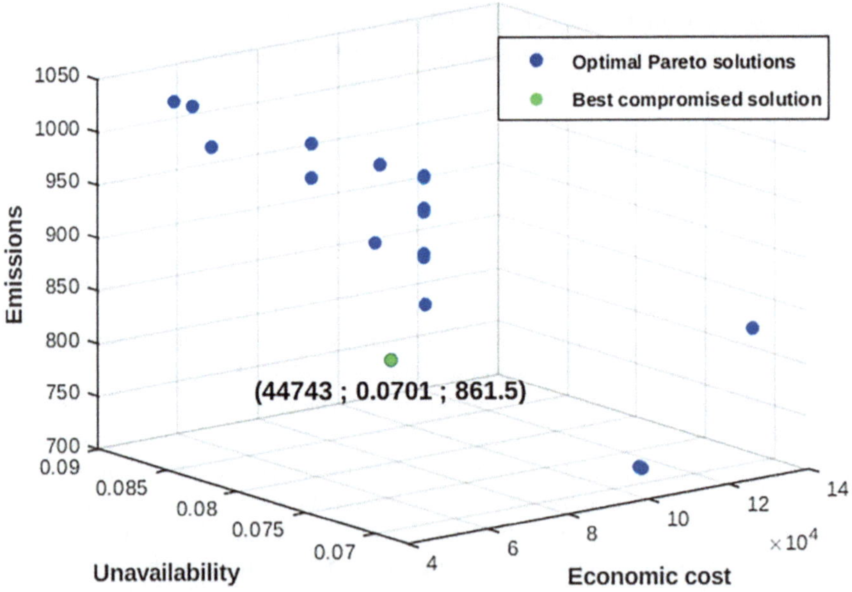

Fig. 3 Optimal Pareto front solutions

Table 9 Optimal integrated in-house M/R, maintenance and outsourced M/R planning with CO2 emissions minimization

Period	1	2	3	4	5	6	7	8
Z_t	0	1	1	0	1	1	1	0
w	0.0333	0.0644	0.07	0.0722	0.0839	0.0797	0.0776	0.0799
a_t	1	1.5	1.75	2.75	2.375	2.1875	2.0938	3.0938
$q^m_{1,t}$	22	0	44	0	45	0	0	0
$q^r_{1,t}$	0	14	0	0	0	0	14	19
$I^s_{1,t}$	0	0	22	0	22	0	0	0
$I^r_{1,t}$	1	0	1	2	3	4	0	0
$I^o_{1,t}$	0	0	0	0	0	0	0	11
$q^m_{2,t}$	25	25	0	46	0	42	0	0
$q^r_{2,t}$	0	0	15	0	0	0	0	20
$I^s_{2,t}$	0	0	0	21	0	20	0	0
$I^r_{2,t}$	1	2	0	1	2	3	4	0
$I^o_{2,t}$	0	0	1	1	0	0	0	10
$q^c_{1,t,3}$	0	20	0	0	0	0	15	30
$q^{or}_{1,t,1}$	0	8	0	0	0	0	6	1
$q^c_{2,t,3}$	0	0	20	0	0	0	0	25
$q^{or}_{2,t,1}$	0	0	7	0	2	0	0	0

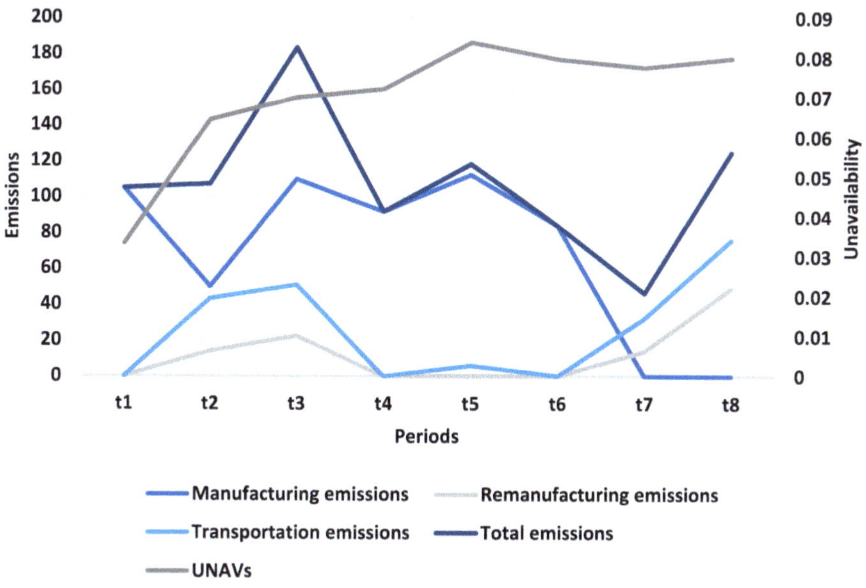

Fig. 4 Effect of maintenance/unavailability and mixture in-house/outsourcing on generated emissions

As an illustrative example, during the last two periods, there is no in-house manufacturing, so the emissions curve is zero. On the other hand, there is in-house and outsourced remanufacturing, as shown in Table 9. This is explained by an increase compared to previous periods. The correlation can be attributed to the adoption of outsourcing practices, particularly the remanufacturing process, which is supposed to be more environmentally friendly in comparison to conventional manufacturing. Emissions linked to the remanufacturing process are low except in a few periods, during which there are slight increases. We mention that variables with zero values in all periods are not represented.

Beyond the influence of in-house and outsourced M/R on overall emissions, another notable factor shaping emissions is the HMRS unavailability. It is noted that as the HMRS unavailability increases, total emissions decrease. In this setting, system unavailability denotes the non-use of internal resources to process a demand within a specified period. Our observation is consolidated by the fact that the trajectory of fossil carbon dioxide emissions underwent a significant alteration due to the effect of COVID-19, i.e., the impact of confinement on the unavailability of production and service systems. In 2020, global CO2 emissions experienced a remarkable reduction, reaching 34 Gt CO2, which is approximately 7% below the 2019 level (Wang et al., 2020; Friedlingstein et al., 2022). Among the world's major emitting economies, the Group of 20 similarly observed a 5.3% diminution in CO2 emissions during the year 2020 (Climate Transparency, 2021; Merchante et al., 2021; Deng et al., 2024).

The unavailability of the manufacturer system tends to slowly increase even after implementing PM operations at almost all periods. Although we seek to minimize unavailability, the results reveal the opposite. For instance, the manufacturer does not opt over time to yield large quantities of items versus its initial state. The increase in unavailability aligns with a reduction in total emissions. As the HMRS experiences a decline in unavailability and a subsequent reduction in capacity for processing, the total manufacturing output diminishes. Thus, fewer items are manufactured or remanufactured in-house, leading to a lower quantity of generated emissions. This is due to the manufacturer's focus on carbon footprint management. The decision to outsource certain processes may be driven by a desire to decrease the overall carbon footprint of the supply chain through green practices.

5.2 *Sensitivity Analysis*

We tackle here the behavior of the implemented mathematical model in terms of several factors having an impact on the HMRS performance. To this end, we pursue a deeper analysis according to the following trials.

5.2.1 First Trial: Number of Period's Effect

In the context of production planning, the horizon could be short, medium or long term, depending on the nature of the production process. It is essential to note that the link between CPU time and the number of planning periods can vary based on the complexity of the optimization model, the size of the problem instance, and the specific employed optimization algorithms.

In Table 10, the first column presents the number of planning periods, while the second column denotes the average CPU time. From this table and Fig. 5 under the parameters settings, it appears that the CPU time is relatively low for short planning horizons of up to 11 periods. The CPU time increased as the optimization algorithm needed to consider a larger number of decisions and constraints. Planning over a

Table 10 Evolution of the CPU time according to the number of periods

T	CPU time
3	2.346
4	8.176
5	27.015
6	44.792
7	71.554
8	184.506
9	464.061
10	718.327
11	1547.218
12	4757.5
13	7430.895
14	15278.23
15	31630.5
16	71629.04

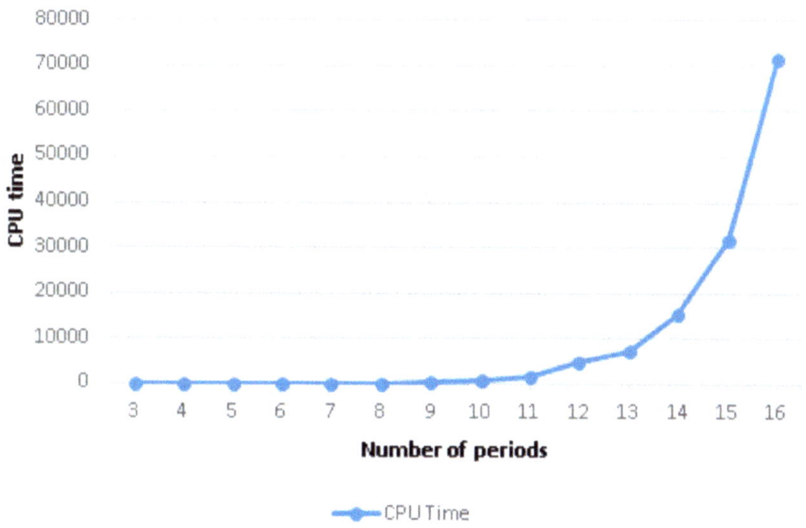

Fig. 5 Effect of periods' number on CPU time

Table 11 Evolution of the CPU time according to the number of products

P	CPU time
1	19.798
2	181.733
3	2650.819
4	140000

long horizon involves considering a larger number of time periods, which significantly increases the computational complexity. The CPU time becomes a limiting factor beyond $T = 15$ associated with large-scale problems. In summary, the evolution of CPU time with respect to the number of planning periods is influenced by the problem's size, complexity, and the efficiency of the optimization algorithm.

5.2.2 Second Trial: Effect of the Products' Number

By analogy to the previous group of tests, it is crucial to emphasize that the correlation between CPU time and the number of products can fluctuate depending on factors such as the complexity of the optimization model, the scale of the problem instance, and the applied optimization algorithms.

In Table 11, the first column displays the number of products and the second one presents the average CPU time. Analyzing this table, given the specified parameter settings, it is evident that the CPU time is comparatively low for the single and two product cases. As the number of products exceeds 3 types, the CPU time increases considerably. Planning multi-product scenarios can significantly amplify the computational complexity. The CPU time imposes a lower bound to the number of products $p = 4$ for which scenarios are considered large-scale problems.

5.2.3 Third Trial: Effect of the Actors' Number

The number of actors can significantly impact the complexity and dynamics of supply chain optimization. Each actor represents a node in the network. As the number of actors increases, the complexity of the optimization problem grows significantly. More actors mean more potential interactions, dependencies, and decision variables. Consequently, the computational resources and time increase.

Table 12 recapitulates the results of the trials. We have defined three levels for upstream and downstream subcontractors, namely, Low, Medium and High, corresponding to 2, 6 and 10, respectively. Data are preserved from the earlier created group whilst supplementary data for the newly inserted actors are generated. We obtained 9 combinations, for each one, we evaluated the CPU time in addition to the value of each objective function, where Fig. 6 depicts the evolution of these indicators.

Table 12 Effect of actors' number

			M/R subcontractors		
			Low	Medium	High
Collection centers subcontractors	Low	CPU time	404.373	703.814	287.029
		ECC	97,110	92,036	122,811
		UNAVs	0.0678	0.0701	0.0675
		EVE	731	663.4	758.7
	Medium	CPU time	141.449	1174.118	480.074
		ECC	37,370	92,816	40,536
		UNAVs	0.0756	0.0707	0.0856
		EVE	876	663.4	828.1
	High	CPU time	176.178	1153.567	480.25
		ECC	86,865	82,711	111,337
		UNAVs	0.675	0.0675	0.0675
		EVE	710.6	657.7	537.7

The case with 2 downstream subcontractors and three levels (2, 6 and 10) of upstream subcontractors is approved as an illustrative case. From Fig. 6a, we compare the LM and LH cases with the first LL; we observe that the case with medium upstream subcontractors generates an economic cost and environmental emissions less than the one generated by the case with 2 and 10 subcontractors. However, the computational time and the unavailability have increased by 74.1% and 3.4%, respectively. These values are deduced in percentage based on the difference between two levels and division by the reference value.

The findings indicate that the total cost of the supply chain is not significantly altered by the number of involved actors. Instead, contractual arrangements are strongly defined by the cost structures (Haoues et al., 2019). The majority of supply chain management considerations revolve around cost reduction at various levels for overall expense minimization, thus capturing additional market share and generating future investment profits.

In practical terms, the optimal number is identified as two subcontractors per function, involving a competitive bidding process and an annual quotation for turnover distribution, with one subcontractor covering 40% and the other covering 60% (Haoues, et al., 2023). Increasing the number of subcontractors elevates the workload associated with monitoring contracts for the manufacturer, encompassing control and administrative processing. However, reducing the number of service providers allows for obtaining sufficient volumes to keep a service provider permanently onsite, thereby reducing waiting times for corrective actions. Conversely, relying on a single subcontractor can be risky, especially if it holds a monopoly position, making it challenging to compare factors such as price, deadlines, and quality. Moreover, a larger number of subcontractors may enhance supply chain resilience by providing more alternative sources, but it also requires better risk management strategies due to increased exposure to disruptions. This can be achieved by focusing on knowledge of the cases or from published references.

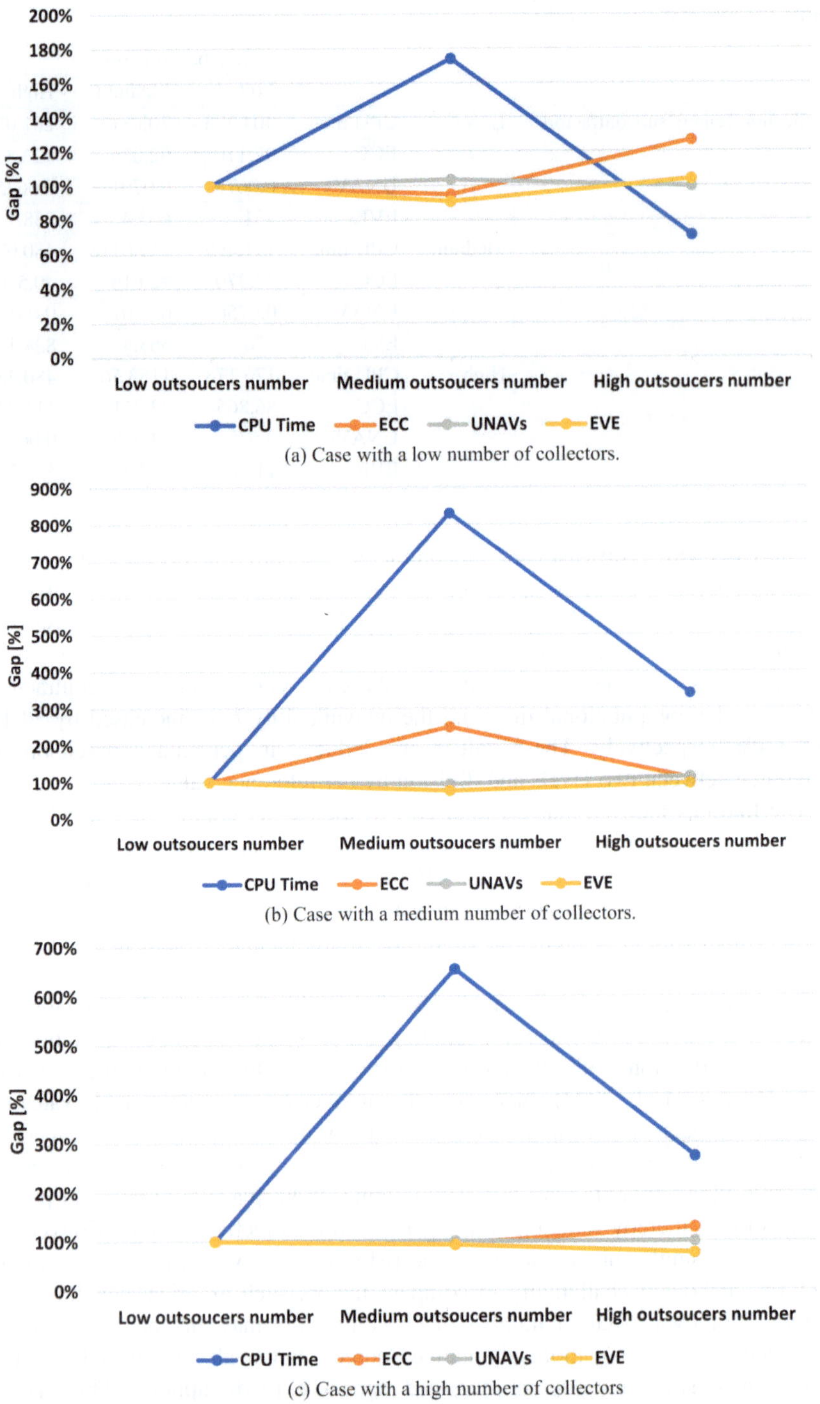

Fig. 6 Effect of the number of actors. (**a**) Case with a low number of collectors. (**b**) Case with a medium number of collectors. (**c**) Case with a high number of collectors

Table 13 Effect of the amount of CO2 emissions

	CPU	ECE	UNAVs	EVE
Low $\left(e_p^m, e_p^r\right)$	405.668	44,362	0.0675	471.7
Medium $\left(e_p^m, e_p^r\right)$	257.379	44,063	0.0675	860.9
High $\left(e_p^m, e_p^r\right)$	214.816	45,116	0.0675	884.4

In summary, the number of actors in a supply chain has a profound impact on the challenges and considerations involved in supply chain optimization. Managing this complexity requires advanced optimization techniques, robust communication channels, and a comprehensive understanding of the dynamics among various actors in the supply chain ecosystem.

5.2.4 Fourth Trial: Effect of the Amount of CO2 Emissions

The amount of CO2 emissions has become a significant factor in supply chain optimization due to increasing consciousness of environmental sustainability and the necessity to address climate change. The manufacturer chooses subcontractors based not only on cost consideration but also on their environmental practices. Collaborating with subcontractors to reduce emissions throughout the supply chain can be a strategic initiative. Table 13 elucidates various global performance measures of different levels related to the amount of CO2 emissions.

The stacked bar chart and the curve in Fig. 7 compare the percentage and the evolution of the total collected products for low, medium and high levels of CO2 emissions.

In addition, for low, medium and high levels of CO2 emissions, the 100% stacked bar charts in Fig. 8 compare the percentage of the contribution of different modes of utilization for each product, both in-house M/R and outsourcing M/R. Besides, the 2D curves display the trend over time for different inventories.

In summary, the amount of CO2 emissions in a supply chain has wide-ranging implications for optimization efforts. Manufacturers are increasingly integrating environmental considerations into their supply chain strategies to align with sustainability goals, comply with regulations, and meet stakeholder expectations.

5.2.5 Fifth Trial: Effect of the System Capacity

The system capacity has a significant impact on decisions related to in-house/ outsourcing M/R strategies. If the internal system capacity is limited or unable to meet demand, the manufacturer chooses to outsource certain tasks to external partners to remedy such shortcomings. Outsourcing allows access to additional manufacturing/remanufacturing or service capabilities without the need for further

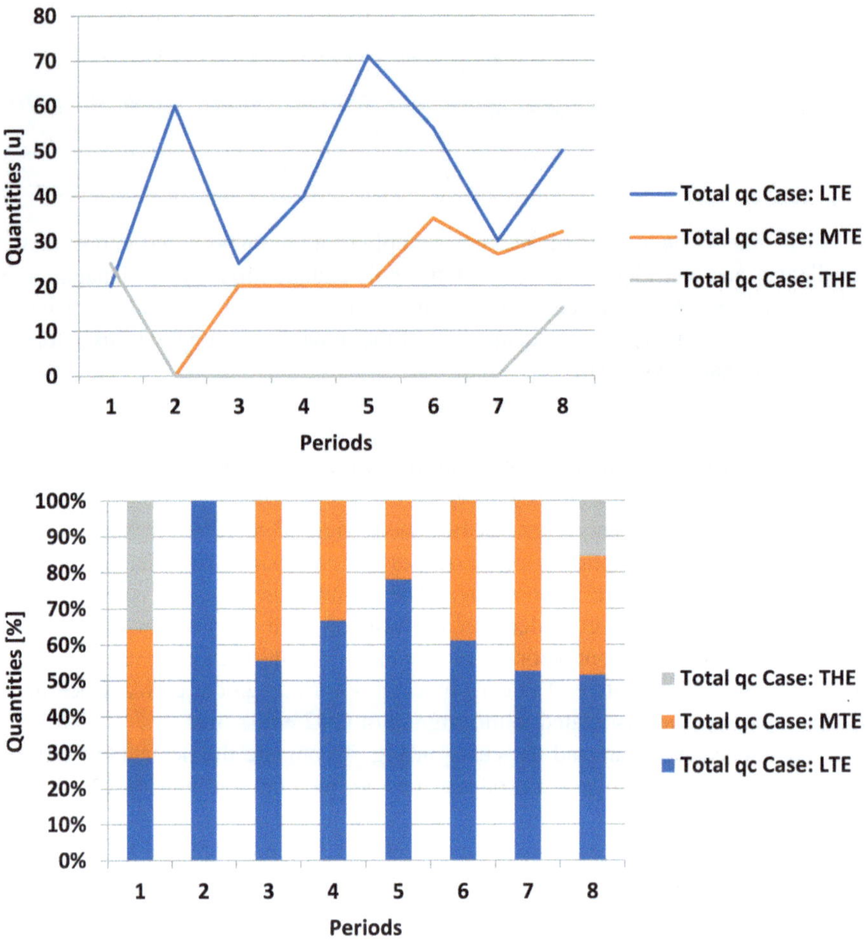

Fig. 7 Evolution of the total collected products for different levels of CO2 emissions

expansion investments. Table 14 introduces global performance assessments for different levels of the system capacity.

In a similar way to the previous trial, we assume three levels of HMRS capacity represent the situations where the capacity is loose, moderate and tight. The stacked bar chart and the curve in Fig. 9 compare the percentage and the tendency of the total collected products for loose, moderate and tight levels of HMRS capacity.

Furthermore, the 100% stacked bar charts in Fig. 10 compare the percentage involvement of diverse modes of employment for each item in-house M/R and outsourcing M/R. On the other hand, the 2D curves demonstrate the tendency over time for diverse inventories.

In summary, the effect of the system capacity on in-house/outsourcing M/R in supply chain optimization originates from many factors, where the manufacturer

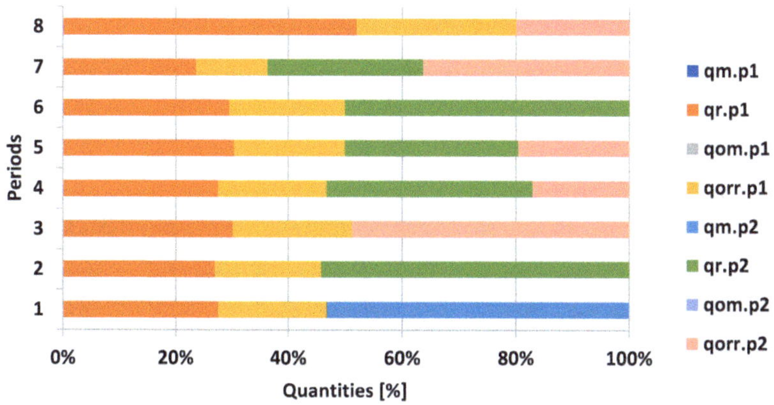

(a1) Percentage contribution of the modes utilization.

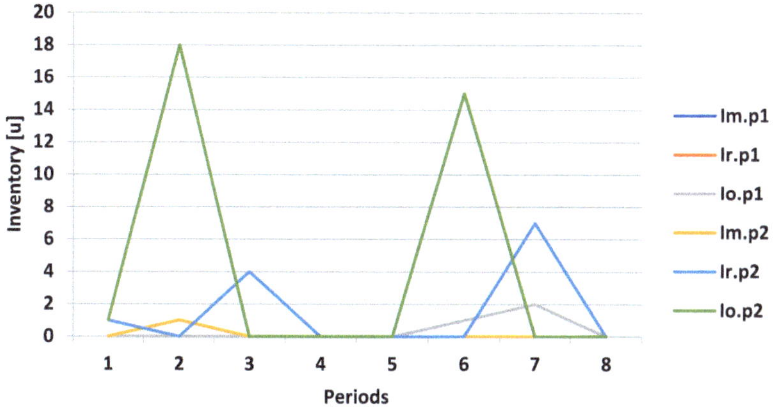

(b1) Evolution over time for different inventories.

Case: Low level of CO2 emissions.

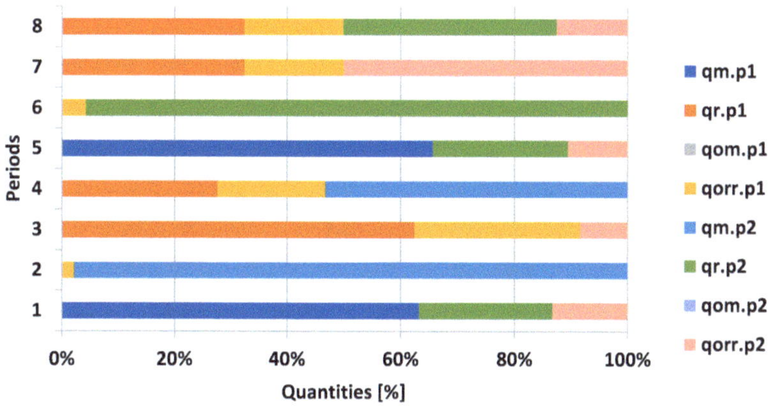

(a2) Percentage contribution of the modes utilization.

Fig. 8 Effect of the amount of CO2 emissions for different levels

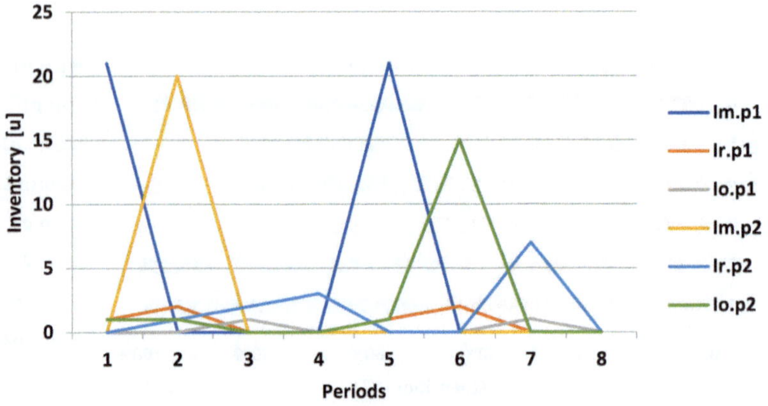

(b2) Evolution over time for different inventories.

Case: Medium level of CO2 emissions.

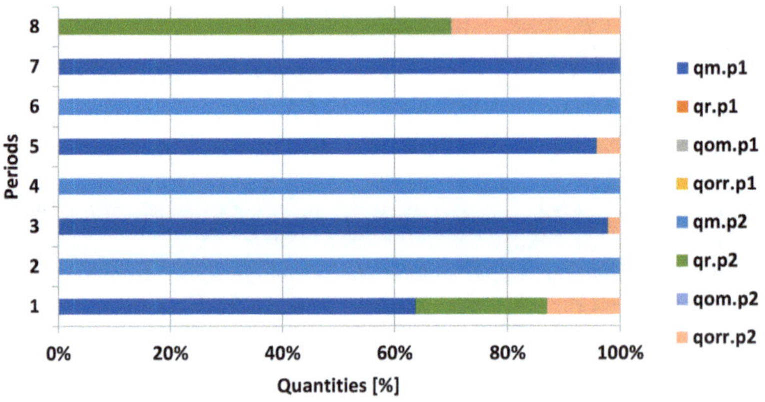

(a3) Percentage contribution of the modes utilization.

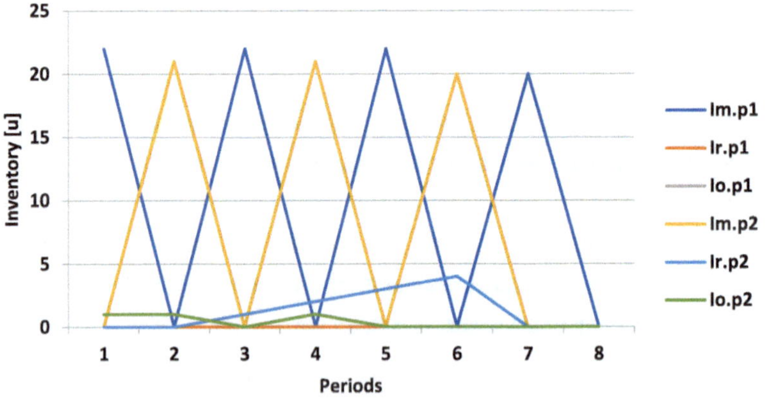

(b3) Evolution over time for different inventories.

Case: High level of CO2 emissions.

Fig. 8 (continued)

Table 14 Effect of the system capacity

	CPU	ECE	UNAVs	EVE
$G = 40$	285.569	44,700	0.0707	904.8
$G = 50$	176.265	44,743	0.0701	861.5
$G = 60$	215.819	44,919	0.0707	832.1

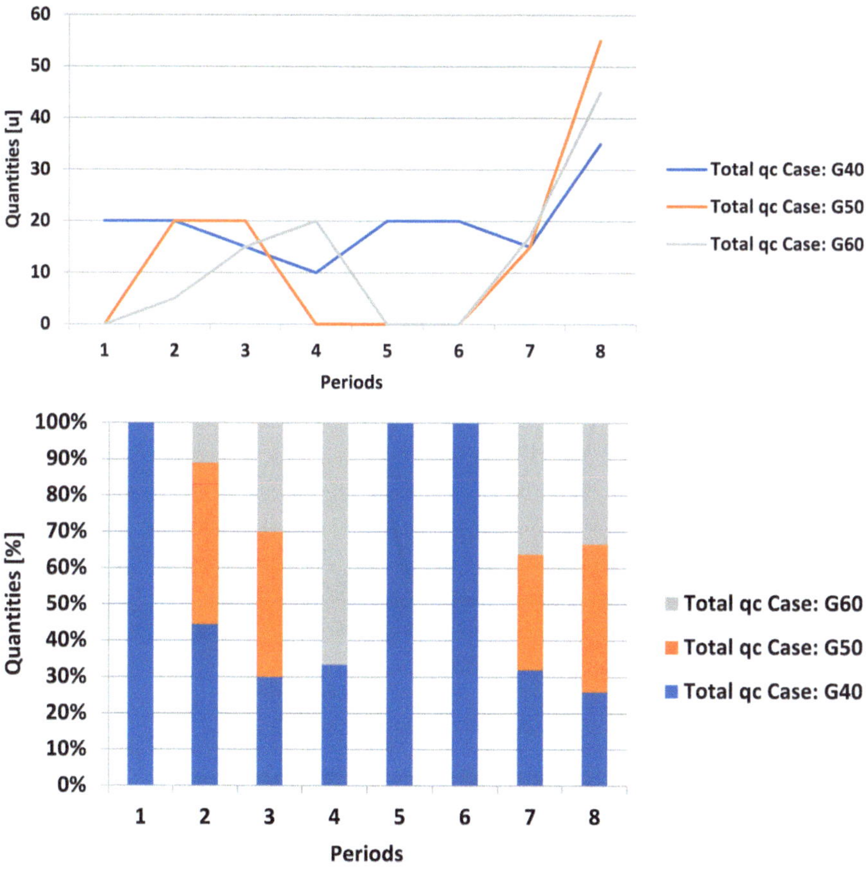

Fig. 9 Evolution of the total collected products for different levels of the HMRS capacity

evaluates its internal capacities and decides on the optimal combination of in-house operations and outsourcing.

5.2.6 Sixth Trial: Effect of the Maximum Amount of Allowed Emissions

The maximum amount of allowed emissions for the manufacturer, often referred to as an emission cap or carbon constraint, can have a substantial impact on decisions

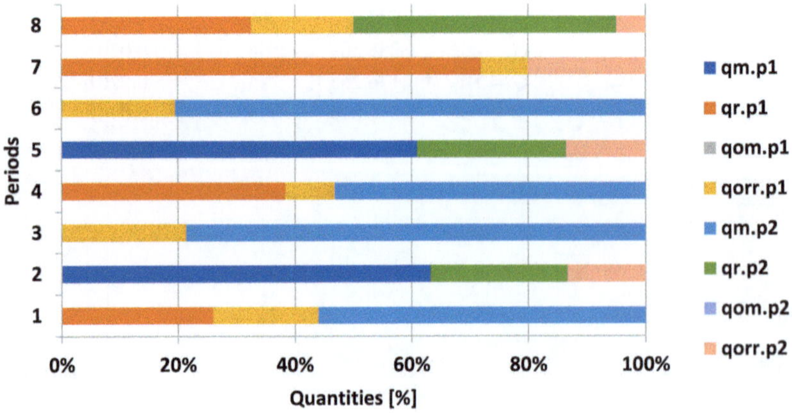

(a1) Percentage contribution of the modes utilization.

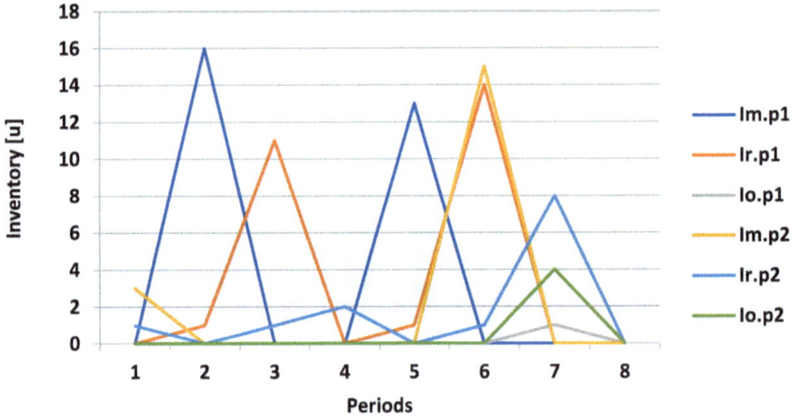

(b1) Evolution over time for different inventories.

Case: Loose system capacity.

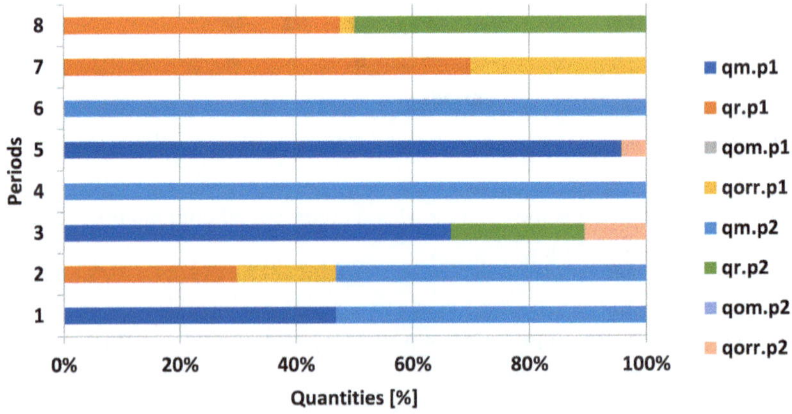

(a2) Percentage contribution of the modes utilization.

Fig. 10 Effect of the HMRS capacity for different levels

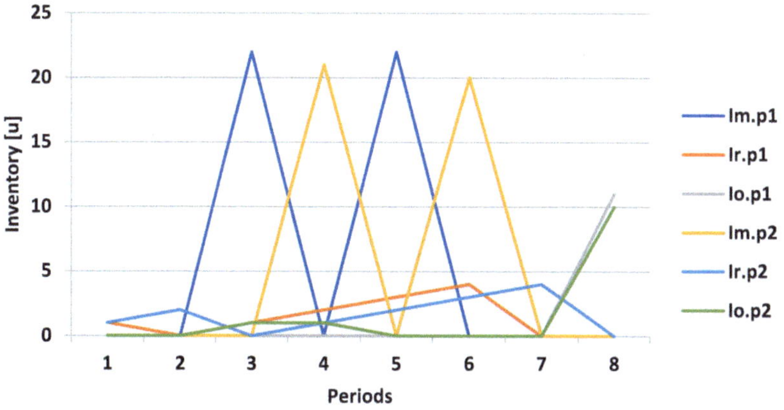

(b2) Evolution over time for different inventories.

Case: Moderate system capacity.

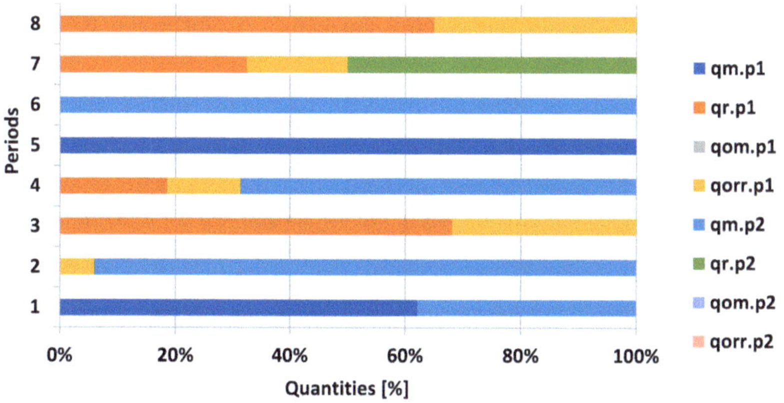

(a3) Percentage contribution of the modes utilization.

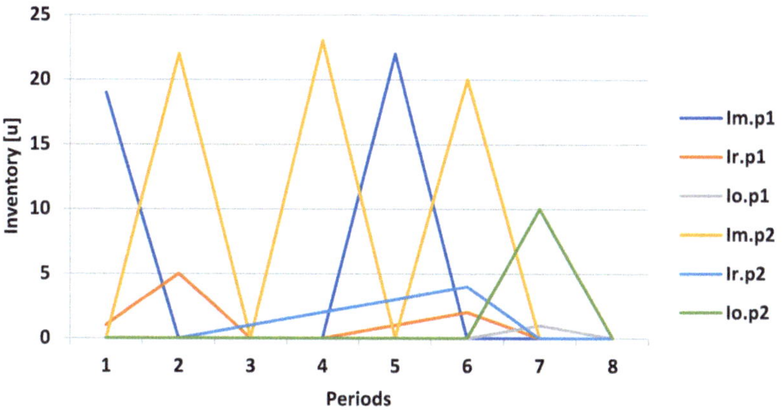

(b3) Evolution over time for different inventories.

Case: Tight system capacity.

Fig. 10 (continued)

Table 15 Effect of the maximum amount of allowed emissions

	CPU	ECE	UNAVs	EVE
$E\max = 2$	54.775	44,919	0.0707	832.1
$E\max = 2.5$	138.021	98,484	0.0675	731
$E\max = 3$	176.265	44,743	0.0701	861.5

related to in-house M/R and outsourcing M/R in supply chain optimization. As environmental sustainability becomes a critical consideration in business operations, including supply chain management, the manufacturer is increasingly constrained by emissions restrictions when making decisions about outsourcing. Table 15 showcases global performance assessments for different levels of the maximum allowed emissions amount.

Three levels of the maximum amount of emissions allowed for HMRS are assumed to be the following states: loose, moderate and tight specifications. The stacked bar chart and the curve in Fig. 11 compare the percentage and the tendency of the total collected products for the loose, moderate and tight level of the maximum amount of emission allowed for the manufacturer.

Additionally, the 100% stacked bar charts in Fig. 12 compare the percentage participation of diverse modes usage for each item in-house M/R and outsourcing M/R. On the other hand, 2D curves are visualized to highlight the trend over time for diverse stocks.

In summary, the maximum amount of emissions allowed for a manufacturer can influence in-house/outsourcing M/R decisions as the manufacturer seeks to align their supply chain operations with environmental sustainability goals and regulatory requirements. Outsourcing to upstream and downstream subcontractors with lower emissions or greener practices is one way the manufacturer can contribute to a more sustainable and eco-friendly supply chain.

5.2.7 Seventh Trial: Effect of Variation in Ordering Costs

For the last three trial sets, several scenarios can be assessed. Thus, we assume that the ordering costs of returns of product 1 are low; however, those of product 2 are considered higher. Also, we take into account the situation where the ordering costs of outsourced manufacturing and remanufacturing of product 1 are high, whereas those of product 2 are considered lower. We adopt the values included within Table 16 for the considered notations.

The 100% stacked bar charts in Figs. 13, 15 and 17 compare the percentage participation of diverse exploitation modes for each item in-house M/R and outsourcing M/R. Curves displayed in Figs. 14, 16 and 18 emphasize the evolution over time periods for diverse stocks, namely serviceable, returned and outsourced inventories.

Table 17 provides the influence of variations occurring at the level of the aforementioned ordering costs.

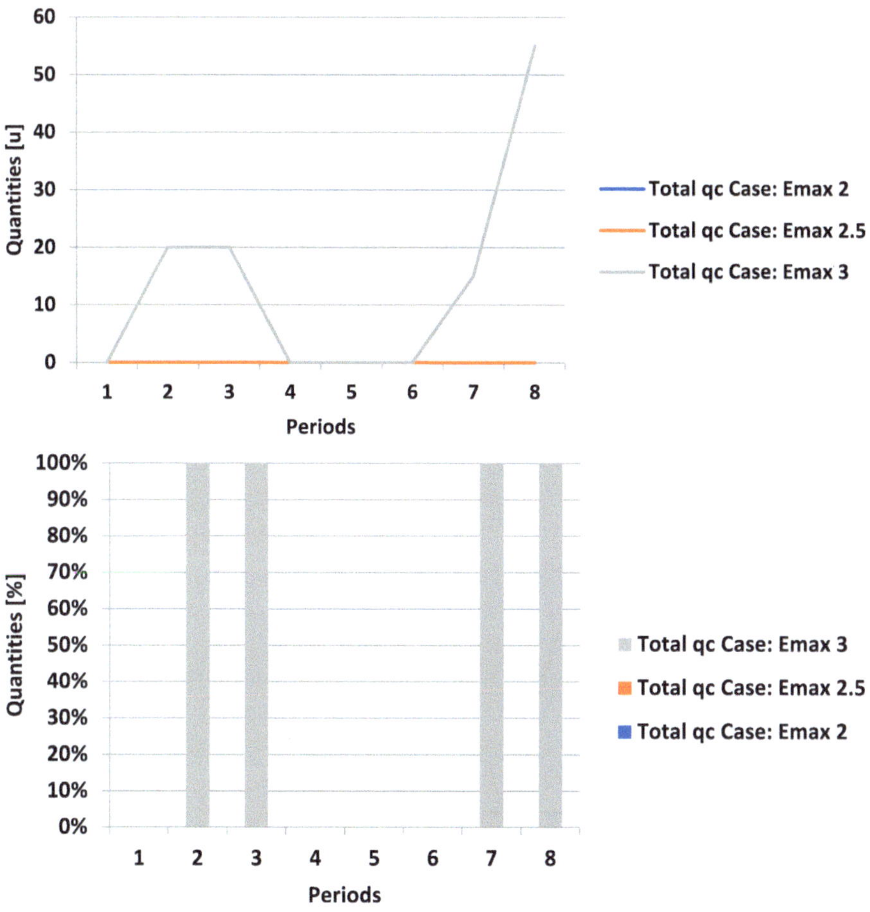

Fig. 11 Evolution of the total collected products for different levels of the maximum amount of allowed emissions

From the realized sensitivity analysis, we can notice that all parameters influence the system's performance. Such impact holds a very complex behavior since it combines the interaction of many correlated variables. This may provide a justification for the lack of studies, as showcased by the research knowledge gap aforementioned at the beginning of this chapter.

6 Conclusion and Future Research Directions

This chapter underscored the pivotal role of outsourcing in enhancing the efficiency of supply chain management. Hence, it is worth elaborating on an integrated strategy for handling constraints originating from distinct sources. To reach this goal,

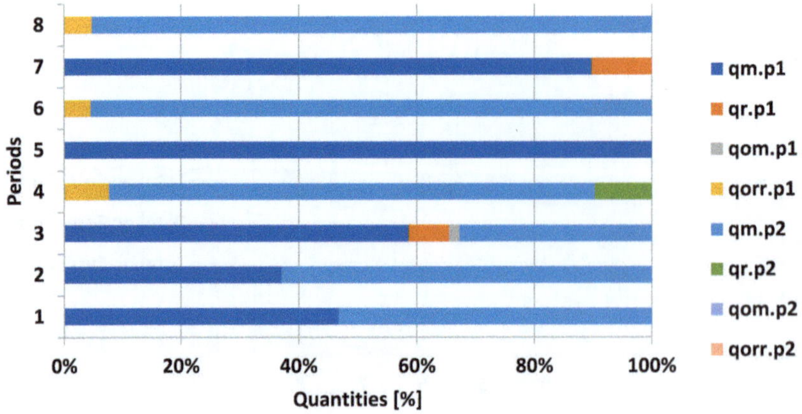

(a1) Percentage contribution of the modes utilization.

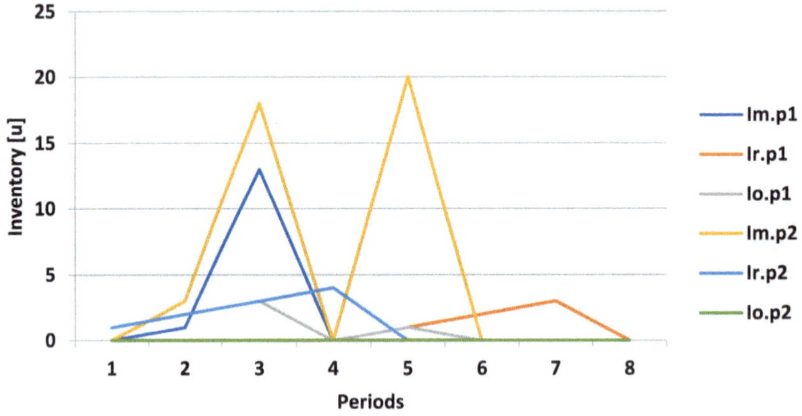

(b1) Evolution over time for different inventories.

Case: Tight maximum amount of allowed emissions.

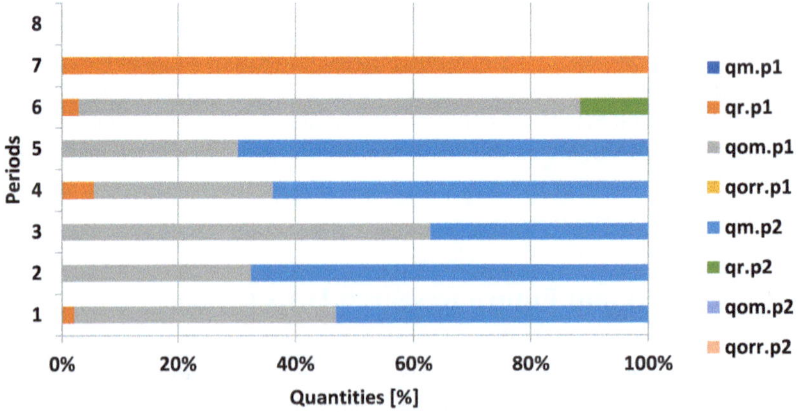

(a2) Percentage contribution of the modes utilization.

Fig. 12 Effect of the maximum amount of allowed emissions for different levels

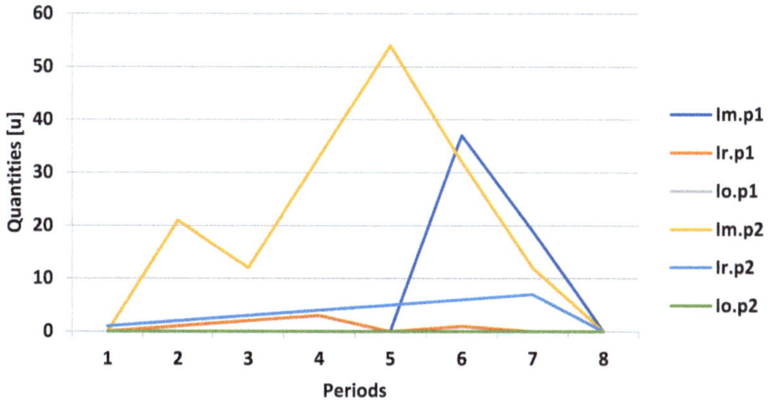

(b2) Evolution over time for different inventories.
Case: Moderate maximum amount of allowed emissions.

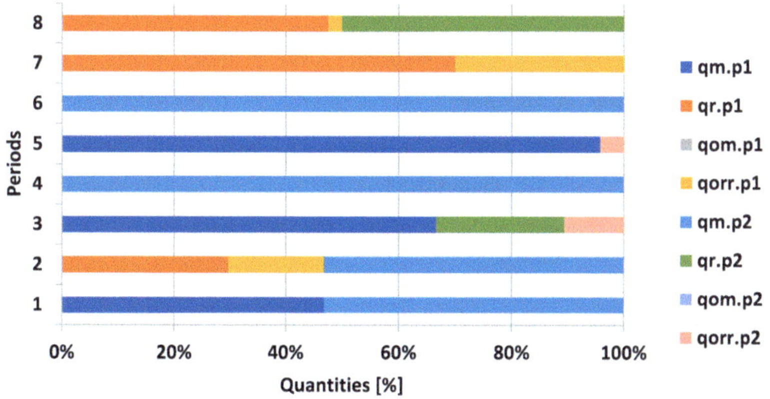

(a3) Percentage contribution of the modes utilization.

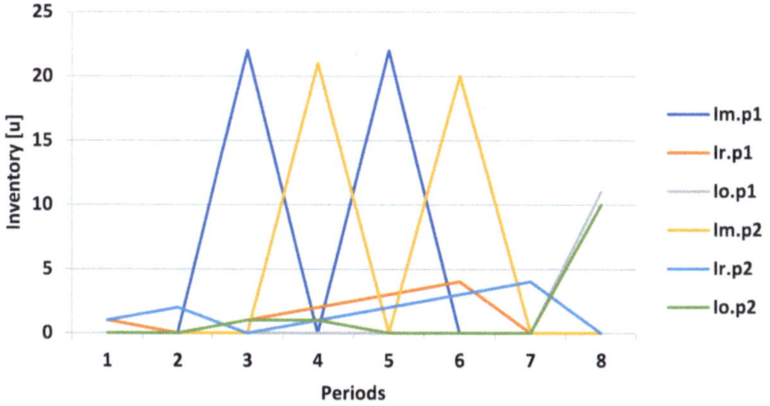

(b3) Evolution over time for different inventories.
Case: Loose maximum amount of allowed emissions.

Fig. 12 (continued)

Table 16 Considered scenarios of ordering costs

Cost/Unit		$o^{c}_{p,t,l}$			$o^{om}_{p,t,s}$				$o^{or}_{p,t,s}$			
Actor		1	2	3	1	2	3	4	1	2	3	4
p	1	4	3	2	470	380	385	475	220	230	235	225
	2	40	30	20	70	80	85	75	20	30	35	25

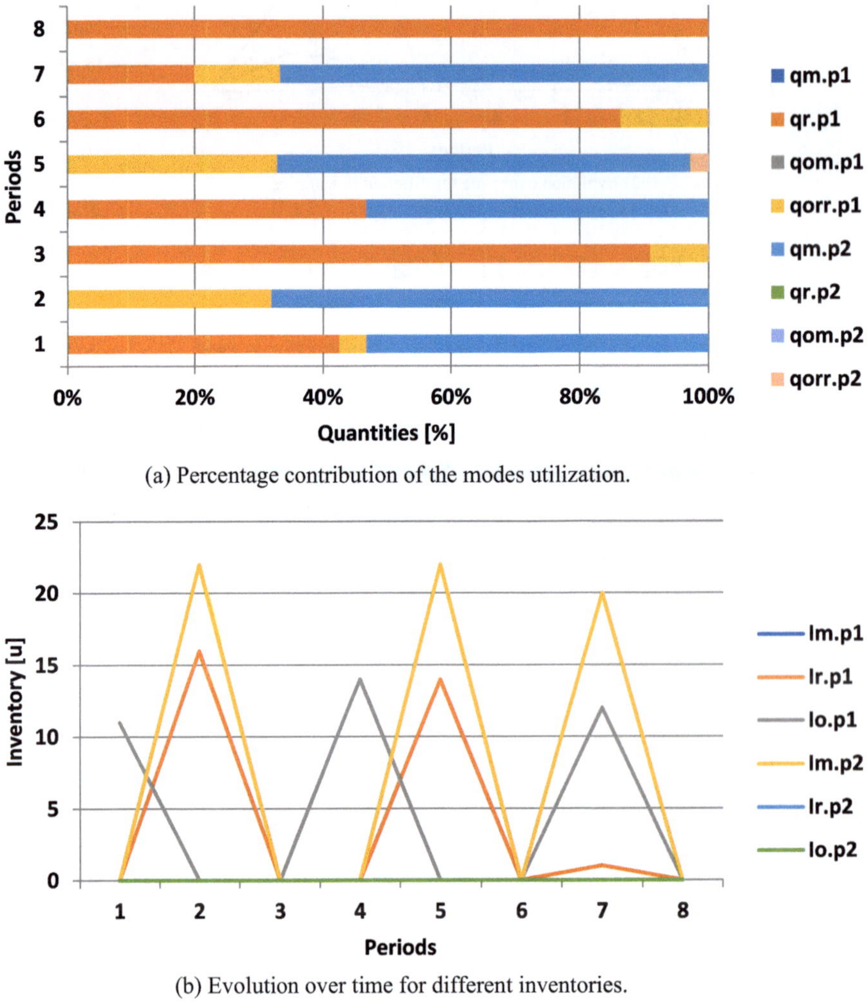

Fig. 13 Effect of variation in ordering cost of returns. (**a**) Percentage contribution of the mode utilization. (**b**) Evolution over time for different inventories

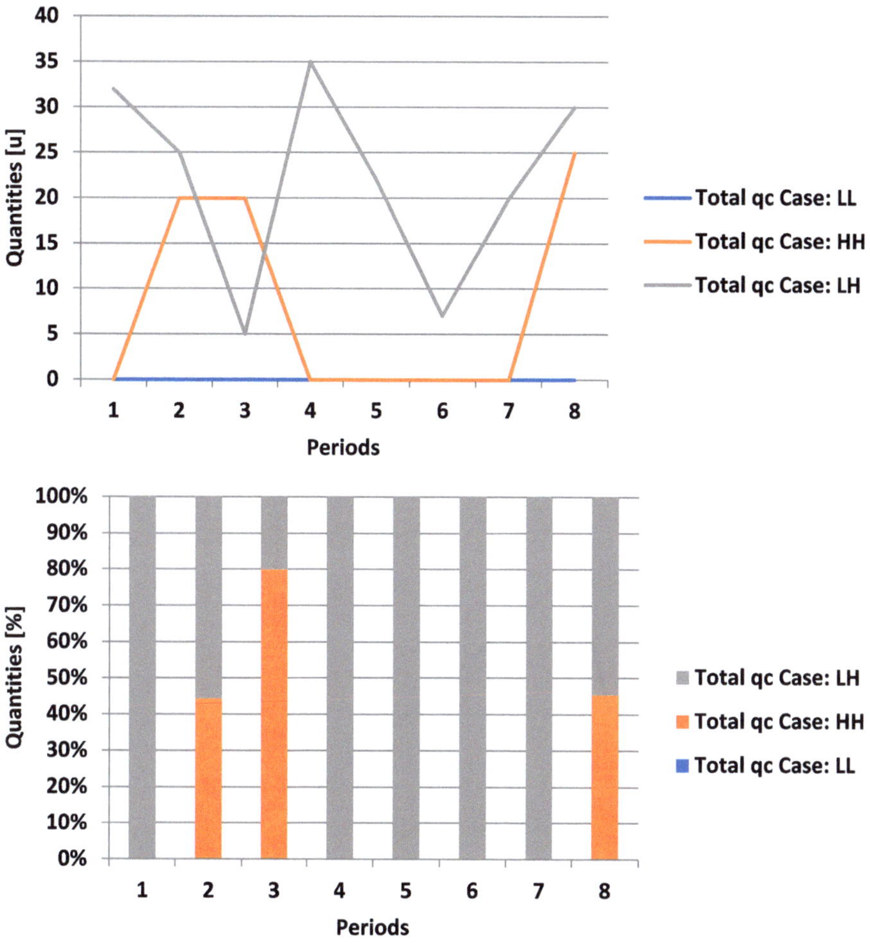

Fig. 14 Effect of variation in ordering cost of outsourced manufacturing. (**a**) Percentage contribution of the mode utilization. (**b**) Evolution over time for different inventories

outsourcing was explored in a product supply chain featuring a single manufacturer with a unique machine subject to random failures necessitating immediate minimal repair. In addition, imperfect PM operations were scheduled to reduce the risk of failure occurrence. A multi-objective mathematical formulation was proposed to account for integrated maintenance/environment-based constraints jointly with outsourcing in both forward and reverse supply chains. In this context, the manufacturer seeks a combined plan to minimize overall economic costs, carbon emissions, and system unavailability. The presented model was solved utilizing the CPLEX solver. Extensive computational experiments were performed to explore the effect of the integrated outsourcing strategy with the consideration of carbon footprints produced by novel and remanufactured items. It is revealed that the

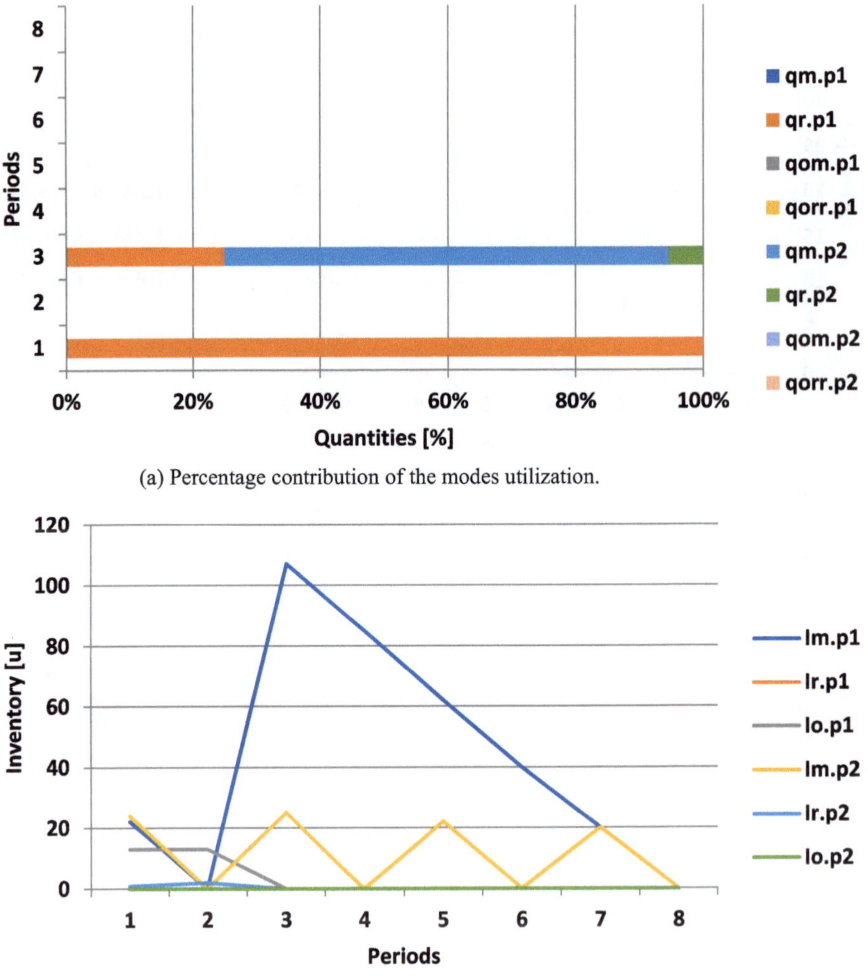

(a) Percentage contribution of the modes utilization.

(b) Evolution over time for different inventories.

Fig. 15 Effect of variation in ordering cost of outsourced remanufacturing. (**a**) Percentage contribution of the mode utilization. (**b**) Evolution over time for different inventories

obtained findings are in good agreement with the mandatory role of integrated outsourcing in yielding significant benefits for demand reduction in terms of new products or substantial resource savings.

For future research directions, exploring the dynamic aspects of outsourcing strategies and their adaptability to evolving market conditions could provide valuable insights. Additionally, shedding light on the quality of returned products in multi-stage systems would contribute to a more comprehensive understanding of the subject. Moreover, it is possible to include uncertain parameters within the outsourcing framework.

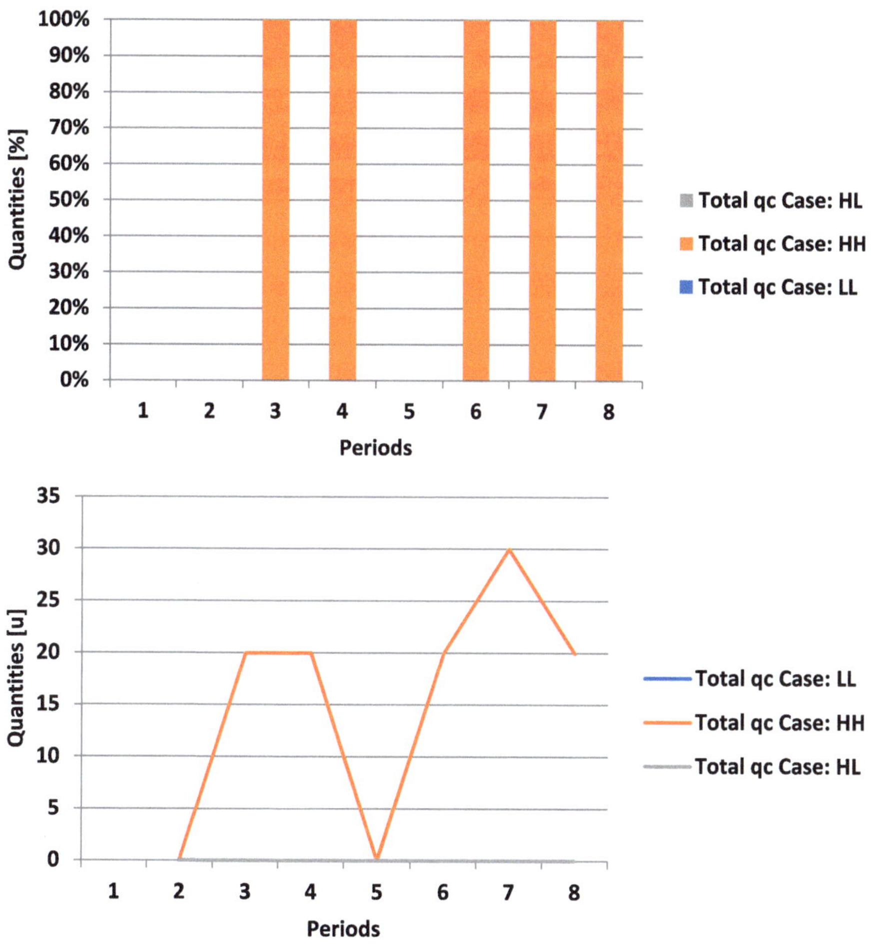

Fig. 16 Evolution of the total collected products for ordering cost of returns variation

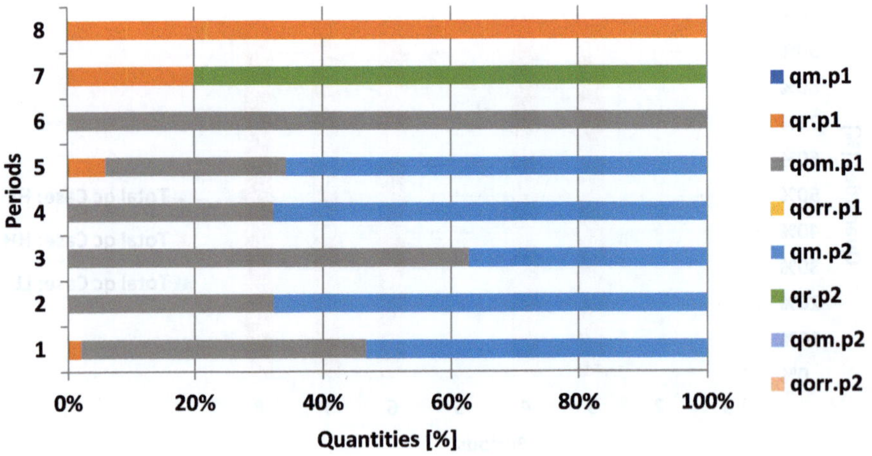

(a) Percentage contribution of the modes utilization.

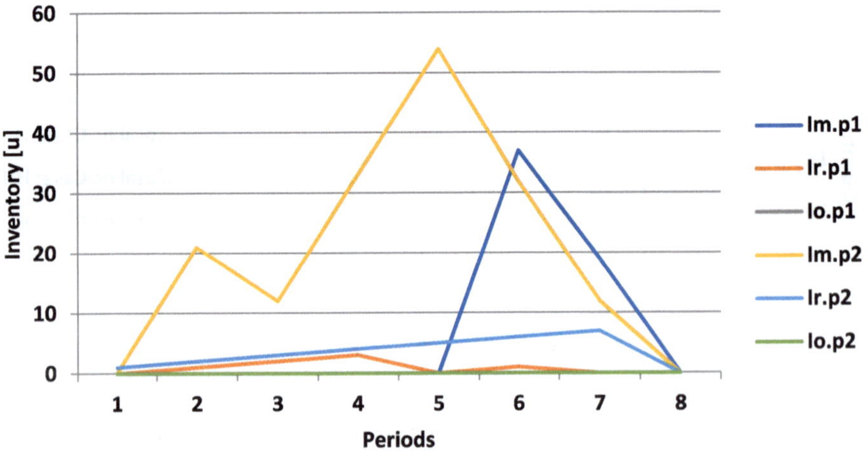

(b) Evolution over time for different inventories.

Fig. 17 Evolution of the total collected products for ordering cost of outsourced manufacturing variation

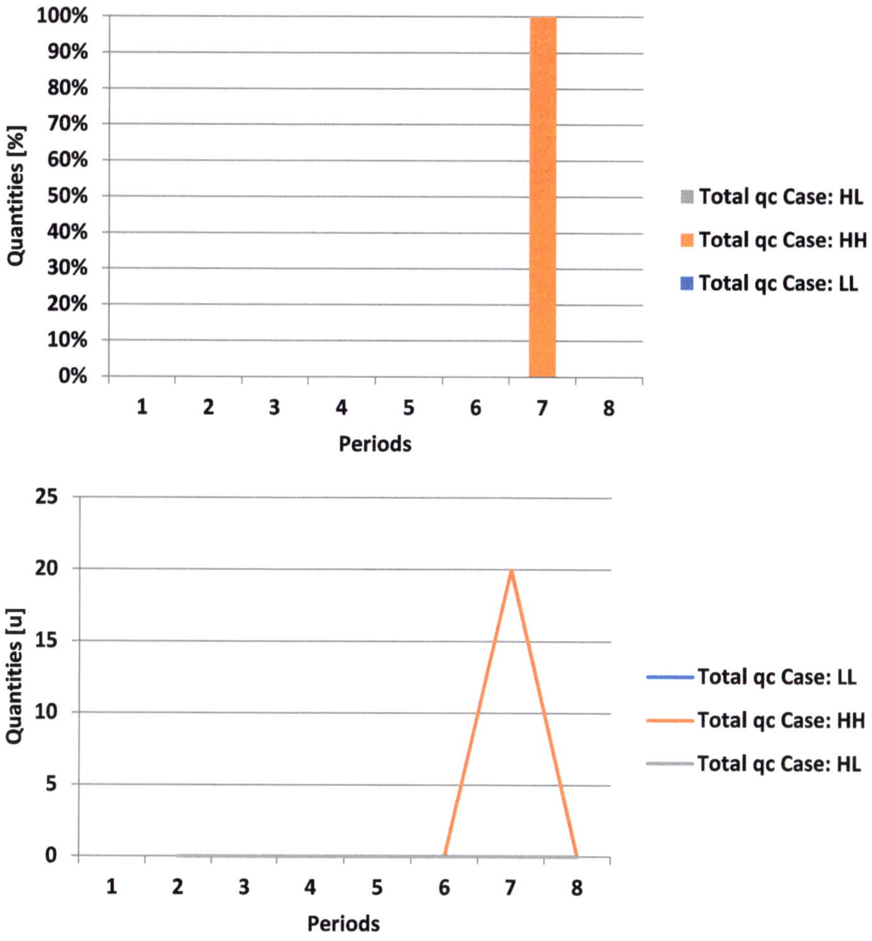

Fig. 18 Evolution of the total collected products for ordering cost of outsourced remanufacturing variation

Table 17 Effect of variation in ordering costs

	CPU			ECE			UNAVs			EVE		
	c	*om*	*or*	*c*	*om*	*or*	*c*	*om*	*or*	*c*	*om*	*or*
LH	–	24.82	80.48	45,039	112,678	98,484	0.0737	0.0675	0.0678	857.7	843	731
LH	131.153	–	–	43,943	–	–	0.0711	–	–	832.2	–	–

References

Absi, N., Dauzère-Pérès, S., Kedad-Sidhoum, S., Penz, B., & Rapine, C. (2013). Lot sizing with carbon emission constraints. *European Journal of Operational Research, 227*(1), 55–61.

Alegoz, M., Kaya, O., & Bayindir, Z. P. (2021). A comparison of pure manufacturing and hybrid manufacturing–remanufacturing systems under carbon tax policy. *European Journal of Operational Research, 294*(1), 161–173.

Amin, S. H., & Zhang, G. (2013). A three-stage model for closed-loop supply chain configuration under uncertainty. *International Journal of Production Research, 51*(5), 1405–1425.

Assid, M., Gharbi, A., & Hajji, A. (2020). Production control of failure-prone manufacturing-remanufacturing systems using mixed dedicated and shared facilities. *International Journal of Production Economics, 224*, 107549.

Assid, M., Gharbi, A., & Hajji, A. (2023). Control policies of changeable manufacturing-remanufacturing systems using two failure-prone production facilities. *International Journal of Advanced Manufacturing Technologies, 125*, 279–297.

Belhocine, L., Dahane, M., & Yagouni, M. (2021). Customer behavior-based multi-objective approach for the recovery and remanufacturing of used products: Application to smartphone reconditioning process. *International Journal of Advanced Manufacturing Technology, 117*, 125–146.

Climate transparency report 2021: Comparing G20 climate action towards net zero. (2021). Climate Transparency.

Dahane, M., Dellagi, S., Clementz, C., & Rezg, N. (2011). Development of joint maintenance and production strategies in a subcontracting environment. *International Journal of Production Research, 49*(23), 1–25.

Dahane, M., Sahnoun, M., Bettayeb, B., Baudry, D., & Boudhar, H. (2017). Impact of spare parts remanufacturing on the operation and maintenance performance of offshore wind turbines: A multi-agent approach. *Journal of Intelligent Manufacturing, 28*, 1531–1549.

Deng, S., Deng, H. X., Chen, H., & Qin, Z. (2024). Estimating fossil CO2 emissions from COVID-19 post-pandemic recovery in G20: A machine learning approach. *Journal of Cleaner Production, 140875*, 140875.

Friedlingstein, P., et al. (2022). Global carbon budget 2021. *Earth System Science Data, 14*(4), 1917–2005.

Ghassemi, A., Asl-Najafi, J., & Yaghoubi, S. (2018). A dynamic bi-objective closed-loop supply chain network design considering supplier selection and remanufacturer subcontractors. *Uncertain Supply Chain Management, 6*(2), 117–134.

Haoues, M., Dahane, M., Mouss, N. K., & Rezg, N. (2012). Integrated maintenance problem in two-stage supply chain coordination with an outsourcing option. In *Proceedings of the 42st International Conference on Computers & Industrial Engineering, Cie & Saiie, Cape Town, South Africa, 16–18 July* (pp. 937–951).

Haoues, M., Dahane, M., & Mouss, N. K. (2019). Outsourcing optimization in two-echelon supply chain network under integrated production-maintenance constraints. *Journal of Intelligent Manufacturing, 30*, 701–725.

Haoues, M., Dahane, M., & Mouss, K. N. (2021). Capacity planning with outsourcing opportunities under reliability and maintenance constraints. *International Journal of Industrial and Systems Engineering, 37*(3), 382–409.

Haoues, M., Merghem, M., Bentrcia, T., & Dahane, M. (2023). Integrated planning for a hybrid manufacturing-remanufacturing system: A multi-objective/fuzzy-satisfying combined approach. In *International Conference on Decision Aid Sciences and Applications (DASA)* (pp. 175–179).

Harris, R. S., Ijomah, W. L., & Windmill, J. F. C. (2023). Evaluation and validation of Damage Assessment Tracking Criteria models within the sector of UK automotive remanufacturing. *Journal of Cleaner Production, 414*, 137494.

Kim, K., Song, I., Kim, J., & Jeong, B. (2006). Supply planning model for remanufacturing system in reverse logistics environment. *Computers & Industrial Engineering, 51*(2), 279–287.

Lahmar, H., Dahane, M., Mouss, N. K., & Haoues, M. (2022a). Production planning optimization in a sustainable hybrid manufacturing remanufacturing production system. *Procedia Computer Science, 200*, 1244–1253.

Lahmar, H., Dahane, M., Mouss, N. K., & Haoues, M. (2022b). Multi-objective production planning of new and remanufactured products in hybrid production system. *IFAC-Papers on Line, 55*(10), 275–280.

Lee, K., & Choi, B. C. (2011). Two-stage production scheduling with an outsourcing option. *European Journal of Operational Research, 213*(3), 489–497.

Marler, R. T., & Arora, J. S. (2010). The weighted sum method for multi-objective optimization: New insights. *Structural and Multidisciplinary Optimization, 41*, 853–862.

Merchante, L. F. S., Clar, D., Carnicero, A., Lopez-Valdes, F. J., & Jimenez-Octavio, J. R. (2021). Real-time CO2 emissions estimation in Spain and application to the COVID-19 pandemic. *Journal of Cleaner Production, 296*, 126425.

Merghem, M., Haoues, M., Mouss, K. N., Dahane, M., & Senoussi, A. (2023). Integrated production and maintenance planning in hybrid manufacturing-remanufacturing system with outsourcing opportunities. *Procedia Computer Science, 217*, 1487–1496.

Mishra, M., Hota, S. K., Ghosh, S. K., & Sarkar, B. (2020). Controlling waste and carbon emission for a sustainable closed-loop supply chain management under a cap-and-trade strategy. *Mathematics, 8*(4), 466.

Ndhaief, N., Rezg, N., Hajji, A., & Bistorin, O. (2020). Environmental issue in an integrated production and maintenance control of unreliable manufacturing/remanufacturing systems. *International Journal of Production Research, 58*(14), 4182–4200.

Ouaret, S., Kenné, J.-P., & Gharbi, A. (2019). Production and replacement planning of a deteriorating remanufacturing system in a closed-loop configuration. *Journal of Manufacturing Systems, 53*, 234–248.

Polotski, V., Kenné, J.-P., & Gharbi, A. (2019a). Production control of hybrid manufacturing–remanufacturing systems under demand and return variations. *International Journal of Production Research, 57*(1), 100–123.

Polotski, V., Kenné, J.-P., & Gharbi, A. (2019b). Joint production and maintenance optimization in flexible hybrid manufacturing–remanufacturing systems under age-dependent deterioration. *International Journal of Production Economics, 216*, 239–254.

Soroudi, A. (2017). *Power system optimization modeling in GAMS*. Springer.

Wang, N., He, Z., Sun, J., Xie, H., & Shi, W. (2011). A single-item uncapacitated lot-sizing problem with remanufacturing and outsourcing. *Procedia Engineering, 15*, 5170–5178.

Wang, Q., Lu, M., Bai, Z., & Wang, K. (2020). Coronavirus pandemic reduced China's CO2 emissions in short-term, while stimulus packages may lead to emissions growth in medium- and long-term. *Applied Energy, 278*, 115735.

Zhao, S., Wang, L., & Zheng, Y. (2014). Integrating production planning and maintenance: An iterative method. *Industrial Management & Data Systems, 114*(2), 162–182.

Zouadi, T., Yalaoui, A., & Reghioui, R. (2018). Hybrid manufacturing/remanufacturing lot-sizing and supplier selection with returns, under carbon emission constraint. *International Journal of Production Research, 56*(3), 1233–1248.

Outsourcing Security in Authoritarian States: Context Sensitivity and the Nodal-Network Framework of Analysis

Engy Moussa

1 Introduction

The continuous expansion of the private security industry, comprising its military and guarding facets, has grown integral to the domestic provision of security services, international security governance and global politics. In the United States of America, the market size of the security services industry in 2023 exceeded 48 billion U.S. dollars (Statista Research Department, 2023), while in the United Kingdom, the market in 2023 encompassed over 10,300 security industry enterprises (Clark, 2023), with the leading company achieving a revenue of approximately 935 million British pounds (Statista Research Department, 2024). The global growth of the private security industry is however far from uniform with wide discrepancies across cases based on where the privatization of security occurs and for what purposes.

In a similar fashion, the literature on the privatization of security is wide-ranging and continuously evolving. It approaches the subject from various angles and offers numerous perspectives on how to comprehend this phenomenon and how to study and evaluate its contemporary manifestations in different countries. Particularly relevant to this chapter is the discussion within this rich literature concerning the three following themes: the relationship between the private security industry and the modern state's monopoly on the means of violence; the traditional versus critical approaches to the processes of outsourcing security; and lastly, the analytical frameworks that are used to study this phenomenon in authoritarian states.

Echoing critical security studies, this chapter affirms the need to closely examine the globally expanding processes of privatizing security, particularly some authoritarian states' decision to outsource the public provision of security. In this vein, the

E. Moussa (✉)
Department of Politics and International Studies, Cambridge University, Cambridge, UK

F. P. García Márquez et al. (eds.), *Outsourcing Using Operations Research and Management Science Methods*, International Series in Operations Research & Management Science 366, https://doi.org/10.1007/978-3-031-91845-2_6

chapter addresses two main questions. First, why do states outsource security, and what are the effects on the state's monopoly over the means of violence and on the relationship between the state and the citizenry? Second, what analytical models or frameworks are most suitable to investigate the privatization and outsourcing of security in authoritarian states? By exploring these questions, this chapter contributes to the growing research on outsourcing security by highlighting the complexities attached to this phenomenon in authoritarian states and proposing an analytical framework that effectively captures these complexities and enables in-depth study that is chiefly informed by the context and specificities of the studied cases.

Toward this end, the chapter starts by briefly tracing the origins of the modern state's monopoly over the means of violence and how it was impacted by the contemporary rise of the private security industry. Next, the chapter discusses some of the traditional approaches to the privatization of security, which are largely linked to the discourse of strong states versus weak states. Seeing the limitations of the traditional approaches, the chapter proceeds to present some of the critical approaches to outsourcing security, particularly highlighting the latter's revisionist views on the public-private dichotomy within the security market, the state-security relationship, and the traditional understanding of the state. This critical section eventually lays the ground for proposing the nodal-network framework of analysis as highly suitable for the study of outsourcing security in contemporary authoritarian states and beyond.

2 Private Security and States Monopoly on Violence

The concept of "security" has, for centuries, been tidily linked to the "modern state." States are traditionally perceived as the sole political actors or entity that possess an uncontested claim over the monopoly of the "legitimate" use of violence. This characteristic of the modern state is captured in Max Weber's (2010, 310–311) famous definition of the state as "a human community which (successfully) lays claim to the monopoly of legitimate physical violence within a certain territory." It is noteworthy that Weber's definition doesn't attribute the monopoly over the means of violence to the "state" but rather to the human community—the association of people forming the state—who "creates monopoly of legitimate coercion in a given geographical area" (Runciman, 2003, 29).

Long before Weber, the idea of the state monopoly over the means of violence finds an earlier niche in Thomas Hobbes' theory of the social contract. In the *Leviathan*, Hobbes asserts that the only prospect to end the state of nature, where continuous war and fear threaten the very existence of humankind, is the establishment of states. States represent the outcome of a social contract where "to become" citizens mutually agree to forfeit their natural right to exercise any form of violence, except in rare, life-threatening circumstances. Subsequently, the established state—the "sovereign"—embraces the responsibility of guaranteeing security and a livelihood of prosperity for all citizens.

According to Elke Krahmann (2009, 2), Hobbes' social control theory depicts the prohibition of the private use of violence as a prerequisite for, but equally a natural outcome of, the state's control of the legitimate use of violence. The public nature of protection, or security as a public good, is thus widely perceived as "among the most important constitutive principles of the modern state and conceptions of sovereignty, and one of the key markers and tests of legitimacy in modern politics" (Abrahamsen & Williams, 2011, 7).

Historically, the state's monopoly over the means of violence undoubtedly played a fundamental role in the emergence of the (Western) modern states. In studying the impact of war-making on the rise of modern European states, Charles Tilly (1990) traced a historical trajectory where continuous wars between European monarchs constituted a catalyst for state-building, marked by the creation of national armies and the imposition of state monopoly over the means of violence. At large, state control over the provision of domestic security proved eventually crucial for state formation and continuity through the abolition of the unregulated use of violence by private entities and individuals. This monopoly progressively evolved to manifest in "the capabilities and legitimization for the centralization of armed force within the institutions of the modern democratic nation-state such as the public police and national armed forces" (Krahmann, 2009, 2).

The modern state's monopoly over the means of violence within a state's own territory equally grew from a sign of state sovereignty into an established international norm. However, the Westphalian ideal of sovereign states with full control over the means of violence is rarely, if at all, found in contemporary politics, regardless of the political system or geographical location examined. For the last few decades, the private security industry has played an increasingly prevailing role in most countries within the private and public sectors alike. The private security industry largely encompasses two main types of companies: private security companies and private military companies. Private military companies are "specialized in military skills, including combat operations, strategic planning, intelligence collection, operational support, logistics, training, procurement and maintenance of arms and equipment" (Schreier & Caparini, 2005, 2).

The private security companies, on the other hand, represent "profit-driven organizations that trade in professional services linked to internal security and protection" (Schreier & Caparini, 2005, 26). The domestic activities of private security companies run across different security domains, including guarding, electronic security, sensor and surveillance, and investigation and risk management, in addition to private intelligence services (Schreier & Caparini, 2005, 27). While an increasing number of companies defy this functional distinction by acting simultaneously as private military and private security companies, the distinction remains useful to effectively analyse the different roles played by individual companies and the nature of their relationship to other actors within the security market.[1]

[1] "Security market" is used in this chapter to substitute for the state-centric "security sector." Unlike the security sector, a security market captures the growing commodification of security and its

The rise of the private security industry, as a contemporary worldwide phenomenon, mirrors profound changes in the global security environment. These included the widespread consolidation of the neo-liberal model of government, the fall of the Soviet Union in December 1991, and a significant increase in inter-state and intra-state wars erupting predominantly in "Third World" countries. In particular, the end of the Cold War impelled "massive reductions in the size of the armed forces on both sides of the Atlantic," which created an abundance of ex-military personnel who found a niche in the private security industry (Krahmann, 2009, 16). The strong emergence of private security companies over the last few decades introduced a set of domestic policies as different countries sought to regulate the expanding industry.

In the meantime, Krahmann (2009) argues that the international understanding of the norm of state monopoly over the means of violence has witnessed a fundamental shift, specifically in respect to the scope and manifestation of this monopoly. Instead of adopting a comprehensive and active monopoly over the means of violence, including its normative and physical display, the norm of state monopoly over the means of violence is currently perceived within the international community of states as largely limited to its legal and regulatory manifestations—a "legal control of the actors who wield armed force to protect others" (Krahmann, 2009, 9).

3 Why Do States Outsource Security?

Privatizing state security functions—outsourcing security—entails a practice whereby "private actors are called upon to take on (supposedly) public functions; and private-sector methods and market mechanisms such as profit and competition are introduced into parts of the public sector dealing with issues such as national security and policing" (Berndtsson, 2009, 9). The nature and scope of the state functions which are being privatized, vary massively across countries, involving many actors and featuring highly dynamic and evolving procedures. In principle, outsourcing security entails the state transferring the ownership of some public security services to a private entity (Westermeyer, 2013, 70). By virtue of being "the contracting agency and initially 'in possession' of the service, the state controls how much ownership it transfers and may set the rules as the contracting agency" (Westermeyer, 2013, 70). In the case of public-private security partnerships, the state shares ownership with, rather than fully transferring to, private actors. Under this co-governance model, the partnerships' shareholdership is managed either by the state or the private entity (Westermeyer, 2013, 70).

---

exchange outside comprehensive state control. It underscores the sector's volatility as the number, identities and activities of its actors continuously evolve; and it stresses the market rationality that increasingly guides public and private security agents. A market perspective also enriches security analyses by contesting the traditional security sector's rigid boundaries and accounting for outsiders, including non-security state actors and ordinary citizens, who interact and influence the security arena.

With respect to why states outsource security, the dominant approach in the security literature follows a functional economic logic and is generally embedded in broader discourses, including "the strong versus weak states." Deborah Avant has written extensively on the contemporary re-emergence of the private security industry, primarily examining the use of private military companies by and within strong and weak states. Taking a comparative approach, Avant (2005) identifies a state's capacity as the crucial variable to understand and evaluate the privatization of security in any given country. State capacity, Avant explains, encompasses three forms of state control: social—reflecting a state's ability to reconcile social values and internal law with the deployment of force; political—"the subjection of the use of force to political or civilian rules and decisions;" and functional—captured in the abilities and effectiveness of the military apparatus (Westermeyer, 2013, 27).

In light of the quick and considerable developments affecting the market for security services, states' control over the means of violence is heavily undermined as many states struggle to develop "a strategy that maximizes all dimensions of control at once" (Avant, 2007, 419). Eventually, managing the security market entails strategies where "individual states find themselves making trade-offs between different elements of control" (Avant, 2007, 419).

In reference to efficient or strong states—depicted as coherent, capable and legitimate (Avant, 2008, 441)—the logic for outsourcing security centres on achieving maximized flexibility, cost-efficiency and enhanced quality. This economic rationale that motivates the outsourcing of security is commonly described as "a direct result of the application of neo-liberal principles to domestic and international security" (Krahmann, 2009, 16). It particularly reflects neo-liberalism's "preference for the small state, free market and maximizing consumer choice" (Krahmann, 2009, 16). Indeed, the rise of neo-liberalism in many countries coincided with a decline in state investment in public services during the 1970s and 1980s. However, as studies later showed, many states, including Britain and the United States of America, actually increased their investment in public policing over this same period (White, 2011, 87).

Considering their advanced capacities and substantive level of control, strong states are generally perceived as equipped to regulate and effectively monitor the private security industry. Nonetheless, Caroline Holmqvist (2005) still identifies four areas of concern with respect to outsourcing security by efficient states. These concerns include establishing clear mandates, ensuring the accountability of private security companies, managing "oversight and control in a skewed market," and achieving "basic and practical coordination of efforts both among private actors and between the private security companies and regular forces" (Holmqvist, 2005, 25).

In a similar vein, the functional economic approach, which seems to largely normalize the privatization of security in strong states, faces intense criticism from academics like Paul Verkuil (2007), who rejects conceiving the field of security just like any other sector affected by state privatization. Specifically, Verkuil, who embraces the traditional view of security as an inherent state function that is closely tied to notions of sovereignty and democratic values, warns of the privatization of security being translated into a loss of sovereignty and a threat to democracy.

Interestingly, even in strong states that are considered non-democratic, the risk of some private security companies escaping the control of the state has attracted considerable attention in recent years, particularly following the short-lived mutiny in June 2023 of the Wagner Group—a Russian private military company that was deployed by the Russian regime to support its military operations in Ukraine, Syria and other places (Schmitt, 2023; Watling et al., 2024).

With respect to weak or fragile states, traditional studies on the privatization of security have regularly framed outsourcing security as the outcome of state incapacity or failure to provide security to its citizens because of inadequate administrative and physical resources. In the meantime, with fragile administrative capabilities, weak states are presumed to fail in properly monitoring the activities of private security and military companies, which can lead to "further fragmentation of authority at the same time that it enhances the power of external actors—whether these be foreign states or private capital—to the detriment of local interests" (Hansen, 2008, 586).

By contrast, many studies highlight a range of benefits that the private security industry brings to weak states. These benefits include supporting these states "to build and defend their territories, institutions, and populations by providing outside resources and transferring skills from countries with more efficient security and military systems" (Hansen, 2008, 586). Nevertheless, the academic proponents of the private security industry still acknowledge the risks attached to the extensive reliance on the private provision of security in weak states. These risks include the creation of a short-term false image of security, having "a skewed distribution of security among populations, and crowding out the establishment of legitimate and functioning state institutions" (Holmqvist, 2005, 12).

While not commonly viewed as a weak state, Tunisia, who faced considerable political and security challenges in the aftermath of the 2010–2011 uprising, offers useful insights into the aforementioned dilemma. In brief, once Zine El Abidine Ben Ali, the former president of Tunisia, was forced out of power in early 2011, the country experienced a strong wave of foreign donors and funding entities who rushed to propose initiatives for security sector reform to the Tunisian authorities. Many of the security reform projects subsequently pursued by the Tunisian state, in collaboration with foreign governments and international agencies, have involved numerous cases of outsourcing to non-state and private security actors (Moussa, 2021, 95).

On the one hand, the internationally sponsored security reform programs implemented in Tunisia from 2011 onward have led to general improvements in the practices and capabilities of the state security forces, as apparent in the enhanced security situation at Tunisia's borders and across its territory. Particularly, progress was noticed in the cooperation between different state security agencies in the way that they share information and that they currently view security threats from a strategic rather than a tactical point of view (Moussa, 2021, 105). On the other hand, the international approach to state security reform in Tunisia has had serious drawbacks, which have restricted the progress and success of the reform projects. These have included the lack of collaboration among the various parties—

governmental and private—who have contributed to the security reform projects, alongside a general preference for capacity-building training and for enhancing tactical security capabilities at the expense of improving security governance and security-society relations (Maryon, 2023; Moussa, 2021, 164–165).

In sum, the discourse concerning "strong states versus weak states" is well established within the security literature. However, this discourse is increasingly viewed as empirically inaccurate and analytically reductionist. The limits of the discourse regularly appear in studies that examine the diverse cases of outsourcing security, political violence and armed conflicts in many developing and under-developed countries. For example, looking at outsourcing security in some African countries, Holmqvist (2005, 12) asserts,

> State incapacity or failure provides only a part of the story ... The private security sector has contributed to maintaining the status quo of inequitable security distribution in weak states—a pattern not exclusive to Africa.

Similarly, Keith Krause and Jennifer Milliken (2009, 216–17), echoing William Reno (2009), underscore the need to critically treat the categories of weak or failed states by examining "how state institutions actually work to provide public order and security (or not), and how states interact with potential and actual challengers to the state's monopoly on the legitimate use of violence."

4 Critical Approaches to Outsourcing Security

Looking at contemporary security provisions across the globe, it is largely evident that not only are private security actors steadily occupying a substantial domestic and international position, but the relationship between the majority of states and the private security industry is generally collaborative, or at the very least not confrontational. Indeed, defying conventional assumptions, states' legitimacy seems to have remained largely intact in the face of the growth of the private security industry, particularly the expanding practice of outsourcing security. As Fred Schreier and Marina Caparini (2005, 65) remark, many states, mostly in the developing world, "are quietly happy about the emergence of the new privatized military industry, all the more if it is a means to keep demobilized or recently retired soldiers busy." These states perceive unemployed former soldiers as a threat to the state, since these soldiers "possess skills that, if they become disaffected, can make them uniquely dangerous and disruptive" (Schreier & Caparini, 2005, 65). This reality has generated substantive revisions within the security literature with respect to the presumed dichotomy between the public and private sectors, the relationship between the modern state and the provision of security, and the traditional understanding of the state.

The sharp dichotomy between the public and private spheres, as well as between states and non-state actors, which underlines both the historical account and the functional economic approach to the privatization of security, fails to account for the significant power acquired by many private actors, which frequently equates them with state representatives. As Rita Abrahamsen and Michael C. Williams (2011, 57) argue, "in security, as in many other spheres, the public–private distinction, as well as the global–local division, is increasingly unhelpful as a means of grasping contemporary international politics." Likewise, Clare Murphy (2001, 7) views the public-private dichotomy as becoming increasingly blurred as states potentially "retain an enlarged but increasingly rational economic function in developing states, but also as political alliances and contests cross over the divide."

Ultimately, the contemporary privatization of security services defies the public-private dichotomy by engaging in broader transformations in governance and "a complex reconfigurations of state power in which the public and private spheres are increasingly entangled" (Østensen, 2011, 371). Additionally, the public-private dichotomy chiefly misses the influential roles occupied by some state representatives within the private security industry and the critical impact these overlapping affiliations introduce to the relationship between the public provision of security and the private security industry.

In regard to the relationship between the modern state and the provision of security, as discussed earlier, security as a public good and an entitlement for all citizens within a state continues to inform and underpin a considerable segment of the security literature, particularly the scholarship on the privatization of security services. Adherents to this view consider the public nature of protection among the defining features of modern states, closely linked to state sovereignty and legitimacy. In this context, the publicness of security remains fundamental to state-building, constituting a political entitlement for all citizens as part of a social contract with the state. Similarly, Paul Jackson (2011, 1813) asserts, "It is an obligation of the state to provide security for its citizens, not to protect personal regimes."

Extending this approach to the study of the privatization of security, the principles of democratic rule, including transparency and state accountability, continue to influence many scholars as they analyse and evaluate the contemporary rise of the private security industry. As Gloria Westermeyer (2013, 27) accurately notes, "the main concern for political scientists with regard to the privatization of security relates to the effects of private actors on governmental control and democratic norms." While many democracies continuously struggle with these ideals when outsourcing security, these ideals are either absent or highly undermined in authoritarian states. Sharing this view, Abrahamsen and Williams (2011, 113) remark,

> The agents and agencies of state security always possess the potential to pose dangers to the very citizens they claim to protect, and they continue to do so today... The publicness of security should also not conceal the extent to which public force was, and often still is, wielded in support of private or sectional interests under the guise of the public good.

In this light, a traditional democratic-based analysis of outsourcing security appears fundamentally unsuitable to understand authoritarian settings. Instead, investigating the rise of the private security industry in many authoritarian countries requires close attention to (1) the internal dynamics of authoritarian rule, (2) the public mistrust in the state's ability or willingness to provide protection, (3) the fear from the abusive and arbitrary power of the state and its security institutions, and (4) the typical lack of serious and widespread public debate about the repercussions of an expanding privatized violence, especially seeing how many authoritarian states continue to lack a comprehensive legal framework to monitor the activities of the private security industry.

Looking at the case of Egypt in earlier publications, I argued that the sharp rise in the privatization and outsourcing of security since the Egyptian uprising in early 2011 has been largely informed by a living legacy of authoritarian politics, including a massive, but internally fragmented, state security apparatus, and a damaged relationship between the state security institutions and the citizenry. In short, the 2011 uprising initially created a public environment of chaos and insecurity, where temporarily missing and generally dysfunctional policing went hand in hand with the growth of the private security industry, as private security actors, including formal private security companies and hired thugs, rushed to fill the security vacuum (Carr, 2013; Sayigh, 2016). Notwithstanding the gradual return of the police forces to their duties as the momentum of the uprising declined, the public sentiment of insecurity hardly improved because the public trust in the competence of the state security forces had been heavily compromised.

On the one hand, for many ordinary citizens and business actors, using private security companies has been an unavoidable solution to a crisis of competence and trust in the state security forces. For others, private security companies seem less corrupt, more efficient and relatively neutral within a large political struggle between the citizenry and the state security forces, whose prime objective has consistently been to protect the regime through exercising widespread oppression. In this regard, relying on private security companies, instead of requesting the services of the state security forces, reflects how many local businesses and international companies sought to avoid the risk of falling into this political struggle and being subsequently harmed (Moussa, 2021, 120). On the other hand, a close examination of the Egyptian regime's increasing resort to outsourcing security, particularly after the 2013 coup d'état, reveals the centrality of regime security and regime interest in directing this phenomenon.

For example, seeing the Egyptian regime's struggle to mitigate a loose control over the state security institutions, which is integral to the security and sustainability of the regime, outsourcing security to carefully selected private security companies seems to offer a parallel source of protection for the regime and the country's president (Moussa, 2021, 145–146). Moreover, outsourcing security effectively enhances the regime's interests by generating substantial economic benefits for different members of the regime and their affiliates, in addition to alleviating widespread economic hardships by offering employment to a great number of people, as well as enhancing the security of private properties and businesses, which stabilizes the country's economy and helps attract foreign investment (Moussa, 2021, 147;). Lastly and most importantly perhaps, the notable expansion of outsourcing of security in Egypt since the 2011 uprising significantly contributes to the regime tightening its control over social and political mobilization by having carefully selected private security companies serve as indirect agents of repression, which ultimately nurtures regime security and leads to overall authoritarian stability (Moussa, 2021, 154–159).

Moving to the traditional understanding of the state, the state is commonly viewed as a cohesive political entity, often represented by a formal government and a set of stable institutions. In this light, the global rise of many influential private actors in the second half of the twentieth century, who became increasingly involved in domestic and global policy-making processes, was a game changer. Among other effects, this global development severely disrupted the traditional view of the state in the political and security literature, which led to the emergence of the concept of governance as a substitute for conventional government. In security studies, the concept of "security governance" is used to depict the evolving role of the state from a "monopoly security provider to an enabler, employer, and regulator of private actors in complex networks" (Krahmann, 2005, 211). The concept equally serves to capture the growing international security agenda that encompasses "a much wider spectrum of threats, such as environmental, economic, and social problems" (Westermeyer, 2013, 26). In this regard, the concept of governance expands the scope of political and security studies to better comprehend the changing nature of the practices of privatisation of security, both domestically and internationally.

While traditional security scholars largely continue to assume a certain hierarchy in favour of states when they interact with non-state actors, the concept of governance underscores "a system of rule, which lacks a hierarchical order with a dominant sovereign entity" (Westermeyer, 2013, 25). Some go even further to declare governance as "the antonym to the rule of government by the nation state" (Westermeyer, 2013, 25). That said, the literature on global and security governance has itself been criticized for remaining widely loyal to the conceptualization of the state as one entity. This uniform version of the state appears increasingly inadequate to match the complex structures of contemporary security governance systems. In this light, the critical scholarship on the privatization of security largely refutes the dichotomous paradigm of state versus non-state actors, opting instead for a disaggregated conceptualization that better captures the evolving nature of the state. Particularly, with regard to outsourcing security, the notion of the state reflects the continuously constructed sum, or aggregation, of a vast number of agents, who despite uniformly carrying the label of "state representatives"—holders of a state capacity by being employed by, or acting on behalf of, the state—embed diverse and volatile interests and allegiances.

This perspective enables a richer account of the internal dynamics driving the processes of outsourcing security, both in terms of state decisions and the vibrant relationships between state representatives and the private security industry. It examines privatizing security through the lens of the vibrant power relations continuously being negotiated among a diverse set of actors, including state representatives, private entities and multiplex actors[2] who connect both. Additionally, it

[2]Within the network analysis model, an actor who simultaneously occupies an active position in more than one network is called a multiplex node (Avant & Westerwinter, 2016, 7). In the

permits a closer and more accurate evaluation of the state provision of security and its relationship to notions of sovereignty and legitimacy. As Abrahamsen and Williams (2011, 9) point out,

> The question becomes not whether the state is gaining or losing sovereignty via private security actors, but how its place and relationship to other actors in a field of power is shifting and how, in the process, state power itself is reconfigured.

In a similar vein, Beatrice Hibou (2004, 19) criticizes the literature, which attributes the privatization and outsourcing of security and other services to a state retreat or loss of sovereignty and legitimacy, of subscribing to a "substantialist and normative view of state power." She alternatively suggests that privatization effectively embodies "a new form of state interventionism," where state power is not uniform and control is not exclusive (Hibou, 2004, 18). This intake on privatization attributes particular attention to the deliberately volatile nature of the process, which centres on a series of formal and informal negotiations, contracts and agreements among the actors of security governance. Notwithstanding the process appearing deeply unstable, secretive and always up for renegotiation, Hibou (2004, 16) affirms,

> This instability is not the result of poor management or other inadequacies, nor is it the expression of external dependency. It is rather at the heart of politics: creating and maintaining conditions for the exercise of power.

In surveying different cases of outsourcing security, the diverse nature of the dynamics driving the privatization process becomes evident. Looking at Cameroon, Hibou (2004) highlights the crucial role played by numerous state representatives in advancing the privatization of security for personal gains. In particular, outsourcing security has translated into direct political and economic benefits for a number of state ministers and senior state agents, who either own or run numerous security services. The situation is comparable in Mozambique, where high-profile state representatives—former senior military personnel and active ministers—tightly monitor the privatization process by controlling "the hierarchical structure of networks, and the shrinking of the political space" (Hibou, 2004, 5). Furthermore, by closely collaborating with the heads of major private security companies, these state representatives manage to secure large economic resources, under the pretext of substituting "for an incompetent police force and undisciplined army" (Hibou, 2004, 6).

Similarly, the case of Egypt, briefly discussed earlier, illustrates how the expanding privatization and outsourcing of security are both directly and indirectly implicated in broad schemes of authoritarian adaptation. Egypt is equally a good example of the blurry line between the public and private spheres with regard to the security market. For instance, Law 86 of 2015 concerning the private security

---

meantime, actors with multiple affiliations within the same network are increasingly visible within the security market. Many examples are found in the public-private security partnerships, where some state representatives are equally part of the private security industry as companies' owners or administrative members. Given this, the concept of multiplex nodes is used in this chapter to refer to actors with simultaneous roles across networks as well as within a single network.

industry exceeds the usual aspects of private security regulations—training, monitoring and issuing licenses—to provide the Ministries of Interior and of Defense, together with the General Intelligence Agency, with the legal power to establish their own private security companies (President of Egypt, 2015). In addition to institutional ownership, the law equally grants former military personnel and police officers unconditional access to administrative positions at private security companies (The Egyptian Ministry of Interior, 2016).

Mirroring many other documented cases, the previous examples underscore the entangled relationship between the state and private actors that shapes the privatization of security across countries, particularly in the case of authoritarian states. As Hibou (2004, 14) remarks,

> local governors, ministers and district police commissioners for the security companies … are privileged contacts for the leaders of these private firms and in fact often closely related to them. When a police chief is replaced, not uncommonly certain companies go bankrupt and others prosper rapidly.

The aforementioned cases also highlight the value of "context sensitivity" for the analysis of the privatization of security. Context sensitivity corresponds to an informed recognition that the privatization of security services and the outsourcing of the public provision of security in different countries inevitably entails variations in terms of the scope and identities of the actors involved alongside the nature of their relationships, which naturally influence the dynamics driving the privatization procedure. As Guntram F. Werther (2007, 322) summarizes, a country's decision to outsource, or not to, "corresponds to a societal choice relating to how governments prefer to manage power."

Context sensitivity is crucial to the analysis of the privatization processes in authoritarian states, where the regime—the continuously dynamic and evolving coalition of different elite factions and their affiliates across the political, economic, social and security domains—heavily depends on the state security institutions to advance their interests and control the citizenry. Within this context, outsourcing security can serve to expand the ruling coalition's governing options by offering new venues to extend their interests and foster political control (Moussa, 2023).

5 The Case for the Nodal-Network Framework of Analysis

To properly investigate the privatization of security, especially amid an evolving security market and under entrenched authoritarian states, researchers require an analytical framework that transcends a simplistic perception of the state and effectively captures the diverse actors—inside and outside the state structure—who shape the political and security arenas. Moreover, seeing the blurry line between the public and private spheres, as well as the close relationship between many authoritarian regimes and the various security actors—both public and private—operating in authoritarian states, closely examining both the identities of different actors within the security market and the dynamics of their relationship is core to an in-depth understanding of the mechanisms and structures that inform, shape and impact the privatization of security as well as a regime's decision to outsource security. In this light, this part of the chapter puts forward the nodal-network framework of analysis as highly suitable to achieve this objective. Acknowledging the nodal and network models as two of the strongest and most useful in studying contemporary security markets, the nodal-network framework of analysis essentially seeks to combine the two models into a holistic framework of analysis that builds on the strengths of both models, thus enabling a more comprehensive study of individual cases as well as in-depth comparative studies.

5.1 The Nodal Governance Model

Influenced by the "network society" theory, Clifford Shearing and Jennifer Wood (2003) introduced the notion of "nodal security governance" to criminology studies in an attempt to expand and enrich the analysis of security privatization and plural policing. These scholars, among others, shortly developed the notion of "nodal security governance" into an elaborate theory that became widely used for the analysis of the privatization of security in criminology and other fields. Regarding the foundational claims of the theory, the following are noteworthy.

Nodal security governance views the new security environment as complex, vibrant and shaped by continuous interactions among a diverse set of actors and nodes. A node is defined "as a site of governance exhibiting four fundamental characteristics: mentalities, technologies, resources and institutional arrangements" (Martin, 2013, 149). Similarly, John Braithwaite (2004, 300) describes a node as "a point in time and space where a cluster of actors collaborates to mobilize pooled resources." Subsequently, since the nodes are not bound by a fixed structure or mode of action, they can encompass individuals, groups, organizations and institutions, among other forms. The various nodes may cooperate or compete or even work in isolation from each other (Shearing & Johnston, 2010, 501). Similarly, a security node is continuously evolving as one, or more, of its characteristics experience change.

Moreover, the theory contests the central and hierarchal position of states in the governance and delivery of security services. It acknowledges the state as simply one node, or a collection of nodes, with no intrinsic conceptual privilege within the large nodal security network (Abrahamsen & Williams, 2011, 83–84). The theory's challenge to the conventional perception of states as the inherent and superior provider of security is attributed to the theory's understanding of power. Tied to Michael Foucault's notion of "disciplinary power," nodal security governance recognizes power "as constitutive of social subjects and as operating through diverse and dispersed social practices" (Abrahamsen & Williams, 2011, 68). Consequently, investigating the various nodes and their relationships translates into an analysis of power relations, where "no set of nodes is given conceptual priority; rather, the exact nature of governance and the contribution of the various nodes to it are regarded as empirically open questions" (Shearing & Wood, 2003, 404).

Based on the theory's former pillars, the value and strength of using a nodal model of analysis when investigating the privatization of security in different cases could be summarized as follows. The nodal security theory provides the researcher with a clear model to effectively investigate individual nodes. Starting with the four fundamental characteristics of each node and then expanding on other features—whether found in related studies or discovered while investigating the case studies—the researcher can steadily advance their study to identify different links and modes of interaction between the nodes, as well as trace the dynamics of the security network. With numerous nodes involved in the security market, not to mention the frequent discrepancy in their structure, objectives and functions, a nodal analysis at the outset enables a rich understanding and appreciation of the processes of privatizing security in the studied case and facilitates identifying the most influential nodes.

Secondly, by approaching all nodes from an equal and neutral standpoint, the theory allows the researcher to fully and evenly engage in the analysis of various nodes. An even approach to all nodes is critical to capture the continuously changing nature and structure of different nodes in the privatization process. Additionally, it enables detecting areas for comparison and contrast across different cases, which might be masked or disregarded due to certain presumptions about the roles or nature of certain nodes.

Furthermore, by decentralizing the position of the state within the security market and treating it evenly with other nodes, the theory permits a critical examination of the changing nature and continuous reconfiguration of the state structure and power. As Abrahamsen and Williams (2011, 84) remark,

> Instead of assuming the presence of a dominant state able to impose and regulate other security actors according to its own governance agenda, nodal governance allows for the possibility that other security actors or nodes may be more influential at particular times or in particular settings.

While not always explicit in the writings of the theory's advocates, the analytical framework, which is proposed in this chapter, treats the state not as one node but as a collection of nodes. This disaggregated view of the state is decisive in conducting more accurate and comprehensive nodal analysis in cases where different state nodes, who are involved in security provision or privatization, carry different agendas, power positions and allegiances.

Moreover, by adopting a dynamic view of power, the theory enhances the scope of analysis. It encourages the researcher to simultaneously focus on the capabilities of individual nodes as well as on the power relations and interactions between different nodes that impact both individual nodes and the processes of privatizing security. Moreover, by seeking to understand the dynamic nature of nodal power relations, the model is not limited to identifying a particular set of nodes or to examining changes affecting their capacities or actions. More importantly, the nodal analytical framework is always alert to the existence or emergence of different or new types of nodes, which distinguishes particular cases or marks a new development in the processes of privatizing security. At times, the newly recognized nodes are not necessarily "new" to the security network; they have been overlooked by traditional state-centric approaches to security. Such actors may encompass informal security nodes, including gangs and militias, citizen patrols, and so forth.

5.2 *From Nodal Models to the Nodal-Network Framework of Analysis*

Notwithstanding the numerous strengths of the nodal security governance model for investigating the dynamics of privatizing security and the governance of the security market more broadly, the model heavily focuses on the nodal dimension at the expense of the network one. Indeed, many security scholars strongly differentiate between nodal and network analyses. As Chad Whelana and Benoît Dupont (2017, 1) remark, "Security network research differs from nodal governance in that it is ... less concerned with the attributes of individual security nodes than it is the relationship between a given set of nodes and the underlying properties of such relationships."

At large, a nodal analysis, which closely explores the various characteristics that distinguish a node, is viewed as a precursor to a network analysis. By providing an in-depth understanding of individual nodes, a nodal analysis enables "addressing vital questions about the behavioural tendencies of individual nodes, as well as their collective functions within a wider context of nodal interaction" (Martin, 2013, 146). Nonetheless, the nodal governance model doesn't on its own offer a sufficiently detailed account of how to investigate the security network, effectively trace its dynamics and distinguish its features. Looking at the contribution of security network research in this regard is integral to the objective of this chapter.

In essence, a network encompasses "a set of nodes and a set of ties representing the presence or absence of relationships between nodes" (Avant & Westerwinter, 2016, 6). The relationship between nodes "may be either formal, based on legal, contractual, or some other kind of organisational arrangement, or informal, depending essentially on the strength of interpersonal trust and relationships" (Whelan & Dupont, 2017, 5). The ties can reflect different kinds and levels of relationships, including "communication between nodes, such as advice and information exchange," or "more substantive transactions, such as resource pooling" (Whelan & Dupont, 2017, 5). Moreover, the ties can signify interactions through which there is a "flow of material and nonmaterial resources, such as money, weapons, information, or advice" (Avant & Westerwinter, 2016, 6).

Similar to the nodal governance model, a network model places "a premium on relational understandings of power; power that derives from and is exercised through actual or potential relationships rather than residing only in a node" (Avant & Westerwinter, 2016, 9). Moreover, "the security network approach frames security as the cumulative outcome of activities undertaken by a broad and diverse range of interdependent institutions" (Whelan & Dupont, 2017, 2). In this light, networking, or the process of building relationships among nodes, constitutes "a dynamic force through which agents can shape their future fates and governance outcomes" (Avant & Westerwinter, 2016, 9).

Looking at various kinds of security networks, in addition to the relationship among some of them, Avant and Westerwinter (2016) identify three key areas of variations to guide the study of security networks: centrality, the distribution of ties within the network, and the quality of ties between nodes. Centrality speaks to the positions which different actors occupy in the studied network; it "is a key mechanism through which nodes garner influence in network theory" (Avant & Westerwinter, 2016, 7). The distribution of ties within the network reflects how centralized or decentralized the network is. For instance, the nodes of a decentralized network usually share a similar pattern of connectedness, and most of them have about the same number of links (Butts, 2008; Barabási, 2014). By contrast, in centralized networks, one or a small number of highly central nodes are usually dominant, with the majority of actors having few relations (Avant & Westerwinter, 2016, 7).

In terms of the quality of ties, this primarily reflects the effectiveness and importance of the ties between different nodes. For instance, some ties can promote "brokerage (enhancing additional connections)," while others affirm "closure (tighten existing connections)," with both—brokerage and closure—representing "forms of social capital" that "activate different social dynamics among network actors" (Avant & Westerwinter, 2016, 8). As this chapter is interested in closely examining the individual nodes within the security network as well as the dynamic processes connecting them and shaping their relationship, using the three areas of variations from the network model to supplement the nodal governance model, outlined earlier, offers a more comprehensive analytical framework for a richer and potentially impactful research.

When adopting the nodal-network framework of analysis (Fig. 1), researchers depend heavily on the first phase of exploring the security market in their chosen cases on the nodal governance model in order to build a comprehensive picture of the key players shaping the security market. Once this foundation is established, the researchers' attention is directed to the security network, which both shapes and is being shaped by the privatization and outsourcing processes. In this vein, the researchers use as analytical tools the three elements of variations identified in the network model: centrality, the distribution of ties within the networks, and the quality of ties between nodes.

With respect to the value of combining the nodal and network models, the following points illustrate some of the benefits of the nodal-network framework of analysis. First, similar to how the nodal model enables comparison between the power and identity of actors within and across networks, the three elements of variations used in the network model permit a deep understanding of the structure and dynamics of single networks, while equally serving as grounds for comparison across different networks, whether these represent the security networks of different

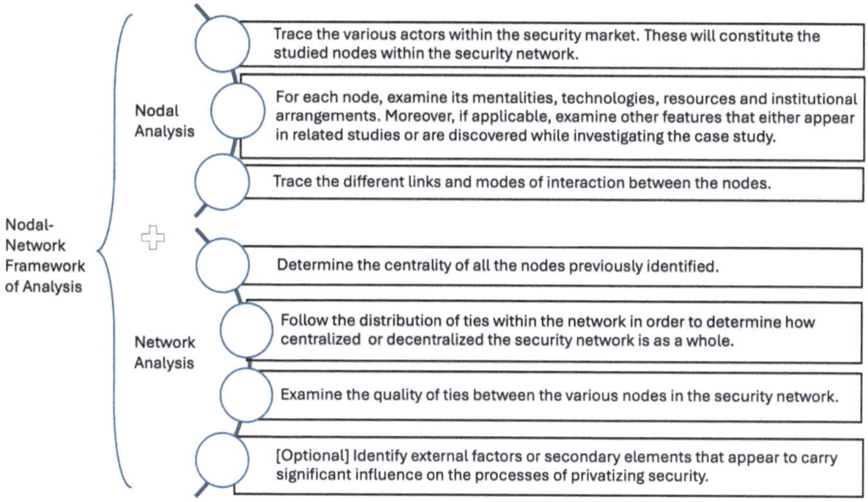

Fig. 1 The nodal-network framework of analysis

case studies, or the security network and other types of networks within the same case.

Secondly, while the nodal model permits numerous and overlapping focus areas for research, including individual nodes, bi-nodal or multi-nodal interactions, researchers can use the network model to widen the scope of their study by paying more attention to external factors or secondary elements that might not be directly identified as part of the nodal security interactions but can be proven of significant influence on the processes of privatizing security. Such elements may encompass domestic or regional economic and social developments, rising unrest or political change in the studied cases, and reconfiguration of state-citizens relationships, among others. Along these lines, Whelana and Dupont (2017, 13), who view networks as central to security governance and network research as "crucial to promoting security," encourage researchers to "concentrate on what makes security networks effective and what causes them to fail, not only as independent units of analysis but in relation to community or society expectations of what specific types of networks should and should not do."

Furthermore, supplementing the nodal analysis with a close examination of the three areas of variations from the network model, as well as considering them together, enables the researchers to identify network structures, which represent "persistent patterns of relations among agents that can define, enable, or constrain those agents" (Hafner-Burton et al., 2009, 561). While largely important, understanding the structures of security networks in authoritarian states carries greater value due to the complexities of the security market in many of these cases, with overlapping identities between state and private security nodes as well as the abuse of some of the relationship inside the network to advance systems of repression, social control and economic exploitation. In this light, going beyond learning about the individual nodes and their mutual relationship to deeply understand the structure and dynamic of the security network as a whole can lead to an impactful contribution by the researcher, which transcends the boundaries of academia and goes into the realm of political activism. After all, one requires an in-depth understanding of the context in which they operate in order to effectively and efficiently shape their strategies of political oppositions, or, at the very least, advance a solid and feasible alternative to authoritarian systems of governance.

6 Conclusion

The public provision of security is traditionally tied to the sovereignty and legitimacy of the modern state. In the meantime, recent decades have witnessed private security actors playing an increasingly substantial role in the domestic and international provision of public and private security. While seemingly at odds, the relationship between the modern state and the private security industry has been generally collaborative, with states' sovereignty and legitimacy remaining largely intact in the face of a growing private security industry alongside a steadily expanding practice of outsourcing security. Against this background, this chapter problematised the study of outsourcing security, particularly in the context of authoritarian states, by addressing two main questions: why do states outsource security, and with what effects on the state's monopoly over the means of violence, and on the relationship between the state and the citizenry? Additionally, what analytical models or frameworks are most suitable to investigate the privatization and outsourcing of security in authoritarian states?

Engaging with these questions, the chapter traced the tension between the contemporary practices of outsourcing security and the provision of security as a "public good" in traditional security studies. In doing so, the chapter highlighted the various limitations of traditional security studies in approaching the processes and dynamics of outsourcing security in contemporary contexts. Alternatively, the chapter underscored some of the approaches adopted by critical security studies regarding how different states use and abuse the privatization of security and the latter's impact on the expression and reconfiguration of state power as well as on the relationship between the state and the citizenry.

In terms of studying the security market, the last part of the chapter proposed the nodal-network framework of analysis as highly suitable for the study of outsourcing security in contemporary authoritarian states and beyond. Acknowledging the nodal and network models of analysis as two of the strongest and most fruitful in studying contemporary security markets, the nodal-network framework of analysis combines these two models into a holistic framework of analysis. This framework firmly enables the researcher to achieve a thorough investigation of the security market in their case studies based on a deep analysis of all the relevant actors as well as the complex network shaping their interactions and defining the security market at large.

Taking the objective of this chapter and the analytical framework it proposes forward, the following represent two important avenues for further research. The first concerns the practicality of implementing the nodal-network framework in authoritarian contexts. Namely, while the chapter accentuates the value of the nodal-network framework in conducting comprehensive studies of individual cases as well as carrying out in-depth comparative studies, researchers often face considerable difficulties in pursuing research in authoritarian states, which might require adjustments to the proposed framework. In this light, reflecting on the availability of resources needed to fully apply the framework and consulting researchers in the field, especially those who engage in fieldwork, to properly articulate the different ways through which the framework can be applied will strongly enhance its implementation in the field.

The second area of interest relates to balancing the emphasis on context sensitivity with the pursuit of generalizable findings. As argued in the chapter, the particularities of each case study mean that the privatization and outsourcing of security in different countries inevitably entail variations in terms of the scope and identities of the actors involved, and the nature of their relationships, which naturally influence the dynamics driving the privatization processes. In the meantime, both the nodal and network models included in the proposed framework enable and encourage researchers to make comparisons across cases, including, for instance, comparing the power and identity of similar actors, as well as comparing similar features of the security network across cases. These comparisons are likely to reveal recurring or consistent trends and patterns, which will make grounds for some generalisations. In this light, making room within the analytical framework for a proactive reflection on the appropriateness, significance, and limitations of drawing generalisations is crucial to ensure the coherence and integrity of the framework.

References

Abrahamsen, R., & Williams, M. C. (2011). *Security beyond the state: Private security in international politics*. Cambridge University Press.

Avant, D. (2005). *The market for force: The consequences of privatizing security*. Cambridge University Press.

Avant, D. (2007). Selling security: Trade-offs in state regulation of the private security industry. In T. Jager & G. Kummel (Eds.), *Private military and security companies: Chances, problems, pitfalls and prospects* (1st ed., pp. 419–442). VS Verlag für Sozialwissenschaften.

Avant, D. (2008). Private security. In P. D. Williams (Ed.), *Security studies: An introduction* (1st ed.). Routledge.

Avant, & Westerwinter, O. (Eds.). (2016). *The new power politics: Networks and transnational security governance*. Oxford University Press.

Barabási, A. L. (2014). *Linked: How everything is connected to everything else and what it means for business, science, and everyday life*. Basic Books.

Berndtsson, J. (2009). *The privatisation of security and state control of force: Changes, challenges and the case of Iraq*. Peace and Development Research, School of Global Studies, University of Gothenburg. https://gupea.ub.gu.se/handle/2077/19412

Braithwaite, J. (2004). Methods of power for development: Weapons of the weak, weapons of the strong. *Michigan Journal of International Law, 26*(1) https://repository.law.umich.edu/mjil/vol26/iss1/10

Butts, C. T. (2008). Social network analysis: A methodological introduction. *Asian Journal of Social Psychology*. Wiley, *11*(1), 13–41.

Cachon, G. P., & Netessine, S. (2006). Game theory in supply chain analysis. In *Models, methods, and applications for innovative decision making* (pp. 200–233).

Carr, S. (2013). Private security firms attempt to fill a gap left by a weakened security apparatus. *Egypt Independent*. https://www.egyptindependent.com/private-security-firms-attempt-fill-gap-left-weakened-security-apparatus/

Clark, D. (2023). Number of VAT/PAYE enterprises in the security and investigation activities sector in the United Kingdom from 2015 to 2023. *Statista.com*. https://www.statista.com/statistics/320460/security-enterprises-in-the-uk/.

Hafner-Burton, E. M., Kahler, M., & Montgomery, A. H. (2009). Network analysis for international relations. *International Organization*. Cambridge University Press, *63*(3), 559–592. https://doi.org/10.1017/S0020818309090195.

Hansen, S. J. (2008). Private security & local politics in Somalia. *Review of African Political Economy, 35*(118), 585–598. https://doi.org/10.1080/03056240802569268

Hibou, B. (2004). *Privatizing the state*. Columbia University Press.

Holmqvist, C. (2005). *Private security companies: The case for regulation* 9. https://www.sipri.org/publications/2005/sipri-policy-papers/private-security-companies-case-regulation

Jackson, P. (2011). Security sector reform and state building. *Third World Quarterly, 32*(10), 1803–1822. https://www.jstor.org/stable/41341200

Krahmann, E. (2005). New threats and new actors in security governance: Developments, problems, and solutions. In *New threats and new actors in international security* (pp. 199–212). Palgrave Macmillan.

Krahmann, E. (2009). *Private security companies and the state monopoly on violence: A case of norm Change?* Frankfurt. https://www.files.ethz.ch/isn/113632/prifrep88_01.pdf

Krause, K., & Milliken, J. (2009). Introduction: The challenge of non-state armed groups. *Contemporary Security Policy*. Routledge, *30*(2), 202–220. https://doi.org/10.1080/13523260903077296.

Martin, J. (2013). Informal security nodes and force capital. *Policing and Society*, Taylor & Francis Group, *23*(2), 145–163. https://doi.org/10.1080/10439463.2012.671821.

Maryon, R. (2023). The role of security assistance in reconfiguring Tunisia's transition. *Mediterranean Politics*. Routledge. https://doi.org/10.1080/13629395.2023.2183666.

Moussa, E. (2021). *Outsourcing security and the reconfiguration of state power after the Arab uprisings*. University of Cambridge. https://www.repository.cam.ac.uk/items/e98c635c-e45c-48af-828d-eb81f5ce2ca1

Moussa, E. (2023). Privatizing security and authoritarian adaptation in the Arab region since the 2010–2011 uprisings. *Contemporary Security Policy*. Routledge, *44*(3), 462–490. https://doi.org/10.1080/13523260.2023.2214757.

Murphy, E. C. (2001). The state and the private sector in North Africa: Seeking specificity. *Mediterranean Politics*. Taylor & Francis Group, 6(2), pp. 1–28. https://doi.org/10.1080/713604511

Østensen, Å. (2011). In from the cold? Self-legitimating the market for private security. *Global Change Peace & Security*. Routledge, *23*(3), 369–385. https://doi.org/10.1080/14781158.2011.601856

President of Egypt. (2015). انون شركاش حراسة المنشآش ون٢ل الأموال ر٢م 86 لسنة 2015٢ [*President decree for law 86 of 2015 on issuing a legislation for the private security companies*]. Egyptian Gazette. https://manshurat.org/node/6575

Reno, W. (2009). Explaining patterns of violence in collapsed states. *Contemporary Security Policy*. Routledge, *30*(2), 356–374. https://doi.org/10.1080/13523260903060250.

Runciman, D. (2003). The concept of the state: The sovereignty of a fiction. In Q. Skinner & B. Stråth (Eds.), *States and citizens: History, theory, prospects*. Cambridge University Press.

Sayigh, Y. (2016). *Dilemmas of reform: Policing in Arab transitions*. Carnegie Middle East Center. https://carnegie-mec.org/research/2016/05/dilemmas-of-reform-policing-in-arab-transitions?lang=en&center=middle-east

Schmitt, M. N. (2023). *Was Russia at war with the Wagner group?* Lieber Institute West Point. https://lieber.westpoint.edu/was-russia-war-wagner-group/

Schreier, F., & Caparini, M. (2005). *Privatising security: Law, practice and governance of private military and security companies*. DCAF Occasional Papers, (6).

Shearing, C., & Johnston, L. (2010). Nodal wars and network fallacies. *Sage, 14*(4), 495–514. https://doi.org/10.1177/1362480610378828.

Shearing, C., & Wood, J. (2003). Nodal governance, democracy, and the new "denizens". *Journal of Law and Society, 30*(3), 400–419. https://www.jstor.org/stable/1410537

Statista Research Department. (2023). Market size of security services in the United States from 2012 to 2022, with a forecast for 2023. *Statista*. https://www.statista.com/statistics/294206/revenue-of-security-services-in-the-us/

Statista Research Department. (2024). Estimated annual revenue of security companies in the United Kingdom from 2021 to 2023. *Statista.com*. https://www.statista.com/statistics/783614/turnover-manned-security-companies-uk/

Tarakci, H. (2016). Two types of learning effects on maintenance activities. *International Journal of Production Research, 54*(6), 1721–1734.

The Egyptian Ministry of Interior. (2016). بشأن إصدار اللائحة الشنفيذية ل٢انون شركاش حراسة المنشآش ون٢ل الأموال [Decree 133 of 2016 on issuing the executive chart of the legislation regulating the private security companies]. *Al-Waqa'i' al-Misriyya*. http://sub.eastlaws.com/GeneralSearch/Home/ArticlesTDetails?MasterID=1825173

Tilly, C. (1990). *Coercion, capital, and European states, AD 990–1990* (1st ed.). Basil Blackwell.

Verkuil, P. R. (2007). *Outsourcing sovereignty: Why privatization of government functions threatens democracy and what we can do about it*. Cambridge University Press.

Watling, J., Danylyuk, O. V., & Reynolds, N. (2024). *The threat from Russia's unconventional warfare beyond Ukraine, 2022–24*. www.rusi.org

Weber, M. (2010). In P. Lassman (Ed.), *Weber: Political writings* (7th ed.). Cambridge University Press.

Werther, G. F. (2007). Back to the future: Private military contractors and political theory in the modern democratic state. In T. Jäger & G. Kümmel (Eds.), *Private military and security companies: Chances, problems, pitfalls and prospects*. VS Verlag fur Sozialwissenschaften.

Westermeyer, G. (2013). *The impact of private actors on security governance: An analysis based on German ISR capabilities for ISAF*. Springer Fachmedien Wiesbaden.

Whelan, C., & Dupont, B. (2017). Taking stock of networks across the security field: A review, typology and research agenda. *Policing and Society*. Routledge, *27*(6), 671–687. https://doi.org/10.1080/10439463.2017.1356297

White, A. (2011). The new political economy of private security. *Sage, 16*(1), 85–101. https://doi.org/10.1177/1362480611410903.

Balancing Cybersecurity and Maintenance Outsourcing: A Profit-Centric Perspective for Manufacturers

Anh Ta, Hakan Tarakci, Victor Prybutok, and Robert Pavur

1 Introduction

In the field of manufacturing operations, machine failures and the resulting production stoppages are inevitable and pose significant challenges. For instance, in the printing industry, where production runs 24/7, machine performance is critical to maintaining consistent output (Alhilman et al., 2017). These issues stem from the complexity of modern manufacturing equipment and the necessity to replace outdated machinery. Such predictable breakdowns cause major problems for manufacturers, including delays in production, wastage of energy, and reduced product quality.

To address this challenge, effective maintenance strategies are essential to minimize downtime and ensure optimal machine performance. The literature strongly supports this view; for example, Madu (1999) highlights the importance of maintenance for operational efficiency, while Tarakci et al. (2014) and Xiang et al. (2014) emphasize their role in ensuring equipment performance and quality output. Optimizing maintenance frequency is strategically important for reducing costs. It not only ensures the functional performance of manufacturing equipment but also significantly improves the overall cost-effectiveness of the manufacturing process. Therefore, a well-planned maintenance strategy is essential for achieving both operational excellence and financial efficiency in the manufacturing industry.

A. Ta (✉)
University of Nebraska Omaha, Omaha, NE, USA
e-mail: Ata@unomaha.edu

H. Tarakci · V. Prybutok · R. Pavur
University of North Texas, Denton, TX, USA
e-mail: Hakan.Tarakci@unt.edu; Prybutok@unt.edu; Robert.Pavur@unt.edu

F. P. García Márquez et al. (eds.), *Outsourcing Using Operations Research and Management Science Methods*, International Series in Operations Research & Management Science 366, https://doi.org/10.1007/978-3-031-91845-2_7

However, the advent of highly connected manufacturing systems introduces additional challenges for maintenance management. The rise of Industry 4.0 and predictive technologies has significantly altered the landscape of maintenance practices (Coleman et al., 2017). The increasing threat of cyber-attacks on manufacturing systems necessitates that manufacturers develop robust outsourcing strategies to address both cyber threats and physical maintenance issues simultaneously (Kane et al., 2022). This dual focus on traditional maintenance and cybersecurity is essential for safeguarding manufacturing operations against a broader spectrum of risks.

Manufacturers must now consider not only the technical aspects of machine maintenance but also the security measures required to protect against cyber threats. This integrated approach to maintenance management ensures that both the physical integrity and the digital security of manufacturing systems are maintained, thereby supporting uninterrupted production and safeguarding valuable assets. As such, developing comprehensive maintenance strategies that encompass both traditional and emerging challenges is imperative for modern manufacturing operations.

The optimization of maintenance frequency is not merely a technical consideration but also a strategic one, bearing direct implications on the financial health of manufacturing operations. Salonen and Deleryd (2011) provided a pertinent perspective on this, estimating that maintenance costs can constitute a staggering 15–70% of total production expenses. Thus, the strategic optimization of maintenance frequency emerges as a pivotal factor in reducing these costs. It serves not only to maintain the functional performance of manufacturing equipment but also significantly contributes to enhancing the overall cost-effectiveness of the manufacturing process.

Evans (2011) described the benefits IoT provides to daily life, business environments, and manufacturing systems. However, despite the benefits, some risks exist, and most cyber-manufacturing systems are inadvertently exposed to potential hacking and cyber-attacks. Data Breach Chronology (2023) shows that from 1/2/2002 to 9/28/2023, there were 35,167 breaches in the U.S. The actual frequency of cyber-attacks is probably greater than reported, as companies might not reveal their cyber breaches due to the absence of uniform regulations governing breach disclosure (Ryan et al., 2012).

The Department of Homeland Security (2016) provided strategies to reduce emerging issues of cyber-attacks on various manufacturing systems. The development of highly connected machines and the lack of cyber security systems resulted in manufacturing becoming the second most hacked industry, only behind healthcare (Wu et al., 2018). Recently, Tuptuk and Hailes (2018) reviewed cyber incidents, discussed types of cyber-attacks on computer-integrated manufacturing systems, and described the vulnerability of current smart manufacturing systems. Consistent with the threat potential, Corallo et al. (2020) and Ta et al. (2023) called for more research articles investigating the business impact and the relationship between security issues and critical assets.

This research seeks to answer the question: How can manufacturers optimize maintenance outsourcing to address both physical machine failures and cyber threats effectively? To explore this, we developed two foundational models addressing maintenance and cybersecurity in manufacturing:

Model 1: This model focuses on a manufacturer navigating the challenges of regular physical breakdowns within a production system, postponing the consideration of cyber threats to a subsequent analysis. This initial framework positions the manufacturer at the helm of a production system, with maintenance responsibilities outsourced to a contractor. The contractor's duties encompass conducting minimal repairs (MRs) upon system failures and executing preventive maintenances (PMs) at predetermined optimal intervals. A simulation study utilizing a non-homogeneous Poisson process (NHPP) was developed to test the effectiveness of the proposed models and offer a genuine assessment of the anticipated system profit performance. Later, an exploratory analysis presents mechanisms for aligning interests between manufacturers and contractors into the design of maintenance outsourcing agreements.

Model 2: This model evaluates the impact of "successful" cyber-attacks that breach a manufacturer's security defenses, resulting in substantial costs without halting production. These attacks typically target the theft of patents or other intangible assets from manufacturers. An illustrative case is a cyber-attack on the U.-S. natural gas pipeline infrastructure, which targeted network data and disrupted communications between operators and their clients, yet left the gas supply uninterrupted (Krauss, 2018). Similar to the first model, to address the conflict of interest between the two parties, the models were enhanced by incorporating channel coordination via cost subsidization. Sensitivity analysis is employed to demonstrate how various parameters influence the optimal time T, security level S, and the contribution of security systems to cost models across diverse scenarios.

The significance of this study extends to various stakeholders in the manufacturing sector, including operations managers, maintenance contractors, and cybersecurity experts. By providing insights into optimizing maintenance strategies in the face of cyber threats, this research aims to enhance operational efficiency and security, ultimately benefiting manufacturers striving for both profitability and resilience.

The rest of the manuscript is organized as follows. Section 2 details the mathematical modeling of maintenance outsourcing, incorporating extensions to address the impact of cyber threats, discussing the integrated approach to maintenance and cybersecurity, and considering channel coordination through cost subsidization. Section 3 presents the numerical analysis conducted to validate the models, exploring various scenarios and conducting sensitivity analyses. Section 4 discusses the results and their implications for both theory and practice, concluding the manuscript by summarizing key findings, identifying limitations, and suggesting directions for future research.

2 Maintenance Outsourcing Mathematical Modeling

In the industrial manufacturing industry, the proficiency in conducting in-house maintenance on complex and costly systems and equipment is often beyond the primary expertise of manufacturers (Wang, 2010). Consequently, the practice of outsourcing maintenance tasks has emerged as a viable alternative, offering access to specialized maintenance personnel and the possibility of reducing human resource expenses. Milgate (2001) notes that outsourcing maintenance to external contractors has become increasingly popular, aiding in maintaining manageable operational costs. Such outsourcing is commonly executed through formalized maintenance-outsourcing contracts.

Maintenance services can be broadly categorized into two types: minimal repair (MR), also known as corrective maintenance, and preventive maintenance (PM). MR, as described by Muchiri et al. (2014), is a failure-based maintenance strategy where intervention occurs solely upon the malfunctioning of manufacturing equipment. Under the assumption that a system's failure rate increases over time (IFR), MR aims to restore the equipment to its functioning state. Post-MR, the failure rate of the equipment is adjusted to a level slightly higher than just before the breakdown, but it does not revert to the initial level of the new system. On the other hand, PM represents a time-based maintenance strategy, where maintenance actions are scheduled at optimally determined intervals (Muchiri et al., 2014). This approach effectively resets the system's failure rate closer to its original level. Additionally, PM facilitates better planning, thereby typically resulting in reduced downtime compared to MR interventions.

2.1 *Models Without Cyber Threats and Without Coordination*

The model development begins with a simple one, in which a manufacturer has to deal only with regular physical breakdowns. The cyber threats will be considered in a later section. This model assumes that a manufacturer controls a production system maintained by a contractor over time. The contractor is responsible for MRs when the system breaks down and PMs when the system reaches the optimal maintenance interval time.

Referring to Fig. 1, a typical cycle consists of three specific events. The system is up and running, the system is down for MRs, or the system is undergoing PMs. After the end of each PM, the system is assumed to be restored to a good-as-new state. The rectangles represent fixed intervals of time for MRs. The beginning of each rectangle represents the point in time at which an MR begins and the end of the rectangle represents the end of the MR. When a failure occurs, the contractor will perform this MR and the production system stops working for time duration, T_R. Thus, T_R is effectively the fixed length of each rectangle in Fig. 1. Note that the exact number of failures is a random variable; however, for illustrative purposes, in the production

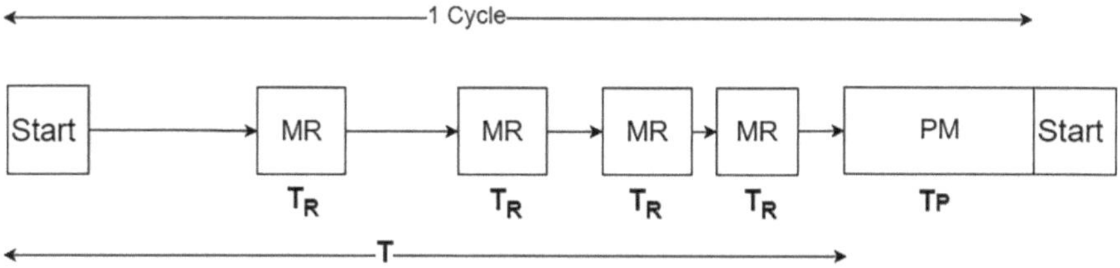

Fig. 1 A typical cycle of a production system with maintenance. *MR* minimal repair, *PM* preventive maintenance, T_R the time of minimal repair, T_P the time of preventive maintenance, *T* the time system is up and running until Preventive Maintenance

cycle, the MR rectangles are spaced increasingly closer to each other. This is on account of the assumption that breakdowns/failures are an increasing function of time. This assumption is very common in the reliability and maintenance literature (Tarakci et al., 2014; Tarakci 2016; Tseng et al., 2009). The cycle repeats itself at the beginning of the next PM epoch (which, in Fig. 1, is the second hexagon to the right).

Let $\lambda_R(t)$ denote the failure rate, which is assumed to be an increasing function of time t. The cost for a minimal repair is C_R. When the system reaches time T, a decision variable, the contractor will execute a PM. This PM will last for a fixed amount of time, T_P, and will cost C_P. The cycle time between the two consecutive preventive maintenance operations will then be $T + T_P$. This can also be gleaned from Fig. 1 as explained earlier. The production system is assumed to generate a net revenue of R dollars per unit of uptime in each cycle. $M_R(T)$ is denoted as the expected number of failures in T units of time, which can be given as $\int_0^T \lambda_R(x)dx$.

As per the renewal reward theorem (Ross, 1983), the expected profit per cycle per unit of time of the system may be computed as follows:

$$\text{Expected profit per cycle per unit of time} = \frac{\text{Expected profit incurred in a cycle}}{\text{Expected duration of a cycle}}$$

Denoting the expected system profit per cycle per unit of time as π_{S1}:

$$\pi_{S1} = \frac{R\,(T - M_R(\mathrm{T}) \cdot T_R) - M_R(\mathrm{T}) \cdot C_R - C_P}{T + T_P} \tag{1}$$

The numerator on the right-hand side of Eq. (1) consists of the difference between the revenue generated and the costs for all possible MRs and a PM for one cycle. The denominator represents the duration for one cycle. Note that $T - M_R(T) \cdot T_R$ represents the amount of uptime and thereby the opportunity to generate revenue.

Lemma 1 Define $h(T) = \lambda_R(T)(T + T_P) - M_R(T)$.

(i) $h(T)$ is always an increasing function of T.
(ii) There exists a unique T^*_{S1}, maximizing system profit π_{s1} and satisfying the following condition:

$$h(T_{S1}^{*}) = \frac{RT_P + C_P}{RT_R + C_R} \tag{2}$$

Proof Please refer to the Appendix for the proofs of all lemmas and corollaries.

According to Lemma 1, for any increasing function of failure rate $\lambda_R(T)$, there is always a unique optimal value maximizing the system profit. Based on Eq. 2, Corollary 1 is introduced to investigate the relationship between T_{S1}^{*} and other parameters such as revenue generated by the system per unit of time and the characteristics of each MR and PM.

Corollary 1 The relationship between T_{S1}^{*} and other parameters is given as follows:

(i) As C_P increases, T_{S1}^{*} will increase, i.e., less frequency of PM operations.
(ii) As C_R or T_R increase, T_{S1}^{*} will decrease, i.e., more frequency of PM operations.
(iii) As R increases, T_{S1}^{*} will increase when $\frac{C_P}{T_P} < \frac{C_R}{T_R}$ or vice versa.
(iv) As T_P increases, T_{S1}^{*} will increase when $\frac{R}{RT_R + C_R} > \lambda_R(T_{S1}^{*})$ or vice versa.

The results found in Lemma 1 and Corollary 1 make several important contributions to the literature. Most significantly, the results are generalizable to any increasing failure rate (IFR) function. These generalizable findings are relatively similar to the ones in Tarakci et al.'s (2006) study, in which they assumed that the failure rate $\lambda_R(T)$ is an increasing Weibull rate function. The findings in this research allow generalizing their mathematical results by showing that the solution in Lemma 1 can apply to not only an increasing Weibull failure rate function but also to any IFR function. The results also show important relationships between the optimal time T_{S1}^{*} and the other parameters. For example, a higher C_P leads to an increase in T_{S1}^{*} (reduction in the rate of PM operations). When PM costs increase, the rate of PM operation decreases to maintain the system profit. In addition, a longer T_R and higher C_R lead to a lower value of T_{S1}^{*} (more frequent PM operations). When the minimal repair duration and cost become high, it is beneficial for the manufacturing system to reset the machine to as-good-as-new condition by increasing PM. In addition, the analysis shows some important results about the relationship between T_{S1}^{*} and the other two parameters, T_p and R. For instance, it is intuitive that, when R increases, the time T_{S1}^{*} should increase to obtain larger uptime for the system. However, this relationship only holds when $T_P C_R - T_R C_P > 0$. Also, when T_P increases, the optimal time T_{S1}^{*} would also increase because higher PM duration means more downtime. To avoid that problem, the system would prefer performing fewer PMs or higher T_{S1}^{*}. While this happens, it is not universal: only if $\frac{R}{RT_R + C_R} - \lambda_R(T_{S1}^{*}) > 0$; otherwise, T_{S1}^{*} goes down. These findings are applied to the numerical analysis in Example 1.

Example 1 Define the failure rate $\lambda_R(T) = kT^l$ with k and $l > 0$. The cumulative distribution function (CDF) of the failure rate should follow this equation, $M_R(T) = \frac{k}{l+1} T^{l+1}$. The costs and duration of PM and MR are $C_P = \$5000$, $C_R = \$500$, $T_P = 1$ unit of time, and $T_R = 0.2$ unit of time. The manufacturer generates \$14,000 per unit of uptime. The failure rate related parameters are $k = 0.05$ and $l=1$. Substituting these values into Eq. (2) in the results of Lemma 1 (ii), the optimum time T should follow this equation, $0.05T^1(T+1) - \frac{0.05}{1+1}T^{1+1} = \frac{14{,}000 \cdot 1 + 5{,}000}{(0.2 \cdot 14{,}000 + 500)}$. Solving this equation provides $T = 14.21$ units of time. In other words, the contractor should operate PM every 14.21 units of time. This example is used to illustrate the results found in Lemma 1 and Corollary 1. In practical application, manufacturers can use historical data to generate the value for each parameter. The failure rate function is a simple form of Weibull distribution which is popularly used in literature (e.g., Tarakci et al., 2013, 2014).

The results for the scenario in Example 1 are derived using deterministic assumptions. To provide a realistic evaluation of the performance of the expected system profit per cycle per unit of time formula in Eq. (1), a simulation study was conducted in which a nonhomogeneous Poisson process was used to generate the times of failure for the machines in Example 1. Ross (2014) provides details about a nonhomogeneous Poisson process. In this example, the intensity function λ(t) for this process is the same as the Weibull failure rate function and is $\lambda_R(\mathrm{T}) = k\,T^l$. Times can be generated by using a CDF inversion approach, noting that the inter-event times have independent Poisson distributions.

In real-world applications, the failure times are not deterministic but follow some probability distribution, usually unknown. To select distributions for the simulation study, distributions from prominent studies involving maintenance and failure times were identified. Wee and Widyadana (2013) developed a solution to a production inventory process optimization assuming stochastic machine maintenance times. Two maintenance time distributions were considered: the uniform distribution and the exponential distribution. The exponential distribution times are used in Poisson processes. The nonhomogeneous Poisson process is often used to model failures occurring over time and events times in service processes (Richards et al., 2015) as the intensity function may be continuous or discrete over time. Furthermore, in the simulation study, the amount of time to repair a machine was allowed to follow a uniform distribution over the interval from 0.1 to 0.3 to provide some variation to the results.

For each of the 2000 replications, the time that provided the maximum profit per cycle per unit time as computed using Eq. (1) was recorded along with the corresponding profit per cycle. From the simulation study, the average profit per cycle was recorded as 10,690.36, with an average optimal time of 13.69. This average profit is less than the computed profit of 11,550.57. The standard deviation of the maximum profit per cycle was 1969.10. The average clock time for optimal time to perform preventive maintenance is less than the 14.21 units of time provided by the equation. The average number of repairs was 5.90 for the optimal stopping time in the simulation. This is close to the $M_R(T = 14.21) = \left(\frac{0.05}{1+1}\right)14.21^{(1+1)} = 5.05$, achieved from Lemma 1. Eq. (1) is derived under a deterministic system and is not expected to be an exact solution for a stochastic process. This simulation study provides support for the use of Eq. (1)

as a guideline with the caveat that results may vary depending on the underlying distribution of the process. It also provides insight into the behavior of the proposed equation of maximum profit per cycle per unit time under known distributional assumptions.

In the Fig. 1 model, it is assumed that the system (both contractor and manufacturer) makes the decision for the frequency of PM operations. However, in practice, when it is not always possible to coordinate the system, the two entities might disagree about the optimal PM frequency. Thus, two extended models are used to investigate the functions of the contractor's and the manufacturer's profit separately. The contractor is assumed to only sign the maintenance contract that meets a minimum expected profit, $P_{\min}$. P is defined as payment per unit of time that the manufacturer has to pay to the contractor; π_m is the expected profit for the manufacturer; and π_c is the contractor's expected profit. The analysis is performed similarly to the previous model in order to investigate the difference between the contractor's and the manufacturer's optimal PM times.

$$\pi_m = \frac{R\left(T - M_R(\mathrm{T}) \cdot T_R\right)}{T + T_P} - P \tag{3}$$

$$\text{s.t.}P - \frac{C_P + M_R(\mathrm{T}) \cdot C_R}{T + T_P} \geq P_{\min}$$

$$\pi_c = P - \frac{C_P + M_R(\mathrm{T}) \cdot C_R}{T + T_P} \tag{4}$$

Lemma 2 Define $h(T) = \lambda_R(T)(T + T_P) - M_R(T)$, then,

(i) There exists a unique T^*_{m1}, maximizing manufacturer profit π_m and satisfying the following condition:
$h\left(T^*_{m1}\right) = \frac{T_P}{T_R}$

(ii) There exists a unique T^*_{c1}, maximizing contractor profit π_c and satisfying the following condition:
$h\left(T^*_{c1}\right) = \frac{C_P}{C_R}$

According to Lemma 2, T_P and T_R affect the manufacturer's optimal profit, while C_p and C_R only influence the contractor maximized profit. This result matches those found in Tarakci et al.'s (2006) study, in which the authors investigated the profit functions with an assumption that the failure rate follows a Weibull distribution. Again, the findings generalize that the study's results for any increasing rate function. Based on Lemma 2, the manufacturer and the contractor have identical optimal time T if and only if T_P/T_R equals C_P/C_R, which rarely occurs in practice. In the uncoordinated case, where the manufacturer and contractor are not acting as a united system, it is assumed that the contractor is the only decision maker in choosing the frequency of PM. Clearly, the contractor would then maximize its own profit. However, the manufacturer can use incentive contracts to influence the contractor to choose a maintenance schedule that maximizes the manufacturing system profit.

2.2 Models Without Cyber Threats, with Channel Coordination Through Cost Subsidization

In the cost subsidization scheme, similar to Tarakci et al. (2006), it is assumed that the manufacturer will partially pay for the cost of minimal repair (C_R) and preventive maintenance (C_P). In this section, we use notation such as T^*_{an}, where * is the optimal value, a is the index of the actor, either m: manufacturer, c: contractor or s: system and n: the model index. Parameters "a" and "b" are defined as the subsidized portion of the cost of C_P and C_R, respectively, with a, $b \in [0, 1]$. This means that the manufacturer will pay aC_P and bC_R, while the contractor will pay $(1 - a)C_P$ and $(1 - b)C_R$ for PM and MR, respectively. While the profit equation of the system will remain the same as the one in the original model in Sect. 2, the two new equations for expected profit per unit of time for the manufacturer and the contractor are:

$$\pi_m = \frac{R\,(T - \mathrm{M}_R(\mathrm{T})T_R) - aC_P - M_R(\mathrm{T})bC_R}{T + T_P} - P \tag{5}$$

$$\text{s.t.} P - \frac{(1-a)C_P - (1-b)M_R(\mathrm{T})C_R}{T + T_P} \geq P_{\min}$$

$$\pi_c = P - \frac{(1-a)C_P - (1-b)M_R(\mathrm{T})C_R}{T + T_P} \tag{6}$$

Applying the results of Lemma 1 and Lemma 2, the optimal PM time T^*_{m2} for the manufacturer's modified profit function in Eq. 5 is achieved when $h(T^*_{c2}) = (1-a)C_P/(1-b)C_R$. Similarly, the optimal time T^*_{c2} for the contractor's modified profit function in Eq. 6 is achieved when $h(T^*_{m2}) = (RT_P + aC_P)/(T_RR + bC_R)$. The relationships among optimal time T^*_{c2}, T^*_{m2}, and T^*_{S1} are given by Lemma 3.

Lemma 3

(i) $T^*_{c2} = T^*_{m2} = T^*_{S1}$ when $a = \frac{b\;C_R\;(RT_P + C_P) + R(\;T_RC_P - T_PC_R)}{C_P(C_R + RT_R).}$

(ii) $T^*_{c2} > T^*_{S1} > T^*_{m2}$, when $a < \frac{b\;C_R\;(RT_P + C_P) + R(\;T_RC_P - T_PC_R)}{C_P(C_R + RT_R)}$ and vice versa

The contractor is the decision maker, so it maximizes its own profit by choosing the optimal time T^*_{c2}. However, the manufacturer can partially subsidize the contractor's cost to manipulate the contractor's decision on the PM interval. In other words, the manufacturer can adjust the values of channel coordinating parameters a and b to maximize system profit by ensuring that the contractor chooses the optimal T^*_{S1}. The a and b values that coordinate the system can be chosen as follows:

$$\frac{(1-a)C_P}{(1-b)C_R} = \frac{RT_P + C_P}{T_RR + C_R}$$

Corollary 2 When channel coordination is achieved through cost subsidization, the manufacturer can choose a value of P to match the contractor's minimum profit demand.

$$\frac{R\left(T_{S1}^{*}-M_R\left(T_{S1}^{*}\right)T_R\right)-aC_P-M_R\left(T_{S1}^{*}\right)bC_R}{T_{S1}^{*}+T_P}-\pi_m\left(T_{c2}^{*}\right)+P_{\min}\geq P$$

$$\geq\frac{(1-a)C_P-(1-b)M_R\left(T_{S1}^{*}\right)C_R}{T_{S1}^{*}+T_P}+P_{\min}$$

The manufacturer has the right to choose the P value that optimizes its goal. If the lower bound of P is chosen, the contractor will earn its minimum required profit ($P_{\min}$). If the upper bound of P is chosen, the manufacturer's profit will be determined by the contractor's optimal PM frequency. In this case, the manufacturer's profit will be equal to $\pi_m\left(T_{c2}^{*}\right)$. The contractor's PM is no longer the only decision because of cost subsidization. To achieve its desired frequency of maintenance and to maximize the system profit, the manufacturer can choose incentive contracts by choosing different values of a, b, and P that are satisfied with the conditions in Lemma 3 and Corollary 2.

2.3 Models Under Cyber Threats Without Coordination

In this section, we extend our models by exploring a manufacturing system that has the option to implement a security system to mitigate potential cyber threats.

The cost, denoted as $C_S(S)$, for establishing a security system is a function of S, security level, which ranges from 0 (no security) to 1 (maximum security). Following the approach of Tarakci et al. (2014), this cost is postulated to be increasingly convex with respect to the security level.

We also assume that physical failures and cyber-attacks are independent events, in which a security breach does not cause physical failures, and vice versa. The security systems are designed to safeguard sensitive company information, leading to a policy where the manufacturer, instead of outsourcing, sets up and manages its own security measures. It is assumed that a higher level of security logically correlates with a reduced frequency of successful cyber-attacks and that, over time, security systems become obsolete as hackers develop new infiltration methods. Therefore, the rate of successful cyber-attacks, $\lambda_A(T, S)$, is assumed to decrease with higher security levels S and increase over time T. Also, this cyber-attack rate is reset following each PM operation, allowing for the installation of the latest security updates.

We define the expected number of cyber-attacks over time T, denoted as $M_A(T, S)$ as the integral $\int_0^T \lambda_A(x, S)dx$ for a given security level S. The cost incurred from each successful cyber-attack is represented by C_A. Under these assumptions, we propose a revised profit equation for the system:

$$\pi_s = \frac{(T - M_R(T) \cdot T_R) \cdot R - C_R \cdot M_R(T) - C_A \cdot M_A(T,S) - C_P}{T_P + T} - C_S(S) \tag{7}$$

Lemma 4 Given that $h(T^*_{S3}) = (T^*_{S3} + T_P) \cdot \lambda_R(T^*_{S3}) - M_R(T^*_{S3})$ and $g(T^*_{S3}, S) = (T^*_{S3} + T_P) \cdot \lambda_A(T^*_{S3}, S) - M_A(T^*_{S3}, S)$. Then, we have

(i) There exists a unique critical point $(T^*_{S3},\ S^*_{S3})$ to maximize π_s, which follows these conditions:

$$C_A \cdot \frac{dM_A(T^*_{S3}, S^*_{S3})}{dS} + C'_S(S^*_{S3})(T^*_{S3} + T_p) = 0 \tag{8}$$

$$g(T^*_{S3}, S^*_{S3}) \cdot \frac{C_A}{RT_R + C_R} + \mathrm{h}(T^*_{S3}) - \frac{C_p + T_p R}{C_R + T_R R} = 0 \tag{9}$$

(ii) The optimal solution for π_s can be uniquely identified as one of the following options:

- The pair $(T^*_{S3},\ S^*_{S3})$.
- The point $(T_1, 0)$ in which $S^* = 0$ and T_1 being the specific T value that maximizes Eq. (7) under the condition $S = 0$.
- The point $(T_2, 1)$ in which $S^* = 1$ and T_2 being the specific T value that maximizes Eq. (7) when S is set to 1.

Because the manufacturer will bear the costs resulting from any "successful" cyber-attacks, the manufacturer's expected profit, measured on a per-time-unit basis, is defined as:

$$\pi_m = \frac{R(T - M_R(T) \cdot T_R) - M_A(T,S) \cdot C_A}{T + T_P} - C_S(S) - P \tag{10}$$

Similar to Lemma 4, there exists a unique critical point (T^*_{m3}, S^*_{m3}) to maximize π_m which follows these conditions:

$$C_A \cdot \frac{dM_A(T^*_{m3}, S^*_{m3})}{dS} + C'_S(S^*_{m3})(T^*_{m3} + T_p) = 0 \tag{11}$$

$$g(T^*_{m3}, S^*_{m3}) \cdot \frac{C_A}{RT_R} + h(T^*_{m3}) - \frac{T_P}{T_R} = 0 \tag{12}$$

The expected profit of the contractor remains the same as in the model that does not account for cyber threats:

$$\pi_c = P - \frac{M_R(T) \cdot C_R + C_P}{T_P + T} \tag{13}$$

Based on the results of Lemma 2 (ii), the contractor's optimal solution, T^*_{c3}, has to satisfy the condition: $h\left(T^*_{c3}\right) = \frac{C_P}{C_R}$. If, as hypothesized in previous section, the contractor alone decides the frequency of PM, the optimal PM frequencies for both the manufacturer and the system will not be realized. This is because they would differ from the contractor's choice, unless coincidentally the numbers align perfectly.

2.4 *Models Under Cyber Threats, with Channel Coordination Through Cost Subsidization*

Similar to what is described in the previous sub-section, the parameters a and b represent the subsidized fractions of the costs of C_P and C_R, respectively, where a and b fall within the range [0, 1]. Consequently, the profit function for the manufacturer is defined as follows:

$$\pi_m = \frac{RT - R\left(T_R M_R(T) + T_A M_A(T,S)\right) - C_A M_A(T,S) - aC_P - bC_R M_R(T)}{T_P + T} - P - C_S(S) \tag{14}$$

Similar to Lemma 4, there exists a unique critical point $\left(T^*_{m4}, S^*_{m4}\right)$ to maximize π_m which follows these conditions:

$$(C_A + RT_A)\frac{dM_A\left(T^*_{m4}, S^*_{m4}\right)}{dS} + C'_S\left(S^*_{m4}\right)\left(T^*_{m4} + T_p\right) = 0 \tag{15}$$

$$g\left(T^*_{m4}, S^*_{m4}\right)\frac{C_A + RT_A}{RT_R + bC_R} + h\left(T^*_{m4}\right) - \frac{RT_P + aC_P}{RT_R + bC_R} = 0 \tag{16}$$

The expected profit of the contractor is as follows:

$$\pi_c = P - \frac{(1-a)C_P - (1-b)C_R M_R(T)}{T_P + T} \tag{17}$$

According to Lemma 2, the contractor's optimal solution, T^*_{c4}, has to satisfy the condition: $h\left(T^*_{c4}\right) = \frac{(1-a)C_P}{(1-b)C_R}$.

Corollary 3 To facilitate channel coordination via cost subsidization, the manufacturer has the capability to modify the values of the coordinating quantities a, b, and P. This adjustment aims to influence the contractor's selection of the optimal values of T and S, which in turn optimize the overall system profit. Therefore, a and b can be strategically selected such that:

$$\frac{R\,T_p + C_p - (C_A + RT_A)\cdot g\left(T^*_{S3}, S^*_{S3}\right)}{RT_R + C_R} = \frac{(1-a)C_p}{(1-b)C_R} \tag{18}$$

where $g\left(T^*_{S3}, S^*_{S3}\right) = \lambda_A\left(T^*_{S3}, S^*_{S3}\right)\left(T^*_{S3} + T_P\right) - M_A\left(T^*_{S3}, S^*_{S3}\right)$.

When the condition for channel coordination via cost subsidization is met, the manufacturer has the option to select a value for P in accordance with the subsequent constraints. These constraints are set to ensure that the contractor's minimum profit requirements are fulfilled:

$$P - P_{\min} \geq \frac{(1-a)C_P - (1-b)M_R\left(T^*_{S3}\right)C_R}{T_P + T^*_{S3}}$$

$$P - P_{\min} \leq \frac{R\left(T^*_{S3} - M_R\left(T^*_{S3}\right)T_R\right) - \left[aC_P + M_R\left(T^*_{S3}\right)bC_R + M_A\left(T^*_{S3}, S^*_{S3}\right)\cdot\left(C_A + RT_A\right)\right]}{T_P + T^*_{S3}} - \left[C_S\left(S^*_{S3}\right) + \pi_m\left(T^*_{c4}\right)\right]$$

The manufacturer holds the right to select the value of P that aligns with its objectives while also meeting the contractor's minimum profit threshold. Choosing the lower limit of P ensures that the contractor receives its required break-even amount, $P_{\min}$, as set in the contract. Alternatively, if the upper limit of P is chosen, the manufacturer's profit hinges on the contractor's optimal time, T^*_{c4}, resulting in a profit of $\pi_m\left(T^*_{c4}\right)$. Thus, the manufacturer has the flexibility to choose any values for a, b, and P that comply with condition (18) and the conditions of Corollary 3 in order to achieve its preferred PM interval.

Example 2 We define the failure rate as $\lambda_R(T) = k\,T^l$, where k and l are both greater than 0. Consequently, the cumulative distribution function (CDF) for the failure rate can be expressed as $M_R(T) = \frac{k}{l+1}\,T^{l+1}$. Additionally, $M_A(T, S)$ is the CDF of $\lambda_A(T, S)$, which decreases with S and increases with T. Therefore, $\lambda_A(T, S)$ can be defined as $gT^h(f - S)$, where both g and h are positive, and f is at least 1. Accordingly, the CDF for the rate of successful cyber-attacks is $M_A(T,S) = \frac{g}{h+1}\,(f-S)T^{h+1}$. The function $C_S(S)$ is convex and increases with S, defined as $C_S(S) = mS^i$, with m and i both exceeding 1. Also, we assume that C_R = \$500, T_R = 0.2 unit of time, C_p = \$5,000, T_p = 1.0 unit of time, C_A = \$3,000, and T_A = 0.2 unit of time. The revenue generated by the manufacturer per unit of system uptime R = \$14,000. The parameters for the system's failure rate are k=0.05 and l = 1, while those for the "successful" cyber-attack rate are f = 1.50, g = 0.15, and h = 1.3. The parameters for the security cost function are i=2.5 and m = 1500. As per Lemma 4, the system's optimal operation point is at T = 4.34 units of time and S = 0.67. Following condition (18), the manufacturer should select values of a and b that meet the condition a + 0.069b = 0.931, indicating an infinite combination of a and b values that can coordinate the system, though with varying profit distributions between the two parties.

3 Numerical Analysis

This numerical analysis examines the effects of altering distinct system parameters on the models' performance, particularly in scenarios involving cyber-attacks. Each numerical analysis involves modifying one specific parameter while maintaining the others as constant, as established in Example 2. The investigation encompasses four key groups of parameters: financial aspects including revenue, costs of PM and MR, and the cost of cyber-attacks. Temporal factors including durations of PM, MR, and cyber-attacks, parameters related to the failure rate, and parameters pertaining to the cyber-attack rate. A variety of metrics are provided for each parameter. For instance, in the financial group, parameters like revenue are scrutinized on an individual basis. The primary emphasis, however, lies in assessing the increase in system profit percentage following the implementation of the security system, and determining the most effective security level for the system.

3.1 *Effect of Financial-Related Aspects*

As illustrated in Table 1, there is a noticeable trend where an increase in revenue correlates with a higher security level, *S*. A plausible explanation for this could be that as revenue rises, the optimal time period *T* increases or the frequency of PM operations decreases. This scenario potentially leads to more frequent successful cyber-attacks. Consequently, to mitigate the impact of these cyber-attacks, a higher security level becomes necessary as revenue escalates. Moreover, the value added by the security system, in terms of enhanced system profits, also grows with increasing revenue.

Table 1 Effect of net generated revenue *R* on the system profit, optimal *S*, and optimal *T*

R ($)	Profit with security system ($)	Profit without security system ($)	% improve in profit by security system	Optimal *T* with security system	Optimal *S* with security system	Optimal *T* without security system
14,000	7880	7317	7.7	4.34	0.67	3.29
15,000	8617	8001	7.7	4.45	0.71	3.32
16,000	9359	8685	7.8	4.57	0.74	3.34
17,000	10,104	9370	7.8	4.70	0.78	3.37
18,000	10,853	10,055	8.0	4.84	0.82	3.39
19,000	11,607	10,740	8.1	5.01	0.86	3.41
20,000	12,366	11,426	8.2	5.21	0.91	3.42

Tables 2, 3, and 4 illustrate how C_P, C_R, and C_A impact the manufacturing process, both with and without a security system in place. The data shows that as the costs of C_P and C_A increase, the utility of the security system also rises. For instance, at a C_P of $5000 or C_A at $3000, the profit enhancement due to the security system is 7.7% and 7.69%, respectively. When C_P escalates to $11,000 or C_A to $6000, the profit increase jumps to 14.46% and 11.13%, respectively. It becomes

Table 2 Effect of C_P on the system profit, optimal *S*, and optimal *T*

C_P ($)	Profit with security system ($)	Profit without security system ($)	% improve in profit by security system (%)	Optimal *T* with security system	Optimal *S* with security system	Optimal *T* without security system
5000	7880	7317	7.7	4.34	0.67	3.29
6000	7696	7086	8.6	4.52	0.70	3.38
7000	7517	6860	9.6	4.71	0.73	3.47
8000	7345	6638	10.7	4.91	0.76	3.55
9000	7179	6420	11.8	5.11	0.79	3.63
10,000	7018	6206	13.1	5.33	0.82	3.71
11,000	6863	5996	14.5	5.57	0.86	3.79

Table 3 Effect of on the system profit, optimal *S*, and optimal *T*

C_R ($)	Profit with security system ($)	Profit without security system ($)	% improve in profit by security system (%)	Optimal *T* with security system	Optimal *S* with security system	Optimal *T* without security system
500	7880	7317	7.7	4.34	0.67	3.29
700	7836	7285	7.6	4.28	0.66	3.27
900	7793	7254	7.4	4.22	0.65	3.25
1100	7751	7223	7.3	4.17	0.65	3.23
1300	7709	7192	7.2	4.11	0.64	3.21
1500	7668	7162	7.1	4.06	0.63	3.20
1700	7628	7131	7.0	4.02	0.62	3.18

Table 4 Effect of on the system profit, optimal *S*, and optimal *T*

C_A ($)	Profit with security system ($)	Profit without security system ($)	% improve in profit by security system (%)	Optimal *T* with security system	Optimal *S* with security system	Optimal *T* without security system
3000	7880	7317	7.7	4.34	0.67	3.29
3500	7737	7145	8.3	4.23	0.69	3.16
4000	7602	6984	8.9	4.13	0.71	3.05
4500	7475	6832	9.4	4.04	0.73	2.94
5000	7355	6687	10.0	3.96	0.75	2.85
5500	7241	6549	10.6	3.90	0.77	2.76
6000	7132	6418	11.1	3.84	0.79	2.68

evident that a rise in the cost of a "successful" cyber-attack underscores the significance of implementing a security system. Table 2 indicates that an increase in C_P leads to a longer optimal time T or a reduced frequency of PM operations, which in turn heightens the rate of successful cyber-attacks. The more frequent these attacks, the greater the advantage the manufacturer derives from the security system. This pattern suggests that the usefulness of the security system is amplified when either C_P or C_A increases.

Table 3 highlights a decline in the effectiveness of a security system as the cost of minimal repair C_R rises. Additionally, an increase in C_R typically leads to a reduction in the optimal time T, or alternatively, an increase in the frequency of PM operations. Consequently, when C_R reaches exceptionally high levels, the benefits derived from maintaining a certain security level become comparatively minimal. Moreover, the level of security, denoted as S, tends to decrease with the escalation of C_R. An analysis of Tables 1, 2, 3, and 4 reveals a consistent trend: the optimal operation time T when a security system is in place is invariably longer than the operation time T without a security system. This finding suggests that, for these four monetary parameters, implementing a security system contributes to reducing the frequency of preventive maintenance.

3.2 Effect of Temporal Factors

Table 5 illustrates how T_P impacts the manufacturing process, both with the inclusion and exclusion of a security system. An increase in T_P corresponds to an increase in the advantages of implementing a security system. For instance, extending T_P from 1 to 2.2 units of time enhances the profit increase due to the security system from 7.7% to 11%. Logically, a longer T_P means the system undergoes preventive maintenance less frequently, or put another way, the optimal operational time

Table 5 Effect of T_P on the system profit, optimal S, and optimal T

T_P	Profit with security system ($)	Profit without security system ($)	% improve in profit by security system (%)	Optimal T with security system	Optimal S with security system	Optimal T without security system
1.0	7880	7317	7.7	4.34	0.67	3.29
1.2	7581	6995	8.4	4.57	0.69	3.41
1.4	7311	6708	9.0	4.78	0.71	3.52
1.6	7065	6449	9.6	4.98	0.72	3.62
1.8	6840	6213	10.1	5.16	0.74	3.71
2.0	6631	5997	10.6	5.33	0.75	3.79
2.2	6437	5798	11.0	5.48	0.76	3.86

T should extend. Moreover, the longer the system operates without interruption, the greater the likelihood of experiencing "successful" cyber-attacks. Therefore, as T_P extends, the necessity for a higher security level becomes apparent.

Table 6 demonstrates that an increase in the duration of minimal repair T_R diminishes the value derived from a security system. Specifically, when T_R nears the duration of T_P, the profit boost attributable to a security system reduces to merely 5.5%. These findings imply that investing in a higher level of security becomes less justified as T_R extends. Table 7 examines the effects of the duration of cyber-attacks T_A on system profits, revealing that a longer T_A enhances the value of having a security system. This observation aligns with the insights from the previous section, indicating that regardless of the specific durations of T_P and T_R, the presence of a security system generally leads to less frequent PM operations within the manufacturing process.

Table 6 Effect of T_R on the system profit, optimal S, and optimal T

T_R	Profit with security system ($)	Profit without security system ($)	% improve in profit by security system (%)	Optimal T with security system	Optimal S with security system	Optimal T without security system
0.2	7880	7317	7.7	4.34	0.67	3.29
0.4	7644	7143	7.0	4.03	0.63	3.19
0.5	7533	7059	6.7	3.91	0.61	3.14
0.6	7426	6977	6.4	3.79	0.59	3.09
0.8	7222	6817	5.9	3.59	0.56	2.99
0.9	7125	6739	5.7	3.51	0.54	2.95
1.0	7031	6663	5.5	3.42	0.53	2.91

Table 7 Effect of T_A on the system profit, optimal S, and optimal T

T_A	Profit with security system ($)	Profit without security system ($)	% improve in profit by security system (%)	Optimal T with security system	Optimal S with security system	Optimal T without security system
0.0	8915	8545	4.3	5.40	0.54	4.46
0.1	8337	7861	6.1	4.75	0.61	3.75
0.2	7880	7317	7.7	4.34	0.67	3.29
0.4	7175	6469	10.9	3.86	0.78	2.71
0.6	6641	5817	14.2	3.67	0.89	2.35
0.8	6221	5285	17.7	3.62	1.00	2.10
1.0	5864	4836	21.3	3.33	1.00	1.91

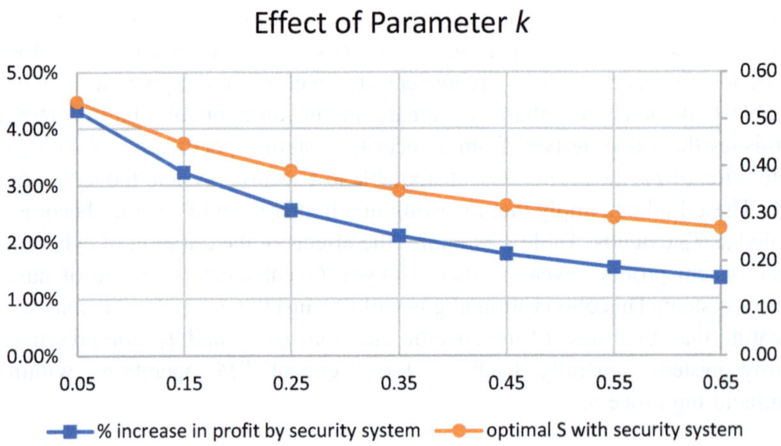

Fig. 2 The influence of parameter *k* on the system profit and optimal *S*

3.3 Effect of Parameters Related to the Failure Rate

An increase in either *k* or *l*, while keeping other parameters constant, leads to a higher failure rate in the manufacturing process. Accordingly, Fig. 2 demonstrates how changes in the *k* and *l* parameters similarly impact the manufacturing system, affecting both the percentage increase in profit and the optimal security level. For instance, with *k* set at 0.05, the profit increase and optimal security level are noted at 7.7% and 0.7, respectively. However, when *k* is increased to 0.65, these values change to 3.23% for profit increase and 0.37 for the optimal security level. Moreover, as *l* rises from 1 to 4, the profit increase diminishes from 7.70% to 2.36%. Figure 2 focuses solely on parameter *k* to illustrate its effect, as both *k* and *l* exhibit parallel impacts on the system. These findings suggest that the advantages of implementing a security system diminish in scenarios where the system's failure rate is elevated.

3.4 Effect of "Successful" Cyber-Attack Rate-Related Parameters

As depicted in Fig. 3, an increase in the parameter *g* implies that the system will face an increased number of cyber-attack threats, necessitating a higher value for the security system and an increased optimal security level accordingly. Conversely, a rise in the parameters h and f results in a decrease in both the optimal security level

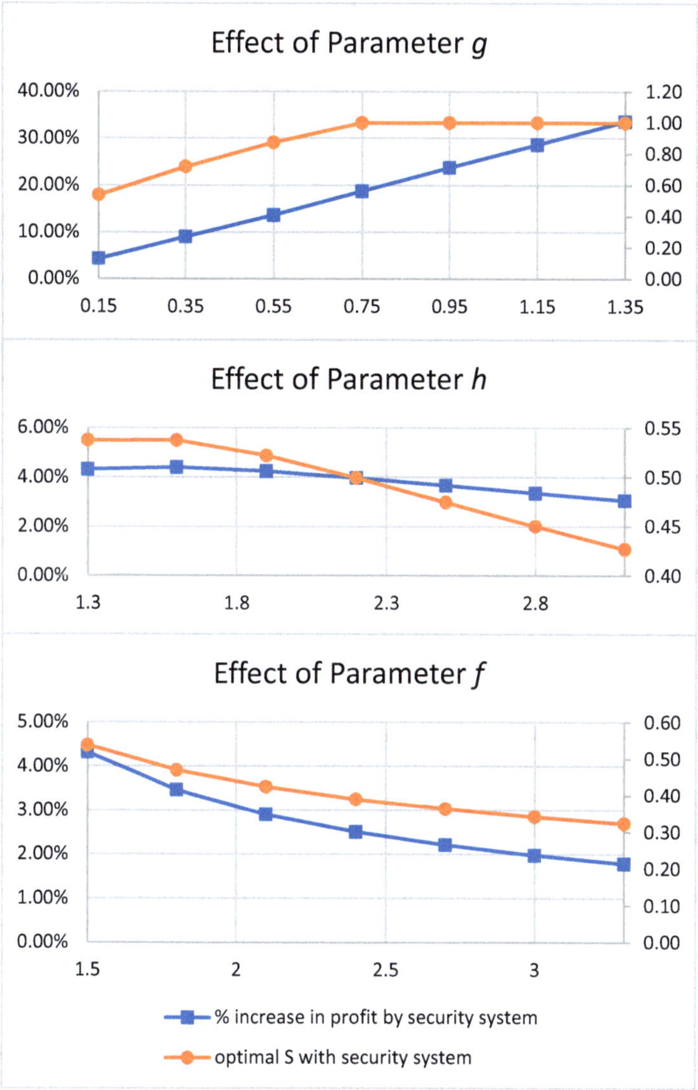

Fig. 3 The influence of parameters related to "successful" cyber-attacks on the system profit and optimal S

and the perceived value of the security system. Figure 3 illustrates that heightened values of these parameters, despite increasing cyber-attack occurrences, necessitate a reduction in the T value to diminish $\lambda_A(T, S)$. This adjustment leads to a more frequent schedule of preventive maintenance (PM) operations, allowing the manufacturer to reduce the optimal level of system security S.

4 Conclusion

Given the complexity and evolving nature of manufacturing systems, particularly with respect to maintenance operations and cybersecurity, the study's exploration into using cost subsidization for achieving optimal maintenance scheduling presents a significant contribution to the field. The findings align with established theories on maintenance optimization and cybersecurity in manufacturing systems, such as those discussed in works by Lee et al. (2006), who investigated the impact of maintenance policies on manufacturing performance, and by Li and Meerkov (2008), which focused on the resilience of production systems against disruptions.

The findings reinforce established theories on maintenance optimization and highlight the importance of integrating cybersecurity into traditional maintenance strategies. The model's suggestion that a unique optimal decision can be made for preventive maintenance (PM) frequency in response to cyber threats is particularly noteworthy. From a managerial perspective, the exploration of cost subsidization schemes offers practical solutions for enhancing system profitability and resilience. Implementing these strategies can help manufacturers better manage maintenance costs and mitigate cyber risks.

The analytical model's extension to include cybersecurity considerations is particularly timely, reflecting a growing recognition of cyber threats in the industrial sector. This approach mirrors insights from studies like the one by Lee et al. (2016), which emphasized the importance of integrating cybersecurity measures into traditional risk management for manufacturing systems. Additionally, the model's suggestion that a unique optimal decision can be made for PM frequency in response to cyber threats echoes the findings of Kim et al. (2017), who highlighted the critical role of physical preventive measures in protecting industrial control systems.

The exploration of cost subsidization schemes to coordinate system operations and achieve optimal profits suggests a novel approach to channel coordination in supply chain management, akin to strategies discussed by Cachon and Netessine (2006). This perspective not only enhances understanding of maintenance and cybersecurity in manufacturing but also offers practical solutions for improving system profitability and resilience.

However, the study's model is based on generated data, which may not capture all real-world complexities, highlighting a limitation that necessitates further validation with empirical data to generalize the findings. Future research directions include testing the model with real datasets to validate its applicability and accuracy, investigating the impact of cyber threats on maintenance policies more comprehensively, and exploring additional cost coordination mechanisms in different manufacturing contexts. The proposal to test the model with real datasets and further investigate the impact of cyber threats on maintenance policies is in line with the call for empirical research by Rajkumar et al. (2010), who stressed the need for data-driven approaches to optimize maintenance and security in manufacturing systems. Also, future research should explore additional cost coordination mechanisms in different manufacturing contexts.

This study contributes to the burgeoning literature on the intersection of maintenance optimization, cybersecurity, and supply chain management in manufacturing systems. Its findings offer theoretical and practical insights that could guide future research and inform the development of more resilient and profitable manufacturing operations.

Appendix

Proof of Lemma 1 (i) By differentiating *h*(*T*) with respect to *T*, we obtain: $\frac{\partial h(T)}{\partial T} = \lambda_R'(T)(T+T_p)$. Given that $\lambda_R(T)$ increases with *T*, $\lambda_R'(T)$ remains positive for all *T*. Consequently, $\frac{\partial h(T)}{\partial T}$ is always greater than 0 for any $T > 0$, indicating that *h*(*T*) consistently rises as *T* increases. (ii) To find the value of *T* that maximizes system profit π_{s1}, we differentiate π_t with respect to *T* and set the derivative equal to zero, yielding: $\lambda_R(T)(T+T_p) - M_R(T) = \frac{RT_p + C_p}{(T_R R + C_R)}$. The right side of this equation is always positive, and since the left side increases with *T*, there exists a unique solution to this equation. If we denote T_{S1}^* as the solution that maximizes system profit, then $\pi_S''(T_{S1}^*) = \frac{-\lambda_R'(T_{S1}^*)(T_R R + C_R)(T_{S1}^* + T_p)^2}{(T_{S1}^* + T_p)^3} < 0$. Thus, T_{S1}^* is the only solution to maximizing system profit.

Proof of Corollary 1 (i) Applying the technique of implicit differentiation, we find that $\frac{\partial h(T_{S1}^*)}{\partial C_p} = \frac{1}{RT_r + C_r}$ and $\frac{\partial h(T_{S1}^*)}{\partial T_{S1}^*}\frac{\partial T_{S1}^*}{\partial C_p} = \lambda'(T_{S1}^*)(T_{S1}^* + T_p)\frac{\partial T_{S1}^*}{\partial C_p}$. Hence, we have $\frac{\partial T_{S1}^*}{\partial C_p} = \frac{1}{RT_r + C_r}\frac{1}{\lambda'(T_{S1}^*)(T_{S1}^* + T_p)} > 0$, indicating an increase in T_{S1}^* as C_p increases. Employing a similar approach for part (ii), we can prove it directly. For part (iii), we have $\frac{\partial T_{S1}^*}{\partial R} = \frac{T_p C_R - T_R C_p}{\lambda_R'(T_{S1}^*)(T_{S1}^* + T_p)(RT_R + C_R)^2}$. If $T_p C_R > T_R C_p$, then $\frac{\partial T_{S1}^*}{\partial R} > 0$ and vice versa. For part (iv), we have $\frac{\partial T_{S1}^*}{\partial T_p} = [\frac{R}{RT_r + C_r} - \lambda_R(T_{S1}^*)]\frac{1}{\lambda'(T_{S1}^*)(T_{S1}^* + T_p)}$. Therefore, if $\frac{R}{RT_r + C_r} > \lambda_R(T_{S1}^*)$, then $\frac{\partial T_{S1}^*}{\partial T_p} > 0$.

Proof of Lemma 2 (i) & (ii) Echoing the approach taken in part (ii) of the proof for Lemma 1, we demonstrate that T_{m1}^* and T_{c1}^* are the unique solutions for maximizing the profit functions of the manufacturer and contractor, respectively. This is achieved by setting the first derivatives of π_m and π_c to zero. The second derivatives of π_m and π_c are found to be: $\pi_m''(T_{m1}^*) = \frac{-\lambda_R'(T_{m1}^*)T_R R(T_{m1}^* + T_p)^2}{(T_{m1}^* + T_p)^3} < 0$ and $\pi_c''(T_{c1}^*) = \frac{-\lambda_R'(T_{c1}^*)C_R(T_{c1}^* + T_p)^2}{(T_{c1}^* + T_p)^3} < 0$, confirming that, T_{m1}^* and T_{c1}^* are indeed the unique solutions for maximizing profits for the manufacturer and contractor, respectively.

Proof of Lemma 3 (i) We establish $T^*_{c2} = T^*_{m2} = T^*_{S1}$ when $h(T^*_{c2}) = h(T^*_{m2}) = h(T^*_{S1})$. By equating $h(T^*_{c2}) = h(T^*_{m2})$, we find $(1 - a)C_p/(1 - b)C_R = (RT_P + aC_P)/(T_R R + bC_R)$. Solving this equation yields the value for a. (ii) Following from Lemma 1, where $h(T)$ is shown to be an increasing function, it follows that $T^*_{c2} > T^*_{m2}$ if $h(T^*_{c2}) > h(T^*_{m2})$ and the reverse is true otherwise. It is logically deduced that T^*_{S1} always lies between T^*_{c2} and T^*_{m2}.

Proof of Corollary 2 Let's consider that channel coordination via cost subsidization is effectively established by the manufacturer through the strategic choice of parameters a and b. Under this arrangement, the contractor is tasked with selecting T^*_{S1} to maximize its profit, represented by the equation $P - \frac{(1-a)C_p - (1-b)M_R(T^*_{S1})C_R}{T^*_{S1}+T_p}$, which must meet or exceed a minimum profit threshold $P_{\min}$. Upon resolving this inequality, we determine the minimum permissible value of P. Simultaneously, the profit for the manufacturer at T^*_{S1} is given by $\frac{R\left(T^*_{S1} - M_R(T^*_{S1})T_R\right) - aC_p - M_R(T^*_{S1})bC_R}{T^*_{S1}+T_p}$, which needs to be at least equivalent to the manufacturer's profit at T^*_{c2} is chosen, denoted as $\pi_m(T^*_{c2}) - P_{\min}$.

Proof of Lemma 4 (i) We begin by differentiating π_s with respect to S to find the first derivative: $\frac{d\pi_s}{dS} = \frac{-C_A}{T+T_P} \cdot \frac{dM_A(T,S)}{dS} - C'_S(S)$. Setting $\frac{d\pi_s}{dS} = 0$ according to the First Order Conditions yields: $\frac{dM_A(T,S)}{dS} \cdot C_A + C'_S(S)(T+T_P) = 0$. Following this, the second derivative with respect to S is $\frac{d^2_{\pi_S}}{d^2_S} = \frac{-C_A}{T+T_P} \cdot \frac{d^2M_A(T,S)}{d^2S} - C''_S(S)$, which, based on our previous assumptions about $C_S(S)$ and $M_A(T, S)$, is always negative, indicating that π_s is concave with respect to S. This means for any fixed T, there's only one S value that satisfies the first derivative equation.

Next, The first derivative of π_s with respect to T is:

$$\frac{d\pi_s}{dT} = \frac{[-\lambda_R(T)(T+T_P)+M_R(T)](RT_R+C_R)+C_A[-\lambda_A(T,S)(T+T_P)+M_A(T,S)]+RT_P+C_P}{(T+T_P)^2}$$

Setting $\frac{d\pi_s}{dT} = 0$ to satisfy the First Order Conditions, we achieve the following equation

$$\lambda_R(T)(T+T_P) - M_R(T) = \frac{R\,T_P + C_P + C_A[-\lambda_A(T,S)(T+T_P) + M_A(T,S)]}{RT_R + C_R} \tag{19}$$

Let $g(T,S) = \lambda_A(T,S)(T + T_P) - M_A(T,S)$, then the Eq. (19) can be simplified as follows:

$$h(T) + \frac{C_A}{RT_R + C_R} \cdot g(T, S) = \frac{R\,T_P + C_P}{RT_R + C_R} \tag{20}$$

Given $h(T)$ and $g(T, S)$ are increasing with T, there exists a unique T which satisfies (20), for any given S.

Then, we take the second derivative of π_s with respect to T, and assume that $X = RT_R + C_R$ and $Y = T + T_p$, we have the following equation:

$$\frac{d^2_{\pi_s}}{d^2_T} = \frac{\left[-\lambda'_R(T)Y^2X + 2\lambda_R(T)YX - \lambda'_A(T,S)C_AY^2 + 2\lambda_A(T,S)C_AY - 2RT_P - 2C_P - 2M_R(T)X - 2M_A(T,S)C_A\right]}{Y^3} \tag{21}$$

Replace T from Eq. (19) to Eq. (21), we obtain:

$$\frac{d^2_{\pi_s}}{d^2_T} = \frac{-\lambda'_R(T)X - \lambda'_A(T,S)C_A}{T + T_P} < 0$$

The result shows that π_s is concave with respect to T at the critical point that satisfies (20). Also, combining the facts that only one S and only one T value satisfy $\frac{dM_A(T,S)}{dS} \cdot C_A + C'_S(\mathrm{S})(T + T_P) = 0$ and $h(T) + \frac{C_A}{RT_R + C_R} \cdot g(T, S) = \frac{R\,T_P + C_P}{RT_R + C_R}$ respectively, we find that there is a unique critical internal point. Moreover, because of the concavity properties, this critical point is (at least) a local maximum.

(ii) Analysis of the Hessian matrix H_S of π_s is *not* globally negative definite, indicating the global optimal solution for π_s could be the unique local maximum identified in part (i) $\left(T^*_{S3}, S^*_{S3}\right)$, or at the endpoints. Evaluating the endpoints, we find that if $T = 0$, then $M_R(T) = 0$ and $M_A(T, S) = 0$. The system profit is negative and equals $\frac{-C_P}{T_p} - C_S(S)$. If $T \to \infty$, then $M_R(T) \to \infty$ and $M_A(T, S) \to \infty$. Then, the system profit is negative infinity. Thus, we eliminate the need to consider T endpoints. However, endpoints involving S need examination, necessitating consideration of $S = 0$ and $S = 1$ as potential global maximizer.

Proof of Corollary 3 It is similar to Corollary 2.

References

Alhilman, J., Atmaji, F. T. D., & Athari, N. (2017). Software application for maintenance system: A combination of maintenance methods in printing industry. In *2017 fifth international conference on information and communication technology (ICoIC7)* (pp. 1–6). IEEE.

Cachon, G. P., & Netessine, S. (2006). Game theory in supply chain analysis. *Models, methods, and applications for innovative decision making* (pp. 200–233).

Coleman, S., Damodaran, S., Chandramoull, M., & Deuel, E. (2017). *Making maintenance smarter predictive maintenance and the digital supply network.* Retrieved from https://www2.deloitte.

com/us/en/insights/focus/industry-4-0/using-predictive-technologies-for-asset-maintenance.html

Corallo, A., Lazoi, M., & Lezzi, M. (2020). Cybersecurity in the context of industry 4.0: A structured classification of critical assets and business impacts. *Computers in Industry, 114*, 103165.

Data Breach Chronology (2023). *Privacy Rights*. Retrieved from https://privacyrights.org/data-breaches?fbclid=IwAR0NdcQqGo_tguu6VGEyaG85-qoJSEBkQLxsLBfRjj_PZjN4ZSAswH9SZ7w

Evans, D. (2011). The internet of things: How the next evolution of the internet is changing everything. *CISCO White Paper*, 1–11.

Kane, A. P., Kore, A. S., Khandale, A. N., Nigade, S. S., & Joshi, P. P. (2022). Predictive maintenance using machine learning. *arXiv preprint arXiv:2205.09402.*

Kim, H. E., Son, H. S., Kim, J., & Kang, H. G. (2017). Systematic development of scenarios caused by cyber-attack-induced human errors in nuclear power plants. *Reliability Engineering & System Safety, 167*, 290–301.

Krauss, C. (2018). Cyberattack shows vulnerability of gas pipeline network. *New York Times*. Retrieved from https://www.nytimes.com/2018/04/04/business/energy-environment/pipeline-cyberattack.html

Lee, J., Ni, J., Djurdjanovic, D., Qiu, H., & Liao, H. (2006). Intelligent prognostics tools and e-maintenance. *Computers in Industry, 57*(6), 476–489.

Lee, J., Bagheri, B., & Jin, C. (2016). Introduction to cyber manufacturing. *Manufacturing Letters, 8*, 11–15.

Li, J., & Meerkov, S. M. (2008). *Production systems engineering*. Springer Science & Business Media.

Madu, C. N. (1999). Reliability and quality interface. *International Journal of Quality & Reliability Management, 16*(7), 691–698. https://doi.org/10.1108/02656719910286198

Milgate, M. (2001). *Alliances, outsourcing and the learning organization*. Quorum.

Muchiri, P. N., Pintelon, L., Martin, H., & Chemweno, P. (2014). Modelling maintenance effects on manufacturing equipment performance: Results from simulation analysis. *International Journal of Production Research, 52*(11), 3287–3302. https://doi.org/10.1080/00207543.2013.870673

Rajkumar, R., Lee, I., Sha, L., & Stankovic, J. (2010, June). Cyber-physical systems: The next computing revolution. In *Proceedings of the 47th design automation conference* (pp. 731–736).

Richards, S. C., Purdy, G., & Woodall, W. H. (2015). Surveillance of nonhomogeneous Poisson processes. *Technometrics, 57*(3), 388–394.

Ross, S. M. (1983). *Stochastic processes* (Series in probability and mathematical statistics) (pp. 61–62).

Ross, S. M. (2014). *Introduction to probability models*. Academic.

Ryan, J. J., Mazzuchi, T. A., Ryan, D. J., De la Cruz, J. L., & Cooke, R. (2012). Quantifying information security risks using expert judgment elicitation. *Computers & Operations Research, 39*(4), 774–784.

Salonen, A., & Deleryd, M. (2011). Cost of poor maintenance: A concept for maintenance performance improvement. *Journal of Quality in Maintenance Engineering, 17*(1), 63–73. https://doi.org/10.1108/13552510910961110

Ta, A., Tarakci, H., Kulkarni, S., Prybutok, V., & Pavur, R. (2023). The effects of cyber threats on maintenance outsourcing and age replacement policy. *Computers in Industry, 144*(103), 787.

Tarakci, H. (2016). Two types of learning effects on maintenance activities. *International Journal of Production Research, 54*(6), 1721–1734.

Tarakci, H., Tang, K., Moskowitz, H., & Plante, R. (2006). Incentive maintenance outsourcing contracts for channel coordination and improvement. *IIE Transactions, 38*(8), 671–684.

Tarakci, H., Tang, K., & Teyarachakul, S. (2013). Learning and forgetting effects on maintenance outsourcing. *IIE Transactions (Institute of Industrial Engineers), 45*(4), 449–463.

Tarakci, H., Ponnaiyan, S., & Kulkarni, S. (2014). Maintenance-outsourcing contracts for a system with backup machines. *International Journal of Production Research, 52*(11), 3259–3272. https://doi.org/10.1080/00207543.2013.870361

The Department of Homeland Security (DHS). (2016). *Recommended practice: Improving industrial control system cybersecurity with defense-in-depth strategies*. Retrieved from https://ics-cert.us-cert.gov/sites/default/files/recommended_practices/NCCIC_ICS-CERT_Defense_in_Depth_2016_S508C.pdf

Tseng, F. S., Tang, K., Moskowitz, H., & Plante, R. (2009). Maintenance outsourcing contracts for new technology adoptions. *IEEE Transactions on Engineering Management, 56*(2), 203–218. https://doi.org/10.1109/TEM.2009.2013824

Tuptuk, N., & Hailes, S. (2018). Security of smart manufacturing systems. *Journal of Manufacturing Systems, 47*, 93–106.

Wang, W. (2010). A model for maintenance service contract design, negotiation and optimization. *European Journal of Operational Research, 201*(1), 239–246. https://doi.org/10.1016/j.ejor.2009.02.018

Wee, H. M., & Widyadana, G. A. (2013). A production model for deteriorating items with stochastic preventive maintenance time and rework process with FIFO rule. *Omega, 41*, 941–954.

Wu, D., Ren, A., Zhang, W., Fan, F., Liu, P., Fu, X., & Terpenny, J. (2018). Cybersecurity for digital manufacturing. *Journal of Manufacturing Systems, 48*, 3–12.

Xiang, Y., Cassady, C. R., Jin, T., & Zhang, C. W. (2014). Joint production and maintenance planning with machine deterioration and random yield. *International Journal of Production Research, 52*(6), 1644–1657. https://doi.org/10.1080/00207543.2013.843037

Evaluation of Resilient 4PL Provider for Online Plant Store: An Intuitionistic Fuzzy DOBI Approach

B. Nila and Jagannath Roy

1 Introduction

E-commerce is becoming increasingly popular, with an increasing number of organizations and consumers performing online purchases. Through e-commerce, customers may easily browse, choose, buy, order, and pay for a large variety of goods available on the international market. There are numerous reasons for the flourishment of e-commerce, which include the reduced hurdles to entry in foreign markets, the quicker establishment of an international presence, streamlined B2B sales cycles, and so forth. E-commerce saves customers money, time, and effort by allowing them to buy goods from around the world. Furthermore, e-commerce offers a plethora of benefits, such as the ease of access to products on a global scale, its quickness, and the convenience of buying from the comfort of one's couch with just a single click (Gurău et al., 2001). However, the delivery of products is often delayed and unsatisfactory due to the complex supply chains (SC) that require physical transportation, time, costs, and various resources and can also encounter abundant risks and disruptions (Delfmann et al., 2002).

E-commerce frequently creates different logistical issues and demands, such as credible product delivery in the least feasible time, competitive rates and delivery circumstances, great quality of products and services, frequent delivery of minor consignments, and product return. It can be claimed that the proper operation of e-commerce depends heavily on logistics and product delivery (Bhattacharjya et al., 2016).

B. Nila · J. Roy (✉)
Department of Mathematics, National Institute of Technology Warangal, Hanumakonda, Telangana, India
e-mail: nb720101@student.nitw.ac.in; jroy@nitw.ac.in

F. P. García Márquez et al. (eds.), *Outsourcing Using Operations Research and Management Science Methods*, International Series in Operations Research & Management Science 366, https://doi.org/10.1007/978-3-031-91845-2_8

E-commerce shipment demands meticulous planning and attention to guarantee their safe arrival at the designated destination when dealing with delicate items like live plants. Timely and secure delivery assumes paramount importance in this case. Online retailers search for novel approaches to distribute goods and effectively satisfy customers' growing demands. One strategy is to hire logistics service providers (LSPs) like fourth-party logistics (4PL) with the skills, resources, and knowledge required to offer and provide all logistical services in SC design, planning, management, and product delivery processes. 4PL involves outsourcing the entire supply chain management to a single external partner. A 4PL provider acts as a strategic intermediary between the client company and multiple logistics service providers, coordinating and managing all aspects of the supply chain, including vendors and technology (Huang et al., 2019). A wide range of companies offer e-commerce logistics services internationally, so choosing the appropriate one is crucial and, at the same time, challenging.

The decision-making process is guided by several concerns pertaining to e-commerce and global SCs. The market requirements, along with logistics and supporting process characteristics, are characterized by a high degree of uncertainty, imprecision, unpredictability, and indeterminacy. Numerous people participate in the processes, which are carried out in various settings and locations. The decision-making process is made more difficult by incomplete, inconsistent, and haphazardly formatted information, as well as input parameters that lack adequate reliability. Furthermore, there have been several obstacles and disruptions to SCs, such as natural disasters, pandemics, trade restrictions, energy and economic crises, and SC concentration. This highlights the resilience of LSPs and all SC contributors. Yet, the mentioned disruptions are challenging to foresee and incorporate into conventional decision-making models. Managing the e-commerce SC demands quicker decision-making than traditional trade, adding complexity to the process.

The aforementioned points make the decision process a Multi-Criteria Decision Making (MCDM) process. The traditional MCDM methods are only partially effective in treating this problem. Instead, new integrated techniques must be developed and put into use. Such techniques are clearly lacking in the existing literature, particularly in real-life scenarios. The primary reason behind authoring this work was to bridge the identified gap, in which the authors attempted to present a novel framework and strategy for assessing a resilient 4PL provider for handling live plants based on the intuitionistic fuzzy Dombi–Bonferroni (DOBI) method for e-commerce demands. The proposed methodology was verified and implemented in evaluating resilient 4PL providers for an online retailer from an Indian city, Kochi, which sells and delivers live plants throughout the country. The primary scientific contribution of this study is the proposed and implemented framework, demonstrated through a practical example. Furthermore, this work makes a substantial contribution by connecting several contemporary and crucial components of the SC, including resilience, e-commerce, and the potential for 4PL providers to improve the delivery of products ordered online.

2 Literature Review

The literature on logistics in e-commerce focuses on SC design, outbound and reverse logistics approaches, warehouse operations, and Information Technology (IT) and data management in e-commerce (Zennaro et al., 2022). The focus is on efficient customer reach through omnichannel, multichannel, or pure e-commerce. Diverse methods and models are employed for SC conformation (Baglio et al., 2020; Govindarajan et al., 2021). Outbound logistics involves the transportation and warehousing of products from businesses to patrons. Various research has been conducted on topics such as last-mile logistics, vehicle routing problems, new trends, environmental impact of transports, outsourcing issues, logistics pooling, and packaging processes (Zennaro et al., 2022; Ranieri et al., 2018; Braekers et al., 2016; Morana et al., 2014). Reverse logistics involves handling the return of products from customers to sellers or manufacturers, including transportation, storage, and disposal. It's crucial in the SC as it impacts business costs and efficiency. Effective management can boost profitability and competitiveness by reducing costs, improving goods retrieval rates, and enhancing buyer service (Stock & Mulki, 2009). Warehousing is another decisive part of the SC, involving intermediate storage between manufacturers and retailers. It ensures smooth goods flow and efficiency in logistics operations (De Koster et al., 2017). An efficient warehouse plan can modernise procedures, minimize employee fatigue, and advance client service (Melacini et al., 2018). E-commerce literature highlights order-picking strategies, mechanisation levels, and warehouse performance as significant issues (Shah & Khanzode, 2017). IT and data management in e-commerce is the use of IT and data management to facilitate e-commerce procedures, offering benefits like increased competition, lower prices, vendor comparison, and easy access. The development of e-commerce has augmented the importance of logistics information systems and SC information systems, which manage and optimize information flow in logistics operations and SCs (White et al., 2014). Integrating these systems improves efficiency and effectiveness by providing real-time data on inventory levels and transportation schedules. Service quality and user satisfaction are crucial aspects of e-commerce (Kilibarda et al., 2020). Studies have shown that logistics service dimensions impact consumer satisfaction, and e-SC management directly impacts customer satisfaction (Vasić et al., 2021). A positive relationship was found between E-SC management and customer satisfaction, E-SC management and service quality, service quality and customer contentment (Abdirad & Krishnan, 2022). Factors influencing satisfaction and reuse intention of 3PL services among online sellers in Malaysia were identified using the stimulus-organism-response theory (Ngah et al., 2021). Sustainability dimensions in e-commerce and logistics are also recognized, along with trends like technological advancements, crowd shipping, operation modes, and policymaking.

The literature offers various interpretations of resilience in the context of SC management. Some define resilience as a system's ability to recover from disturbances within an acceptable timeframe, while others view it as a company's capacity to withstand disruptions and successfully recover (Ralston & Blackhurst, 2020; Park et al., 2022; Blackhurst et al., 2011). Another perspective suggests that resilience is the ability to return to the original state or transition to a new state after disturbances. In conclusion, resilience can denote a system's capability to rebound from disruptions promptly, a company's adeptness at enduring and bouncing back from disturbances, or the capacity to revert to the initial state or adapt to a new one after disruptions. Recent studies emphasize that responding to disruptions requires restructuring, adaptation, or reconfiguration of the SC network. Various research efforts evaluate the resilience of SC networks, exploring relationships among global SC risks, resilience, and mitigating strategies (Cano et al., 2022). In recent years, studies on product SC resilience have shown significant progress, but there is a gap regarding the supply aspect of logistics services (Zhang et al., 2022a). The authors highlight the distinctive nature of logistics services' supply, which significantly influences collaboration in the SC. Game theory and other models are employed to analyse decision-making for optimal returns under bounded rationality (Diehlmann et al., 2021). From an interdisciplinary perspective, some researchers classify resilience into engineering and socioecological perspectives. The engineering perspective treats the SC as a closed system, emphasizing optimization, quick response to disruptions, and swift recovery while the socioecological perspective views the SC as an open system influenced by the changing environment, emphasizing transformation and adaptation (Wieland & Durach, 2021; Novak et al., 2021). The LSPs are recognized as key contributors to SC resilience. LSPs' integration and cooperation along the global SC play a vital role, but disruptions impact their resilience and operations significantly (Panayides & So, 2005). Research focuses on LSPs' resilience in the face of various challenges, including port strikes, COVID-19, and logistics outsourcing vulnerabilities (Carvalho et al., 2018; Iyengar et al., 2021; Herold et al., 2021). However, limited research exists on how LSPs specifically contribute to building resilience in SCs, particularly while dealing with live plants. This study aims to address this gap and contribute to the existing literature.

The literature review in this paragraph focuses on the selection and evaluation of 4PL providers. Very limited research exists on this topic, but notable contributions include Aydin et al.'s proposal of a neutrosophic MCDM method for assessing 4PL providers' performance (Aydın et al., 2022). This method utilized a defined neutrosophic language scale for expert evaluations. Bhatti et al. employed Taguchi's loss function to create a model for the selection of 3PL by 4PLs (Bhatti et al., 2010). Caglar and Aydin explored the capabilities and role of 4PL in SC agility and company's performance, emphasizing the benefits of partnerships with 4PL (Çağlar & Aydın, 2020). Buyukozkan et al. proposed an analytical MCDM approach based on the 2-additive Choquet integral to evaluate 4PL operating models (Büyüközkan et al., 2009). Zhang et al. established a mixed-integer nonlinear programming model for multiperiod distribution network design from a 4PL perspective (Zhang et al., 2022b). Few papers focus on 4PL resilience, with Huang et al. considering a 4PL network creation problem accounting for ambiguous disturbances (Huang et al., 2011). Regarding SC resilience, Yazdi et al. explored critical success factors for transportation service providers, offering a method based on the Best-Worst Method

(BWM) and Multi-Attributive Border Approximation Area Comparison (MABAC) (Karbassi Yazdi et al., 2023). Naseem et al. developed an approach combining Grey Relational Analysis and Technique for Order Preference by Similarity to Ideal Solution (TOPSIS) for selecting the best LSP for e-commerce firms (Naseem et al., 2021).

Based on the literature mentioned above, it is evident that numerous studies have been conducted on e-commerce. Nevertheless, it is noteworthy that the specific domain of e-commerce pertaining to live plants remains relatively underexplored. There exists a notable gap in the literature concerning factors such as consumer behaviours, logistical challenges, ecological considerations, and the unique characteristics of live plants as commodities in the online marketplace and opportunities associated with its online trade. This unexplored territory serves as a compelling motivation for the present research, offering the potential to uncover insights and contribute to the evolving landscape of digital commerce, especially in the context of horticulture and the live plant market.

3 Methodology

3.1 Intuitionistic Fuzzy Sets

Atanassov pioneered the concept of an Intuitionistic Fuzzy Set (IFS), comprising degrees of membership and non-membership, both values falling within the unit interval [0, 1], with their sum constrained to 1 (Atanassov & Atanassov, 1999). IFSs offer a superior means of capturing fuzziness and offer a broader framework compared to traditional fuzzy sets. Thus, in IFS-based MCDM, decision-makers can express not only the degree of membership but also the level of non-membership between the alternatives and criteria. By incorporating hesitation, IFS-based MCDM offers a more nuanced approach to decision-making, enabling the consideration of both positive and negative perceptions simultaneously (Li, 2005). This methodology has found applications in diverse fields such as engineering, finance, and healthcare, where decision-makers often face complex, uncertain, and conflicting information. The fundamental principles of IFSs are outlined as follows (Atanassov & Atanassov, 1999):

Definition 1 Let I be an IFS in the universe of discourse X (Atanassov & Atanassov, 1999). Then,

$$I = \{(X, \mu(x), \nu(x)) | x \in X\}$$

where $\mu(x)$ and $\nu(x)$ represents the membership and non-membership degrees such that $0 \leq \mu(x) + \nu(x) \leq 1; \forall\, x \in X$ and $\mu(x), \nu(x) : X \rightarrow [0, 1]$.

3.2 IF-DOBI Method

Step 1. The decision-makers evaluate the criteria using intuitionistic fuzzy linguistic terms (IFLT). The obtained results are given in Eq. (1)

$$D_k = \left(\left(\mu_1^k, \nu_1^k\right),\ \left(\mu_2^k, \nu_2^k\right),\ \cdots\ \left(\mu_m^k, \nu_m^k\right)\right) \tag{1}$$

where, $k = 1, 2, \ldots, t$ (Seikh & Mandal, 2021).

Step 2. Aggregate the decision-makers' opinions by taking the average to obtain the IF weights of the criteria.

$$\left(\mu_j, \nu_j\right) = \frac{\left(\mu_j^1, \nu_j^1\right) + \left(\mu_j^2, \nu_j^2\right) + \cdots + \left(\mu_j^t, \nu_j^t\right)}{k} \tag{2}$$

Step 3. The criteria weights are calculated using Eq. (3).

$$w_j = \frac{\left(\mu_j, \nu_j\right)}{\sum_{j=1}^{m} \left(\mu_j, \nu_j\right)} \tag{3}$$

Step 4. The decision-makers evaluate the alternatives with respect to the criteria using IFLT.

$$D_k = \begin{pmatrix} \left(\mu_{11}^k, \nu_{11}^k\right) & \left(\mu_{12}^k, \nu_{12}^k\right) & \cdots & \left(\mu_{1n}^k, \nu_{1n}^k\right) \\ \vdots & \vdots & \ddots & \vdots \\ \left(\mu_{m1}^k, \nu_{m1}^k\right) & \left(\mu_{m2}^k, \nu_{m2}^k\right) & \cdots & \left(\mu_{mn}^k, \nu_{mn}^k\right) \end{pmatrix} \tag{4}$$

Step 5. Aggregate the decision-makers' opinions by taking the average to obtain the initial decision matrix.

$$\left(\mu_{ij}, \nu_{ij}\right) = \frac{\left(\mu_{ij}^1, \nu_{ij}^1\right) + \left(\mu_{ij}^2, \nu_{ij}^2\right) + \cdots + \left(\mu_{ij}^t, \nu_{ij}^t\right)}{k} \tag{5}$$

Step 6. Normalize the initial decision matrix.

$$\left(\mu_{ij}', \nu_{ij}'\right) = \begin{cases} \left(\mu_{ij}, \nu_{ij}\right), \text{if } j \text{ is benefit type} \\ \left(\nu_{ij}, \mu_{ij}\right), \text{if } j \text{ is cost type} \end{cases} \tag{6}$$

Step 7. Compute the weighted IF-DOBI averaging function $\wp_i^{(1)\alpha_1,\alpha_2,\rho}$ and weighted IF-DOBI geometric function $\wp_i^{(2)\alpha_1,\alpha_2,\rho}$ (Seikh & Mandal, 2021).

$$\wp_i^{(1)\alpha_1,\alpha_2,\rho} = \left(\begin{array}{c} \sum_{i=1}^{n} \mu'_{ij} - \dfrac{\sum_{i=1}^{n} \mu'_{ij}}{\left\{ 1 + \left\{ \dfrac{1}{w_i w_j (\alpha_1+\alpha_2)} \dfrac{1-w_i}{\sum\limits_{\substack{i,j=1 \\ i \neq j}}^{n} \dfrac{1}{\alpha_1 \left(\frac{f(\mu'_i)}{1-f(\mu'_i)} \right)^{\rho} + \alpha_2 \left(\frac{f(\mu'_j)}{1-f(\mu'_j)} \right)^{\rho}}} \right\} \right\}^{1/\rho}}, \\ \dfrac{\sum_{i=1}^{n} \nu'_{ij}}{\left\{ 1 + \left\{ \dfrac{1}{w_i w_j (\alpha_1+\alpha_2)} \dfrac{1-w_i}{\sum\limits_{\substack{i,j=1 \\ i \neq j}}^{n} \dfrac{1}{\alpha_1 \left(\frac{1-f(\nu'_i)}{f(\nu'_i)} \right)^{\rho} + \alpha_2 \left(\frac{1-f(\nu'_j)}{f(\nu'_j)} \right)^{\rho}}} \right\} \right\}^{1/\rho}} \end{array} \right) \quad (7)$$

$$\wp_i^{(2)\alpha_1,\alpha_2,\rho} = \left(\begin{array}{c} \dfrac{\sum_{i=1}^{n} \mu'_{ij}}{\left\{ 1 + \left\{ \dfrac{1}{w_i w_j (\alpha_1+\alpha_2)} \dfrac{1-w_i}{\sum\limits_{\substack{i,j=1 \\ i \neq j}}^{n} \dfrac{1}{\alpha_1 \left(\frac{1-f(\mu'_i)}{f(\mu'_i)} \right)^{\rho} + \alpha_2 \left(\frac{1-f(\mu'_j)}{f(\mu'_j)} \right)^{\rho}}} \right\} \right\}^{1/\rho}}, \\ \sum_{i=1}^{n} \nu'_{ij} - \dfrac{\sum_{i=1}^{n} \nu'_{ij}}{\left\{ 1 + \left\{ \dfrac{1}{w_i w_j (\alpha_1+\alpha_2)} \dfrac{1-w_i}{\sum\limits_{\substack{i,j=1 \\ i \neq j}}^{n} \dfrac{1}{\alpha_1 \left(\frac{f(\nu'_i)}{1-f(\nu'_i)} \right)^{\rho} + \alpha_2 \left(\frac{f(\nu'_j)}{1-f(\nu'_j)} \right)^{\rho}}} \right\} \right\}^{1/\rho}} \end{array} \right) \quad (8)$$

Step 8. Evaluate the integrated value of IF-DOBI function $\Im_i$.

$$\Im_i = \frac{\wp_{\mathrm{i}}{}^{(1)\alpha_1,\alpha_2,\rho} + \wp_{\mathrm{i}}{}^{(2)\alpha_1,\alpha_2,\rho}}{1 + \left\{\frac{1}{2}\left(\frac{1-\wp_{\mathrm{i}}{}^{(1)\alpha_1,\alpha_2,\rho}}{\wp_{\mathrm{i}}{}^{(1)\alpha_1,\alpha_2,\rho}}\right)^{\tau} + \frac{1}{2}\left(\frac{1-\wp_{\mathrm{i}}{}^{(2)\alpha_1,\alpha_2,\rho}}{\wp_{\mathrm{i}}{}^{(2)\alpha_1,\alpha_2,\rho}}\right)^{\tau}\right\}}; \tau \geq 0 \quad (9)$$

Step 9. The alternatives are ranked on the basis of $\Im_i$. We use the score function of IF numbers, given by Eq. (10) for comparing $\Im_i$.

$$\Phi(\mu, \nu) = \mu - \nu \quad (10)$$

4 Case Study

The proposed strategy was put to the test using the example of an online merchant from Kochi that sells live plants all over India. The company relies on multiple logistics providers across the country. The company has been engaged in a mission for a while now involving the hiring of a 4PL provider, who would handle all aspects of SC planning, design, and management, as well as product delivery to end users through the process of logistics outsourcing. The company has partnered with four decision-makers ($D1$, $D2$,..., $D4$) who are logistics industry specialists with over a decade of experience in SC management. The task is to find a reliable and effective 4PL partner with whom the organization can actively collaborate over the long term. With the guidance of these experienced DMs, we compile a dataset comprising 10 essential criteria ($C1$, $C2$,..., $C10$), as outlined in Table 1. In the table, whether it is a minimization (cost) criterion or maximization (benefit) criterion. For a cost criterion, the minimum is the better and for a benefit criterion, the maximum is the better. Ten 4PL suppliers responded to the company's request for bids after it published an advertisement. Six of these companies were deemed feasible options by the experts. These six service providers were identified as $A1, A2, A3, A4, A5$, and $A6$.

4.1 Evaluation of Criteria

In accordance with the concepts of IFLT (see Table 2), the expert panel evaluated the 10 criteria. Table 3 gives the ratings done by the experts. The IFLTs are converted to IF numbers, and then the average of the opinions is calculated. The weights of the criteria are found by employing Eq. (3). The obtained weights are given in Table 4. An example of the calculation is given below.

Table 1 Description of criteria

Criteria	Description	Type
Service time (C1)	Order-to-delivery time for end consumers	Min
Service price (C2)	Cost of delivering the product	Min
Technological expertise (C3)	Several solutions facilitating real-time monitoring, visibility, and information across the entire SC	Max
Supply chain design (C4)	The distribution and network reach of 4PL	Max
Redundancy (C5)	Number of 3PLs with which the 4PL collaborates	Max
Risk management (C6)	The quality standards of the 4PL	Max
Flexibility (C7)	The variety of product types a 4PL can transport, their responsiveness, and the resource capacity	Max
Geographical expertise (C8)	Proficiency in managing the complexities of transporting live plants, and the knowledge of geographical challenges, climate fluctuations, and compliance with regional regulations	Max
Service quality (C9)	Service quality was assessed using three dimensions: past faults, the charges of damage, and on-time delivery	Max
Inventory facilities (C10)	4PL storage facilities needed in case of unpredicted situations	Max

Table 2 Intuitionistic fuzzy linguistics terms and their values for evaluation of criteria (Karagoz et al., 2020)

IF Linguistic term		Value
VI	Very Important	(0.8,0.1)
I	Important	(0.7,0.2)
M	Medium	(0.5,0.4)
U	Unimportant	(0.3,0.6)
VU	Very Unimportant	(0.1,0.8)

Table 3 Ratings done by the experts

	C1	C2	C3	C4	C5	C6	C7	C8	C9	C10
D1	VI	U	M	I	VU	M	I	I	VI	U
D2	U	VI	I	M	I	M	M	U	M	I
D3	VI	I	M	VI	M	VI	I	I	I	VI
D4	I	I	M	I	I	M	M	I	I	I

Consider column 1 corresponding to criteria 1 in Table 3. Here, the experts rated the criteria as VI, U, VI, and I. First, we convert the IFLTs into IF numbers as (0.8,0.1), (0.3,0.6), (0.8,0.1), and (0.7,0.2), respectively. Then, take the average of the opinions as $\frac{(0.8,0.1)+(0.3,0.6)+(0.8,0.1)+(0.7,0.2)}{4} = (0.65,0.25)$. Now, using Eq. (3), the weight of criteria 1 is calculated as

$$w_1 = \frac{(0.65, 0.25)}{(0.65, 0.25) + (0.625, 0.275) + \cdots + (0.625, 0.275)} = (0.1070, 0.0412)$$

Table 4 Weights of criteria

Criteria	Weights
C1	(0.107,0.041)
C2	(0.103,0.045)
C3	(0.091,0.058)
C4	(0.111,0.037)
C5	(0.082,0.066)
C6	(0.095,0.053)
C7	(0.099,0.049)
C8	(0.099,0.049)
C9	(0.111,0.037)
C10	(0.103,0.045)

Table 5 Intuitionistic fuzzy linguistics terms and their values for alternative ranking (Karagoz et al., 2020)

IF Linguistic term		Value
EP	Extremely poor	(0.1,0.9)
VP	Very Poor	(0.2,0.7)
P	Poor	(0.3,0.6)
MP	Medium Poor	(0.4,0.5)
M	Medium	(0.5,0.4)
MG	Medium Good	(0.6,0.3)
G	Good	(0.8,0.1)
VG	Very Good	(0.9,0.1)
EG	Extremely Good	(1,0)

Table 6 Ratings done by one expert

	C1	C2	C3	C4	C5	C6	C7	C8	C9	C10
A1	EP	P	G	M	MG	VG	G	G	M	P
A2	MG	M	VG	G	G	P	MG	G	M	VP
A3	EG	MG	VG	G	VG	G	VP	MG	G	MP
A4	MG	G	VG	MG	MG	P	EG	MP	G	G
A5	G	MG	MG	MG	MP	VP	MG	G	P	VG
A6	EP	P	M	MG	VP	G	MG	M	MG	MP

4.2 Evaluation of Alternatives

The expert panel evaluated these providers' performances concerning the ten criteria based on the concepts of intuitionistic fuzzy linguistic variables (Table 5). Table 6 gives the ratings done by one expert. Next, aggregate the decision makers' opinions by taking the average to obtain the initial decision matrix. Normalize the initial decision matrix using Eq. (6). Now, execute the additive normalization and compute the weighted IF-DOBI averaging function $\wp_i^{(1)\alpha_1,\alpha_2,\rho}$ and weighted IF-DOBI geometric function $\wp_i^{(2)\alpha_1,\alpha_2,\rho}$ using Eqs. (7) and (8), by employing the parameters $\alpha_1 = \alpha_2 = \rho = 1$. Next, use Eq. (9) to calculate the IF-DOBI function

Table 7 Results

	Z1	Z2	R	Rank
A1	(0.568,0.068)	(0.563,0.085)	(0.64,0.139)	*1*
A2	(0.516,0.08)	(0.51,0.091)	(0.526,0.191)	*5*
A3	(0.559,0.064)	(0.552,0.071)	(0.618,0.123)	*2*
A4	(0.559,0.071)	(0.552,0.087)	(0.618,0.149)	*3*
A5	(0.545,0.081)	(0.543,0.092)	(0.592,0.188)	*4*
A6	(0.459,0.099)	(0.455,0.111)	(0.417,0.285)	*6*

integrated value, $\Im_i$Then, by using Eq. (10) we determine the score of $\Im_i$. The 4PL providers are ranked on the basis of the computed $\Im_i$ Table 7 provides the weighted IF-DOBI averaging and geometric functions values, and the integrated value of IF-DOBI function. Steps 5 and 6 in IF-DOBI calculations are done using MS Excel and the remaining steps are done using Python.

5 Results and Discussions

Robustness analysis helps us understand how sensitive the primary solution is to changes in model parameters. Robustness analysis assesses the validity of a system or model by examining how it performs under various conditions, uncertainties, and perturbations. It helps identify weaknesses, vulnerabilities, and potential failure points, enabling the development of more reliable and resilient systems or strategies (Wang & Triantaphyllou, 2008). By examining the impact of different parameter values, we can determine if the chosen solution remains effective and reliable across various scenarios. Additionally, robustness analysis allows us to identify potential weaknesses or vulnerabilities in the primary solution, enabling us to make informed decisions and adjustments if necessary. We investigate the effect of parameters α_1, α_2, ρ and τ on the alteration of the initial solution, given that the parameters rely on arbitrary evaluation.

5.1 *Impact of Parameters* α_1 *and* α_2

Variations in the integrated value are noted as the stabilization parameters α_1 and α_2 changes from 1 to 100. Figure 1 depicts the changes in the IF score functions and the response of $\Im_i$ to alterations in parameters $1 \leq \alpha_1, \alpha_2 \leq 100$ on alternative $A1$ is shown in Fig. 2. We can observe that the rankings remain unchanged for all the alternatives. This indicates that there is an adequate advantage among the alternatives under consideration and that alternatives $A1$ and $A3$ stand out as the prominent ones among all the alternatives. This stability in the rankings indicates that our method consistently produces reliable results.

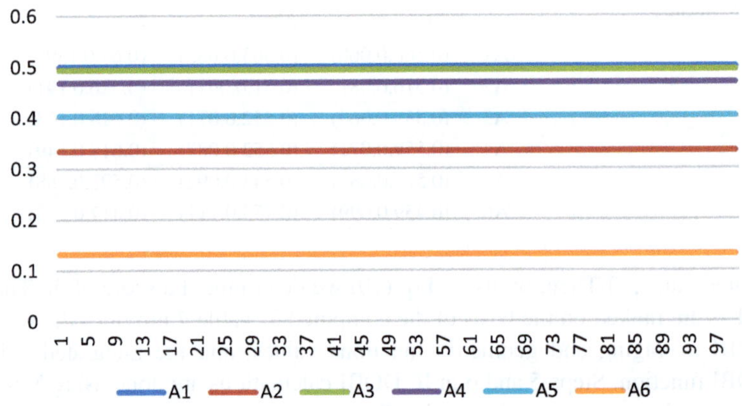

Fig. 1 Response of integrated values to the alterations in parameters $1 \leq \alpha_1, \alpha_2 \leq 100$

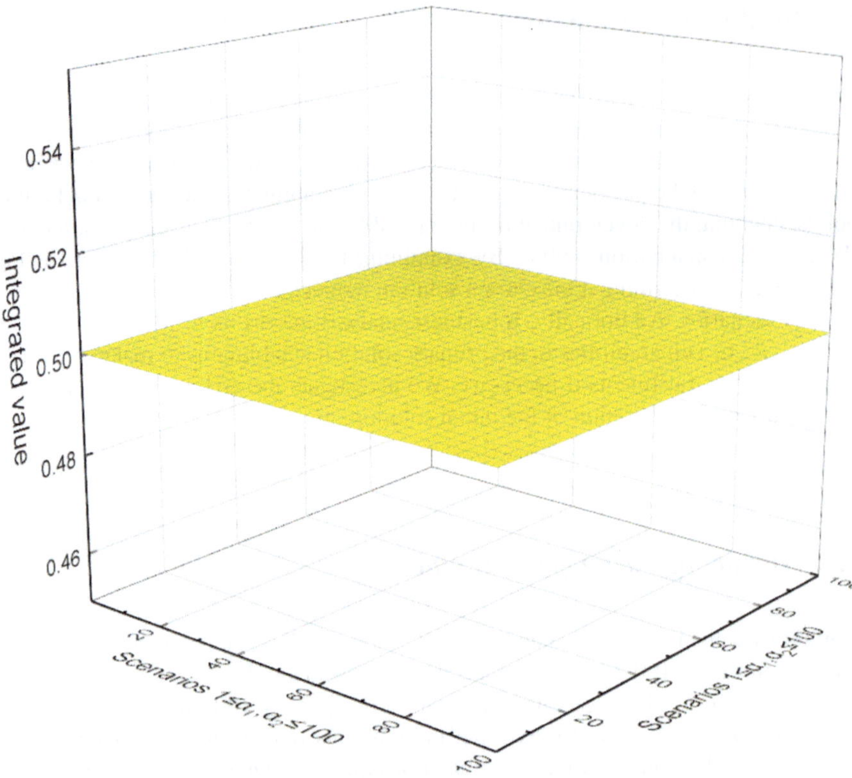

Fig. 2 Response of $\Im_i$ to alterations in parameters $1 \leq \alpha_1, \alpha_2 \leq 100$ on alternative $A1$

5.2 *Impact of Parameter* ρ

Here, the parameter ρ is varied in the range $1 \leq \rho \leq 100$ by keeping the other parameters $\alpha_1 = \alpha_2 = \tau = 1$. The response of $\mathfrak{I}_1$ to changes in parameter $1 \leq \rho \leq 100$ on alternative $A1$ is shown in Fig. 3. The variations in the $\mathfrak{I}_i$ for all the alternatives are depicted in Fig. 4. We can observe that the rank remains unchanged when $\rho > 25$ and produces stable results. The stability of the initial solution grows as the parameter value increases.

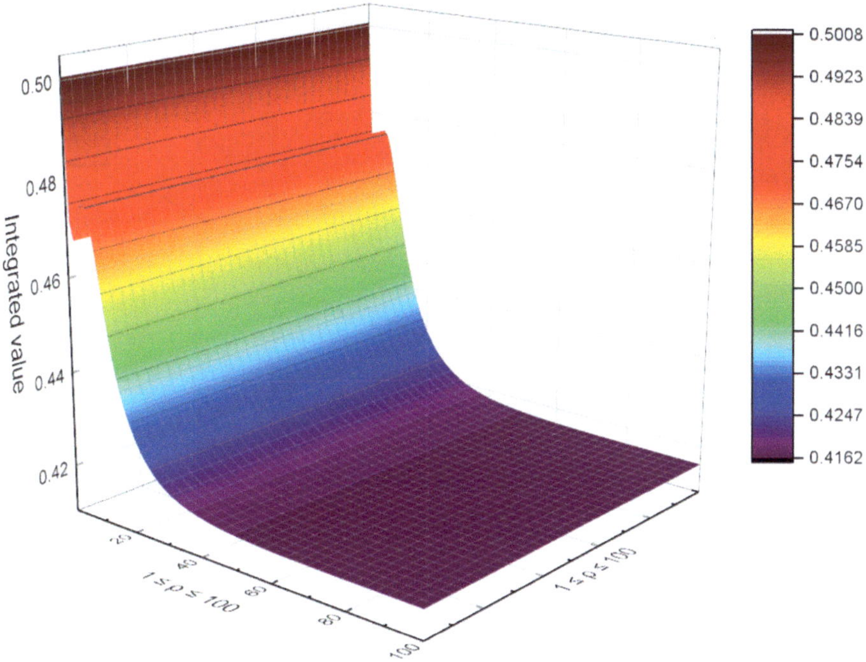

Fig. 3 Variations in the $\mathfrak{I}_i$ for all the alternatives for $1 \leq \rho \leq 100$

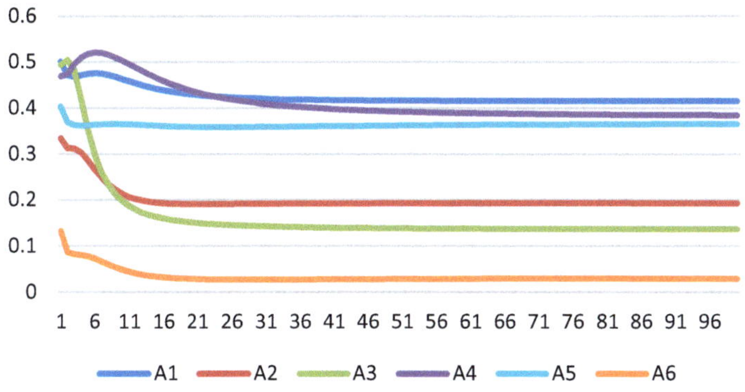

Fig. 4 Response of $\mathfrak{I}_1$ to changes in parameter $1 \leq \rho \leq 100$ on alternative $A1$

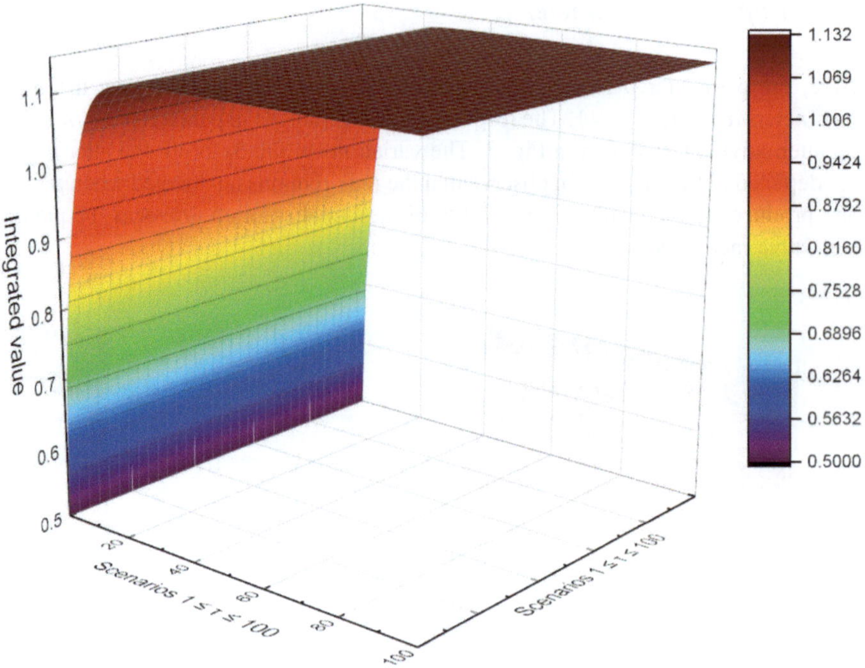

Fig. 5 Response of $\mathfrak{I}_1$ to changes on alternative $A1$ for $1 \leq \tau \leq 100$

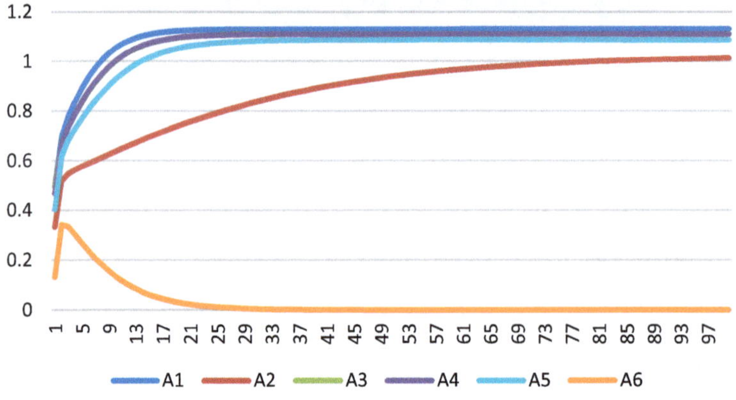

Fig. 6 Variations in the $\mathfrak{I}_i$ for all the alternatives for $1 \leq \tau \leq 100$

5.3 *Impact of Parameter* τ

The response of $\mathfrak{I}_1$ to deviations in the parameter in the range $1 \leq \tau \leq 100$ by keeping the other parameters $\alpha_1 = \alpha_2 = \rho = 1$ is noted. The plot of the response of $\mathfrak{I}_1$ to changes on alternative $A1$ is shown in Fig. 5. The variations in the $\mathfrak{I}_i$ for all the alternatives are depicted in Fig. 6. It is clear that the rank remains unchanged when $\tau > 2$ and produces stable results. It is evident that the stability of the initial solution grows as the parameter value increases. These findings suggest that the alternative $A1$ is the best choice since it has a substantial advantage over the other alternatives in the group.

5.4 *Comparison with Other MCDM Methods*

This section presents a comparative analysis of outcomes with other MCDM techniques, employing various methodologies for data standardization. Models such as TOPSIS, Ranking of Alternatives through Functional mapping of criterion sub-intervals into a Single Interval (RAFSI), and MABAC were evaluated alongside the IF-DOBI model under identical conditions. Results depicted in Fig. 5 validate the consistency of the IF-DOBI model, showing a high degree of agreement with Spearman Correlation Coefficient values ranging from 0.83 to 1.0. While slight divergences were observed with the TOPSIS model due to its vector algorithm for standardizing information, the DOBI, RAFSI, and MABAC models exhibited close alignment. Notably, these traditional MCDM techniques utilize linear aggregation functions, potentially overlooking mutual relationships between decision attributes, unlike the nonlinear functions employed by DOBI. This nonlinear approach enhances the model's ability to perceive the complexities of real-world dynamics within a dynamic environment, demonstrating higher flexibility and adaptability compared to conventional methods like TOPSIS, RAFSI, and MABAC.

Expanding the scope of the problem is acknowledged to elevate the complexity of mathematical models employed for resolution. Additionally, nonlinear MCDM models, handling attribute interactions and information uncertainties, are recognized to possess higher complexity than their linear counterparts. While this can pose challenges in implementing the IF-DOBI model, the advantages of obtaining an objective perspective, flexibility, and the capability to simulate risks in information underscore the evident potential of this presented MCDM framework (Fig. 7).

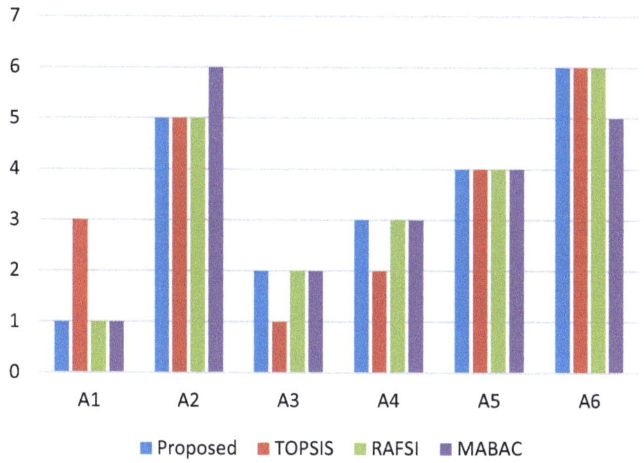

Fig. 7 Comparison of proposed method with other MCDM methods

6 Conclusion

The selection of an appropriate 4PL provider is crucial, particularly for firms facing challenges in meeting customer demands in the realm of e-commerce for live plants. Outsourcing these services to a resilient 4PL provider offers advantages and opportunities for enhancing delivery services, especially in the face of SC risks. The decision to engage a 4PL provider requires careful consideration, necessitating the use of scientific approaches and methods to address the complexities of SCs. Beyond standard criteria like price and service quality, this paper emphasizes the importance of resilience-related criteria such as service time, technological expertise, inventory facilities, and risk management. The evaluation framework proposed in this study incorporates the IF-DOBI method to assess the resilience of a 4PL provider and the overall SC, ensuring uninterrupted delivery even in unexpected situations. Balancing efficiency and resilience in selecting a 4PL provider is essential to ensure optimal performance while mitigating risks and disruptions in the supply chain. While efficiency-focused providers may prioritize cost savings and streamlined operations, resilient providers offer robustness and adaptability in the face of unforeseen challenges. By carefully evaluating the trade-offs between efficiency and resilience, firms can choose a 4PL provider that not only meets their immediate delivery needs but also safeguards against potential disruptions, ultimately enhancing customer satisfaction and competitive advantage in the e-commerce market for live plants.

The methodologies employed in this study effectively evaluate 4PL providers in e-commerce. A robustness analysis confirms result stability, indicating minimal changes in the final ranking. The proposed approach serves as a valuable decision-support tool, addressing a gap in the literature by offering a model for assessing resilient 4PL providers. While the model is adaptable for various decision-making scenarios by adjusting criteria and alternatives, it has limitations, notably in not considering other methods for determining criteria weights or alternative ranking. Future research could explore applying the methodology to other logistics problems with uncertainty, experimenting with different MCDM methods, and developing a methodology for evaluating and selecting distribution channels in e-commerce.

References

Abdirad, M., & Krishnan, K. (2022). Examining the impact of E-supply chain on service quality and customer satisfaction: A case study. *International Journal of Quality and Service Sciences, 14*(2), 274–290. https://doi.org/10.1108/IJQSS-08-2020-0131

Atanassov, K. T., & Atanassov, K. T. (1999). *Intuitionistic fuzzy sets* (pp. 1–137). Physica-Verlag HD.

Aydın, S., Yörükoğlu, M., & Kabak, M. (2022). Fourth party logistics firm assessment using a novel neutrosophic MCDM. *Journal of Intelligent & Fuzzy Systems, 42*(1), 529–539. https://doi.org/10.3233/JIFS-219209

Baglio, M., Perotti, S., Dallari, F., & Garagiola, E. R. (2020). Benchmarking logistics facilities: A rating model to assess building quality and functionality. *Benchmarking: An International Journal, 27*(3), 1239–1260. https://doi.org/10.1108/BIJ-01-2019-0029

Bhattacharjya, J., Ellison, A., & Tripathi, S. (2016). An exploration of logistics-related customer service provision on Twitter: The case of e-retailers. *International Journal of Physical Distribution & Logistics Management, 46*(6/7), 659–680. https://doi.org/10.1108/IJPDLM-01-2015-0007

Bhatti, R. S., Kumar, P., & Kumar, D. (2010). A loss function based decision support model for 3PL selection by 4PLs. *International Journal of Integrated Supply Management, 5*(4), 365. https://doi.org/10.1504/IJISM.2010.035643

Blackhurst, J., Dunn, K. S., & Craighead, C. W. (2011). An empirically derived framework of global supply resiliency. *Journal of Business Logistics, 32*(4), 374–391. https://doi.org/10.1111/j.0000-0000.2011.01032.x

Braekers, K., Ramaekers, K., & Van Nieuwenhuyse, I. (2016). The vehicle routing problem: State of the art classification and review. *Computers & Industrial Engineering, 99*, 300–313. https://doi.org/10.1016/j.cie.2015.12.007

Büyüközkan, G., Feyzioğlu, O., & Şakir Ersoy, M. (2009). Evaluation of 4PL operating models: A decision making approach based on 2-additive Choquet integral. *International Journal of Production Economics, 121*(1), 112–120. https://doi.org/10.1016/j.ijpe.2008.03.013

Çağlar, K. M. B., & Aydın, K. (2020). The role of 4PL provider as a mediation and supply chain agility. *Modern Supply Chain Research and Applications, 2*(2), 99–111. https://doi.org/10.1108/MSCRA-09-2019-0019

Cano, J. A., Londoño-Pineda, A., & Rodas, C. (2022). Sustainable logistics for e-commerce: A literature review and bibliometric analysis. *Sustainability, 14*(19), Article 19. https://doi.org/10.3390/su141912247

Carvalho, H., Machado, V. H., Barroso, A., Azevedo, S. G., & Cruz-Machado, V. (2018). Resilience of logistics service providers facing a port strike: A case study. In *Proceedings of the International Conference on Industrial Engineering and Operations Management, IEOM 2018*. IEOM Society.

De Koster, R. B. M., Johnson, A. L., & Roy, D. (2017). Warehouse design and management. *International Journal of Production Research, 55*(21), 6327–6330. https://doi.org/10.1080/00207543.2017.1371856

Delfmann, W., Albers, S., & Gehring, M. (2002). The impact of electronic commerce on logistics service providers. *International Journal of Physical Distribution & Logistics Management, 32*(3), 203–222. https://doi.org/10.1108/09600030210426539

Diehlmann, F., Lüttenberg, M., Verdonck, L., Wiens, M., Zienau, A., & Schultmann, F. (2021). Public-private collaborations in emergency logistics: A framework based on logistical and game-theoretical concepts. *Safety Science, 141*, 105301. https://doi.org/10.1016/j.ssci.2021.105301

Govindarajan, A., Sinha, A., & Uichanco, J. (2021). Joint inventory and fulfillment decisions for omnichannel retail networks. *Naval Research Logistics (NRL), 68*(6), 779–794. https://doi.org/10.1002/nav.21969

Gurău, C., Ranchhod, A., & Hackney, R. (2001). Internet transactions and physical logistics: Conflict or complementarity? *Logistics Information Management, 14*(1/2), 33–43. https://doi.org/10.1108/09576050110363176

Herold, D. M., Nowicka, K., Pluta-Zaremba, A., & Kummer, S. (2021). COVID-19 and the pursuit of supply chain resilience: Reactions and "lessons learned" from logistics service providers (LSPs). *Supply Chain Management: An International Journal, 26*(6), 702–714. https://doi.org/10.1108/SCM-09-2020-0439

Huang, M., Li, R., & Wang, X. (2011). Network construction for fourth-party logistics based on resilience with using particle swarm optimization. In *2011 Chinese Control and Decision Conference (CCDC)* (pp. 3924–3929). https://doi.org/10.1109/CCDC.2011.5968907

Huang, M., Tu, J., Chao, X., & Jin, D. (2019). Quality risk in logistics outsourcing: A fourth party logistics perspective. *European Journal of Operational Research, 276*(3), 855–879.

Iyengar, D., Nilakantan, R., & Rao, S. (2021). On entrepreneurial resilience among micro-entrepreneurs in the face of economic disruptions… A little help from friends. *Journal of Business Logistics, 42*(3), 360–380. https://doi.org/10.1111/jbl.12269

Karagoz, S., Deveci, M., Simic, V., Aydin, N., & Bolukbas, U. (2020). A novel intuitionistic fuzzy MCDM-based CODAS approach for locating an authorized dismantling center: A case study of Istanbul. *Waste Management & Research, 38*(6), 660–672.

Karbassi Yazdi, A., Mehdiabadi, A., Wanke, P. F., Monajemzadeh, N., Correa, H. L., & Tan, Y. (2023). Developing supply chain resilience: A robust multi-criteria decision analysis method for transportation service provider selection under uncertainty. *International Journal of Management Science and Engineering Management, 18*(1), 51–64. https://doi.org/10.1080/17509653.2022.2098543

Kilibarda, M., Andrejić, M., & Popović, V. (2020). Research in logistics service quality: A systematic literature review. *Transport, 35*(2), Article 2. https://doi.org/10.3846/transport.2019.11388

Li, D. F. (2005). Multiattribute decision making models and methods using intuitionistic fuzzy sets. *Journal of Computer and System Sciences, 70*(1), 73–85.

Melacini, M., Perotti, S., Rasini, M., & Tappia, E. (2018). E-fulfilment and distribution in omni-channel retailing: A systematic literature review. *International Journal of Physical Distribution & Logistics Management, 48*(4), 391–414. https://doi.org/10.1108/IJPDLM-02-2017-0101

Morana, J., Gonzalez-Feliu, J., & Semet, F. (2014). Urban consolidation and logistics pooling. In J. Gonzalez-Feliu, F. Semet, & J.-L. Routhier (Eds.), *Sustainable urban logistics: Concepts, methods and information systems* (pp. 187–210). Springer. https://doi.org/10.1007/978-3-642-31788-0_10

Naseem, M. H., Yang, J., & Xiang, Z. (2021). Selection of logistics service provider for the e-commerce companies in Pakistan based on integrated GRA-TOPSIS approach. *Axioms, 10*(3), Article 3. https://doi.org/10.3390/axioms10030208

Ngah, A. H., Anuar, M. M., Rozar, N. N., Ariza-Montes, A., Araya-Castillo, L., Kim, J. J., & Han, H. (2021). Online sellers' reuse behaviour for third-party logistics services: An innovative model development and e-commerce. *Sustainability, 13*(14), Article 14. https://doi.org/10.3390/su13147679

Novak, D. C., Wu, Z., & Dooley, K. J. (2021). Whose resilience matters? Addressing issues of scale in supply chain resilience. *Journal of Business Logistics, 42*(3), 323–335. https://doi.org/10.1111/jbl.12270

Panayides, P. M., & So, M. (2005). Logistics service provider–client relationships. *Transportation Research Part E: Logistics and Transportation Review, 41*(3), 179–200. https://doi.org/10.1016/j.tre.2004.05.001

Park, Y. W., Blackhurst, J., Paul, C., & Scheibe, K. P. (2022). An analysis of the ripple effect for disruptions occurring in circular flows of a supply chain network*. *International Journal of Production Research, 60*(15), 4693–4711. https://doi.org/10.1080/00207543.2021.1934745

Ralston, P., & Blackhurst, J. (2020). Industry 4.0 and resilience in the supply chain: A driver of capability enhancement or capability loss? *International Journal of Production Research, 58*(16), 5006–5019. https://doi.org/10.1080/00207543.2020.1736724

Ranieri, L., Digiesi, S., Silvestri, B., & Roccotelli, M. (2018). A review of last mile logistics innovations in an externalities cost reduction vision. *Sustainability, 10*(3), Article 3. https://doi.org/10.3390/su10030782

Seikh, M. R., & Mandal, U. (2021). Intuitionistic fuzzy Dombi aggregation operators and their application to multiple attribute decision-making. *Granular Computing, 6*, 473–488.

Shah, B., & Khanzode, V. (2017). A comprehensive review of warehouse operational issues. *International Journal of Logistics Systems and Management, 26*(3), 346–378. https://doi.org/10.1504/IJLSM.2017.081962

Stock, J. R., & Mulki, J. P. (2009). Product returns processing: An examination of practices of manufacturers, wholesalers/distributors, and retailers. *Journal of Business Logistics, 30*(1), 33–62. https://doi.org/10.1002/j.2158-1592.2009.tb00098.x

Vasić, N., Kilibarda, M., Andrejić, M., & Jović, S. (2021). Satisfaction is a function of users of logistics services in e-commerce. *Technology Analysis & Strategic Management, 33*(7), 813–828. https://doi.org/10.1080/09537325.2020.1849610

Wang, X., & Triantaphyllou, E. (2008). Ranking irregularities when evaluating alternatives by using some ELECTRE methods. *Omega, 36*(1), 45–63.

White, G. R. T., Afolayan, A., & Plant, E. (2014). Challenges to the adoption of e-commerce technology for supply chain management in a developing economy: A focus on Nigerian SMEs. In E. Lacka, H. K. Chan, & N. Yip (Eds.), *E-commerce platform acceptance: Suppliers, retailers, and consumers* (pp. 23–39). Springer International Publishing. https://doi.org/10.1007/978-3-319-06121-4_2

Wieland, A., & Durach, C. F. (2021). Two perspectives on supply chain resilience. *Journal of Business Logistics, 42*(3), 315–322. https://doi.org/10.1111/jbl.12271

Zennaro, I., Finco, S., Calzavara, M., & Persona, A. (2022). Implementing e-commerce from logistic perspective: Literature review and methodological framework. *Sustainability, 14*(2), Article 2. https://doi.org/10.3390/su14020911

Zhang, G., Wang, X., Wang, Y., & Kang, J. (2022a). Research on the resilient evolutionary game of logistics service supply chain with government participation. *Mathematics, 10*(4), Article 4. https://doi.org/10.3390/math10040630

Zhang, Y., Gao, Z., Huang, M., Jiang, S., Yin, M., & Fang, S.-C. (2022b). Multi-period distribution network design with boundedly rational customers for the service-oriented manufacturing supply chain: A 4PL perspective. *International Journal of Production Research, 62*(20), 1–20. https://doi.org/10.1080/00207543.2022.2140220

Stank, T. P., [illegible] (2020). [illegible] *Journal of Business Logistics*, [illegible]. https://doi.org/10.1002/[illegible]

Vasic, N., Kilibarda, M., Andrejić, M., & Jović, S. (2021). Satisfaction is a function of users of logistics services in e-commerce. *Technology Analysis & Strategic Management*, *33*(7), 813–828. https://doi.org/10.1080/09537325.2020.1849610

Wang, X., & Triantaphyllou, E. (2008). Ranking irregularities when evaluating alternatives by using some ELECTRE methods. *Omega*, *36*(1), 45–63.

White, G. R. T., Afolayan, A., & Plant, E. (2014). Challenges to the adoption of e-commerce technology for supply chain management in a developing economy: A focus on Nigerian SMEs. In E. Lacka, H. K. Chan, & N. Yip (Eds.), *E-commerce platform acceptance: Suppliers, retailers, and consumers* (pp. 23–39). Springer International Publishing. https://doi.org/10.1007/978-3-319-06121-4_2

Wieland, A., & Durach, C. F. (2021). Two perspectives on supply chain resilience. *Journal of Business Logistics*, *42*(3), 315–322. https://doi.org/10.1111/jbl.12271

Zennaro, I., Finco, S., Calzavara, M., & Persona, A. (2022). Implementing e-commerce from logistic perspective: Literature review and methodological framework. *Sustainability*, *14*(2), Article 2. https://doi.org/10.3390/su14020911

Zhang, G., Wang, L., Wang, Y., & [illegible] (202[illegible]). [illegible]

Outsourcing Ancillary Services on the Municipal Level in Slovakia

Beata Mikušová Meričková, Nikoleta Jakuš Muthová, and Juraj Nemec

1 Introduction

Prior to the implementation of fundamental changes in the functioning of the public sector at the end of the last century, it was basically taken for granted that the state would both finance and implement its activities. However, experience has shown that this approach is associated with a high potential for inefficiency (Hodge, 2000 or Van der Valk, 2023). The theory and the practice started to understand that the fact that the state is the provider of a service does not automatically mean that the state also has to produce and finance that service (Hammerschmid et al., 2019; Lapuente & Van De Walle, 2020).

The choice of the appropriate form of service provision, taking into account the nature of the service and the specific needs and conditions in which the service is provided, affects the efficiency of production and the quality of the service provided. However, this choice can only be realised in the conditions of a pluralistic system of services in the public sector based on the principle of competition of ownership forms of their producers (Cullis & Jones, 1992 or Blomqvist & Winblad, 2022),

B. M. Meričková
Faculty of Economics, Matej Bel University, Banska Bystrica, Slovakia

Faculty of Economics and Administration, Pardubice University, Pardubice, Czech Republic
e-mail: beata.mikusovamerickova@umb.sk

N. J. Muthová
Faculty of Economics, Matej Bel University, Banska Bystrica, Slovakia
e-mail: nikoleta.jakusmuthova@umb.sk

J. Nemec (✉)
Faculty of Economics, Matej Bel University, Banska Bystrica, Slovakia

Faculty of Economics and Administration, Masaryk University Brno, Brno, Czech Republic
e-mail: juraj.nemec@umb.sk

F. P. García Márquez et al. (eds.), *Outsourcing Using Operations Research and Management Science Methods*, International Series in Operations Research & Management Science 366, https://doi.org/10.1007/978-3-031-91845-2_9

allowing for the implementation of alternative approaches to the provision of services in the public sector.

According to literature (like Van der Valk, 2023), the basic types of alternative approaches to public service delivery are: contracting out public sector services, public-private partnership investment projects, public benefit organisations (non-governmental organisations in the non-profit sector), and vouchers. Outsourcing services in the public sector (the provision of internal—ancillary—services in a public sector organisation by private organisations) is one of the forms of contracting out in the public sector.

Outsourcing of ancillary service production has its origin in the process of organisational management, where both public and private organisations often face the question "to provide the service with their own capacities, or to buy the service?" (Prager, 1994, p. 176). An organisation has two options: to produce a service internally—with its own capacities—or to use the option of external provision—contracting out the service/outsourcing the service.

According to Prager (1994), the two key reasons for internal production lie in the creation of economies of scale and the increased need for direct control in the service production process. As long as economies of scale of production are generated by producing the service internally and the issue of control in the service production process is of utmost importance, then the decision to produce the service internally is indeed justified. In some cases, outsourcing the production of a service for reasons of efficiency may be a more profitable solution. According to Prager, a general rule of thumb is "to internalise a service only if we assume that the cost of producing it internally is lower than the cost of externalising the production of the service" (Prager, 1994, p. 184).

The pros and cons, factors, barriers and limits of outsourcing on the local level are investigated by several already existing studies; however, in most cases, it is in the conditions of the developed countries, where the liberal democracy and the market function well. The goal of our chapter is to analyse the outsourcing of ancillary services in the post-transitional country of Slovakia. Slovakia switched from the centralised model of economy and governance in 1989 and in 2004 the country was accepted as a European Union member. The experiences from this change are unique. Moreover, the past still impacts the current conditions (path dependency). Detailed information about the size, results and purposes for results of outsourcing in these specific conditions represents important value added to the current state of knowledge.

2 Outsourcing Ancillary Services

The impacts of externalisation (contracting and outsourcing) on the efficiency of service delivery in the public sector are the subject of a large number of foreign studies (Brudney et al., 2005; Hodge, 2000; Kamerman & Kahn, 1989; Savas, 1987; Sclar, 2000; Siegel, 1999; Bel et al., 2010; Bel & Rosell, 2016; Gradus et al., 2014;

Petersen et al., 2018; Bel & Gradus, 2018), as well as domestic studies in the conditions of Slovakia (Kopričet al., 2018; Meričková & Nemec, 2007).

According to the results of existing studies, the success of outsourcing ancillary/supportive services, the provision of which is essential for the operation of public organisations providing public services (e.g. cleaning, building management and maintenance, catering for employees, transport, information technology management, security services) depends on the proper response to two critical questions:

1. Make or buy the service?
2. How to manage the outsourcing process?

The theoretical background for the first question can be found in the transaction cost theory (Prager, 1994; Hefetz & Warner, 2012; Brown et al., 2015; Djikgraaf & Gradus, 2018). The principal agent theory (Pratt & Zeckhauser, 1986; Arrow, 1985; Braun & Guston, 2003; Perunović & Pedersen, 2007; Quinn, 2011; Gradus et al., 2014; Petersen et al., 2018; Blomqvist & Winblad, 2022) is crucial regarding the second question.

2.1 Transaction Cost Theory

When choosing the specific provision form of the production of ancillary services in public organisations (external versus internal production), the public organisation should decide on the basis of the economic nature of the service as well as on the impact of the form of provision on the efficiency of production and quality of the service, and the possibility of public control of the production of the service. The choice of the appropriate form of service provision should take into account the nature of the service and the specific needs and conditions in which the service is provided. It affects the efficiency of production and the quality of the service provided. In the context of outsourcing in the public sector, it is necessary to address the issue of transaction costs, as stated by several authors, Bailey (1995), Prager (1994), Ferris and Graddy (1991), Brown et al. (2015), Hefetz and Warner (2012), Djikgraaf and Gradus (2018).

Transaction costs can be understood as all costs that are associated with the implementation of an external form of service delivery beyond production costs. Without incurring transaction costs, this form would never have been realised or these costs would never have been incurred without the formation of an external form. A generally accepted definition of transaction costs has not yet been recognised. As Hirsch (1991, pp. 56–57) states, there are two types of transaction costs:

1. Costs associated with the invitation to tender for the service, with the evaluation of the tender documents submitted by the bidders, with the selection of the supplier and the formation of the contractual relationship.
2. Costs with the further monitoring and control of the outsourcing of the service

Transaction costs are reflected in the relationship between the public organisation and the external supplier. It is important to note that the costs associated with the implementation of service provision through outsourcing are "the sum of the actual costs associated with the production of the service and the transaction costs" (Williamson, 1986, p. 110). If the decision in favour of outsourcing is to be efficient, then these costs must not outweigh the economic benefits of preferring an external form of provision over an internal form of service provision.

The amount of transaction costs can vary depending on the nature of the outsourcing management and the type of service in which the outsourcing occurs (Williamson, 1986; Ferris & Graddy, 1991; Hefetz & Warner, 2012; Tejedo-Romero & Aruajo, 2023). The nature of outsourcing management is influenced by the type of public organisation. Williamson (1986, p.105) argues that simple outsourcing management is typical of a public organisation with a simple structure and demanding outsourcing management is typical of a public organisation with a complex structure. By analogy, demanding outsourcing management in the case of a public organisation of simple structure leads to unwarranted transaction costs and easy outsourcing management in the case of a public organisation of complex structure leads to strain. Limiting the growth of transaction costs is influenced by effective management of outsourcing, which in turn can affect the efficiency and quality of service delivery.

According to Williamson (1986, p.108), the amount of transaction costs that is relevant in public organisations' decisions about how to provide services are influenced by three factors: the specificity of the service, the measurability of the outputs of the service, the frequency with which the service is outsourced. The first two factors are key in this regard. When assessing the specificity of a service, it can be logically assumed that the more specific the provision of a service, the more exceptional and monopolistic the position of the contractor becomes in that area of service provision. The monopoly position favours the contractor in the negotiating relationship with the public organisation, which implies increased transaction costs on the part of the public organisation. In the case of the measurability of service outputs, an inversely proportional relationship can be identified between the level of transaction costs and the measurability of outputs. The increase in transaction costs gives rise to costs for monitoring service outputs.

In some cases, the benefits of production cost savings in service delivery through outsourcing fall short of the transaction costs incurred in implementing this form of service delivery. For this reason, it is not appropriate to deliver this type of service through external forms of provision and, despite the undeniable claims of greater efficiency of the externalisation services, the internal forms, i.e., "self-delivery," should continue to be retained. The most appropriate services for outsourcing are services characterised by low specificity and easy measurability of outputs. Conversely, the least suitable services in terms of outsourcing are services with high specificity and demanding measurability of outputs.

2.2 *Principal Agent Theory*

Outsourcing is based on the establishment of a contractual relationship between the client/principal (in our case, a public organisation) and an external supplier/agent (private organisations). Both the principal and the agent pursue their own objectives, which may not (and usually do not) align (MacNeil, 1978; DeHoog, 1990; Sclar, 2000; Andersen et al., 2008; Bel & Gradus, 2018). The mismatch between the goals of the principal and the agent is the cause of the problems or the potential risks associated with outsourcing services (Pratt & Zeckhauser, 1986). If the contracting authority does not directly monitor the activities of the contractor, this leads to a reduced level of safety in the provision of services. The public organisation loses direct control over the production of the service. This manifests itself in the form of:

1. Moral hazard or the problem of hidden activities
2. The problem of wrong choice or the problem of hidden information (Arrow, 1985; Aben et al., 2021; Guruganesh et al., 2021; Owusu-Manu et al., 2021)

Moral hazard: the problem of hidden activities arises when the activities of the contractor are not adequately monitored and controlled, which is reflected in the scope and quality of the service provided, or by other behaviour of the external contractor that is contrary to the public interest. This problem should be solved by compliance with the defined principles of public procurement and continuous control of the production of the service (contractor) by the public organisation (the contracting authority).

The problem of incorrect selection or hidden information can be referred to as information asymmetry. A specialised service provider has information (usually of a professional nature) that is not available to the public organisation and, by using it, can influence the public organisation in its decision to select a supplier. For example, the public authority is interested in selecting from potential suppliers the one that best meets the requirements for efficiency and quality of service production but does not have the necessary information to be able to evaluate the candidate ex-ante in this respect. Bailey (1995, pp. 290–292) also mentions this problem as one of the risks associated with the externalisation of service production in the public sector. External service producers bidding for a service contract may deliberately underestimate the real costs of service production when calculating the price for the service, which, if the contract is awarded, leads to problems in providing the service to the extent and quality required.

In addition to the risks of moral hazard, information asymmetry, losses from the wear and tear of public assets and transaction costs, Bailey (1995, pp. 290–292) mentions other potential risks associated with outsourcing an ancillary service in a public organisation: employee demotivation, rigidity of upgrading qualifications and skills and stalling of capital investment.

Van der Valk (2023) summarises the situations that pose risks to outsourcing success as follows: information asymmetry between principal and agents, the amount and distribution of transaction costs, calculation and allocation uncertainty and risks, management of the risks that the contractor seeks to protect the investment, for example by price or contract length (some risks can be reduced by legal guarantees on both sides), and the motivation of the public organisation when outsourcing services. Avoiding the above risks, particularly those associated with moral hazard and information asymmetry, can be achieved by efficiently managing the process of outsourcing services in the public sector.

In this sense, several authors list the factors or determinants of the quality of contract management for outsourcing ancillary services. The most critical factors are as follows:

- The degree of competition in being awarded a public contract—it can be simplistically assessed according to the procurement procedure used (Savas, 1987; Kettl, 1993; Hodge, 2000; Brown et al., 2015; Bel et al., 2014; Glas & Essig, 2021).
- Ex-ante evaluation of a bidder for a public contract (Rehfuss, 1989; Romzek & Johnston, 2002; Yescombe & Farquharson, 2018).
- A clearly defined subject of procurement (Rehfuss, 1989; Brown et al., 2015; Petersen & Ostergaard, 2018).
- The extent and intensity of monitoring of external production (Rehfuss, 1989; Prager, 1994; Hefetz & Warner, 2004; Johansson et al., 2016; Keller et al., 2021).
- Penalties for non-compliance with contract terms (MacNeil, 1978; DeHoog, 1990; Brown et al., 2015; Johansson et al., 2016).
- The contracting authority's knowledge and experience in contract management (DeHoog, 1990; Rehfuss, 1989; Yescombe & Farquharson, 2018).
- The expertise of the contracting authority on the technical parameters of the procured service (Kettl, 1993; Yescombe & Farquharson, 2018).

The conventional view of outsourcing from the perspective of the principal-agent theory, where the relationship between the service provider, the purchaser of the service, and the producer, the supplier of the service, is seen as managerial or controlling (due to the divergence of the objectives of the parties involved and their efforts to enforce them) represents one line of the existing research. In other literature (Williamson, 1986; DeHoog, 1990; Sclar, 2000; Johansson et al., 2016; Rose-Ackerman & Palifka, 2016), we also find a perspective that sees the relationship between the provider and purchaser as a partnership based on flexible collaboration. In this concept, other internal factors stand out as determinants of the benefits of contracting out:

- The frequency of communication between the service provider and the service producer (Behn & Kant, 1999; DeHoog, 1990; Johansson et al., 2016; Lima & Cruz, 2019).
- Collaborative problem-solving (Sclar, 2000; Johansson et al., 2016; Martiniello et al., 2020).
- Mutual trust, shared values, and a move away from penalties to negotiation (MacNeil, 1978; Hefetz & Warner, 2012; Rose-Ackerman & Palifka, 2016).

The absence of systemic contract management is one of the reasons, among others, why the impacts of outsourcing on the efficiency and quality of service production in the public sector are controversial (Hodge, 2000; Sclar, 2000; Brudney et al., 2005; Bel et al., 2014; Bel & Rosell, 2016) or even negative (Kamerman & Kahn, 1989; Gradus et al., 2014; Petersen & Ostergaard, 2018). However, if everything "works as it should," outsourced services in the public sector are delivered more efficiently and with higher quality compared to services provided in-house by so-called "in-house" capabilities (Savas, 1987; Gradus et al., 2014; Kopric et al., 2018; Hammerschmid et al., 2019; Lapuente & Van De Walle, 2020).

3 Methodology

The goal of this chapter is to analyse the outsourcing of ancillary services on the Slovak municipal level. Slovakia is a small post-socialist country with 5.5 million inhabitants. After the change of the regime in 1989 the real municipal system was established and today Slovak municipalities have full freedom to decide within the scope of the large scale of their competences (see, for example, Plaček et al., 2020). Three research questions are formulated to reflect the main research goal, covering the three most critical aspects of outsourcing ancillary services on the Slovak municipal level (scale, results and purposes determining the results). Regarding the set of purposes, the quality of the contract management was selected (see the explanation in the analytical part of the text):

RQ1: What is the scale of outsourcing of ancillary services on the Slovak municipal level?
RQ2: What are the results of outsourcing ancillary services on the Slovak municipal level?
RQ3: What is the quality of the contract management of outsourcing ancillary services on the Slovak municipal level?

We decided to focus on selected ancillary services in municipal bodies (cleaning, building management and maintenance, catering and transport of employees, IT administration, and security services) in different research samples of municipalities in different years. The selection was determined by the importance of these services from the contextual and financial point of view (services which can be simply externalised, and which represent an important percentage of costs of the municipal budget). The research includes contracting out data for 1860 ancillary services.

The primary data collection through a questionnaire survey in Slovakia concerning outsourcing of ancillary services took place in the period 2009, 2010, 2020, 2021 (the years were not selected intentionally; these are the years when the researchers obtained research grants to cover the costs of data collections). The data are obtained by primary data collection between 2009 and 2021 are equally related to the provision of ancillary services in public organizations—the data collected are not available in any database and the only possibility to obtain them is via direct

Table 1 Research on outsourcing ancillary services in the public sector in Slovakia

Research implementation period	Research sample
	Contracting out ancillary services in public service organisations
2009	114 public service organisations
2010	141 town and municipal authorities
2020	115 town and municipal authorities
2021	54 town and municipal authorities

Source: Author's primary research

research. The selected municipalities were contacted personally in 2009 and 2010 by random selection. All municipalities in Slovakia were contacted electronically between 2020 and 2021. Municipalities filled out an electronic questionnaire survey created via Google Forms. The reason for the chosen 10-year period is to see how we have changed the situation over a longer period of time. The research sample in Slovakia is described in Table 1.

The scale of outsourcing (RQ1) is assessed by a simple percentage. The results of outsourcing (RQ2) are assessed by (i) simple comparison of the costs of internalisation with the costs of outsourcing services per employee and per the performance indicator; and (ii) by the multi-criteria analysis, combining data for the costs and the quality (the best value criteria method). The multi-criteria analysis is easily applicable to the conditions of public sector service evaluation and is a typical weighted sum algorithm.

The first step in applying this method is to define n criteria against which we will evaluate each service provision alternative (we denote the number of criteria by m). We evaluate two service provision alternatives—internalisation and contracting out. We evaluate these alternatives on the basis of the defined criteria. In our research, we have chosen three criteria. The first criterion is the expenditure on service provision per citizen (for local public services) and per employee (for ancillary services); the second criterion is the expenditure per performance indicator.[1]

The third criterion is the quality of the service. To monitor this, we have used the consumer-based evaluation methodology described above. In the case of local public services, citizens evaluated the services; in the case of ancillary services, employees of public organisations.

Thus, we have m alternatives A_i $(i = 1\ldots m)$ evaluated on the basis of n criteria $K_j(j = 1\ldots n)$. Two alternatives and three criteria. We assign to each criterion (expressed by the corresponding indicator) a value for its fulfilment by a particular alternative. The criteria evaluated thus take on different values x_{ij} for each alternative (where $i = 1\ldots m; j = 1\ldots n$).

[1] Due to a number of factors affecting the complexity and nature of the data obtained, we cannot work with the total cost of service provision indicator when generating results (public organisations do not monitor the comprehensive cost of service provision indicator). In this case, we can use the expenditure from the organisation's budget on service provision per employee or per performance indicator as an approximate measure.

As the degree of the fulfilment of each criterion is expressed by a different indicator on a different scale, we need to ensure that these criteria are comparable with each other in a comprehensive evaluation. This is achieved by normalising the values of x_{ij}, thus obtaining their normalised values a_{ij} from the interval (0;1>), as follows:

1. If the best value of criterion K_j is its maximum value $x_{\max}$, we obtain the normalised value a_{ij}, as the quotient of the specific value of the j-th criterion of the i-th alternative and this maximum value of the value set:

$$a_{ij} = \frac{x_{ij}}{x_{\max}} \tag{1}$$

2. If the best value of the criterion K_j is its minimum value $x_{\min}$, the value of a_{ij} is determined as the quotient of this minimum value and the specific value x_{ij}:

$$a_{ij} = \frac{x_{\min}}{x_{ij}} \tag{2}$$

We set the relative weights v_j of individual criteria so that:

$$\sum_{j=1}^{n} v_j = 100 \tag{3}$$

We determine the weights on the basis of the level of importance of each criterion in terms of meeting the objectives to be achieved by the service provision. We can use any of the existing approaches to determine the weights, e.g., scoring method, ranking method, pairwise comparison method, etc. (Fiala et al., 1994, pp. 33–43). We will use the Saaty method, which is a combination of the scoring method and the pairwise comparison method (Saaty et al., 1983).

By the medium of the Saaty matrix $S = (s_{ij})$, we compare the criteria using a scale with a range of 1 to 9, where:

1) $s_i = s_j$ (the criteria are of equal value)	}	(Even numbers are intermediate)
3) s_i criterion is weakly preferred over s_j		
5) s_i criterion is strongly preferred over s_j		
7) s_i criterion is very strongly preferred over s_j		
9) s_i criterion is absolutely more important than s_j		

After constructing the Saaty matrix, we calculate for each i the value

$$S_i = \prod_{j=1}^{k} S_{ij} \tag{4}$$

Table 2 Saaty matrix and calculation of multi-criteria evaluation weights

Criteria	K1	K2	K3	s_i	R_i	v_i (weight of the i-th criterion)	Weight of the i-th criterion v %
Expenditure per citizen/employee on the provision of the service K1	1	1	1/3	1/3	0.693	0.3	30
Expenditure on service provision per citizen/employee per performance indicator K2	1	1	1/3	1/3	0.693	0.3	30
Employee satisfaction rate with quality-of-service K3	3	1/3	1	1	1.000	0.4	40
Σ					2.387	1	100

Source: Author's own

Then for each i value:

$$R_i = (S_i)^{\frac{1}{k}} = \sqrt[k]{S_i} \tag{5}$$

Next we determine the weights of the criteria according to the relationship:

$$v_i = \frac{R_i}{\sum_{i=1}^{k} R_i} \tag{6}$$

Table 2 shows the criteria and their weights used in the multi-criteria evaluation of the efficiency of the provision of the selected ancillary services.

The normalised values of a_{ij} are then written in the form of a matrix, which is then multiplied by a column vector of the normalised values of the relative weights v_j for each criterion:

criteria | weight of the criteria | final evaluation

alternative

$$\begin{array}{c} \mathrm{K}_1 \;\; \mathrm{K}_2 \;\; \mathrm{K}_3 \;\; \mathrm{K}_4 \;\; \ldots \;\; \mathrm{K}_n \\ \begin{bmatrix} a_{11} & a_{12} & a_{13} & a_{14} & . & a_{1n} \\ a_{21} & a_{22} & a_{23} & . & . & a_{2n} \\ a_{31} & a_{32} & . & . & . & a_{3n} \\ . & . & . & . & . & . \\ . & . & . & . & . & . \\ a_{m1} & a_{m2} & . & . & . & a_{mn} \end{bmatrix} \end{array} \cdot \begin{pmatrix} v_1 \\ v_2 \\ v_3 \\ . \\ . \\ v_n \end{pmatrix} = \begin{pmatrix} h_1 \\ h_2 \\ h_3 \\ . \\ . \\ h_m \end{pmatrix} \tag{7}$$

The result is a column vector whose values h_i determine the order of preference for the implementation of the alternatives considered. The most efficient in terms of the set criteria is the alternative for which the value of h_i takes the maximum value h_{max} – in our case the more efficient service provision alternative, which reaches a higher value in the evaluation.

Through the evaluation of the established criteria, we can determine the most efficient alternative for the provision of a particular form of service among all those considered, and we can also find out the ranking of the alternatives according to the degree of efficiency. The predictive power of the evaluation process depends primarily on the appropriateness and scope of the set of evaluation criteria chosen and the way they are quantified through individual indicators.

In monitoring the quality of contracted-out services, we use the methodology of several studies (Bowaird & Loffler, 2003; Potůček et al., 2005), which consider citizens'/employees' satisfaction with these services as the basic criterion for evaluating the quality of public services. Employees evaluated the quality of the service provided by expressing their level of satisfaction with the quality of the service on a rating scale:

Completely satisfied	100%	Degree of satisfaction
Satisfied	80%	↓
More satisfied than dissatisfied	60%	
More dissatisfied than satisfied	40%	
Dissatisfied	20%	
Completely dissatisfied	0%	

The quality of the contract management (RQ3) is also measured by the multi-criteria analysis. Following the information provided in the literature review, we established a system of criteria that reflect the generally accepted risks of the process: the risk of information asymmetry, the risk of moral hazard, and the risk of non-transparency (Table 3). This list of criteria is based on the existing literature, which provides a large set of possible criteria and groups them according to the main risks connected to contract management. From all possible criteria listed in the literature, we selected our set of seven criteria, taking into account the individual importance of a criterion (based on the literature review) and the possibility to operationalise their measurement. This full set of seven criteria was used to measure the quality of contract management for ancillary services.

Table 3 presents our methodological approach for quantifying the criteria of the quality of contracting out ancillary services concerning the contracting out risks. The criteria were defined as qualitative characteristics; we transformed them into a quantitative form according to the selected features for the research.

The quantification was determined using Saaty's method (expert method of determining weights—Saaty, 1994). To each of the determinants we assigned a qualitative (Qualitative characteristic) and a quantitative (Quantification) form of

Table 3 Methodology for assessing the quality of contract management

Risk	Criterion	Qualitative characteristic	Quantification
Non-transparency	X1: degree of competition for the award of a public contract	Public tender	100
		Restricted competition	70
		Negotiating procedure	50
		Price tender	30
		Direct award	0
Hidden information	X2: ex-ante evaluation of the contractor for the public contract	The most economically advantageous offer	100
		Lifecycle costs	50
		Lowest price	0
	X3: the municipality staff involved in the contracting out process have sufficient expertise in the technical parameters of the service to be procured	Fundamentally agree	100
		Agree	50
		Disagree	0
		Fundamentally disagree	0
Risk of hidden activity	X4: frequency of monitoring of the output of the contracted service (how often the service is inspected by the municipality)	Regularly	100
		On an ongoing basis as required	50
		Without monitoring	0
	X5: the procedure to be followed by the municipality in the event of non-compliance with the obligations of the contract	Cancellation of the contract—termination	100
		Financial penalties	70
		Demanding redress	30
		Other procedures	0
	X6: duration of the contract—length of the contract	Up to and including 1 year	100
		Up to and including 2 years	70
		Up to and including 5 years	30
		Indefinitely	0
	X7: the method of payment to the external supplier for the service	Payment for performance	100
		Fixed payment + performance, i.e. a combination	50
		Fixed payment	0

Source: Own primary research

evaluation—a weight-in relation to its impact on the quality of the contract management. Individual values were assigned based on the evaluation by a group of experts on contracting out in the public sector (Appendix Table 10). The main criteria for the competence of the experts were considered to be their professionalism, degree of education, and experience in the subject matter.

4 Results

4.1 Scale of Outsourcing

The first question on which the research focuses is defining the scale of outsourcing) of ancillary services on the Slovak municipal level. The higher efficiency of outsourcing should lead to the predominance of outsourcing over internalization. Whether this is really the case in practice is shown by the scale of outsourcing, i.e., how many % of all forms of service provision outsourcing of selected ancillary services account for. Figure 1 presents the results.

The low value in Fig. 1 reflects a low scale of outsourcing. The above data document the developments in the outsourcing rate of ancillary services in public service organisations and municipal and town councils. For ancillary services in public service organisations, the most commonly contracted services are catering, security services and IT administration services. The undisputed reason for this is the limited staff and capital capacity of local authorities. The solution to the problem lies in harnessing the capacities of the private sector and switching from an internal to an external mode of service provision—outsourcing services. Again, these are services whose in-house provision would place increased demands on the capital or staff capacity of public organisations. Conversely, some services are dominated by in-house provision (cleaning, maintenance and management of buildings from among support services in public organisations).

4.2 Results of Outsourcing

Figure 2 compares expenditures from the budgets of public organisations, among them town and municipal authorities, on the internalisation of services with expenditures on outsourcing services per employee. The values represent the percentage of the indicator observed for outsourcing services, with the value of the indicator for internalisation of services being 100%. For the lower percentage, the cost-effectiveness per employee of the outsourced service was rated as better, and for the higher percentage, conversely, the cost-effectiveness per employee was rated as worse.

The assessment of the cost-effectiveness of ancillary services is in favour of outsourcing, although IT and transport management services are significantly more expensive when outsourced in Slovakia. On the other hand, the transaction costs

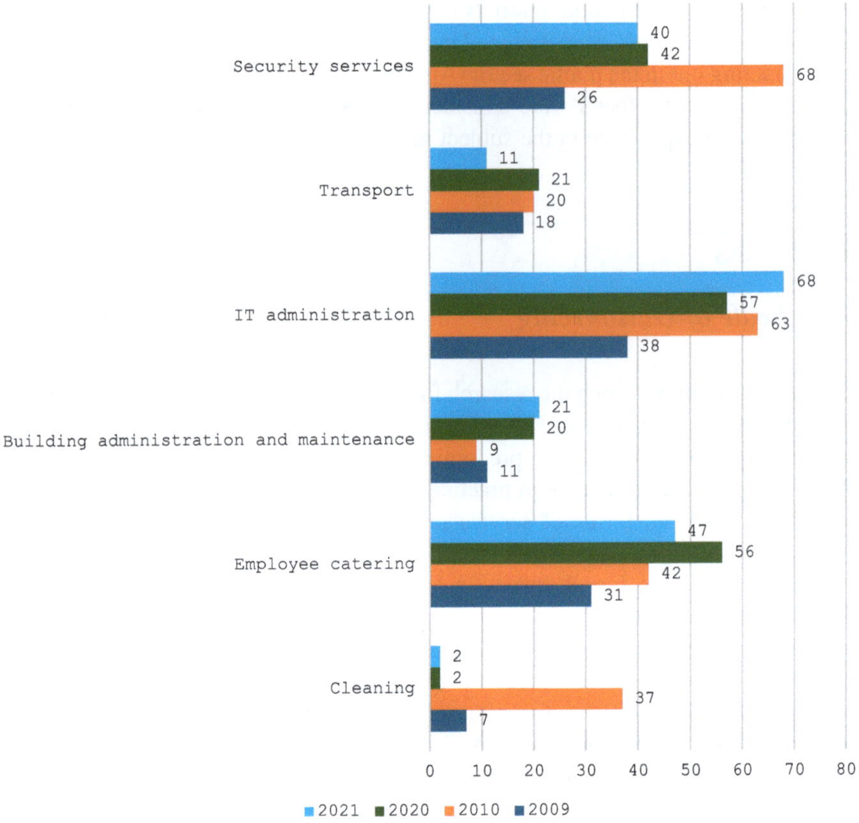

Fig. 1 Scale of outsourcing of ancillary services in public organisations, town and municipal offices (in %)

associated with the process of procuring the service and the subsequent monitoring of the external output are not included in the outsourcing costs, so the real costs of outsourcing are even higher. The data on the cost-effectiveness of outsourcing ancillary services in public organisations in Slovakia show large, even unrealistic, differences between internal and external provision of services. Therefore, we also deliver the comparison of expenditure per performance indicator. The selected performance indicators for ancillary services are described in Table 4.

A comparison of the expenditure on the provision of the monitored ancillary services attributable to the above performance indicators is presented in Fig. 3. The values represent the percentage of the observed indicator for contracting out services, while the value of the indicator for service internalisation is 100%.

The results again show different pictures for different services and for different time periods, but at least they look more realistic. Outsourcing cleaning services and IT administration are significantly more expensive in public organisations in Slovakia. Security services are outsourced significantly cheaper in Slovakia. The

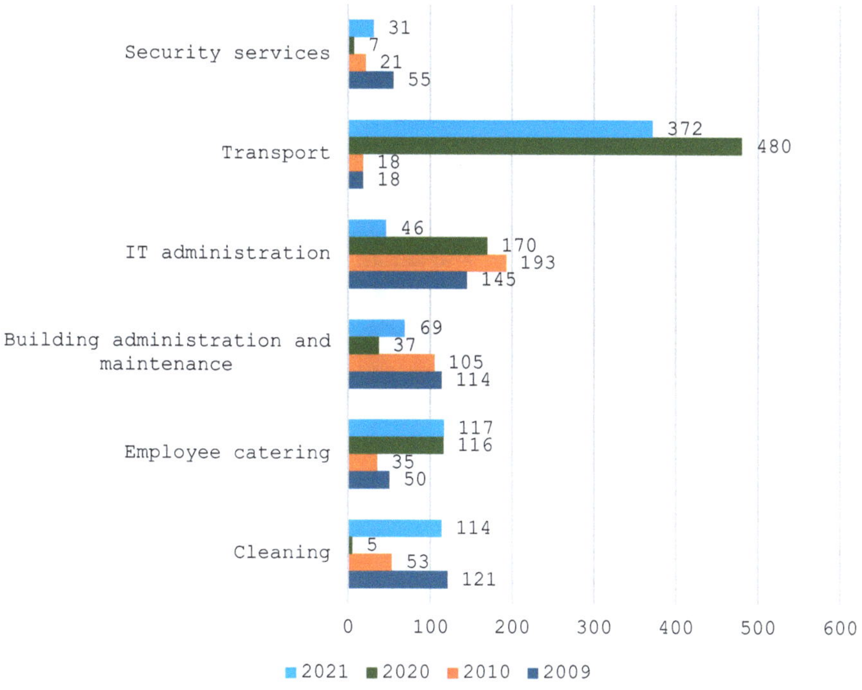

Fig. 2 Cost-efficiency of contracting out ancillary services in public organisations in Slovakia in % (*expenditure per employee*)

Table 4 Performance indicators for local public and ancillary services

Ancillary service	Performance indicator
Cleaning	m^2
Catering for employees	Number of diners—employees
Building management and maintenance	Average number of service interventions per year
IT administration	Average number of service interventions within IT management per year
Transport	Average number of kilometres travelled per year
Security services	m^2 of guarded area

Source: Author's research

inconclusive results led us to the need for further improvement of the methodology for assessing the efficiency of contracting out public sector services.

They may indicate that the results are different for different municipalities, and they may be biased by the limitations of our approach. The main critical problem is the comprehensiveness of capturing the cost-of-service provision indicator, which cannot be guaranteed, given the available data, either when tracking internalisation costs (absence of cost centres in the first years of the research, their formal

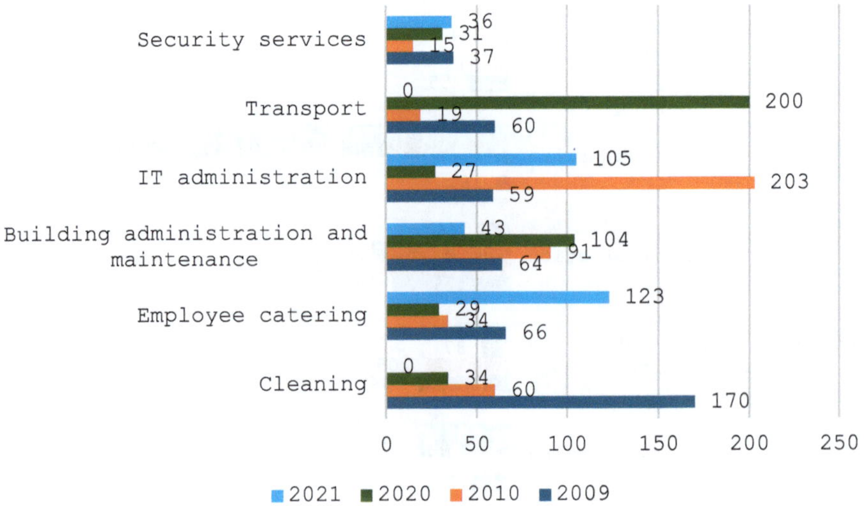

Fig. 3 Cost-effectiveness of contracting out ancillary services in public organisations in Slovakia in % (*expenditure per performance indicator*)

Table 5 Quality of contracted out ancillary services in Slovakia

Service	2009	2010	2020	2021
Cleaning	4	2	15	X
Employee catering	−2	0	−1	15
Building administration and maintenance	−2	−4	2	11
IT administration	−3	−7	−1	30
Transport	−11	−2	−1	X
Security services	−3	12	1	−8

Source: Author's research
X missing data

functioning in the later years of the research) or when tracking outsourcing costs (municipalities do not track transaction costs associated with public procurement or subsequent monitoring of external production).

As the last step we used a multi-criteria evaluation method—the best value criteria method. To apply it, we measured the quality of delivered ancillary services by direct quantification based on the multiple criteria evaluation method. The results show that outsourced ancillary services are rated as lower quality by the staff of public organisations (Table 5).

Minus values represent lower quality ratings for contracted-out services. The negative values point to the fact that the impacts of outsourcing on service quality are even more controversial than in the case of cost-effectiveness. However, the question of the impact of outsourcing on the efficiency of ancillary service delivery remains unanswered.

Table 6 Results of the multi-criteria evaluation of the efficiency of the provision of ancillary services in 2009, 2010, 2020, 2021

Services	Form	2009	2010	2020	2021
Cleaning	Internalisation	94.34	56.40	67.36	100.00
	Outsourcing	91.30	92.85	40.00	62.90
Employee catering	Internalisation	79.22	73.04	87.08	96.10
	Outsourcing	97.41	81.19	49.40	88.30
Building administration and maintenance	Internalisation	88.81	90.78	91.22	64.90
	Outsourcing	89.23	74.97	33.74	100.00
IT administration	Internalisation	74.09	98.88	61.71	76.90
	Outsourcing	95.25	77.83	76.86	98.00
Transport	Internalisation	83.15	78.86	77.52	100.00
	Outsourcing	97.67	99.91	63.48	44.50
Security services	Internalisation	76.10	64.43	64.64	53.70
	Outsourcing	96.29	97.73	76.71	70.00

Source: Author's research

The results of the complete multi-criteria evaluation of the efficiency of outsourcing ancillary services in Slovakia (Table 6). To calculate the results, the first criterion is the expenditure on service provision per employee, the second criterion is the expenditure per performance indicator, and the third criterion is the quality of services assessed on the basis of the satisfaction of consumers (employees) of the service. The highest possible score is 100.

A multi-criteria assessment of the efficiency of outsourcing ancillary services just reconfirms that it is not possible to see any common trend regarding the results of outsourcing in the Slovak municipal conditions. However, the data at least confirm that the results of outsourcing are problematic in Slovakia.

4.3 *Quality of Contract Management*

The data show that outsourcing is, in many cases, more expensive and outsourced services of lower quality, despite the fact that the general economic theory, expecting gains from the competition, assumes the opposite. The following part evaluated one possible purpose for this situation—to calculate the quality of contract management by our own methodology, described above. Tables 7, 8, and 9 characterise the situation regarding the quality of management of contracts for ancillary services town and municipal authorities in Slovakia for three samples (2010, 2020 and 2021). The sample 2021 was collected to ensure that the trend between 2010 and 2020 (marginal, if any improvements) is somehow realistic.

The results in Slovakia indicate serious problems in the quality of management of outsourcing ancillary services, which increase the risks associated with outsourcing. The risk of non-transparency of public procurement processes, as indicated by inappropriately chosen procedures and unclearly defined subjects of public

Table 7 Evaluation of the quality of contract management of ancillary services in public organisations in Slovakia in 2010 in %

Quality of risk management	Non-transparency	Hidden information		Hidden activity/moral hazard			
Ancillary service	Degree of competition for the award of public contracts	Ex-ante evaluation of the contractor for the public contract	Expertise	Frequency of monitoring of the production of the service	Procedure in the event of non-compliance with the contractual obligations	Length of contract	Type of payment to the external supplier for the service
Cleaning	45.28	58.34	48.06	56.95	57.22	43.89	31.39
Catering for employees	32.91	73.90	69.69	55.25	67.46	30.54	56.32
Building management and maintenance	52.11	73.83	74.16	63.43	50.32	56.08	74.81
IT administration	38.52	71.39	64.53	58.97	51.39	44.74	58.02
Transport	28.81	69.58	58.97	71.25	48.25	60.56	75.00
Security services	37.14	57.25	66.50	59.52	45.76	33.05	47.05
Average	39.13	67.38	63.65	60.9	53.4	44.81	57.1

Source: Author's primary research

Table 8 Evaluation of the quality of contract management of ancillary services of town and municipal offices in 2020 in %

Quality of risk management	Non-transparency	Hidden information		Hidden activity/moral hazard			
Ancillary service	Degree of competition for the award of public contracts	Ex-ante evaluation of the contractor for the public contract	Expertise	Frequency of monitoring of the production of the service	Procedure in the event of non-compliance with the contractual obligations	Length of contract	Type of payment to the external supplier for the service
Cleaning	14.62	56.52	30.77	44.00	25.50	24.00	41.65
Catering for employees	32.88	46.49	36.73	45.37	39.85	28.24	45.89
Building management and maintenance	25.67	57.50	48.81	44.44	33.09	47.27	73.18
IT administration	27.71	50.70	41.13	47.79	32.09	40.69	62.61
Transport	25.29	56.94	27.78	38.24	32.52	39.29	71.45
Security services	27.59	51.79	40.63	46.08	32.16	19.49	41.08
Average	25.63	53.32	37.64	44.32	32.53	33.42	55.98

Source: Author's primary research conducted in 2020

Table 9 Evaluation of the quality of contract management of ancillary services of town and municipal offices in 2021 in %

Quality of risk management	Non-transparency	Hidden information		Hidden activity/moral hazard			
Ancillary service	Degree of competition for the award of public contracts	Ex-ante evaluation of the contractor for the public contract	Expertise	Frequency of monitoring of the production of the service	Procedure in the event of non-compliance with the contractual obligations	Length of contract	Type of payment to the external supplier for the service
Cleaning	X	25.00	16.67	35.00	34.67	X	61.60
Catering for employees	19.55	34.78	32.35	43.75	35.20	37.50	37.82
Building management and maintenance	17.14	42.86	45.00	41.67	33.78	33.33	75.67
IT administration	19.00	48.44	34.48	45.59	18.14	33.33	59.45
Transport	33.75	50.00	12.50	27.78	17.33	25.00	68.00
Security services	27.50	20.00	47.06	45.45	31.79	14.29	53.10
Average	23.39	36.85	31.34	39.87	28.49	28.69	59.27

Source: Author's primary research conducted in 2021
Remark: *X* data not available

procurement, may cause the contracting authority/principal not to select the most suitable supplier/agent for external production of services. In this case, this happens for subjective reasons on the part of the principal—the contracting authority "does not want" to choose the most advantageous tender. However, incorrect selection of the supplier may also occur for objective reasons in case of high risk of hidden information, unless there is an ex-ante evaluation of the contractors for the public contract—the contracting authority "does not know" how to choose the most advantageous tender. Both risks can manifest themselves at the first stage of the outsourcing process, during the selection of the service supplier, and seriously jeopardise the final effect of outsourcing, its impact on the efficiency of service provision.

The outsourcing process does not end with the selection of the supplier. This is forgotten by many public institutions outsourcing services. Inappropriately defined contractual conditions (in particular the length of contract, penalties, type of payment) together with insufficient monitoring of external production increase the risk of hidden activities and moral hazard. Moral hazard creates room for the external service provider to pursue its own interests at the expense of the interest of the contracting authority, which should be the economic, efficient, effective use of public funds to provide the service.

The biggest gaps in the quality of contract management of the contracts assessed by us in terms of the above risks can be seen in the process of public procurement of the service. Open tendering is not dominant, often a price bid or direct award is chosen as the procurement procedure, moreover, often there is no clear definition of the subject of public procurement and the criterion used for the evaluation of tenders is the lowest price.

The results of the research document some worsening in favour of the use of public procurement by public tender. See Tables 7, 8, and 9 columns "degree of competition for the award of public contracts." The average degree of competition for the award of public contracts for selected ancillary services was evaluated as 39.13% in 2010; 25.65% in 2020 and only 23.39% in 2021. We have evaluated contracts according to the scale: public tender 100%, restricted competition 70%, negotiating procedure 50%, price tender 30%, and direct award 0%. Results document a return to public procurement procedures with a lower degree of competitiveness of bidders for the public contract—direct award. The situation is similar also in the case of selection criterion (see Tables 7, 8, and 9 columns "ex-ante evaluation of the contractor for the public contract") evaluated as 67.38% in 2010; 53.22% in 2020 and only 36.85% in 2021. We have evaluated contracts according to the scale: the most economically advantageous offer is 100%, lifecycle costs 50%, and the lowest price 0%. The criterion of the lowest price remains dominant, which disproportionately increases the risk of a decrease in the quality of the service due to the problem of information asymmetry associated with contracting out. The choice of the lowest price criterion is often the choice of a simpler procedure for evaluating the tenders submitted, given the complexity and often incomprehensibility of the evaluation procedure defined by law. In practice, it often happens that contracting authorities make mistakes in choosing the most economically advantageous tender evaluation criterion, which is criticised by the inspection bodies due to the ambiguity of the legal definition of the evaluation procedure. The choice of the lowest price criterion is therefore a simpler option, although not the right one. It leads to restrictions on the quality of the service provided.

The other most critical issues are the process of monitoring the external production of the service and solving the identified problems (irregular control of the external production, "soft" penalties of the external contractor in the event of a breach of contract by the provider, limited room for negotiation, or limited room for changing the supplier due to disproportionate length of the contract).

5 Conclusions

Our goal was to evaluate the outsourcing of ancillary services on the municipal level in Slovakia. The data about the scale of outsourcing (RQ1) are relatively reliable and show that outsourcing is regularly used, and in some cases, it may even be the dominant mode of production (especially for IT services).

The data about the results of outsourcing are very problematic. There are more reasons for such a situation. First, the municipalities do not keep the proper evidence about the full costs of internal production. Moreover, the data related to the quality of a service represent the subjective opinion of respondents, not any objective measure.

The results may indicate that the situation regarding the real results of outsourcing differs on a case-by-case principle. What is most important is the data, independently from their critical limitations, a document that the results from outsourcing are not "as good, as the New Public Management theory preferring competition suggests." Based on the data obtained, we can be fully sure that in many cases outsourcing increases the costs and decreases the quality of the production of ancillary services on the municipal level in Slovakia.

Our data about the quality of contract management document the situation related to one of the possible factors behind the low success of outsourcing. These data are almost fully reliable, as most of them have "hard" character and were collected via the analysis of existing contracts by authors. The quality of contract management related to outsourcing by the Slovak municipalities is very low and has not improved over time (the results from 2010 and 2020 show similar patterns and the control sample from 2021 just confirms this).

Our findings are related to three samples from Slovakia, but the policy lesson based on them can be generalized for the country and probably also for the region, independently from all methodological problems connected with our research. Few existing studies from other countries of the region (see, for example, Kopřič et al., 2018) indicate that the problems of "post-communist" countries are very similar. Limited accountability and rent-seeking (path-dependency factors), low quality of local public financial management (institutional factor) and over-bureaucratisation can be mentioned as core general problems. In countries with highly fragmented territorial structures (Czech Republic, Slovakia, Hungary), the limited management capacity of small municipalities should be added.

The findings directly suggest the policy lessons. Accountable governmental institutions and accountability watchdogs (like the National Audit Offices) should learn from our results. The current non-systematic approach to contracting should be replaced by a systematic logic of necessary implementation steps.

At the start, the "market" and the character of a service should be investigated to respond to the question, "Make or buy the service?" This step includes a comprehensive evaluation with the aim of comparing internalisation and outsourcing from the point of efficiency and quality of the service production—service testing. The service testing should be based on the information obtained through comprehensive market research and exact knowledge of one's own situation. In most countries the real costs of production of ancillary services in public organisations are not known, as the public organisations do not use full costs accounting approaches and cost centres are not created. Without proper cost data, the high-quality search for the optimum solution is the "mission impossible."

The specific step in the process of comparing in-house production and outsourcing is the estimation of transaction costs in the eventual contracting of the service. However, most public organisations in less developed countries may not even understand the term "transaction costs." In Slovakia most municipalities have less than 1000 inhabitants. Without external expertise, the obtainment of proper data in such a situation is "mission impossible."

The first step decision-making process should, of course, also include an assessment of the public institution's material, technical, and personnel capacities to provide the service required for internalisation of the service and the risks connected with outsourcing.

The results from the market testing represent a perfect source for the next steps of the contract management process. They should serve as inputs for the comprehensive definition of the procurement approaches; for example they may provide inputs for the estimation of the value and the price of the public contract.

Regarding the public procurement process, open, transparent, fair, and effective competition is the legal rule; moreover, such an approach should lead to critical savings. The lowest cost selection criterion should be used only in extraordinary cases. The most advantageous bid (MEAT method) should be the principal selection criterion.

As critically important, municipalities (public organisations in general) must remember that the contract management process does not end with the selection of the winner (supplier), but it shall also continue after the conclusion of the contract. The external production shall be monitored based on the contract conditions and on building working relationships with the external supplier. Non-compliance shall be detected, discussed, and, if needed, penalised according to the contract conditions. In the end, each decision on outsourcing and each contract should be re-evaluated periodically. The time period for this depends on the character of the service.

Acknowledgement The research in this study is supported by the project VEGA 1/0003/24 Inter-municipal Cooperation in the Provision of Local Public Services

Appendix

Table 10 List of experts involved in assigning weights to indicators

	Position	Expertise/education	Length of practice (years)
SK1	Retired civil servant	PhD degree in public administration	50
SK2	City lord-mayor	MA degree in business	30
SK3	Municipal mayor	MA degree in public administration	25
SK4	Municipal financial officer	PhD degree in public administration	35
SK4	Policy advisor	PhD degree in public policy	25
SK5	Academia	Professor of public administration	45
SK6	Academia	Professor of public policy	35
SK7	Academia	Professor of public management	40

References

Aben, T. A., Van Der Valk, W., Roehrich, J. K., & Selviaridis, K. (2021). Managing information asymmetry in public–private relationships undergoing a digital transformation: The role of contractual and relational governance. *International Journal of Operations & Production Management, 41*(7), 1145–1191.

Andersen, B., Spjelkavik, I., & Henriksen, B. (2008). Benchmarking applications in public sector principal-agent relationships. *Benchmarking: An International Journal, 15*(6), 723–741.

Arrow, K. J. (1985). The economics of agency. In J. W. Pratt & J. Zeckhauser (Eds.), 1986. *Principals and agents: The structure of business*. Harvard Business School Press.

Bailey, S. J. (1995). *Public sector economics*. Macmillan. ISBN 0-07-70345-2.

Behn, R. D., & Kant, P. A. (1999). Strategies for avoiding the pitfalls of performance contracting. *Public Productivity and Management Review, 22*, 470–489.

Bel, G., & Gradus, R. (2018). Privatisation, contracting-out and inter-municipal cooperation: New developments in local public service delivery. *Local Government Studies, 44*(1), 11–21.

Bel, G., & Rosell, J. (2016). Public and private production in a mixed delivery system: Regulation, competition and costs. *Journal of Policy Analysis and Management, 35*(3), 533–558.

Bel, G., Fageda, X., & Mur, M. (2014). Does cooperation reduce service delivery costs? Evidence from residential solid waste services. *Journal of Public Administration Research and Theory, 24*, 85–107.

Blomqvist, P., & Winblad, U. (2022). Contracting out welfare services: How are private contractors held accountable? *Public Management Review, 24*(2), 233–254. https://doi.org/10.1080/14719037.2020.1817530

Bowaird, T., & Loffler, E. (2003). Evaluating the quality of public governance. *International Review of Administrative Sciences, 69*(3), 33–60.

Braun, D., & Guston, D. H. (2003). Principal-agent theory and research policy: An introduction. *Science and Public Policy, 30*(5), 302–308.

Brown, T., Potoski, M., & Van Slyke, D. (2015). Managing complex contracts: A theoretical approach. *Journal of Public Administration Research and Theory, 26*(2), 294–308.

Brudney, J. L., Fernandez, S., Ryu, J. E., & Wright, D. S. (2005). Exploring and explaining contracting out: Patterns among the American states. *Journal of Public Administration Research and Theory, 15*, 393–419.

Cullis, J., & Jones, P. (1992). *Public finance and public choice*. McGraw – Hill Book Co. ISBN 0-07-7070400-9.

Dehoog, R. H. (1990). Competition, negotiation, or cooperation: Three models for service contracting. *Administration and Society, 22*, 317–340.

Djikgraaf, E., & Gradus, R. (2018). Collusion in the Dutch waste collection market. *Local government studies, 33*(4), 573–588.

Ferris, J., & Graddy, E. (1991). Production costs, transaction costs, and local government contractor choice. *Economic Inquiry, 25*(6), 541–554.

Fiala, P., Jablonský, J., & Maňas, M. (1994). *Vícekriteriální rozhodování*. VŠE.

Glas, A., & Essig, M. (2021). Management of performance-based contracting. In T. Choi, J. Li, D. Rogers, J. Rungtusanatham, T. Schoenherr, & S. Wagner (Eds.), *The Oxford handbook of supply chain management* (pp. 236–264). Oxford University Press.

Gradus, R., Dijkgraaf, E., & Wassenaar, M. (2014). Understanding mixed forms of refuse collection, privatization, and its reverse in the Netherlands. *International Public Management Journal, 17*(3), 328–343.

Guruganesh, G., Schneider, J., & Wang, J. R. (2021). Contracts under moral hazard and adverse selection. In *Proceedings of the 22nd ACM Conference on Economics and Computation* (pp. 563–582).

Hammerschmid, G., Van De Walle, S., Andrews, R., & Mostafa, A. M. S. (2019). New public management reforms in Europe and their effects: Findings from a 20-country top executive survey. *International Review of Administrative Sciences, 85*(3), 399–418.

Hefetz, A., & Warner, M. E. (2012). Contracting or public delivery? The importance of service, market, and management characteristics. *Journal of Public Administration Research and Theory, 22*(2), 289–317.

Hirsch, W. Z. (1991). *Privatizing government services: An economic analysis of contracting by local governments*. Institute of Industrial Relations, Publications Center, University of California.

Hodge, G. A. (2000). *Privatization: An international review of performance*. Westview Press.

Johansson, T., Siverbo, S., & Camén, C. (2016). Managing cooperation, coordination, and legitimacy: Control of contracted public services. *Accounting Auditing & Accountability Journal, 29*(6), 1012–1037.

Kamerman, S. B., & Kahn, A. J. (1989). *Privatization and the welfare state*. Princeton University Press.

Keller, A., Lumineau, F., Mellewigt, T., & Ariño, A. (2021). Alliance governance mechanisms in the face of disruption. *Organization Science, 32*(6), 1542–1570.

Kettl, D. F. (1993). *Sharing power – Public governance and private markets*. The Brookings Institution. ISBN 0-8157-4906-6.

Koprič, I., Wollmann, H., & Marcou, G. (2018). *Evaluating reforms of local public and social Services in Europe*. Palgrave Macmillan. ISBN 978-3-319-61091-7.

Lapuente, V., & Van De Walle, S. (2020). The effects of new public management on the quality of public services. *Governance, 33*(3), 461–475.

Lima, B., & Cruz, C. O. (2019). The challenge of monitoring PPP projects: Proposal of a conceptual 5-dimension KPI's model. *The Journal of Modern Project Management, 7*(2), 108–117.

Macneil, I. R. (1978). Contracts: Adjustments of long-term economic relations under classical, neoclassical and relational contract law. *Northwestern University Law Review, 72*, 855–905.

Martiniello, L., Morea, D., Paolone, F., & Tiscini, R. (2020). Energy performance contracting and public-private partnership: The importance of technological advanced systems for performance monitoring. In *Socio economic ecosystems-challenges for sustainable development in the digital era*. Business Systems Laboratory.

Meričková, B., & Nemec, J. (2007). Contracting-out local public services – Situation and trends in Slovakia and the Czech Republic. In *Lessons and recommendations for improvement* (NISPAcee Yearbook, pp. 191–204). Central and Eastern European Public Administration and Public Policy, NISPAcee. ISBN 978-80-89013-31-9.

Owusu-Manu, D. G., Kukah, A. S., Boateng, F., Asumadu, G., & Edwards, D. J. (2021). Exploring strategies to reduce moral hazard and adverse selection of Ghanaian public–private partnership (PPP) construction projects. *Journal of Engineering, Design and Technology, 19*(2), 358–372.

Perunović, Z., & Pedersen, J. L. (2007). Outsourcing process and theories. In *POMS 18th Annual Conference* (p. 10).

Petersen, B., & Ostergaard, K. (2018). Reconciling contracts and relational governance through strategic contracting. *Journal of Business and Industrial Marketing, 33*(3), 265–276.

Petersen, O. H., Hjelmar, U., & Vrangbaek, K. (2018). Is contracting out of public services still the great panacea? A systematic review of studies on economic and quality effects from 2000 to 2014. *Social Policy & Administration, 52*(1), 130–157.

Plaček, M., Ochrana, F., Nemec, J., & Půček, M. J. (2020). *Fiscal decentralization reforms: The impact on the efficiency of local governments in Central and Eastern Europe*. Springer International Publishing.

Potůček, M., et al. (2005). *Veřejná politika*. SLON.

Prager, J. (1994). Contracting out government services: Lessons from the private sector. *Public Administration Review, 54*(2), 176–184.

Pratt, J. W., & Zeckhauser, R. J. (1986). Principals and agents: The structure of business. *Journal of Economic Literature, 24*(4), 1788–1789.

Rehfuss, J. A. (1989). *Contracting out in government*. Jossey-Bass. ISBN 0124413528.

Romzek, B. S., & Johnston, J. M. (2002). Effective contract implementation and management: A preliminary model. *Journal of Public Administration Research and Theory, 12*, 423–453.

Rose-Ackerman, S., & Palifka, B. J. (2016). *Corruption and government: Causes, consequences, and reform* (2nd ed.). Cambridge University Press. ISBN 978-1107441095.

Saaty, T. L. (1994). How to make a decision: The analytic hierarchy process. *Interfaces, 24*(6), 19–43.

Savas, E. S. (1987). *Privatisation: The key to government*. Chatman House. ISBN 0-385-460821-X.

Sclar, E. D. (2000). *You don't always get what you pay for: The economics of privatization*. Cornell University Press. ISBN: 978-0-8014-8762-0.

Tejedo-Romero, F., & Aruajo, J. F. F. E. (2023). Critical factors influencing information disclosure in public organisations. *Humanities and Social Sciences Communications, 10*, 1–12.

Van Der Valk, W. (2023). Public sector contracting. In J. Grandia & L. Volker (Eds.), *Public procurement. Theory, practices and tools* (pp. 121–135). Palgrave Macmillan.

Williamson, O. E. (1986). *Economic organization: Firms, markets, and policy control*. New York University Press.

Yescombe, E. R., & Farquharson, E. (2018). Public-sector contract management. In *Public-private partnerships for infrastructure: Principles of policy & finance* (pp. 261–274). Butterworth-Heinemann.

Unravelling Threads: The Decline of Bhagalpur Silk Art

Ruchi Kumari and Meghna Dutta

1 Introduction

1.1 History of Bhagalpur Silk

This city of Bhagalpur has a long history of silk weaving and is renowned for its "Tussar silk" and Bhagalpuri silk sarees, which have gained popularity nationally and internationally. The textile sector ranks second to agriculture in its contribution to national income and employment generation (Kulkarni, 2015). The silk industry in Bhagalpur dates back several centuries, with the region being known for its expertise in silk weaving and production. The traditional silk weaving techniques have been passed down through generations, contributing to the industry's rich heritage. Bhagalpur's geographic location provides it with a natural advantage for silk production. The region's climate and soil are conducive to mulberry cultivation, which is the primary food source for silkworms. This favourable environment supports the growth of silkworms and contributes to the availability of high-quality silk cocoons. The silk production process in Bhagalpur involves multiple stages. It begins with the rearing of silkworms to obtain silk cocoons, followed by the extraction of silk threads through sericulture. These silk threads are then spun into yarn, dyed in various colours, and woven into exquisite sarees and other silk products. Bhagalpur's textile industry primarily relies on handloom weaving. Skilled artisans work on traditional handlooms, carefully weaving intricate designs

R. Kumari
School of Liberal Education, Galgotias University, Greater Noida, India
e-mail: ruchi.kumari@galgotiasuniversity.edu.in

M. Dutta (✉)
Humanities and Social Sciences, Indian Institute of Technology Patna, Patna, India
e-mail: meghna@iitp.ac.in

F. P. García Márquez et al. (eds.), *Outsourcing Using Operations Research and Management Science Methods*, International Series in Operations Research & Management Science 366, https://doi.org/10.1007/978-3-031-91845-2_10

and patterns into the fabric. This craftsmanship requires precision and attention to detail, producing high-quality silk products. The silk products from Bhagalpur are known for their unique designs and patterns. The weavers incorporate traditional motifs, such as floral patterns, peacock motifs, temple and geometric designs, into the fabric. These designs have cultural significance and showcase the artistic heritage of the region. Bhagalpur, situated on the southern bank of the river Ganges, is of historical importance. Over 100 years of weaving tradition in Bhagalpur gave this city a distinct picture, often called the "Silk City." It has been a family tradition among the lower-income group to take up weaving. Weaving in Bhagalpur is traditionally confined to the social group Other Backward Class (OBCs), who are Muslims (Ansaris), Scheduled Castes and some more local tribes. Silk has an excellent dye absorbent property, making it possible to make infinite shades, finishes and designs. The high-interest rate charged by the self-help groups also discourages loans (Kumar, 2013; Nath, 2022). Consequently, the owners rely on middlemen and friends for their credit needs.

Five types of silk are found in India: Mulberry, Tussar, Muga, Eri and Matka. Bhagalpur produces the most significant quantity of "Tussar Silk" in India, popularly known as "Bhagalpur Silk." It is also known as "Desi Khewa." It is found in live forests or food plants like Jamun and Oak and is famous for its deep, royal golden colours. Now, Tussar silk is replaced by Chinese silk, Koria, Viscose, and synthetic staples, which have all taken hold of our market. Bhagalpur is known globally for making different types of sarees, stoles, scarves, dupattas, blankets and dress materials.

The data for this study is obtained from a primary survey conducted in Bihar, India. The fieldwork that served as the basis for this article was carried out in the summer of 2022 in two villages in Bhagalpur district. Bhagalpur in Bihar is one of India's oldest industrial districts, famous for producing silk and is known as the "silk city." We studied two villages, Champanagar and Nathnagar. To understand the existing situation, we have done a cross-sectional study of these villages in Bhagalpur. This information is crucial for assessing this sector's needs, challenges and opportunities. This cross-sectional study is an essential tool for understanding the current state of the population and identifying the problems for further intervention. The textile cluster in the Bhagalpur district ranks second in the country in terms of the production and exports of silk fabrics. The state produces the unique Tussar silk in the Bhagalpur cluster, which commands high prices in international markets. Its final products include different types of sarees, stoles, blankets, scarves, and dupattas and dress materials from Tussar silk. Major cluster regions in the district of Bhagalpur that produce silk yarn are Nathnagar, Champanagar, Aliganj, Dariapur, Shekhpura, Puraini and Mirzafari. Of these, Nathnagar and Champanagar are two significant weaving centres. These villages had extensive handloom weaving in earlier days, but now the producers have shifted to power looms. We surveyed about 125 such firm owners from Champanagar and Nathnagar based on the random sampling method through a structured questionnaire. In both villages, informal home-based production units have proliferated in the villages (the periphery) surrounding the city (the center), where bigger formal sector firms are located. These villages have congested roads far from the main market and highway. The condition of the roads is also deplorable, and there is very infrequent passenger transport service. However, this art is now in decline (Khan, 2020).

The industry has established strong supply chains and distribution networks to cater to domestic and export markets. However, it is extensively plagued by credit issues and labour unavailability. Gang et al. (2022) found that financial access is crucial in promoting entrepreneurship among informal sector firms in India. Morris et al. (2001) discovered that the lack of financing for small firms is primarily due to institutional and organizational failure. To see how these issues affect informal firms' growth, we conducted a primary survey in the two villages of Bhagalpur, Nathnagar and Champanagar.

In this case study, the data consists of 125 individual interviews with the firm owner in the textile industry of Bhagalpur. We found some prominent cases in the study villages, which we have elaborated on here. These include problems like credit constraints, lack of work, lack of market access, increase in yarn price, decrease in wages, seasonal demand and shortage of yarn, which were found to persist in these villages.

Case 1: A producer in Nathnagar, who is 60 years old, said, "I had one power loom and two handlooms. After 2019, all looms were shut down due to scarcity of yarn and order. I have two sons and two daughters. My sons went to Mumbai in 2021 because they had no work or money to continue their business here." In the region where there is no textile park, he mentioned that middlemen have a dominant influence. According to them, a small percentage of weavers (around 3–5% at most) receive work orders directly from traders. Conversely, the more significant portion, constituting the majority, relies on middlemen to secure work opportunities from big firms.

Case 2: Eight looms are owned by another respondent in Nathnagar. Out of them, seven looms have been non-operational since 2019. The last order he received was before the first lockdown for COVID-19 started in 2019. His younger son manages only one loom. "we are given raw materials such as yarn and dye by the middlemen who place the orders, and we are only paid wages for the production," he said. The government subsidies intended for silk-making businesses in Bhagalpur are siphoned by middlemen and a small group of influential people. While the Government introduces numerous credit programs to improve the community's well-being, common weavers often face difficulties obtaining loans due to bureaucratic obstacles and rigorous paper requirements imposed by banks. The advantages tend to be enjoyed solely by influential people who are not part of the weaving profession. Those who successfully secure loans are often compelled to pay substantial bribes to officials.

Case 3: In Champanagar, another respondent said, "We faced the problem of the high price of yarn and had no orders during or after Covid 19." He had nine power looms, but four were not in use because of a lack of order, and his business was on the verge of collapse. During Covid-19, they spent their money on daily expenses, which they had kept for emergencies. He also said that we encounter challenges in obtaining loan approvals from banks, leaving us with no choice but to resort to borrowing from local moneylenders. Due to a lack of work opportunities and accumulating financial obligations, we face difficulties meeting repayment obligations.

Case 4: Silk weaving has traditionally been a household-based family business that involves the entire family. A respondent complained, "We are facing order issues and financial crunch; the younger generations are moving away from this work because they see it as labour intensive and unremunerative work." The respondent, along with his two sons, owns six looms. In addition to the shortage of operational funds, the surging costs of yarn have emerged as a significant hurdle for local weavers. The prices of yarn and other essential raw materials have escalated to a point where these expenses are beyond the means of small-scale weavers. As a result, they rely on middlemen and traders who supply them with the necessary raw materials. He also mentioned that they receive orders only during the festival seasons in the country for the rest of the months; they sometimes receive fewer or no orders.

Case 5: In Champanagar, 11 looms owned by a respondent have remained idle for more than 2 years due to the lockdown. "We would earlier get paid Rs 70–80 for weaving a mixed silk saree, measuring 7 m, at approximately Rs 7 per meter. As a result of the present work order crisis, the exploitation now has reached the extent that we get only Rs 50–55 per saree and give Rs 30 to the workers." With many corporate entities entering this sector, the instances of exploitation have risen. Allegedly capitalizing on the vulnerable position of the impoverished weavers, these corporations are reportedly providing meagre wages. Faced with limited alternatives, the economically disadvantaged weavers are compelled to accept these dismal wages for work.

Case 6: An owner of ten power looms said he got paid Rs. 150 for weaving a pure silk saree measuring 7 m and paid Rs. 60 to the workers before COVID-19. However, after the pandemic, he got only Rs. 100 for weaving a 7-m saree and gave Rs. 45 to the workers. The weavers of Bhagalpur find themselves in a precarious situation due to a combination of factors, including a scarcity of credit, persistent power shortages, and heightened rivalry from alternative silk production hubs. Moreover, the subsidies designated by the Government for the local silk manufacturing units in Bhagalpur are reportedly being redirected by corporate people or moneylenders. Specific looms rely on generators for operation, a cost that smaller weavers struggle to bear. The prevalent issue of frequent power outages in the state further exacerbates this challenge.

Case 7: A female respondent said that she took 100 cocoons from the Mahajan and spun them, for which she got less than 30 rupees before the pandemic, but after the pandemic, it went down to 10–20 rupees. The workforce involved in the meticulous tasks of silk thread extraction from cocoons and yarn spinning for garment weaving comprised approximately 100,000 weavers. However, due to the migration of numerous handloom weavers to other states seeking better opportunities amidst financial hardships, this workforce has now been diminished by half.

Case 8: A girl who recently completed her intermediate school from Nathnagar said that she and her parents worked for 18 h on the bobbin machine and wrapped two bundles of cotton yarn in a day. For this, the middleman gave them 50 rupees before the pandemic, but after the pandemic, they got 40 rupees per bundle (1 bundle = 5 kg of yarn). Her father notes that previously, he would purchase a 400-g bundle of cotton yarn for 800 rupees. However, the same bundle is being sold at a range of 1400 rupees to 1600 rupees. According to him, wholesalers are raising the price of the yarn without a clear basis.

Case 9: "The looms we have are upgraded versions of handlooms. They are outdated. If the Government wants us to stay in the competition, we must be given new machines based on the latest technologies. To give the dying sector a new life, there must be an easy flow of credit at lower interest rates. The bank processes must be eased so that the benefit can reach many firm owners. The Government currently gives us a loan of Rs.10 lakhs with a 50% subsidy through an online application. The shortlisted applicant is called for an interview, but only those who bribe officials can get financial help. The majority of us are illiterate and not able to apply online. It would be a great help if these processes are eased," complained another respondent.

Case 10: A respondent said that the industry was so profitable earlier that his father left his government teaching job to take forward family work of weaving. His uncle left his well-paid job to help in the family business. However, now, the same industry is facing a scarcity of capital, forcing them to live miserable lives and preventing them from educating their offspring. To fulfil their daily need, they are bound to sell their power looms one by one. They barely get their marginal wage to fulfil their daily needs.

2 Discussion

The cases presented highlight various challenges the weaving community faces in the study villages. These challenges revolve around issues such as credit constraints, lack of work, market access, fluctuating yarn prices, declining wages, seasonal demand, and structural factors like the dominance of middlemen and corporate influence.

2.1 *Emergence of Middleman*

The dominance of middlemen in the supply chain allows them to exert control over the weavers' access to work orders and raw materials. This results in a situation where weavers receive only wages for their labour, while the profits generated from the final product primarily benefit these intermediaries, known as middlemen. Textile firms in Bhagalpur often rely on middlemen or intermediaries to sell and distribute their products. This dependence can lead to reduced profit margins and limited control over pricing and market access. The work in the Bhagalpur silk industry is often seasonal, with fluctuations in demand throughout the year. Weavers may face periods of low demand and limited orders, which reduces their income potential. The irregular nature of work makes it challenging for weavers to earn a consistent and stable income. The weavers face challenges accessing broader markets and selling their products directly to consumers. They often rely on intermediaries or middlemen who take a significant portion of the profit margin, leaving limited earnings for the weavers. This dependence on intermediaries reduces earnings for the weavers due to the additional costs and commissions involved. Weavers face difficulty obtaining loans from formal financial institutions due to bureaucratic hurdles and stringent paperwork requirements. This lack of access to credit restricts their ability to invest in their businesses, upgrade their equipment, and improve their overall productivity. Establishing direct customer relationships or exploring online platforms can help firms overcome this challenge.

2.2 *Women and Young Generation*

Women have conventionally not been the primary firm owners in Bhagalpur. However, their labour is crucial at all stages of silk production, such as boiling the cocoons, extracting the yarn, and filling the bobbins. These works require intense and skilled labour. Gender norms and stereotypes can limit women's participation in specific roles within the industry. However, their roles in silk production are often invisible and undervalued. Their work is not acknowledged as essential, leading to a lack of appreciation and respect. This invisibility further contributes to the perpetuation of low wages and poor working conditions. While women contribute skilful labour to various stages of silk production, they lack opportunities to upgrade their skills or learn new techniques. They are confined to specific tasks deemed suitable for them, restricting their chances to diversify their skills and contribute more significantly. However, their daily wage rate in both villages is as low as Rs. 30, and their role in making this silk is nearly invisible. Despite performing intense and skilled labour in various stages of silk production, women receive disproportionately low wages. This wage disparity is a result of gender bias, limited bargaining power, and a lack of recognition for their contributions. This prevents them from adapting to changing market demands and advancements in the industry. The younger generation, too, leaves the villages due to a shortage of work. Even if there is work, it is not remunerative. As a result, the industry is losing out on a potential labour force, and the communities are facing a decline in traditional skills and knowledge. Only if there is some credit can a producer expand this work. The Covid-19 pandemic has also dealt a blow to these workers, who now lack new orders. The Covid-19 pandemic has significantly impacted the Bhagalpur textile industry. Lockdowns, disrupted supply chains, and reduced demand have led to job losses and decreased income for women workers. The pandemic has highlighted the vulnerability of these workers and the need for more decisive social support systems.

2.3 Credit Issues

Despite the industry's rich legacy, the textile sector in Bhagalpur faces various challenges. These include limited access to finance, inadequate infrastructure, outdated technology, and a lack of skilled labour. One factor that affects a firm's ability to grow is the availability and cost of financing (Oliveira & Fortunato, 2006; Binks & Ennew, 1996). A firm's performance is affected by sources of financing (such as an informal loan from moneylenders) and access to credit (Beck et al., 2005; de Maffioli et al., 2017; Allen et al., 2019). Access to credit and financing is a significant challenge many workers and businesses face. This challenge often arises due to several factors, including the informal nature of the industry, lack of collateral, and limited financial literacy among workers. However, there are opportunities for growth once these challenges are addressed and modern advancements in technology for marketing and design are leveraged. During our survey, many respondents reported being denied a loan or receiving a lower loan from a formal institution after many struggles (Kaplan & Zingales, 1997; Cao & Leung, 2020). Many firms also struggle to access adequate financial resources for business expansion, technology upgradation, and modernization. Constrained access to formal banking services and difficulty obtaining loans or credit hinder growth opportunities. One standard solution that has emerged to address credit issues in the Bhagalpur textile industry is the involvement of middlemen and relatives as funding sources. These intermediaries often play a crucial role in facilitating loans and credit for workers and small businesses.

Due to limited access to formal credit sources, most textile businesses in Bhagalpur resort to informal financing channels, such as local moneylenders. As a result, they may resort to outsourcing as a strategy to overcome these constraints (Dutta & Dhar, 2020). These firms lack formal contracts and legal protection. The potential for exploitation is also high due to its informal nature. The region's traditional handloom weaving techniques, unique designs, and favourable geographic conditions contribute to the industry's success. With proper support, the textile industry in Bhagalpur can continue to thrive and contribute to the region's economic development. Inadequate infrastructure, such as transportation and logistics facilities, poses a considerable challenge for this industry. Timely delivery of raw materials and finished products is often affected, leading to disruptions in the supply chain and increased costs.

2.4 Lack of Demand and Order

Across the cases, a common challenge is the scarcity of work orders. This can be attributed to various factors, including market fluctuations, changing consumer preferences, and increased competition from alternative production hubs. The economic situation of silk weavers is precarious due to several factors, such as reduced payments, high costs of raw materials (especially yarn), and irregular income. This situation is worsened by the lack of consistent orders and exploitation by intermediaries, resulting in financial insecurity for the weavers and their families. As local Tussar producers have nearly disappeared, China has established a monopoly over Tussar yarn manufacturing. According to traders, the historic Bhagalpur silk industry, with a century-long legacy, has become highly reliant on importing cheap raw materials from China. By increasing the cost of these raw materials, China seems to be on the verge of weakening the foundation of the local industry. Cheaper silk from China captured the market. Weavers consistently face a reduction in orders for their products, leading to idling of looms and economic instability.

3 Conclusion

Small firms often face difficulties obtaining credit from formal financial institutions due to their limited collateral or lack of credit history. This credit constraint hampers their ability to invest in raw materials, machinery, and other production inputs. Middlemen step in by providing credit to these small firms. They may offer financial assistance through loans, advances, or extended payment terms. This access to credit helps small firms overcome their credit constraints and continue their production activities. In addition to providing financial support, middlemen also act as suppliers of raw materials to small firms. As a part of the credit arrangement, they may offer raw materials to small firms on credit, allowing them to commence production without needing upfront payment. This is particularly crucial for small firms that lack the financial resources to purchase raw materials independently. By supplying raw materials on credit, middlemen enable small firms to operate and fulfil orders from larger formal firms. Middlemen play a coordinating role in production fragmentation. They act as intermediaries between small and more significant formal firms, facilitating the flow of information, orders, and specifications. They help small firms align their production processes with the requirements and standards of the larger firms. This coordination ensures that the products produced by small firms meet the quality and quantity expectations of the formal firms they serve. Another aspect of production fragmentation is the role of middlemen in connecting small firms with larger formal firms, thereby providing market access. The middlemen serve as a distribution channel, helping small firms reach the customer base of the larger formal firms. They handle logistics, marketing, and sales, ensuring that the products manufactured by small firms are efficiently delivered to the formal firms and, ultimately, to the end consumers. Credit constraints in the textile sector lead to production fragmentation, with small firms relying on middlemen as intermediaries. These middlemen address credit constraints by providing small firms with financial support and raw materials. They also coordinate production processes and enable market access by connecting small firms with larger formal firms. As a result, middlemen emerge as crucial connectors, facilitating the functioning of production networks and supporting the integration of small firms into the value chain of the textile sector. It is important to note that while middlemen and relatives can offer a temporary solution, they might not provide the long-term financial stability and growth opportunities that formal banking institutions can offer. Encouraging financial literacy and awareness, improving access to formal credit, and promoting the establishment of microfinance institutions tailored to the needs of the textile industry could contribute to more sustainable solutions for addressing credit challenges in Bhagalpur's textile sector.

References

Allen, F., Qian, M., & Xie, J. (2019). Understanding informal financing. *Journal of Financial Intermediation, 39*, 19–33.

Beck, T., Demirguc-Kunt, A., & Levine, R. (2005). SMEs, growth, and poverty: Cross-country evidence. *Journal of Economic Growth, 10*(3), 199–229.

Binks, M. R., & Ennew, C. T. (1996). Growing firms and the credit constraint. *Small Business Economics, 8*(1), 17–25.

Cao, S., & Leung, D. (2020). Credit constraints and productivity of SMEs: Evidence from Canada. *Economic Modelling, 88*, 163–180.

de Maffioli, A., Negri, J. A., Rodriguez, C. M., & Vazquez-Bare, G. (2017). Public credit programmes and firm performance in Brazil. *Development Policy Review, 35*(5), 675–702.

Dutta, M., & Dhar, N. S. (2020). Credit constraint and intra-country production reorganization–evidence from the unorganized textile industry in Maharashtra. *Journal of Economic Studies, 47*(2), 217–230.

Gang, I. N., Raj Natarajan, R., & Sen, K. (2022). Finance, gender, and entrepreneurship: India's informal sector firms. *The Journal of Development Studies, 58*(7), 1383–1402.

Kaplan, S. N., & Zingales, L. (1997). Do investment-cash flow sensitivities provide useful measures of financing constraints? *The Quarterly Journal of Economics, 112*(1), 169–215.

Khan, S. H. (2020). Loss of traditional industry and a state of urban decay in small-scale industrial cluster: A case study of Bhagalpur, Bihar, India. *Journal of Urban Regeneration and Renewal, 13*(4), 389–405.

Kulkarni, S. (2015). A brief report on the textile industry in India. The report, ASA and Associates.

Kumar, N. (2013). Cost components of the interest rate charged by Indian self-help groups financed by not-for-profit microfinance institutions. *Journal of Global Economy, 9*(4), 302–322.

Morris, S., Basant, R., Das, K., Ramachandran, K., & Koshy, A. (2001). *The growth and transformation of small firms in India*. Oxford University Press.

Nath, M. (2022). Credit risk in colonial India. *The Economic History Review, 75*(2), 396–420.

Oliveira, B., & Fortunato, A. (2006). Firm growth and liquidity constraints: A dynamic analysis. *Small Business Economics, 27*(2), 139–156.

MIX
Papier aus verantwortungsvollen Quellen
Paper from responsible sources
FSC® C105338

If you have any concerns about our products,
you can contact us on
ProductSafety@springernature.com

In case Publisher is established outside the EU,
the EU authorized representative is:
Springer Nature Customer Service Center GmbH
Europaplatz 3, 69115 Heidelberg, Germany

Printed by Libri Plureos GmbH
in Hamburg, Germany